# CRIMINAL JUSTICE:
## An Introduction to the Criminal Justice System in England and Wales

DAVIES, CROALL AND TYRER

# CRIMINAL JUSTICE:

## AN INTRODUCTION TO
## THE CRIMINAL JUSTICE SYSTEM IN
## ENGLAND AND WALES

LONGMAN

LONDON AND NEW YORK

Longman Group Limited
Longman House, Burnt Mill,
Harlow, Essex CM20 2JE, England
*and Associated Companies throughout the world.*

*Published in the United States of America
by Longman Publishing, New York*

© Longman Group Limited 1995

First published 1995

ISBN 0 582 247691 CSD
ISBN 0 582 247683 PPR

**British Library Cataloguing-in-Publication Data**
A catalogue record for this book is
available from the British Library

**Library of Congress Cataloging-in-Publication Data**

Set by 8 in 10/12pt Plantin
Printed and bound by Bookcraft (Bath) Ltd

# CONTENTS

# LIST OF FIGURES

# PREFACE

In the last ten years criminal justice has emerged as a new field of study in Britain. New degree courses in criminal justice studies have been set up, and careers advisers point to an industry with over a quarter of a million employees; bigger than the British army and legal profession combined. As sure as night follows day, the arrival of new degree courses is followed by a demand for student textbooks. But what type of textbook is needed for criminal justice? It was our observation as lecturers on one of the first criminal justice degree courses in Britain that many texts were neither introductory nor comprehensive in coverage as they focused on particular aspects of the criminal justice process.

We felt that an introductory textbook, written for students, practitioners and volunteers, new to the subject, should provide basic information about the various agencies of the criminal justice system: police, Crown Prosecution Service, magistrates' courts, Crown Court, probation and prisons. We also felt that it was important to outline the basic elements of criminal law and procedure which define crime and the responses to it in England and Wales, along with an exploration of the philosophies, principles and models of criminal justice on which these are based. In addition we also wished to look at the many non-legal factors which affect the operation of these agencies and finally we wanted to identify some of the policy issues involved in the control of crime and the pursuit of justice which interest the public and practitioners.

The aims of this book are therefore to:

- introduce readers to the agencies of the criminal justice process in England and Wales and to outline their legal responsibilities and tasks;
- help readers to understand the contextual constraints which influence the operations of these agencies;
- explain the legal and sociological factors which have shaped the operations of the criminal justice agencies in England and Wales;
- illustrate the relationship between these agencies and their interdependency;
- by the inclusion of study exercises and review questions, to aid understanding.

In this text we will therefore describe the legislation, history and organisational forms of the agencies operating within the criminal justice system. We did not wish our approach to be straightjacketed by any one academic discipline, be it law, sociology, criminology or administrative studies. We have therefore included insights into the principles of criminal law and its procedure provided by criminal lawyers, along with empirical studies of how these laws are implemented on a day-to-day level. Thus we have included findings of empirical research and statistical data in the hope of moving beyond an understanding of law as discussed in books to an appreciation of law in action. Moreover, we felt that readers should have an awareness of the system as a whole. The criminal justice system is more than the sum of its parts and an awareness of the interdependencies between the agencies in the system is as important as an understanding of the role of individual agencies.

Our approach is therefore intended to be both introductory and comprehensive. Thus we have included the role and functions of police, prosecutors and the trial and have looked beyond these into the working of the probation and prison services. These agencies and processes are all part of the criminal justice system, and their work is interdependent. They are all affected by the pervasive logic of the adversarial system, and by the goals and principles which shape the criminal justice process. The policies and procedures adopted at one stage of the system affect later stages.

This book is not, however, meant to be a detailed guide to either criminal law and procedure or criminology – many other texts perform this task adequately. It is intended to provide readers with a broad introduction to the present criminal justice system, to the principles which underlie it and to the many conflicting pressures on criminal justice policy to which current legislative changes and reviews are a response. Thus it should be regarded neither as a law nor criminology text, but rather as drawing on elements of law, sociology and criminology to introduce the many aspects of criminal justice and to place these in a broader socio-legal context.

The first three chapters aim to introduce students to the key elements of criminal justice and to the many ways of defining, explaining and measuring crime. Chapters 4-7 deal with the agencies and processes involved in investigating and prosecuting crime and determining the guilt or otherwise of those accused of having committed crimes. Chapters 8 and 9 explore sentencing and penal policy, introducing students to the main aims of punishment, and the many influences on sentencing decisions. The aims and purpose of imprisonment are considered in Chapter 10. The criminal justice process however has many limitations and recent pressures to reduce crime have led to the development of many initiatives involving the community in relation to crime prevention, punishment and policing. These will be discussed in Chapter 11. Finally, the implications of changing influences on policy for the future of criminal justice will be explored in Chapter 12.

Each chapter is followed by a number of review questions directed towards the student reader. In addition there are a series of exercises which student readers may attempt in order to further their understanding of some of the concepts and processes which we have explored. A list of key further reading also follows each chapter, to enable readers to increase their knowledge and understanding of the agencies or processes introduced.

We have included the many far-ranging changes to the criminal law and its procedures brought about by the Criminal Justice and Public Order Act 1994. The political controversy surrounding this hotch-potch Act was apparent in the debates in Parliament and in the street protests over the legislation. We do not think that the political implications of the criminal justice system can be ignored. However, we do not see our task as being to simplify issues as is apparent in the many partisan debates on topics of criminal justice, nor do we intend to present the text from any one theoretical or ideological perspective.

We are conscious that issues of criminal justice are now centre stage in the political drama and that the five Criminal Justice Acts passed in the 13 years since 1982 reveal not only a heightened audience interest on matters of crime and justice, but a desperate search to stage a happy ending – the retreat on unit fines was a prime example.

Given the continual review of aspects of criminal justice, it is possible that by the time this book is published, further changes will have taken place. No text can ever be fully up-to-date. It is hoped however that readers will be able to place such recent changes in the context of the many influences on policy that will be explored in this text.

Malcolm Davies,
Hazel Croall,
Jane Tyrer,
*January 1995*

We would like to dedicate this book to Michael Molyneux
on his retirement from the Law School at Thames Valley University
for his inspiration as a teacher to generations of
students and colleagues.

# ACKNOWLEDGEMENTS

We are most grateful to the following scholars, researchers and practitioners who commented on the manuscripts: Bill Brown, penal policy lecturer at Thames Valley University; Jacqueline Burns and Jane Grant, research associates at the Criminal Justice Centre at TVU; Michael Molyneux, retired law teacher; Dr Alex Weich, from Westminster University; Clive Welsh of the Prison Service: and the three anonymous readers of the manuscript for their helpful comments and suggestions.

We are entirely beholden to Angela Legg, the administrator of the Criminal Justice Centre at Thames Valley University, for her tireless help with this book. To our students of criminal justice at Thames Valley we offer our thanks for their part in the development of this book.

# TABLE OF CASES

# CHAPTER 1

# CRIMINAL JUSTICE

Defining Criminal Justice
Criminal Justice in England and Wales
Principles, Systems and Models of Criminal Justice
Criminal Justice Legislation

## INTRODUCTION

Is the British system of justice the best in the world? A survey conducted for the *Solicitors Journal* (1993), found that only 21 per cent of a sample of 1,000 people in England and Wales said that it was, while 43 per cent disagreed. It could of course be asked what these answers mean. Did respondents have sufficient knowledge to assess the British system of justice? Is it likely that they had much of an understanding of a foreign criminal justice system? Nonetheless, responses could be taken to indicate some lack of public confidence in the system. How can this be interpreted?

Answers could reflect concern about miscarriages of justice illustrated by cases such as the Birmingham Six or the Guildford Four. In these cases men and women convicted of terrorist offences were later released after serving substantial periods in prison because of procedural errors or misconduct in the investigation and prosecution of incidents. Initial appeals had been turned down but public campaigns on behalf of the accused contributed to the decision to reappraise the convictions.

Some respondents may have thought that the system is intrinsically unjust and unfair to some groups such as the poor or ethnic minorities. Others might have believed that the criminal law in this country is too intrusive. Critics point to our high levels of imprisonment when compared with other European countries, and argue that tougher treatment of juvenile offenders may propel them into a life of crime. Tougher powers against squatters, rave parties and new age travellers introduced in the Criminal Justice and Public Order Act 1994 attracted a wave of public protest.

It was apparent nevertheless that respondents did not share the anxieties

1

of some of these critics as they overwhelmingly (84 per cent) wanted to see more, not fewer police being put on the beat. In response to specific questions about sentencing, 90 per cent believed that judges were too lenient in sentencing rapists, and 72 per cent thought that the average sentence of 12.9 months for burglary was too low.

A number of complex issues are raised by a question which asks whether British justice is the best in the world. In the first place, we need to clarify some terms. There are not one but three criminal justice systems in Britain, with Scotland and Ulster having different criminal procedures from those in England and Wales, which is a single jurisdiction. Furthermore, European institutions also affect the operations and policy of criminal justice in this country.

Examining the criminal justice system involves many issues. Political issues are raised in asking what the aims of the system are and in whose interests it is run. Criminal justice also inevitably raises issues of fairness and freedom, as the system seeks to control and repress criminal behaviour. If it does this too vigorously, citizens may be arbitrarily arrested and unfairly accused of a crime they did not commit. We are all at risk however if crime is tolerated and the system cannot deal effectively with it. This in turn raises questions about how we understand and define crime, how we measure the extent of crime, the number of criminals and victims, and the effects of crime on victims and the community at large.

Before these questions are addressed we must first define what we mean by the phrase 'criminal justice system', understand how it works, what it is trying to achieve, and with what effect. This book sets out to examine these issues, and this chapter will define these questions more specifically. Criminal justice systems in all countries involve a vast and growing organisation, including many different agencies responsible for the detection and trial of suspected criminals and the punishment of those who are found to be guilty.

In this chapter the main agencies of the criminal justice system will be described and their expansion in recent years outlined. To comprehend criminal justice fully we also need to understand the principles underlying the system, and how these principles affect policy and practice. Like any other institution, criminal justice has to be organised and managed in the context of political and public pressures along with financial and resource constraints. Different models of criminal justice, which illustrate its conflicting aims, and the pressures these place on policy, will be explored. Finally, recent legislation will be briefly outlined to illustrate the conflicting pressures surrounding contemporary criminal justice. A short chronology of significant criminal justice legislation will complete this introductory chapter.

# DEFINING CRIMINAL JUSTICE

How can a criminal justice system be defined and described? What does it do? What are its key elements? To explore these questions we must first look at what criminal justice is a response to – activities which are against the criminal law. We must also look at how criminal justice is organised and the functions performed by its constituent agencies. Furthermore we can analyse the nature of a criminal justice system by examining what happens to those convicted and sentenced in terms of the types and extent of the punishments used. These are the key elements in any criminal justice system, although there may be variations between different countries, or in legal terms, jurisdictions.

## Content of the criminal law: what is penalised?

In most countries, particular kinds of behaviour are criminalised through the criminal law, formulated in some countries by a penal code. As we shall see in Chapter 2 there is no simple way of defining what behaviour is criminal, and this may vary between different countries and over time. Nonetheless, in most Western societies similar kinds of behaviour are considered to be criminal including homicide, rape, arson, kidnapping, robbery, burglary, assault, theft, fraud and motoring offences. Thus according to Knut Sveri, 'if a person does something which is considered to be a crime in Sweden, it will practically always be considered to be a crime in New York' (Sveri 1990).

## Form and process: criminal procedure and criminal justice agencies

It is in 'comparing the system of criminal procedure that we do find differences stemming from different legal traditions. The role of the parties involved in the criminal justice system differs' (Sveri 1990: 11).

Thus different countries have very different ways of investigating and prosecuting criminal cases, based on different principles and rules. Varying procedures and regulations govern such matters as the investigation of crime, the arrest and interrogation of suspects, prosecution decisions, bail procedure, trial procedures, rules of evidence and the role of the jury, if there is one. There are also differences in how courts decide on the guilt or otherwise of defendants.

This is in part because other countries have different agencies dealing with these matters. In France an investigating magistrate, the *juge d'instruction*, conducts investigations into serious crime, in contrast to the UK where the police have this responsibility. In Germany the public prosecutor, the *staatsanwalt*, has overall responsibility for pre-trial proceedings and advises the examining judge on bail and remand decisions. There is no equivalent in

England and Wales to the Scottish Procurator Fiscal who also has an investigating and prosecuting role. Across the USA, each of the 50 states has its own penal code and each county within a state has its own criminal justice agencies such as district attorneys and sheriffs, in addition to the state and federal agencies.

It is important to appreciate how criminal justice agencies define and interpret their role and legal responsibilities. The criminal law does not enforce itself. To understand a system we need to consider how law enforcers, prosecutors, lawyers, magistrates, judges, probation officers and prison officers perceive their job and their function within the system. How they work will not only be affected by their official role but by political, financial, organisational and cultural influences. While Parliament and judges may create and interpret the criminal law, they do not implement it on a day-to-day basis. An appreciation of the everyday world of those who translate the law as described in books into the law in action is therefore essential to an understanding of how criminal justice agencies operate.

### Functions and aims of the criminal justice system

In exploring what a criminal justice aims to do, we need to distinguish between the goals of the system as a whole, and the functions of the different agencies who make up the system. Agency specific functions are shown in Figure 1.1. Cross-system goals include:

- Protecting the public by preventing and deterring crime, by rehabilitating offenders and incapacitating others who constitute a persistent threat to the community.
- Upholding and promoting the rule of law and respect for the law, by ensuring due process and proper treatment of suspects, arrestees, defendants and those held in custody, successfully prosecuting criminals and acquitting innocent people accused of a crime.
- Maintaining law and order.
- Punishing criminals with regard to the principles of just deserts.
- Registering social disapproval of censured behaviour by punishing criminals.
- Aiding and advising the victims of crime.

### Mode and distribution of punishment

Finally, variations between systems include differences in the modes and distribution of punishment, recognising that different societies punish offenders in different ways. If one point of distinction in defining a criminal justice system is to establish what is punished, another is to describe the types or mode of punishment used.

**Fig 1.1** Agency Specific Functions

- **Police**:
  Investigating crime
  Preventing crime
  Arresting and detaining suspects
  Maintaining public order
  Traffic control
  Responding to criminal and non-criminal emergencies

  Some of these tasks are also carried out by private and other public law enforcement agencies such as Customs and Excise and environmental health and trading standards departments of local authorities.

- **Prosecution**:
  Filtering out weak cases
  Preparing cases for prosecution
  Prosecuting cases in the magistrates' courts
  Preparing cases for trial in the Crown Court by liaising with barristers for the prosecution before and throughout a trial

- **Courts**:
  Handling and processing cases efficiently
  Deciding on bail, remands, and mode of trial
  Protecting the rights of the defendant
  Deciding on guilt
  Passing sentence
  Hearing appeals against conviction and sentence
  Providing a public arena so that justice can be seen to be done

- **Prisons**:
  Holding persons remanded in custody by the courts
  Holding sentenced offenders
  Maintaining proper conditions for those held in custody
  Preparing inmates for release
  Attempting to rehabilitate offenders

- **Probation**:
  Preparing pre-sentence reports
  Providing bail facilities for and information to the courts on offenders' appropriateness for bail
  Working with offenders given a probation, community service, or combination order
  Running probation centres
  After-care and pre-release work with inmates in custody

The main penal sanctions or court sentencing options are imprisonment, fines, probation, community penalties, discharges, admonitions and cautions. The death penalty was abolished in this country in 1965, and has also been abolished in most European countries although it is still in use in some states in the USA and in African and Asian countries.

The most noticeable difference between countries however is not merely in the mode of punishment but in the distribution of punishment, that is the range of sentences routinely given for particular offences. What is acceptable to a Swedish, British or USA court in terms of typical sentencing practice varies greatly.

If we look at different cultures, differences in what punishments are seen as appropriate become evident. A good illustration of this is provided in the extract from the *Daily Telegraph* (Figure 1.2) which looks at differences within Australia between the European and Aboriginal attitude towards punishment.

## CRIMINAL JUSTICE IN ENGLAND AND WALES

The organisation and jurisdictional limits of criminal justice in England and Wales are determined by constitutional distinctions within the UK. In the UK, although Parliament passes legislation which may apply throughout, there are three distinctive criminal justice systems with separate procedures and agencies: England and Wales, Scotland, and Northern Ireland. Different government departments are responsible for criminal justice in these three regions – the Home Office for England and Wales, the Scottish Office and the Northern Ireland Office.

Other government departments such as the Lord Chancellor's Department and the Attorney General's Office are involved in the administration of criminal justice. Local councils have a statutory duty to establish a Social Services Department employing qualified social workers to deal with children in trouble with the criminal law. Criminal inquiries are not made exclusively by the police but also by many other agencies such as investigators for the Department of Trade and Industry, the Serious Fraud Office, HM Customs and Excise and various local government bodies such as the Environmental Health and Trading Standards Departments.

In England and Wales criminal justice agencies such as the police, prisons and probation are funded primarily from central government sources. Policy is established primarily by civil servants who advise ministers and by legislation enacted by Parliament. For administrative purposes agencies are divided into regional areas. The main agencies are briefly described below:

- *The police.* There are 43 regional police forces each under the direction of a chief constable and, except for the Metropolitan Police and the City of London police, local police authorities. Forces vary in size – the biggest

**Fig 1.2** Tribal elders punish Aborigine car thieves

BY GEOFFREY LEE MARTIN IN SYDNEY

Six Aborigines have been beaten for stealing cars after Northern Territory police let their elders handle the matter in a traditional way.

The six, aged 15–25, were beaten with rubber hoses in front of the local council chambers in an Aboriginal community near Darwin.

Since the incident three months ago, only one minor offence of theft has been committed in the town.

It was not the first time Aborigines in the Territory have been handed over to elders by the Australian justice system for tribal punishment.

Earlier this year, Mr Brian Martin, the Chief Justice of the Territory, asked the Department of Correctional Services to monitor the tribal 'payback' spearing through both thighs of Wilson Jagamara Walker, an Aboriginal convicted of manslaughter. Mr Martin's decision was influenced by petitions from the man's tribal council and a group of senior women at Yuendumu, 150 miles southwest of Alice Springs, who warned him that innocent members of the man's family would be speared instead of him if he was jailed.

Taking this into account, the judge released Walker on a bond and asked that correctional services report on whether the spearing took place.

However, the judicial outcome remained unclear after officials said that the victim's family had decided not to proceed with the spearing even though Walker was prepared to submit to the punishment.

Mr Martin gave Walker a three-year suspended jail term and allowed six months, which expires in August, for the payback to occur. In the ritual, the convicted man will be speared through the thighs in front of the tribe by the younger brother of a man he stabbed to death in Alice Springs in a family feud last year.

Walker, who has accepted the tribal law and is said to be happy with the judge's decision, is now being cared for by relatives at an isolated settlement. He is said to be ready to return to Yuendumu for the spearing when preliminary tribal ceremonies have been completed.

Mr Kevin Kitchener, a barrister with the North Australian Aboriginal Legal Aid Service, said: 'Maybe we should go back to the old traditional ways. They seem to work.' Mr Kitchener, who related the beating incident to a conference on Aboriginal justice issues in Townsville, Queensland, said the youths had been surrounded in the street by Aboriginal male adults. They had not been seriously hurt because the adults knew how to beat them without causing permanent injuries.

'It sounds barbaric', he said, 'but the instant justice had an important further deterrent effect. They know that if they get into trouble again the same thing will happen. But next time women will be wielding the rubber hoses, which will give them an even greater sense of shame.'

Mr Kitchener said the day before the public beating another group of Aboriginal youths had been arrested in Darwin for similar offences.

'They told friends they were very glad to be facing white man's justice – not one of them wanted to face Aboriginal punishment,' he said.

(Daily Telegraph, 18 June 1994: 13)

being the Metropolitan Police with 28,000 uniformed officers. The Home Office is the government department responsible for the police.

● *Prosecutors.* The Crown Prosecution Service was set up in 1985 and is organised into 13 areas. The Attorney General is answerable in Parliament for the Crown Prosecution Service which is headed by the Director of Public Prosecutions, a senior lawyer.

● *Courts.* Most criminal cases have to go to the magistrates' courts although more serious cases are ultimately dealt with in the Crown Courts. Officials in these courts include judges, magistrates, magistrates' clerks and ushers. The criminal courts come under the authority of the Lord Chancellor's Department which is responsible for the appointment of magistrates and judges.

● *Probation.* The Probation Service is responsible for preparing pre-sentence reports for courts, supervising probation orders and helping prisoners adapt to community life following release. There are 55 probation areas, and the service comes under the control of the Home Office.

● *Prisons.* The Prison Service is an executive agency, with policy direction from the Home Office and is organised into 15 regional areas, with responsibility for 130 prisons in 1994.

As well as the professions and officials in these agencies, many private citizens are involved in criminal justice. These include lay visitors to police stations, neighbourhood watch groups, victim support volunteers, members of juries and prison boards of visitors. Perhaps the most important group is lay magistrates of which there were 30,008 in 1995.

There is also a growing army of employees in private security firms. Group 4, Pinkerton's, Securicor and Wells Fargo are the best known of the companies undertaking crime prevention work for profit. In 1993 there were estimated to be 7,482 private security firms. These are mainly smaller businesses, such as private detectives, locksmiths, bailiffs and credit investigation and information services. Although it is extremely difficult to estimate the total number of employees in this sector some have estimated the number to be as high as 250,000 although the most reliable estimate gives a figure of 162,303 (Jones and Newburn 1994). The higher figure is about the same size as the numbers working for all government criminal justice agencies, thus the private sector plays a major and growing role in crime prevention. It is also becoming increasingly involved in other sectors of the system. In November 1991, Group 4 signed a contract to run the first private prison, the Wolds Remand Prison in Humberside. The second to be opened was Blakenhurst, a local prison, and Doncaster opened in 1994. Twelve prisons were initially planned to be put in private hands by the Prison Service.

8

Finally, the legal professions are a vital part of criminal justice. Barristers and solicitors are the two branches of this powerful professional group which is independent of government. Barristers are primarily court advocates whereas solicitors advise clients on a variety of matters and deal with clients prior to trial. The majority of advocacy in the Crown Court is done by barristers and the higher courts have only recently been open to solicitors as advocates. Both solicitors and barristers have the right to appear and represent clients, ie rights of audience, in the magistrates' court, where much of the work is undertaken by solicitors. A member of the public cannot directly seek advice from a barrister without first instructing a solicitor. A survey by the Law Society (1989) showed that of the 26,670 solicitors in private practice, 62 per cent dealt with criminal matters. In 1992 there were 7,150 practising barristers, most of whom will have represented criminal clients in their career, and some of whom specialise entirely in criminal cases.

## Expansion of the criminal justice system in the 1980s and 1990s

Whether we assess growth by expenditure, output or number of employees, the agencies making up the criminal justice system in England and Wales have all grown steadily over the last decade. Figure 1.3 illustrates the growth of employees in some of the main sectors, showing that in 1993 there were a quarter of a million employees. To this must be added the estimated 162,000 private sector employees.

In addition to the quantitative growth of this occupational sector, a qualitative change is also occurring as pressure mounts for greater professionalisation through degree level entry and an increasing emphasis on training. This is most evident in the police, prison and court services. This demand for greater professionalism reflects the greater complexity of the work of criminal justice employees in the 1990s. It is recognised for example that officials need to be responsive to the changing demands of society and the increasing complexities of the system. Social change and community demands have resulted in continual reviews and a re-examination of the function and practice of many agencies and professions. Further changes can be expected as the implications of greater European and international co-operation are examined. The introduction of new technology has increased demands for a more highly trained and flexible work force.

The volume of recent legislation, government reports and commissions on aspects of criminal justice, which will be referred to throughout this book, reflects this state of change. The Criminal Justice Act 1991 continued the emphasis on expanding the use of punishment in the community. The Royal Commission on Criminal Justice chaired by Lord Runciman examined options for reform of criminal procedure and reported in 1993. The Lord Chancellor's Department has established an agenda of reforms for the legal profession and the court services. Reviews of recruitment, functions and training are taking place in both the police and prison services. In 1994, two

9

**Fig 1.3** Employment in Criminal Justice

|  | *1986–87* | *1993–94*\* | *Growth* |
|---|---|---|---|
| Prisons | 28,180 | 37,750 | 9,570 |
| Police officers | 121,542 | 128,524 | 6,982 |
| Police civilians | 45,185 | 53,855 | 8,670 |
| Magistrates' court manpower | 9,523 | 10,638 | 1,115 |
| Probation officers | 5,630 | 6,790 | 1,160 |
| CPS | 2,243 | 5,390 | 3,147 |
| TOTAL | 212,303 | 242,947 | 30,644 |

\* Relates to planned growth

(*The Government's Public Expenditure Plans 1991–92 to 1993–94 for the Home Office and the Charity Commission*, February 1991. Cm 1509. London: HMSO)

major Acts were passed, the Police and Magistrates' Courts Act and the Criminal Justice and Public Order Act. These have many implications which will be explored later in this chapter, indicating that virtually every aspect of the system is currently undergoing change.

This expansion has meant that the law and order budget has grown steadily. In the financial year 1991/92 the Home Office, Lord Chancellor's Department and the Attorney General's Office spent £8,770 million on criminal justice services. This compares with £25,557 million spent on health, £26,894 million on education and £23,025 million on defence. In recent years the Home Office has sought to improve the cost effectiveness of the system by contracting out some services and utilising performance measures and auditing techniques. The restructuring of the management of the magistrates' court services and the reform of legal aid have been influenced by fiscal pressures to reduce public expenditure.

It is clear therefore that criminal justice is currently undergoing considerable change, brought about by a number of different and often conflicting pressures. These also affect the perceived role and function of criminal justice and its many agencies. Before discussing this, we need to examine the principles on which the criminal justice system is based, and the different ways of looking at its role.

# PRINCIPLES, SYSTEMS AND MODELS OF CRIMINAL JUSTICE

## Principles of criminal justice

Unlike many other countries, England and Wales has no written penal code or definitive statement of the principles of criminal justice. Nonetheless some important principles guide criminal justice procedure. A crucial feature of

10

criminal justice in England and Wales is the adversarial system, which determines how guilt should be established. A central aspect of this is the acceptance that the individual has rights; whether as a suspect, defendant or convicted person. The adversarial system starts with the premise that a person is innocent until proven guilty or has admitted guilt. The use of the word innocent in this context is an assumption of the adversarial trial process, which determines its logic and procedure.

In adversarial systems a trial does not establish whether the accused is innocent of the offence he or she has been charged with, but whether the evidence is sufficient, beyond reasonable doubt, to establish guilt. Criminal appeals examine the same issue, a point is explained by Professor Michael Zander in the context of a Court of Appeal decision which overturned the conviction of Winston Silcott for the murder of PC Blakelock during the Broadwater Farm riot of October 1985.

In a letter to *The Times*, Zander explains the key logic of the adversarial system :

### Guilt or Innocence?

Sir, In writing about compensation for Winston Silcott (August 3) Janet Daley says, 'He has now been declared innocent of one particular crime'. This commonly held view is incorrect.

Mr Silcott, whose conviction for another murder still stands, had his conviction for murder in the case of PC Blakelock quashed by the Court of Appeal. This no more represents a declaration of innocence than does acquittal by a jury.

A jury acquittal means that in the jury's view the prosecution have not proved beyond reasonable doubt, or that even if guilt has been established they are unwilling to convict. The quashing of a conviction by the Court of Appeal means that for one of a large number of possible reasons the conviction cannot stand. Very often the reason is that the judge directed the jury wrongly on law. In the Silcott case, the reason related to documents which the Court of Appeal considered had been tampered with.

Many people, including many commentators in the media, have confused these issues.

*The question of whether someone is innocent is not one that is addressed in a criminal trial in our legal system* (emphasis added).

(*The Times*, 12 August 1994: 15)

In the same way as the trial questions whether guilt has been established on the basis of evidence presented, an appeal after conviction considers whether the trial process was flawed. In neither case does the court ask 'Is the defendant innocent?'.

Other guiding principles can be found in policy statements by parliamentary bodies such as the Select Committee on Home Affairs and in the written aims of separate agencies in the system. General statements can also be found in policy documents such as White Papers or as preambles to legislation. The Home Office and the Lord Chancellor's Department have overall responsibility for many aspects of the criminal justice system, but unlike other more centralised systems, a policy document from these departments is not regarded as a definitive statement of policy to be followed slavishly. This is partly because this would conflict with other principles such as the independence of the judiciary, professional autonomy and divisions of responsibility for the management and funding of criminal justice.

In contrast to our system, some countries have penal codes which contain clearly stated principles. An example of this is Finland where the basic principles of the criminal justice system have been set out in the Penal Code of 1889. Although these have been amended over the century, the Finnish Ministry of Justice identifies the fundamental principles in Finnish criminal law and procedure:

> Today, the fundamental principles in criminal law include the principles of legality, equality, predictability and proportionality. Among the consequences of the strict interpretation given the principle of *legality* in Finland is that the court may not impose forms of punishment that are not specified for the offence in question. *Equality* demands that all cases falling within a specific category are dealt with in the same way. *Predictability* demands that it is possible to assess, in advance, the certainty and level of punishment for a given act. Predictability increases if the law is simple and legal practice is uniform. *Proportionality* requires that the sanction for an offence is in proportion to its blameworthiness. This principle, which also requires that consideration be taken of all official and unofficial penal and non-penal consequences of an offence, establishes the maximum punishment. It is not seen to prevent mitigation of punishment where this is deemed reasonable.
>
> In Finland, as in all of the Nordic countries, it is generally felt that punishments primarily have, and should have, a general preventive effect. General prevention can be enhanced by two components, the *certainty* and *severity* of punishment. Finnish criminal policy emphasizes certainty, but not severity. General prevention also involves the maintenance of standards of morality through the public disapproval that punishment directs at criminal behaviour. Individual prevention, as a primary goal of punishment, has been rejected. The coercive rehabilitation of offenders was found to be based on flawed arguments and to raise problems with legal safeguards and the control of discretion.
>
> (Joutsen 1990: 2)

Without a penal code or its equivalent the principles that govern criminal justice in England and Wales evolve from the system of parliamentary sovereignty and the principles of the rule of law. The system of parliamentary sovereignty means that parliament is the supreme authority and the final arbiter of legality as defined by the enacted laws of the land. In recent years, since the Treaty of Rome, Parliament has not been the only source of rules and regulations and some aspects of the sovereignty of the British Parliament have been ceded to European institutions.

The basic principles of the rule of law were articulated by A V Dicey, who wrote:

No man is punishable or can be lawfully made to suffer in body or goods except for a distinct breach of law established in the ordinary legal manner before the ordinary courts of the land.

... no man is above the law, but . . . every man whatever be his rank or condition, is subject to the ordinary law of the realm and amenable to the jurisdiction of the ordinary tribunals.

... the general principles of the constitution (as for example the right to personal liberty, or the right to public meeting) are with us as the result of judicial decisions determining the rights of private persons in particular cases brought before the courts.

(Dicey 1959: 188–195).

The rights of the defendant, and the victim and the public at large, are derived from the provisions enacted by Parliament and interpretations of the ordinary courts. A primary principle of the rule of law is that everyone is subject to the law including those who enforce it. They can claim no special status unless given by the law and must always be answerable to the law.

In England and Wales official objectives are typically expressed in Home Office documents, such as *Criminal Justice: A Working Paper* (Home Office, May 1984). In the foreword the then Home Secretary, Leon Brittan, specified four objectives for criminal justice which would contribute towards sustaining the principle of the rule of law:

A fair and effective criminal justice system marks the distinction between a civilised society and anarchy. If it works well, we as citizens can live our lives peacefully, and enjoy the rewards of our labours; if it works badly, many of us – particularly the elderly and the vulnerable – will have our lives marred by the fear, and sometimes the experience, of crime. . . .

We needed a strategy. . .

The central objectives of this strategy are to sustain the rule of law:

a. by preventing crime wherever possible;
b. when crimes are committed, by detecting the culprit;
c. by convicting the guilty and acquitting the innocent;
d. by dealing adequately and appropriately with those who are guilty and by giving proper effect to the sentences or orders which are imposed.

Principles of criminal justice, whether set out in penal codes, legislation or policy documents, attempt to capture a complex set of issues in grand statements which are supposed to guide the policies and actions of participants in the system. However, the world of human behaviour is not so easily captured into a few phrases and reality is necessarily more complex. The presumption of innocence, for example, sounds simple but raises complex questions. One of these is how many guilty criminals we are prepared to allow to escape apprehension and punishment in order to ensure that no innocent person is unjustly arrested and punished. We could punish those whom we are absolutely certain have committed an offence, but victims may feel aggrieved when cases fall on seeming technicalities and the release of too many apparently guilty persons could encourage vigilantism. Then the chances of justice being done would be even less likely.

13

Principles of criminal justice are abstractions which portray what ought to happen. Anecdotal insights, be they from police officers, solicitors, barristers, probation officers or recidivists, are frequently stories of the way the system failed to work as it is supposed. Empirical studies by criminologists and social scientists in recent years have given credence to some of these insights by revealing the gap between principles and reality.

It is very important for a student of criminal justice not to treat the principles as facts, but to regard them instead as criteria by which to judge the performance and practices of any system of criminal justice.

## Systems approaches to criminal justice

We have used the term 'criminal justice system', and must now look at what this implies. The term 'system' is often used to describe a designed unit such as a central heating or a recording system, or a natural phenomenon such as the solar system. It has also been used by social reformers who applied the term to the education or welfare systems and talked in terms of social engineering. The word 'system' conveys an impression of a complex object with interconnected parts and subdivisions with a flow from beginning to end.

Would it be accurate to describe criminal justice as a system? Certainly looking at the flow charts in Figures 1.4–1.7 below, it could well appear that there is a system at work which has a beginning and a number of predictable stages. The agencies in the criminal justice system are interdependent. One agency's output is another agency's input. Those who leave the courts with a prison sentence become the intake into the prisons at the back-end of the system. The role of each agency depends on its particular function in the overall scheme of things. For instance, policing cannot be fully understood without an awareness of the role of the police in the overall context of the system. The system may therefore be seen as greater than the sum of its parts.

It is also useful to view criminal justice as a system when considering planning, organisation and policy. During the 1980s for example there were a number of attempts to encourage a systems approach towards criminal justice. The Home Secretary, Leon Brittan, in evidence to the Home Affairs Committee of the House of Commons declared:

> . . . on taking office I decided that we needed a strategy which would enable us to establish and pursue our priorities and objectives in a deliberate and coherent way. . . . Our principal preoccupation is, and I believe it ought to be, the criminal justice system which, incidentally, I wish to see treated in all that we do as a system.
>
> (Home Affairs Select Committee, 23 January 1984)

There are several implications of regarding criminal justice as a system. It recognises that agencies are interdependent. Hence, the work of the prison and probation services depends on the work of the courts who in turn depend on the filtering role of the Crown Prosecution Service, the generation of cases by the police and initially by the activities of lawbreakers. It is very important for financial and resource planning and is particularly crucial when considering reforms to recognise the interdependency of the system. Thus reforms proposed for one part of the system will often have an impact on other agencies not directly involved in the proposed changes.

This can be seen by considering how the prison population can be affected by changes in the law. In the last 50 years, the advent of the motor car has created the need for more regulation by the criminal law, as cars not only provide opportunities for theft, but also necessitate regulation of driving if others are not to be endangered or inconvenienced. This increases the number of people brought to court, which in turn affects the number in prison. Motoring offences have resulted in a rise in the number of receptions into prisons of those convicted of serious motoring offences such as causing death by dangerous driving, along with many fine defaulters initially convicted of a comparatively trivial motoring offence. In 1991 of the 18,973 receptions of fine defaulters into prisons, 5,293 (28 per cent) were for motoring offences. Thus decisions at the front-end of the system will affect the back-end – the prisons.

A systems approach also encourages inter-agency consultation and co-operation. One recommendation from the Woolf Inquiry into the series of prison riots during 1990 was the need for greater co-operation and liaison between agencies in the criminal justice system. Thus prisons cannot be effectively managed without the fullest co-operation of all agencies responsible for dealing with offenders. The report recommended that a Criminal Justice Consultative Council (CJCC) be set up. This was done in 1991 and includes senior members of most of the agencies. Since then 24 local committees have been formed. The aim of establishing Area Committees was to encourage better communications between agencies and to improve strategic planning by identifying common areas of concern, receive reports, collect and distribute information on agency and cross-agency activities, disseminate information regarding available resources and be a forum for addressing strategic developments that affect all agencies.

Greater co-operation between criminal justice agencies and external organisations was also encouraged during the 1980s in respect of crime prevention. Many partnerships were set up, encouraged by the Home Office, involving links between official criminal justice agencies, local government and the voluntary and business sectors. These will be explored in Chapter 11.

How systematic is criminal justice in England and Wales? First, we have to recognise that the multiple and competing aims of the system mean that different goals may be simultaneously pursued by different participants. These aims are not easy to reconcile, either in the system as a whole or within specific agencies. For example, should the judge give a sentence that deters the future lawbreaker or one that rehabilitates past lawbreakers?

These multiple aims also affect how those working in agencies see their role, and how, over time, they have developed their own ways of working within conflicting constraints. Thus agencies have developed what can be described as a distinctive working culture or professional ideology. One example of these kinds of conflicts can be found in the implementation of parts of the Criminal Justice Act 1991, which enacted curfew orders and electronic monitoring but did not provide details as to how or when they were to come into effect. These new sanctions were not popular with some sections of the probation service who regard themselves as a profession whose aim is to help or care for offenders, rather than to supervise or control them. So the central problem of describing criminal justice as a system is to recognise the practical implications of these conflicting goals.

Secondly, problems may arise where agencies are expected to co-operate with each other. There may for example be competition between agencies over the allocation of responsibilities or funding. Different working cultures which derive from different perceptions of the goals of the system may lead to mistrust between agencies. This may mean that they are reluctant to co-operate with each other and may inhibit the exchange of information, which affected the initial relationship between the police and the Crown Prosecution Service when it was established in 1985. Differing models, as described below, may be followed: the police, who have traditionally been seen as following a crime control model, may have difficulties in communicating with lawyers whose role derives from the due process model, or with social workers, who may be more committed to a rehabilitative model.

Thirdly, a certain level of conflict is designed into the system by the *adversarial* nature of criminal trials. It is the duty of the prosecution to prove the guilt of the accused 'beyond reasonable doubt', whereas it is the duty of the defence lawyer to plant that 'reasonable doubt' in the minds of the magistrates or the jury and so secure an acquittal. This adversarial nature of criminal trials has important consequences for other parts of the system. It affects the way the police, prosecutors and the probation service perceive and discharge their respective roles.

As we have seen, the trial seeks not to establish the truth, but provides a process for the conviction or acquittal of the accused which affects the kind of evidence the police must secure. The logic of the adversarial style of trial explains why the defence lawyer may cross-examine victims of crime, for example in rape cases, in a way that appears at times to be brutal and insensitive.

## Flow charts of the criminal justice system

The interrelationships between agencies and stages in the system can be represented in flow charts which provide a helpful snapshot of the process to enhance understanding of the jigsaw of interrelationships in the system.

Figures 1.4–1.7 illustrate the flow and system process diagrams designed in recent years, and are a useful indicator of aggregate flows and stages.

Flow charts however provide a misleadingly simplistic picture of a system that involves encounters between human beings, all coming into the system with their own motives, be they criminals, victims or criminal justice officials. Each encounter involves an individual story, and has significance in the overall drama of society's response to crime. The drama, morality and social consequences of crime and punishment cannot be portrayed easily in such charts. In addition, while they show some of the ways in which agencies and the stages of the system interrelate, they cannot always reflect the complexities of how one decision, taken by one agency at a particular point in the system affects later decisions.

Some prefer to see criminal justice as a process – through which a case or a defendant passes. In this process all stages, each governed by a set of discrete rules, are interrelated and affect the eventual outcome. Whether a defendant pleads guilty or not guilty for example affects not only whether they are convicted, but whether and how evidence must be prepared, whether they are given bail, and it will almost certainly affect any sentence. At the same time, defendants' decisions about whether or not to plead guilty, and if so, when to plead guilty, will be affected by what might happen at later stages.

## Models of criminal justice

Models of criminal justice are essentially different perspectives on, or different ways of looking at, criminal justice, derived from the work of writers from a variety of legal, sociological, or administrative backgrounds. They provide a way of looking at criminal justice in terms of some general characteristics, principles or themes of a system. They help the person new to a system to come to terms with its complexities and to make some sense of it. But it should be remembered that like all models, they are a scaled down version of the real thing and will not capture all its complexities.

Herbert Packer first identified two alternative models – a crime control model which stressed the role of criminal justice in terms of the efficient controlling of crime (the conveyor belt), and a due process model (the obstacle course), which stressed the importance of the rule of law and procedural safeguards (Packer 1968). These ideas were extremely influential, and later writers identified further models such as Michael King who outlined six such models (King 1981).

The first model, originally developed by Packer is the *due process* model, which represents an idealised version of how the system should work derived from the ideas inherent in the rule of law. It encompasses the principles of the defendant's rights found in textbooks and constitutional documents. It incorporates principles conveyed in well-known phrases such as the presumption of innocence, the defendant's right to a fair trial, equality before

**Fig 1.4** The criminal process: from suspicion to conviction

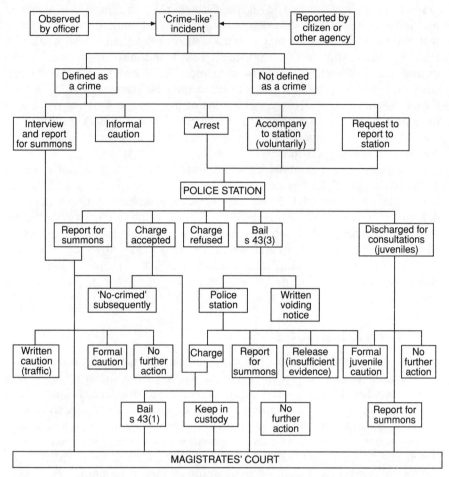

(Bottomley K and Pease K. (1986) *Crime and Punishment – Interpreting the Data.*
Milton Keynes: Open University Press: 63. Adapted from Femmill and Morgan-Giles
(1980). fig 2.2: 14 and Ashworth (1984) fig 2: 13)

the law and that justice should be seen to be done. These phrases embody
principles that underlie and allow us to interpret the many rules surrounding
both the trial and the pre-trial processes. They protect defendants in order
that the innocent may be acquitted and only the guilty convicted.

The second model is the *crime control* model identified by Packer and earlier explored by Jerome Skolnick in his book *Justice without Trial* (Skolnick
1966). This stresses the role of the system in reducing, preventing and curbing crime by prosecuting and punishing those who are guilty of offences. It
also stresses the importance of protecting citizens and serving the public by

**Fig 1.5** The criminal process: first court appearance to sentence

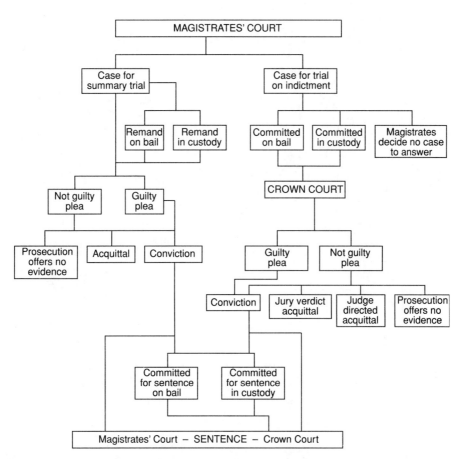

(Bottomley K and Pease K. (1986) *Crime and Punishment – Interpreting the Data.*
Milton Keynes: Open University Press: 72. Adapted from Ashworth (1984)
fig 2: 13)

crime reduction. Thus the police and prosecution agencies may interpret
their role primarily as crime fighters responsible for ensuring that the guilty
are brought to justice. However, problems arise if this aim is pursued regardless of rules protecting the rights of the suspect. Fabricating evidence or
neglecting to use search warrants could be seen as justifiable in order to
ensure that an offender whom the police 'know' to be guilty is found guilty.
This problem underlies many laws governing police procedure, seen most
recently in legislative reforms of the 1980s. The Police and Criminal
Evidence Act 1984 introduced the procedure under which the police tape
recorded interviews with suspects in police stations, and the Prosecution of

19

**Fig 1.6** Flow model – Pullinger

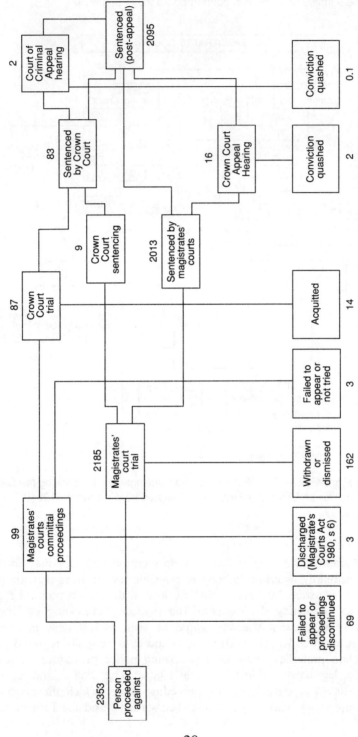

(Pullinger H (1985) *Research and Planning Unit Paper No 36* London: Home Office)

20

**Fig 1.7** Models of criminal justice

| Social function | Process model | Features of court |
|---|---|---|
| 1. Justice | Due process model | a) Equality between parties<br>b) Rules protecting defendants against error<br>c) Restraint or arbitrary power<br>d) Presumption of innocence |
| 2. Punishment | Crime control model | a) Disregard of legal controls<br>b) Implicit presumption of guilt<br>c) High conviction rate<br>d) Unpleasantness of experience<br>e) Support for police |
| 3. Rehabilitation | Medical model (diagnosis, prediction, and treatment selection) | a) Information collecting procedures<br>b) Individualisation<br>c) Treatment presumption<br>d) Discretion of decision-makers<br>e) Expertise of decision-makers or advisers<br>f) Relaxation of formal rules |
| 4. Management of crime and criminals | Bureaucratic model | a) Independence from political considerations<br>b) Speed and efficiency<br>c) Importance of and acceptance of records<br>d) Minimisation of conflict<br>e) Minimisation of expense<br>f) Economical division of labour |
| 5. Denunciation and degradation | Status passage model | a) Public shaming of defendant<br>b) Court values reflecting community values<br>c) Agents' control over process |
| 6. Maintenance of class domination | Power model | a) Reinforcement of class values<br>b) Alienation of defendant<br>c) Deflection of attention from issues of class conflict<br>d) Differences between judges and judged<br>e) Paradoxes and contradictions between rhetoric and performance |

(King M (1981) *The Framework of Criminal Justice.* London: Croom Helm: 13)

Offences Act 1985 led to the establishment of a prosecution agency independent of the police – the Crown Prosecution Service.

For many decades it has been accepted that offenders may not be wholly responsible for their own actions but that their criminality may spring from individual characteristics or social factors. These may be psychological disturbance or problems related to their family circumstances or the social environment. It may make little sense to punish such offenders without at the same time attempting to deal with these underlying issues. This is reflected in King's third model, that of *rehabilitation,* which has affected many parts of the criminal justice process. Under this model one of the major considerations at each stage is how best to deal with the individual offender, assuming that their criminality can be reduced by taking a rehabilitative approach. Thus it might be more desirable for the police to divert some offenders, especially young offenders, from the system, in circumstances where they feel that no benefit will be served by prosecution. The police have powers to caution offenders and refer them to social work agencies which may also help adult offenders. Social workers and probation officers become involved at the sentencing stage, by preparing pre-sentence reports on the offender's circumstances and outlining sentencing options which may involve counselling and treatment rather than punishment.

Rehabilitation therefore individualises decisions, requiring that the needs of the offender are taken into account. It gives all agencies far greater amounts of discretion. This may well conflict with other goals – for example with those of due process which seek to ensure that all offenders are treated equally, or with the crime control model which stresses the need to punish the guilty.

King's fourth model reflects the pressure on criminal justice officials to implement rules and procedures within the many constraints imposed by limited resources and public pressure to solve crimes. Agencies must therefore establish measures of *bureaucratic efficiency.* They must ensure that defendants are tried and sentenced as speedily and efficiently as possible. If defendants spend too long in prison before they come to trial, if trials take too long and are too costly, or if it is argued that too many defendants are acquitted or that there are miscarriages of justice, agencies and courts will come under considerable criticism. The cost effectiveness of law enforcement and court administration has become a major concern of the government in the 1990s.

Balancing the interests of due process with those of crime control and bureaucratic efficiency is not always easy. It is difficult for example to subject abstract principles such as justice to tests of cost effectiveness. How many defendants should be acquitted? How many should be tried rather than plead guilty? There are no straightforward answers to these questions – no yardstick against which to assess the efficiency of the system. Indeed in some instances the interests of justice may conflict with those of efficiency – as can be seen in the example of not guilty pleas. If the defendant pleads not guilty, the prosecution and the defence have to prepare a case which may involve collecting evidence, summoning witnesses and preparing the many documents involved in a trial. If the defendant pleads guilty, much of this work can be avoided. Guilty pleas are therefore cost effective and save the time of victims, witnesses, police, courts and the Crown Prosecution Service. But any pressure on defendants to plead guilty could deprive them of their right to trial. However, if more defendants insisted on their right to trial the system could become overloaded and more costly.

On the other hand the police might not have sufficient admissible evidence to proceed against a person they suspect is guilty. The due process model would result in no action being taken. However, there may be some concern about the resources expended on an investigation with no result. The tension between these models will result in a difficult decision on whether to charge the person and hope that they plead guilty or to drop the case.

Some would argue that offenders should be publicly tried and sentenced in order to reflect the community's moral disapproval of offending behaviour. This is reflected in the fifth model identified by King – the *denunciation and degradation* model. In this model, public trial and punishment are necessary to underline the law abiding values of the community. Some sociologists have argued that the criminal justice system serves an important social function in reinforcing social values. While this may conflict with the aims of rehabilitation, it can be argued that such public punishment and expression of society's disapproval can in itself be rehabilitative, as it may induce feelings of shame in offenders – a prerequisite for rehabilitation. John Braithwaite argues in favour of re-integrative shaming – offenders should feel ashamed of their offences but shaming should not be so extreme that it stigmatises offenders to a point where they cannot be re-integrated into the community (Braithwaite 1989).

Analysing criminal justice systems also raises questions about who makes the law and whose interests criminal justice serves. This is reflected in King's last model, the *power* model. Some, using a marxist or conflict perspective, which will be outlined in Chapter 2, argue that criminal justice systems essentially reinforce the role of the powerful – those who make the laws and who are served by the many agencies of the system. Thus criminal law and its enforcement are influenced by the interests of dominant classes, elites, races or gender, depending on the particular version of domination used. The state is regarded in this model as acting in the interest of the dominant group who use the criminal law to further these interests. Advocates of this approach point to the over-representation of those from poorer sections of the community as defendants in the criminal justice system.

To King's six models of criminal justice we would add a seventh: the *just deserts* model. Combining elements of retribution for offenders with a notion of proper respect for the treatment of the accused or defendant, this model stresses the importance of punishing offenders in terms of their blameworthiness and the seriousness of their offence, not through crude revenge or incapacitation, but in response to the wrongfulness of their act. This brings together the principles of respect for the offender as a human being with certain rights, the need to establish the offender's culpability for the offence so as to punish only the guilty, and the right of society to exact retribution from those who have done wrong. This links punishment and crime to issues of morality and control.

How useful are these models of criminal justice? To an extent they focus on and magnify one feature of the system. They do however illustrate different ways of looking at the system and indicate very different influences on policy and practice. Most of these models have been developed by different academic disciplines such as criminology, sociology or law and more recently from systems analysis utilised by experts in management and auditing techniques. Not surprisingly these disparate disciplines provide different snapshots of bits of the system from their own perspective. Lawyers focus mainly on procedures before and during trial. Sociologists emphasise the informal influences that can lead to inequalities and injustice. Criminologists focus on crime statistics and explanations of crime. Systems analysts trace the aggregate flow of cases through the system, management consultants look at problems of accountability and effectiveness, whilst accountants examine the cost effectiveness of the entire system and agencies within it. This has led to the development of management by objectives and the use of auditing techniques in the criminal justice system.

These different models indicate the many different influences on policy which often conflict. It might be better to understand a criminal justice system by starting with its multiple goals and by understanding the influences on the agencies that seek to implement these goals, be they legal, political, administrative, professional or economic. The next section will briefly outline recent legislation and reports which have had an important impact on the system, and which illustrate these conflicting policy pressures.

## CRIMINAL JUSTICE LEGISLATION

'The first five Criminal Justice Acts of the century were spaced out over nearly 50 years, from 1925 to 1972, whereas the last five have come in less than 20 years since 1972 and the current Act is the third in only five years.' Wasik and Taylor wrote this in 1991 since when there have been two more Criminal Justice Acts. The last decade has seen a series of reviews, inquiries and proposals for legislative reform involving virtually every aspect of criminal justice.

This section aims to outline briefly recent developments in the 1990s, highlighting how these reflect the many conflicting goals and models of the system and their effect on policy. These are the Criminal Justice Act 1991, subsequently amended, the report of the Royal Commission on Criminal Justice published in July 1993, and the Criminal Justice and Public Order Act 1994. The final section of this chapter gives a chronology of key legislation and events which have had a significant impact on the system – many of which will be discussed in later chapters. But first let us look at the remarkable history of one recent example of criminal justice legislation, the Criminal Justice Act 1991.

## Criminal Justice Act 1991

This Criminal Justice Act (CJA 1991) was preceded by an unprecedented amount of research, planning, consultation and training. An experiment on unit fines was carried out in magistrates' courts in Hampshire, and extensive training was given to those who were to enforce the Act. But despite the research and consultation that went into the Act, within seven months of its implementation the Home Secretary announced that amendments were to be made to it.

The Act developed out of the recommendations of several reports and extensive consultations preceded the eventual legislation. These included the report of the Carlisle Committee, *The Parole System in England and Wales: Report of the Review Committee* (1988), the government's Green Paper, *Punishment, Custody and the Community* (1988) and the White Paper, *Crime, Justice and Protecting the Public*, published in February 1990.

The CJA 1991 was hailed as a far-reaching systematic reform of sentencing, although it reflected many existing shifts in penal philosophy and sentencing policy. The underlying themes of this change were expressed in the 1990 White Paper, *Crime, Justice and Protecting the Public*, and included the need for more consistency in sentencing policy and for sentences to be proportionate to the offence. In addition it introduced what has come to be known as a 'twin track' approach to sentencing making a clearer distinction between property offences and violent crime. The former were to be dealt with by a greater use of punishment in the community, while the latter, with a view to crime prevention, could result in longer prison sentences. The overall framework for sentencing otherwise was provided by a philosophy of 'just deserts': punishing in accordance with the current offence, rather than past crimes or possible future ones.

An example of this approach was the introduction of the unit fine system under which sentencers were to allocate points reflecting the severity of the offence. These points would then be related to the offender's income, producing a specific amount of fine. This was in part to alleviate the problems of imposing fines on offenders with very different means where the same fine could have a severe impact on poorer defendants, while representing little loss for wealthier ones. The application of the formula would also, it was argued, achieve more consistency.

Unit fines almost immediately attracted criticism. The calculation for translating points into actual amounts meant that fines were not only higher overall, but that they were particularly severe for those on middle incomes, typically convicted for traffic offences. In a review of the impact of the CJA 1991 Martin Wasik comments that 'people on average incomes found themselves in the top band' (*The Magistrate*, October 1993: 15).

Vociferous criticism was made of another aspect of the sentencing reforms introduced by the CJA 1991. Section 29 had prevented judges and magistrates taking into account past convictions when sentencing except in limited circumstances. Furthermore, they could only take into account two offences

25

when assessing seriousness for a person convicted of multiple incidents. Thus the burglar convicted of 20 burglaries would actually be sentenced on the basis of the worst two burglaries. Sentencers felt unable to reflect the frequency and history of offending in their disposals.

Most of the provisions of the Act came into effect on 1 October 1992. By Easter 1993, Kenneth Clarke, the then Home Secretary, announced that the unit fine system was to be abandoned. Legislation to this effect was added to the Criminal Justice Bill already before Parliament. Thus the CJA 1993, which dealt primarily with measures to combat anti-terrorist acts, drug trafficking and insider dealing, was used to amend the CJA 1991. Section 65 abolished the two main planks of the 1991 Act, unit fines and s 29. The new Act provides that sentencers must take account of means when fining, and adjust fines up or down as appropriate, but without imposing a framework for doing so. In addition, the court can now consider all offences before the court and offenders' previous convictions or any failure to respond to earlier sanctions can be used by the courts when deciding on a sentence.

## Royal Commission on Criminal Justice 1993

While the 1991 Act was primarily directed towards sentencing policy, successive revelations of miscarriages of justice in the 1980s and concerns about police procedures led to the setting up of a Royal Commission chaired by Lord Runciman. Its brief was:

> to examine the effectiveness of the criminal justice system in England and Wales in securing the conviction of those guilty of criminal offences and the acquittal of those who are innocent, having regard to the efficient use of resources. . .

It was also to consider whether there should be changes in aspects of the system including the conduct of police investigations; the role of the prosecutor and issues involving advanced disclosure to the defence; the role of experts such as forensic scientists; the possibility that courts might have an investigative role prior to the trial; the duties of the court in respect of considering evidence – especially uncorroborated confession evidence. Finally, it was to consider the role of the Court of Appeal and arrangements for considering and investigating allegations of miscarriages of justice.

Many research projects were commissioned to examine these issues and the Commission reported in July 1993. It considered that both legislative change and significant changes in attitudes and conduct were necessary. It made 352 recommendations, the most significant of which were:

- To set up an independent Criminal Cases Review Authority which would consider allegations of miscarriages of justice, supervise investigations of them by police forces and refer cases to the Court of Appeal.
- To maintain the right to silence in police custody and to tighten the rules of confession evidence but not to require supporting evidence for such confessions.

- To introduce continuous video recording of police custody suites.
- To establish a 'helpline' scheme in all police forces to enable officers to report concerns about possible malpractice.
- To require defendants to disclose any defence prior to trial.
- To abolish committal proceedings in their present form in magistrates' courts.
- To abolish the defendant's right to choose trial by jury in triable either way cases – that is cases which can be heard either in the magistrates' court or the Crown Court.
- To allow judges in exceptional cases to order selection of a jury containing up to three people from ethnic minority communities.
- To introduce a more open system of sentence discounts with earlier pleas of guilty attracting higher discounts.
- To tighten up arrangements to ensure that convicted defendants get legal advice on their prospects of appeal.

Many of these proposals are currently under review. In March 1994 the government published a discussion paper on the independent body to consider alleged miscarriages of justice, and other proposals including those dealing with sentencing discounts are included in the Criminal Justice and Public Order Act 1994 (CJPOA 1994). Other recommendations, such as the recommendation to retain the so-called right to silence of the accused, have been disregarded by provisions introduced by the CJPOA 1994.

The Royal Commission with its emphasis on preventing miscarriages of justice whilst at the same time paying regard to securing the conviction of the guilty raises issues fundamental to the conflict between crime control and due process. Particularly controversial for example has been the issue of the right to silence. This right, seen as essential to protect the innocent, is also seen as a barrier to conviction of the guilty. Other aspects of the system have also been the subject of intense controversy. Concerns about rising rates of persistent offending by children and teenagers have led to attempts to toughen the powers of the courts in respect of such offenders. Thus, in October 1993 the Home Secretary announced at the Conservative Party Conference that he would be seeking new legislation in respect not only of the right to silence, which he wished to see abolished, but also in respect of young offenders. Thus he argued:

> I have been reviewing too the powers we need to deal with persistent young offenders. We are all sick and tired of reading about young hooligans who have endlessly stolen cars, burgled houses and terrorised communities. As things stand they can cock a snook at authority. Magistrates are powerless to deal with them. It is time to untie their hands and give the public the protection they need. . .

Announcing a variety of proposals he said:

> In the last 30 years the balance in the criminal justice system has been tilted too far in favour of the criminal and against the protection of the public. The time has

come to put that right. I want to make sure that it is criminals that are frightened, not law abiding members of the public.

These issues were to be part of what was hailed as a comprehensive package on law and order including two Acts, the Police and Magistrates' Courts Act 1994 and the CJPOA 1994. Both Acts were passed following considerable controversy, including the defeat of some proposals in the House of Lords.

## Criminal Justice and Public Order Act 1994

This Act deals with many aspects of the criminal justice system. Details of its provisions will be given in relevant chapters. Below are its main provisions:

- The introduction of a secure training order for 12–14-year-old persistent offenders. The first half of this order is to be spent in secure training units, five of which are to be provided, mainly from the private sector. The second half will be spent under compulsory supervision in the community.
- The doubling of the maximum sentence for 15–17-year-olds of detention in a young offender institution from one to two years (see Chapter 5).
- Curbing the right to silence by allowing a court to draw inferences from a defendant's silence during police questioning or in court.
- Section 25 of the Act provides that bail cannot be granted to defendants charged with or convicted of homicide or rape or who have a previous conviction for such an offence. Section 26 provides that persons accused or convicted of committing an offence while on bail need not be given bail (see Chapter 6).
- Pilot projects for curfew orders and electronic monitoring.
- Further contracting out of prisons and prisoner escorts.
- Changes to court procedure – the Act abolishes the present system of filtering out cases in magistrates' courts before they go to the Crown Court, known as committal proceedings. These are to be replaced by transfer proceedings. This was recommended by the Royal Commission on Criminal Justice.
- With regard to sentencing, s 48 of the Act, which deals with discounts for guilty pleas, requires the courts to take account of the timing and circumstances of a guilty plea in line with the recommendations of the Royal Commission.
- Changes in police powers in relation to obtaining intimate samples and, more controversially, increased powers of stop and search where the police believe that serious incidents of violence may take place (see Chapter 4).
- Tougher powers against trespassers and unauthorised camping – directed at new age travellers and rave parties of more than 100 people. A new offence of aggravated trespass is created in ss 68 and 69. In addition, the

enhanced protection for property owners against squatters effectively amounts to the criminalisation of squatting.

- Changes to the laws in relation to obscenity to incorporate child pornography produced on computers and some restrictions on the classification of video recordings – directed against what are commonly known as 'video nasties'.
- Changes to sexual offences – s 142 of the Act redefines the offence of rape which may now cover non-consensual intercourse with either a woman or a man – thus effectively recognising the offence commonly known as 'male rape'. Section 145 lowers the age of consent for homosexual acts from 21 to 18.
- The Act creates other new offences including a new offence of intentionally causing harassment, alarm or distress by using threatening, abusive or insulting words, behaviour or displays, intended to apply to racial harassment. Other changes deal with the use of embryos or foetuses, ticket touting at football matches and touting for car hire services.

Other legislation has dealt with a range of matters. The Police and Magistrates' Courts Act 1994 proposed a number of changes in the organisation of the police and magistrates' courts, including proposals for reorganising police authorities and the introduction of performance related pay for magistrates' clerks. In addition, the government sought to oversee appointments to magistrates' courts and to police authorities.

This spate of legislation illustrates several of the issues raised in this chapter, and reveals the constant tension between the different goals and models of criminal justice. The Home Secretary's comments quoted above clearly reflect an emphasis on crime control. Thus he stresses the need for tougher controls on young offenders and criticises the due process emphasis on defendant's rights. At the same time however the Royal Commission was set up in the light of allegations that police procedures and miscarriages of justice indicated that defendants' rights were not sufficiently protected. Many of the measures in the CJPOA 1994 have been inspired by increasing concern over persistent offending by young persons, offences committed while on bail, and others, such as the provisions in relation to inferences from silence and police powers and public order, clearly reflect a crime control perspective. Others derive from the bureaucratic efficiency model, most notably the provisions to abolish committal proceedings. Provisions which allow the greater involvement of the private sector by providing prison escort services and secure units are further indications of a belief that such involvement is cost effective.

The controversy surrounding the passage of the CJPOA 1994 also revealed the conflicts between the models of criminal justice, with critics of the legislation seeking to protect the right to silence and resisting what was seen as a shift towards a more punitive approach to justice for young offenders, seen by others as vital for crime control, just deserts and denunciatory purposes. But tougher sentencing powers add to the cost of criminal justice as more offenders head for prison, and any proposals to toughen police powers inevitably raise issues of due process. The provisions directed against squatting, rave parties and new age travellers have been particularly controversial and have provoked much public protest. They have led to accusations that the government is seeking to criminalise young people's life-styles, illustrating the power model discussed earlier.

In this chapter, we have suggested that to understand how a criminal justice system operates it is necessary to identify its many aims, to be able to describe its procedures, modes of punishments and the behaviour criminalised and to appreciate the interdependencies between agencies, which at a minimum allow us to call it a system. We have also indicated through the models of criminal justice many of the influences and principles that guide criminal justice agencies and placed this into the context of the political, economic and cultural factors that shape participants' views and actions, be they offenders, judges, police or probation officers. Finally we have illustrated how models of criminal justice help us to come to terms with the tensions between the formal goals and the real practices that go on in the world of those who enforce, interpret and implement the criminal law. That world is complex, given its many manifestations, aspirations and everyday encounters, and no one theory, model or principle will do justice to that reality. This book will attempt to reflect these many issues as we look at specific agencies and stages of the system.

## CHRONOLOGY OF KEY DATES IN THE DEVELOPMENT OF CRIMINAL JUSTICE IN ENGLAND AND WALES

What follows is a list of significant dates referred to in this book. Added comments indicate key developments in the criminal justice system in England and Wales.

| | |
|---|---|
| 1717 | Transportation Act |
| 1779 | Penitentiary Act |
| 1784 | Transportation Act |
| 1816 | Millbank penitentiary opened in London |
| 1824 | Vagrancy Act |
| 1823 | Gaol Act |
| 1829 | Metropolitan Police Improvement Act. The Metropolitan Police Force was established |
| 1833 | Factory Act |
| 1842 | Pentonville prison opened |
| 1853 | Penal Servitude Act. Ends short terms of transportation and Park-hurst Prison opens with a regime designed for young offenders |

| 1854 | Reformatory School Act |
|---|---|
| 1856 | County and Borough Police Act |
| 1861 | Offences Against the Person Act |
| 1867 | End of transportation |
| 1877 | Prison Act. The Prison Commission was established with responsibility for all prisons in the country: the first chairman was Sir Edmund Du Cane |
| 1878 | Criminal Investigation Department (CID) of the Metropolitan Police was established |
| 1879 | Prosecution Offences Act |
| 1895 | Gladstone Committee Report |
| 1898 | Prison Act |
| 1898 | Criminal Evidence Act |
| 1901 | Borstal experiment introduced |
| 1907 | Probation of Offenders Act |
| 1908 | Prevention of Crime Act. Borstal system and preventive detention introduced |
| 1908 | Children Act. Restrictions on the imprisonment of children |
| 1913 | Mental Deficiency Act. Mentally deficient persons were diverted out of the prison system |
| 1919 | Police Act followed the Police Strike and the formation of the Police Federation |
| 1925 | Criminal Justice Act |
| 1933 | Children and Young Persons Act. Reformatories and industrial schools were replaced by approved schools |
| 1936 | Open prison was established near Wakefield<br>Prison Officers' Association was founded<br>End to arrows on uniforms and treadmills |
| 1936 | Public Order Act |
| 1948 | Criminal Justice Act. Abolished penal servitude, prison with hard labour and whipping. Introduced corrective training, preventive detention and detention centres |
| 1949 | Royal Commission on Capital Punishment |
| 1957 | Homicide Act |
| 1961 | Criminal Justice Act. Minimum age of imprisonment was raised from 15 to 17. Greater use was encouraged of borstal training instead of prison for offenders under 21 |
| 1962 | Royal Commission on the Police |
| 1963 | Prison Commission abolished and replaced by the Prison Department |
| 1964 | Criminal Procedure (Insanity) Act |
| 1964 | Police Act |
| 1965 | Murder (Abolition of Death Penalty) Act |
| 1966 | Mountbatten Report. Following the escape of the Russian spy George Blake from Wormwood Scrubs prison, Earl Mountbatten conducted an inquiry into prison security |

1967    Criminal Justice Act. Introduction of the suspended sentence and discretionary parole. Courts were empowered to suspend any sentence of imprisonment not exceeding two years. Parole allowed an inmate to apply for parole after serving one third of their sentence. Abolition of preventive detention and corrective training and corporal punishment in prisons. Introduction of majority jury verdicts

1968    Firearms Act

1968    Criminal Appeal Act

1969    Children and Young Persons Act. Introduced care and supervision orders and replaced approved schools and remand homes with community homes

1971    Misuse of Drugs Act

1971    Courts Act. Abolished Assizes and Quarter Sessions and established the Crown Court

1972    Road Traffic Act. Introduced the breathalyser

1972    Criminal Justice Act. Introduced community service orders

1974    Juries Act

1974    Rehabilitation of Offenders Act

1976    Bail Act

1977    Criminal Law Act. Allowed the court to suspend a sentence of imprisonment in part.

1979    Report of the May Committee on the Prison Services. A policy of positive custody was advocated

1980    Magistrates' Courts Act

1981    Scarman Report

1981    Contempt of Court Act

1981    Royal Commission on Criminal Procedure

1982    Criminal Justice Act. Reduction of the parole eligibility criteria from 12 to 6 months. Statutory criteria for sentencing young offenders to custodial sentences. Borstal training replaced by youth custody

1983    Mental Health Act

1984    Police and Criminal Evidence Act

1985    Prosecution of Offences Act. Established the Crown Prosecution Service

1986    Public Order Act

1988    Criminal Justice Act. Extension of statutory criteria for custodial sentences for young offenders

1988    Legal Aid Act

1988    Road Traffic Act

1990    White Paper, *Crime, Justice and Protecting the Public*

1991    Criminal Justice Act. Introduced the combination order and the unit fine

1991    Report on the Prison Disturbances of April 1990 (chairman, Lord Justice Woolf). It recommended wide-ranging changes to the nature of prison regimes and the need for greater co-ordination throughout the criminal justice system.

1991     Criminal Procedure (Insanity and Unfitness to Plead) Act
1993     Royal Commission on Criminal Justice (chairman, Lord Runciman)
1993     Bail (Amendment) Act
1993     Criminal Justice Act repeals the unit fine
1994     Sexual Offences Act
1994     Police and Magistrates' Courts Act
1994     Criminal Justice and Public Order Act

## Review questions

1. Identify and outline the characteristics of the seven models of criminal justice defined in Chapter 1.
2. Identify current issues and controversies affecting criminal justice (for example a current case, issue or debate in Parliament, statement by politicians or other public figures) and consider:
   (a) To what extent these reveal the conflicting goals of the criminal justice system.
   (b) How these would be approached by the different models of criminal justice outlined above.

## Further reading

Ashworth A (1994) *The Criminal Process*. Oxford: Clarendon Press
King M (1981) *The Framework of Criminal Justice*. London: Croom Helm
Sanders A and Young R (1994) *Criminal Justice*. London: Butterworths

# Chapter 2
# IMAGES OF CRIME

Images and Definitions of Crime
Criminal Liability and Criminal Defences
Influences on Public Perceptions of Crime
Theories of Criminal Behaviour

## INTRODUCTION

What is crime? This is not such an easy question to answer as it might at first appear because a number of different images are associated with the words crime and criminal. In this chapter we will look at the different uses of the word, from the legal conception of crime used to establish a person's liability for criminal conduct, to the wider conception of crime used by the public and the media. This wider conception reflects the reality that most crime does not end up with a criminal being convicted because much is unnoticed, unrecorded or unsolved. The sources of information about crime which shape these public perceptions will be explored and we will finally look at many of the theories put forward by criminologists, psychologists and sociologists to explain crime. These accounts of crime filter into everyday consciousness and affect the public's notions about the causes of crime and policies which aim to 'do something about crime'. They also influence the way that the professions involved in the criminal justice process think about crime, be they probation officers or judges.

## IMAGES AND DEFINITIONS OF CRIME

Legally, a crime is any act or omission proscribed by the criminal law and thus punishable by the state through the criminal justice process. The criminal law and its associated punishment are used against a very wide range of behaviour – from murder, rape and assault to driving with excess alcohol, parking on a yellow line and failing to comply with a plethora of health and safety regulations. While few would dispute that murder is and should be an offence, not all members of the public would think of someone who drives with excess alcohol in their blood as a criminal.

The public have a commonsense view of what they regard as crime. Behaviour which people disapprove of is often described as criminal to emphasise its seriousness and unacceptability. These commonsense images tend to be associated with the deliberate infliction of physical harm often involving a confrontation between an offender and a victim. Dishonesty, cheating or theft are also a key part of these commonsense notions of crime. Everyday conceptions of the criminal carry connotations of the wrongdoer who should be stigmatised. Stigma means that a person is not considered normal, or is deviant and should be censured as a person who behaves badly.

Yet not all activities proscribed by the criminal law are necessarily regarded as crimes, or their perpetrators as criminal. In the workplace for example employees may regularly fiddle the books or engage in petty pilfering. These activities are described euphemistically as perks or fiddles rather than as theft or fraud. Members of the public may inflate insurance claims or fail to disclose their full earnings to the Inland Revenue without regarding themselves as criminals, or being viewed as such by others. Drivers may regularly infringe road traffic laws without considering their behaviour as deviant. Different groups therefore may have different conceptions of where to draw the line between acceptable behaviour and crime.

Even where individuals are injured and killed as a result of illegal actions they may not always be regarded as victims of crime. Many injuries and deaths in the workplace are caused by neglect of health and safety regulations. Yet these are regularly dealt with as accidents rather than as crimes, and those responsible are rarely sanctioned as criminals (Wells 1988; Croall 1992). This may be because there is no immediate confrontation between offender and victim and because those responsible intended no harm. Many are also physically injured within the home, by the actions of their spouses, lovers, parents or children. Yet domestic violence was for many years not widely perceived as being as serious as other violent crime – partly because it takes place in the private sphere of the home.

Although there is considerable overlap between legal and everyday conceptions of crime there is therefore no necessary equation between the two. Public tolerance of different activities changes over time and legal categories are subject to change. The criminal law in our society is not based on a fundamentalist or absolutist conception of morality but shifts according to changes in public attitudes. This is reflected in political pressures to change legislation that defines crime. Thus over the last 50 years the way in which the law has dealt with drunk driving, homosexuality, prostitution and domestic violence has changed. Changes in the public's tolerance of activities leads to campaigns to criminalise some behaviours and to decriminalise others. As seen in Chapter 1, parts of the Criminal Justice and Public Order Act 1994 aim to curb the activities of new age travellers and organisers of raves, while lowering from 21 to 18 years the age at which men may lawfully perform homosexual acts in private.

Hence the legal conception of crime is subject to change and depends, in a parliamentary democracy, on political as well as moral considerations. However, if the criminal law does not express and reflect public morality and concerns about harm to the community the public would have little regard for the law – it would lose its legitimacy. Furthermore it would be seen as unduly oppressive – as an instrument of social control and political domination. Such laws are unlikely to inspire public trust, confidence or legitimacy. They would be difficult to enforce and would undermine confidence in the criminal justice process.

To avoid confusion between the more technical and legal conception of crime used by lawyers and its everyday usage, we suggest the following definition of a criminal.

> A person whose behaviour is in breach of legally prescribed rules which renders that person liable to criminal proceedings.

As a starting point this definition is useful because it focuses on the three elements that are indispensable if we are to understand and explain crime. They are: behaviour, rules and enforcement.

## Behaviour

Criminal law is essentially concerned with the regulation of behaviour. This may involve prohibitions on some kinds of behaviour such as stealing another person's property or harming them deliberately. Other laws may require a specific action, such as having insurance when driving a car, or complying with regulations. In some instances it is the combination of behaviour with a particular situation that defines a crime such as being drunk in a public place. In others it is the combination of status with behaviour such as the purchase of alcohol by someone under 16 years of age.

Illegality covers a multitude of actions, responsibilities, circumstances and statuses and hence the diversity of acts that may be characterised as criminal is considerable. Thus it is impossible to offer a simple explanation of why someone acts criminally. Furthermore, people do not act in an identical fashion. Some people are more prone to self-indulgence, others are more violent in character. Later in this chapter we will look in more detail at the attempts to explain crime by identifying individual and social characteristics that are thought to lead to criminal behaviour, for example, unemployment or poor environmental conditions.

## Rules

The rules which determine whether or not behaviour is criminal are found in legislation passed by Parliament or in decisions of the courts. These form the starting point for understanding crime as they provide the legal definition of criminal acts. As we have seen, these rules may change over time, and the number of potentially illegal acts may increase as more behaviour, for example failure to wear a seat belt in a car, is criminalised.

There are two sources of law in England and Wales: legislation and law based on decided cases. Legislation consists of Acts of Parliament (statutes) and statutory instruments (often called subordinate legislation). Case law is law that has been built up over the years by decisions of the courts in individual matters: these may include decisions on the meaning of statutes. The law of England and Wales is thus based on the accumulation of previous cases and is described as a common law system, which distinguishes it from European systems which are based on codes established by legislation.

Although many offences are now governed by, or were created by, statutue, the general principles of criminal law are still matters of the common law, which also governs some of the most serious crimes, for example murder. The idea that the common law evolves from the piecemeal interpretation of the law by judges is an integral part of the legal tradition in England and Wales.

## Enforcement and criminal proceedings

Behaviour is not self-defining nor are rules self-enforcing. Laws do not have any impact unless they are enforced, or unless there is the anticipation of enforcement. How then is behaviour interpreted as breaking the rules? By whom and how are rules interpreted and applied? The criminal law specifies who can enforce the law and what procedures are necessary to investigate and prosecute crime, adjudicate on guilt and decide on an appropriate sentence. Enforcement is the responsibility of specialist agencies or organisations specifically given the right to enforce the law, such as the police, Customs and Excise Officers and Crown prosecutors. Although the basic procedures and guidelines for law enforcement are set out in statutes and case law, it is inevitable that these cannot cover every situation. That is why it is important to understand that many factors in addition to legal rules influence the way the criminal law is put into action.

Resources are required to fund the agencies and organisations that enforce the law. To learn how these agencies operate it is necessary to establish how they deploy these resources and how they interpret their formal goals and objectives. Professional loyalties, training and commonsense notions of crime and the crime problem will influence the way they decide on priorities and interpret their responsibilities. Also as officials in criminal justice agencies do not normally come from outside the society in which they work, many of the taken-for-granted prejudices of the wider culture also influence how they see their role.

Edwin Schur wrote, 'Once we recognise that crime is defined by the criminal law and is therefore variable in content, we see quite clearly that no explanation of crime that limits itself to the motivation and behaviour of individual offenders can ever be a complete one.' (Schur 1969: 10)

The three elements that constitute a criminal act, behaviour, rules and the enforcement of rules, are further refined by the concept of criminal liability. Not all actions by a person, that might appear to be in breach of the criminal law, are necessarily criminal because there may be an excuse or acceptable reason for their behaviour. In commonsense terms and in a legal sense they may not be blameworthy or culpable. Establishing the culpability of a defendant is therefore central to the criminal process and explains the central role of the trial as the mechanism of establishing criminal liability.

## CRIMINAL LIABILITY AND CRIMINAL DEFENCES

One of the most fundamental principles of criminal law is that a person should not be punished unless they have both committed the act or omission in question and are blameworthy. This means that in order to be considered culpable, it must be established that an offender has not only committed an offence but is responsible for it. These two aspects are usually referred to as the *actus reus*, the guilty act, and the *mens rea*, the guilty mind. Both the act and the intention are generally required before someone is deemed to be guilty of a crime.

Some crimes, called crimes of strict or absolute liability, do not require a guilty mind. These include offences such as speeding, drinking and driving, and applying a false trade description to goods. These types of crimes tend not to attract the same level of blame or culpability as offences that involve intention.

To illustrate the concepts of *actus reus* and *mens rea*, it is useful to analyse the offence of theft, which is now defined by s 1 of the Theft Act 1968 which states:

A person is guilty of theft if he dishonestly appropriates property belonging to another with the intention of permanently depriving that other of it.

It can be seen that two different elements make up the offence. First, the act of appropriating property belonging to another person, and secondly the mental element of dishonesty and the intent to permanently deprive another person. If any of these elements is missing, the offence is not committed. This can be highlighted by examining the modern problem of taking another person's car for the purpose of using it as a conveyance, popularly known as joyriding. After such use, the car is abandoned. The taker never intended to keep the car, thus they cannot be guilty of theft, having no 'intention to permanently deprive'. Therefore a different offence had to be created if this conduct was to be punished as a crime. The offence, now in s 12 of the Theft Act 1968, is, 'Taking a conveyance without the owner's consent'. This provision states:

... a person shall be guilty of an offence if, without having the consent of the owner or other lawful authority, he takes any conveyance for his own or another's use or, knowing that any conveyance has been taken without authority, drives it or allows himself to be carried in or on it.

Different offences relating to similar behaviour, for example assault, may reflect different levels of intent and seriousness. This can be illustrated by examining the different crimes relating to offences of violence, the seriousness of which is determined both by the injury inflicted and the level of intention, thereby combining an assessment of actus reus and mens rea in determining culpability.

Common assault is the least serious, and only be tried in the magistrates' court and is punishable by up to six months' imprisonment. It is defined as the intentional or reckless causing of another to fear immediate unlawful violence. More serious is the offence of occasioning actual bodily harm under s 47 of the Offences Against the Person Act 1861 (OAPA 1861). This can be tried either in the magistrates' court or the Crown Court and is punishable with a maximum sentence of five years' imprisonment. It is not necessary to establish that the accused intended the kind of injury that occurred. Actual bodily harm means any physical harm.

Another offence, higher up the ladder of seriousness, although attracting the same maximum penalty, is the offence under s 20, OAPA 1861 of unlawfully and maliciously wounding or inflicting grievous bodily harm. Grievous bodily harm means really serious harm. More serious still, triable only on indictment, and attracting up to life imprisonment, is the offence under s 18, OAPA 1861 of malicious wounding or causing grievous bodily harm with intent to do grievous bodily harm.

It is not possible to analyse these provisions in detail here, but it can be seen that varying combinations are possible depending on the level of injury and the level of intent to do harm of the kind that resulted – the mens rea. Did the defendant mean to do any harm at all, or, were they reckless as to what harm was caused? Did they intend to cause harm of the level inflicted? What was the level of harm inflicted?

The most serious offence known to the criminal law is, of course, murder, which is punishable with a mandatory life sentence. This means that once a conviction is recorded, only a life sentence can be passed by the judge. However the law has long recognised that deaths can be caused, even intentionally, in many different circumstances, not all equally blameworthy. This is reflected in the number of categories of homicide, including murder, manslaughter and infanticide. Murder is described as unlawful killing involving intention to kill or cause grievous bodily harm. Murder can be reduced to manslaughter (for which the sentence is variable) because of 'provocation' by virtue of s 3 of the Homicide Act 1957. This recognises that under pressure people may lose control and provocation is defined as a 'sudden temporary loss of self-control'. This provision has recently been the subject of much criticism. Particularly problematic has been the situation of women who have been systematically brutalised by partners and have planned to kill them. Decisions against these women have highlighted the requirement that in order to plead provocation any loss of control must be sudden. Thus Kiranjit Ahluwalia was convicted of the murder of her husband and sentenced to life imprisonment in 1989 despite claiming she was 'provoked' by 10 years of abuse at his hands.

Murder is also reduced to manslaughter when killing takes place as a result of diminished responsibility, defined as an abnormality of mind which impairs the mental processes, or under a suicide pact. Both these circumstances are referred to as voluntary manslaughter, where the intent was to kill but in less blameworthy circumstances. Some abused women have succeeded in arguing that they should be convicted of manslaughter rather than murder as a result of diminished responsibility brought on by the abuse. Kiranjit Ahluwalia's conviction was thus reduced to manslaughter on appeal in 1992.

Manslaughter includes all other forms of unlawful killing when there was a lesser degree of intent than that required for murder. Manslaughter is therefore committed when death results in the course of an unlawful act, for example, burglary, and in other circumstances where death was not actually intended. Many different combinations of circumstances can be envisaged and have come before the courts: the defendants who threw a brick from a motorway bridge to deter a 'blackleg' (*R v Hancock and Shankland* (1986)) and the defendant who played 'Russian Roulette' with tragic consequences for his step-father (*R v Mahoney* (1985)).

The role of the law is to develop rules that reflect moral blameworthiness. But as the following case illustrates, it is not always easy to apply these principles in cases involving the deliberate commission of a dangerous act resulting in death. In one recent case the Court of Appeal, seeking to clarify the application of principles, listed the kinds of situation in which this type of offence, sometimes called involuntary manslaughter, arises (*R v Sulman and Others* (1993)). This particular case arose after a patient died following a negligently conducted operation. There had been negligence – did that create a criminal offence? Negligent inattention in the sense of mere inadvertence does not create criminal liability; the degree of fault has to be gross negligence, such as:

- indifference to a known risk
- foresight of a risk which is nevertheless undertaken
- appreciation of the risk, and an intention to avoid it, but coupled with a high degree of negligence in the attempted avoidance
- inattention to a serious and obvious risk.

Infanticide is also recognised as a special case by the law which provides that a different offence, less culpable than murder is committed where a woman kills her child in the first year of its life, when the balance of her mind is affected by the birth.

Another situation recognised by the law is where death occurs as a result of a road accident. Legislation has taken a variety of approaches to these situations, the current position being that it is an offence to cause death by dangerous driving. Dangerous driving is defined as driving at a standard far below that of a competent and careful driver and where it would be obvious to such a driver that driving in that way would be dangerous.

The problem of basing criminal culpability on the offender's intention and not on the result of the offence can be seen in the increasing number of cases in which pedestrians or other car users are killed by a driver subsequently convicted of careless driving. While careless driving can kill, in many cases it has either no adverse consequence or only a trivial one. Outraged relatives have been appalled when drivers who have killed a member of their family have been given non-custodial sentences or even a fine. This outrage is further added to when the driver is proved to have been drinking and has a past record of driving with excess alcohol. Lee Taziker was 'over the limit' and driving at 56 mph when he swerved a 28-ton articulated lorry and hit and killed 17 year-old John Smith on a Somerset road in October 1993. Taziker was sentenced to 240 hours of community service and banned from driving for three years. Judge Willis, who gave the sentence, said, 'I do not think any useful purpose would be served by sending you to prison.' The victim's father, Steve Smith is quoted as saying, 'I simply cannot believe it ... It just makes a mockery of the law. You get more than that for thumping somebody.' (*Daily Telegraph*, 13 August 1994: 9).

## Criminal defences

In criminal trials the defence may argue that although the defendant did commit the act they had an excuse for so doing. These excuses reflect an acceptance that in certain circumstances the defendant could not help acting in a particular way, was somehow forced into the action, or could not control his or her behaviour and is therefore not to blame. The mens rea element of the criminal trial focuses on blameworthiness or moral culpability and the defence counsel may use arguments known as criminal defences in an attempt to show that the defendant was not responsible or blameworthy for the act they did indeed commit.

Where the mental capacities of the individual are impaired for example by mental illness, or not fully developed – as with a young person, the law may attach less – or no – blame. Children under the age of 10 years and those certified as mentally ill are not regarded as responsible for their actions in criminal matters.

A similar approach applies when we examine defences to criminal prosecutions. *Duress* refers to situations where people are compelled to do something that would otherwise be a crime as a result of threats made, or the circumstances they find themselves in. The threat or danger must be severe – such as death or serious personal injury and this will excuse all offences other than murder and treason. In these circumstances, although the offence is in one sense voluntary, it is said that the offender's will is overborne, so they are not regarded as responsible.

A situation commonly found in criminal acts is that the defendant was affected by alcohol or drugs. The mere fact of being drunk is not a defence, even though it is recognised that drinking may reduce inhibitions. It may however be a defence where the alcohol or drugs had the effect that the offender was not able to form the intent required for the commission of the crime, such as murder or wounding 'with intent'.

If an act normally regarded as illegal occurs when a defendant cannot control their physical acts, such as during an epileptic fit, they will not be held blameworthy. They are said to be in a state of *automatism*. Defendants are also not held blameworthy when responding to another person's aggressive actions, merely to defend themselves, that is in *self-defence*. The scriptures might require a person to turn the other cheek, the law does not.

## Sentencing mitigation

Even where a legal defence – which removes all blame – is not available or has not been accepted by the jury or magistrates, other factors may reduce culpability. After a defendant has been found guilty or has pleaded guilty, the defence may offer a plea in mitigation to the court. This will introduce factors suggesting that the seriousness of the offence is not as great as it might be, or that the offender is less blameworthy.

Mitigation may relate to the offence: that the offender played a limited part, was led into the offence by others, or that it happened almost by accident. Defendants may claim they forgot to renew a licence or their motor vehicle insurance. Mitigation might also relate to the personal circumstances of the offender. It may be argued that the offender is in such difficult circumstances that they should not be blamed or punished any more than has already happened because they might have lost their job or have been deserted by their family. If you sit in court for any length of time you might be surprised to hear the same mitigation repeated, such as the number of recently convicted people who are starting a job next week or whose girlfriend has just discovered she is pregnant. This part of the criminal process allows the convicted person the opportunity to minimise their culpability for the offence and so increase their chance of a more lenient sentence.

The court must take all these factors into account in passing sentence, which may mean that individual sentencing decisions are unpopular. Some sentencing decisions cause outrage and public anxiety and have been widely criticised in the press, Parliament or on the radio and television. It is important to appreciate that members of the public may have very different perceptions of criminal responsibility from those of the court. Questions of crime and criminal responsibility generate many strong opinions and public conceptions may well conflict with legal concerns. Public views of crime are not necessarily informed by the somewhat narrow legal conceptions of culpability and blameworthiness outlined above, nor do the public always appreciate the technicalities of requirements to prove intent or to focus on the act rather than the result. Public discussion tends to be more general than legal discussion – therefore it is necessary to look at the nature of debates outside the world of the criminal lawyer and the criminal court. It is also important to explore how the opinions of the public are influenced by information which they receive about crime from a variety of sources.

# INFLUENCES ON PUBLIC PERCEPTIONS OF CRIME

Some people find out about crime and form views on the basis of their own experiences or those of their family, friends or neighbours. In large part however their views are influenced by information in newspapers or on television. This may include coverage of individual cases, and some may follow discussions on crime by politicians and commentators. Before looking at the official criminal statistics in Chapter 3, it is important to explore how politicians, pressure groups and experts reflect and influence public assumptions about the extent and causes of crime.

## Crime in the mass media

Most people come to know about crime through the mass media – newspapers, television, books or films. This is because the majority of the public have little first-hand knowledge about crime or the criminal justice system unless they are victims or perpetrators. Newspapers and television coverage of crime stories will influence people's knowledge about crime and may enhance their fear of becoming a victim. Media coverage in itself may affect people's behaviour – women and the elderly for example are often scared to walk the streets at night for fear of being raped or mugged, and parents may be frightened to let their children out of the house alone through fear of kidnapping, sexual assault or murder. In reality of course the chance of such events happening is very small, and fears emerge from high profile media coverage.

Crime is a popular subject in the mass media, and as many point out, crime, especially sexual crime, sells newspapers (see for example, Schlesinger and Tumber 1994; Soothill and Walby 1991). Crime dramas are also extremely popular, as seen in the high ratings given to TV detectives such as Inspectors Morse, Taggart or Wexford. Few of course believe that drama gives a real picture of crime or policing – otherwise the murder rate in Oxford, Glasgow or Kingsmarkham would be the subject of national concern and police clear up rates would be vastly improved! How real is other, supposedly factual, reporting of crime?

In 1992 a series of injuries to horses in certain areas of the country caused great public outrage and anxiety, with newspaper articles about such attacks. Many routine equine injuries were attributed to 'horse-slashers'. Yet of course, horse slashing, however unpleasant for its victims, is scarcely a typical crime.

This selectivity means that a very unrepresentative picture of crime may be given by the media. From all the possible news stories about crime, the media can only select a small number. This selection will depend on decisions as to whether or not such stories are newsworthy. What makes a story newsworthy is likely to be its novelty or dramatic elements. Thus cases reported in newspapers are likely to be unusual or have elements capable of providing drama or titillation (Chibnall 1977; Soothill and Walby 1991). Most researchers would appear to agree for example that sexual and violent crimes, which play on the public's fear, are more likely to be reported than more common kinds of crime such as theft or vandalism (Ditton and Duffy 1983). In addition, these kinds of crime are also selectively reported with an over-emphasis on, for example, serial killers or rapists (Soothill 1993). Many have argued that the reporting of rape tends to focus on the 'sex fiend' who attacks women in public places – whereas in reality women are more likely to be raped in private places, by people they know (Soothill 1993).

Newspaper reports also tend to simplify crime stories, providing little by way of extended analysis (Schlesinger and Tumber 1994). News reports about crimes are necessarily abbreviated accounts of events, focusing on those aspects considered likely to attract the public's attention. This is also the case when the criminal statistics are reported. Although these are complex documents requiring careful interpretation, reports in the media tend to focus on simple questions about whether some kinds of crime have risen or fallen.

The media may also set in train what is called a moral panic about a particular kind of crime (Cohen 1980). This happens where a spectacular incident or series of incidents, for example a riot, a series of child abuse cases, or someone being killed by joyriders, alerts the public to a particular problem. The media may effectively create a new form of crime as the example of horse slashers demonstrates. Once the public has been alerted, there may be a tendency for more of these crimes to be reported both to the police and by the media, as they have now been defined as newsworthy. This gives the impression that there has been an increase in these crimes, which may be far from the truth. Following this the media may then report comments of the police, judges, and academic experts in an attempt to further explore this new problem. Often however the problem is not new – it has simply not been seen as newsworthy before. Moral panics often involve folk devils, like football hooligans, lager louts or new age travellers, who become the focus for wider anxieties about the crime problem, the nature of contemporary morality or the state of society (Cohen 1980).

Thus for example, rising rates of crime by young offenders are often seen as a symptom of declining standards of education or discipline, the increase in permissiveness, the decline in family and community or the effects of popular entertainment such as, in contemporary society, video nasties (Pearson 1994). It is interesting to note however that these kinds of sentiments have been voiced for well over a century – they appeared, for example, following the industrial revolution where hooliganism was attributed to these kinds of factors and to the adverse effects of popular music hall entertainment (Pearson 1983; 1994).

## Politicians

Politicians quite properly talk about issues which worry the public and there can be little doubt that crime is a major issue. The publication of criminal statistics attracts a lot of public attention. Apparent rises and falls in the rate of crime are discussed with the government of the day claiming credit for any fall in crime and disputing the reliability of any recorded rises. The opposition party in Parliament routinely blames government policies for any increase in crime and disputes any fall.

In the UK, crime has become more of an election issue since the 1970s. In the 1979 General Election campaign the Conservative Party, on advice from Saatchi and Saatchi, ran a poster campaign on the theme of crime and whether it was safe to vote for Jim Callaghan's Labour government. The poster, see Figure 2.1, made use of official statistics to highlight the growth of mugging, robbery and criminal damage.

The Conservative Party won the 1979 General Election. Despite its boast of being the party of law and order crime figures rose steadily. Between 1979 and 1992 the total amount of crime recorded has risen from 2,377,000 offences to 5,413,300. The number of robberies recorded in 1979 was 13,730. This increased to 47,700 in the year ending 31 March 1992.

The rise in recorded crime, which will be examined more closely in Chapter 3, has meant that crime has continued to be seen as a political issue with politicians arguing about the significance of the statistics and about the causes of crime. There has been for example, considerable political controversy over the extent to which rising crime can be attributed to greed or badness on the part of individuals, to family problems or problem families or whether it is related to wider social factors such as unemployment. The Conservative Party expressed the following view during the 1987 General Election:

> The origins of crime lie deep in society in families where parents do not support or control their children; in schools where discipline is poor and in the wider world where violence is glamourised and traditional values are under attack.
>
> (1987 Conservative Manifesto, quoted in Loveday 1992: 301)

Suggestions of a link between crime and unemployment, poverty or deprivation are dismissed as, in effect, excusing crime. In 1988 the then Prime Minister, Margaret Thatcher, commented that:

If anyone else is to blame it is the professional progressives among broadcasters, social workers and politicians who have created a fog of excuses in which the mugger and burglar operate.

(Loveday 1992: 302)

More recently, any suggested link between poverty and crime was rejected by the Employment Secretary, David Hunt, writing in a Conservative Political Centre pamphlet:

some of the so called cultures springing up in our country reject all decency and civilised values . . . the bulk of thieving today, of course, has nothing to do with poverty. It is the result of wickedness and greed.

(*Guardian*, 21 March 1994)

Tony Blair, as Labour Party spokesman for Home Affairs, popularised the slogan that governments should be 'tough on crime and tough on the causes of crime'. These causes may well include wider social factors. Thus he argued:

nobody excuses crime because of social conditions but it is plain common sense that if young people are brought up in a culture of no job prospects, poor education, violence, drug abuse and family instability then they are less likely to grow up as individually responsible citizens.

(*Guardian*, 21 March 1994)

As we shall see later empirical research has found that there are no simple explanations for crime. It is important to realise however that explanations of crime may have political significance and affect criminal justice policy.

**Fig 2.1** Conservative Party publicity on crime in the 1979 General Election

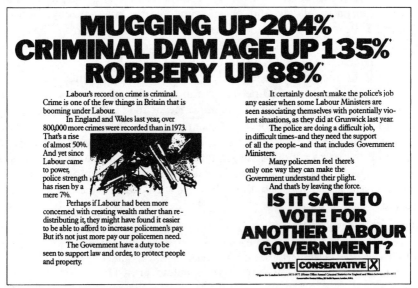

## Pressure and interest groups

Political parties are not the only representative groups to engage in debates about crime. A number of other bodies representing professional interests also contribute to discussions of crime policy. They may participate officially in Royal Commissions, appear on current affairs programmes or contribute newspaper articles. These bodies include the Police Federation which represents the rank of police constable, the Association of Chief Police Officers (ACPO), the Bar Council, the Law Society, the National Association of Probation Officers (NAPO), the Justices' Clerk Society and the Prison Officers' Association (POA). Voluntary groups such as the Magistrates' Association and the National Association of Victim Support Schemes also contribute in this way.

Pressure groups also have a key role in shaping attitudes about penal policy. The Howard League for Penal Reform, the Prison Reform Trust and the National Association for the Care and Resettlement of Offenders (NACRO) have played a key role in changing opinions. NACRO, for example, carries out research, sponsors projects, runs conferences and provides much useful information to its members, along with schools, colleges, journalists, policy makers, politicians and academics. NACRO aims to ensure that the case for improved prison conditions and less frequent use of custodial sentences is put effectively.

Pressure groups such as NACRO and professional interest groups such as the POA provide insights into the running of the criminal justice system, but they are first and foremost interest groups who aim to influence debates and policies. No information is thus entirely objective, a point which applies equally to the academics who comment on the criminal justice system.

## Academics and policy makers

Academics and policy makers also contribute to public impressions about the nature and causes of crime. Their commonly accepted theories filter into the public domain through publications and reports of research offered to the government and reported in the media. Thus their views influence many journalists, politicians, officials and practitioners.

Ways of looking at a problem such as crime alter over time according to changing assumptions about the causes and consequences of crime. This 'way of looking' is called a paradigm and the main shift in the penal paradigm in the 20th century will be further explored in Chapter 9. During the early decades of the 20th century the growing science of criminology promoted the view that crime resulted from genetic and environmental causes. Criminologists believed that crime could be cured by identifying the psychological and social determinants of crime, similar to the way medical practitioners diagnosed the causes of sickness, and they believed that criminals could be rehabilitated by the application of correctional policies. By the 1970s this view fell out of favour and gave way to the idea that rehabilitation was not easy to achieve. Other theorists pointed out that this emphasis on the offender had been at the expense of other goals such as punishment. Even so it was felt by most theorists that criminals should be treated justly and fairly. This led to the justice approach to punishment.

Academics may not agree amongst themselves over what priority to accord to the many factors associated with crime and views change over time in the light of new evidence, problems and changes in perspectives on crime. But the agenda of intellectual debate about crime, in part influenced by academics, has an impact beyond the walls of academia and helps to inform public debates on crime issues.

So far in this chapter we have examined what constitutes crime both in the narrow legal sense and in the broader views of the public. It is the task of the criminal justice system to respond to crime by following the procedures laid down by the law. As we have seen however, there is no simple definition of crime, and law enforcement agencies need to take account of wider public perceptions. The rest of this book will look at these aspects in more detail.

The remaining section of this chapter provides a summary of the major criminological approaches which have attempted to explain criminal behaviour. A full examination of these theories lies beyond the scope of this book, and interested readers should consult one of the sources in the reference list. It is important however to explore briefly these different approaches to crime as they inform the views of the law makers and enforcers whose work we will be looking at in subsequent chapters.

## THEORIES OF CRIMINAL BEHAVIOUR

As we have seen, public and political discussions incorporate a variety of notions about the causes of crime. Some see individual criminals as inherently bad or wicked. Others blame a general lack of discipline, particularly within families. Yet others argue that the culture of modern society, with its emphasis on materialism and individual success, may be associated with crime, along with socio-economic factors such as unemployment or social deprivation. Academic theories, based on disciplines such as criminology, sociology or psychology are related to these commonsense notions, attempting to subject them to the tests of empirical validation through research. As argued above, however, it is clear that no one single set of factors can fully account for the wide variety of actions defined as crime.

There are, therefore, many different ways to approach the task of explaining criminal behaviour. We can start with individual offenders and ask whether they differ from law abiding individuals. Early criminologists likened criminality to a disease. Thus much research focused on the characteristics of offenders, looking at their biological make up, psychological characteristics or personal, family or social circumstances.

Individuals however live within a social environment in which they learn the values of a culture. As we have already seen, there may be a gap between legal notions of crime and what is defined as criminal among different groups within society. Some forms of crime may be tolerated and not seen as deviant within some groups. Thus, whatever their individual circumstances, some offenders may participate in lawbreaking behaviour because it is seen as acceptable, even desirable, within a culture or what is often called a subculture.

The way in which society is organised and structured may also affect crime. Modern societies are organised hierarchically, and material goods and rewards are distributed unevenly. This can produce a situation in which those at the bottom see themselves as failures, particularly if they live in a culture which encourages high aspirations. Crime may be a response to such feelings and may therefore be related to wider socio-economic trends. Care must be taken in how we link the causes of crime to an explanation of crime. By making the link, we suggest that crime is a product of forces beyond the control of individuals. Thus, if crime is caused by poor schooling or as a result of a personality disorder, then blame falls on the cause not the person. This approach to explaining crime has important implications for the notion of an individual's responsibility for their own actions.

The logic of this approach is that crime can be cured not by the exercise of self-restraint but by the diagnosis of the correct causal factors. This approach follows the medical metaphor and a belief in the power of science to diagnose causes. It may also result in crude stereotyping. If unemployment causes crime, then must all unemployed people be criminals? However, attempts to provide a simple explanation of the motivations of the criminal are frustrated when the wide range of activities covered by the criminal law is appreciated. Greed may well be an explanatory factor in property crimes but it would not help to account for many spontaneous acts of violence. Finally, it ignores the fact that behaviour itself is only criminal if it is in breach of the rules set out in the criminal law. The following sections will briefly outline some of the many approaches to explaining criminal behaviour.

## Born criminal – biological theories

It has always been a popular notion to attribute criminality to an offender's biological make up and to ask whether criminality, like height, weight or hair colour can be inherited. One of the earliest researchers to attempt to apply scientific methods to the study of crime was the Italian criminologist, Cesare Lombroso, who studied the characteristics of convicts in prisons. He claimed that criminal men were distinguished by what he called physical stigmata such as long arms, shifty glances, droopy eyelids, bushy eyebrows, large ears, twisted noses and abnormal mouths and skulls. Criminals, he argued, were atavistic – biological throwbacks to an earlier stage of evolution. His theories were later discredited, particularly as many similar characteristics were found in the general population, but they stimulated further research relating criminality to physical characteristics. Later criminologists for example claimed to find a positive relationship between a tendency to act aggressively and a muscular or mesomorphic body shape (see, for example, Williams 1991). These theories however had many limitations, not least the fact that many people with such shapes had committed no crimes.

The notion that criminality could be inherited also inspired studies of twins. If criminality is assumed to be inborn, then identical twins should be more likely both to become criminal than non-identical twins. While some studies did suggest this, the evidence was not convincing and it proved virtually impossible to screen out the effects of the environment. In other words was it heredity that was causing the similarity in behaviour, or the similar way in which twins were being brought up? (Sanderson 1992; Williams 1991). Was the Kray twins' life of crime influenced by their common genetic inheritance or socialisation? Other genetic factors have been linked to criminality. For example, great excitement greeted the discovery of what was thought to be the criminal gene, when a number of psychiatrically disturbed prisoners were found to have an extra Y chromosome. They were also bigger than the norm. However, as research progressed, a number of otherwise normal, if tall, men were found to possess this genetic abnormality.

Biological factors other than genetic inheritance may affect criminality. Some studies suggest for example that the bio-chemical effects of vitamin deficiencies or food allergies can indirectly lead to delinquency. Low blood sugar or food allergies can produce hyperactivity which in turn may produce hallucinations and violent behaviour. Children so affected it is argued, may be less likely to learn social skills, be difficult to discipline and more likely to be seen as problem children (Sanderson 1992; Williams 1991). In a celebrated case in the USA a defendant claimed in mitigation that he had a chemical imbalance in his brain caused by eating too much junk food – the so-called 'Twinkie defence', called after the offending sweet bar (Williams 1991: 119). Again however it may be an interaction between biological factors and the environment which produce any links with delinquency – for example, children showing these behavioural symptoms may be labelled as difficult, a label which may in itself produce a delinquent response. Others have sought to link criminality to brain damage and other brain disorders such as epilepsy. The evidence to support these links is somewhat inconclusive, and it is clear that many are related to environmental factors. Even where links can be established, they only account for a tiny minority of offences.

### Are criminals mad?

Another popular explanation of criminality is to imply that in some way criminals are mad, psychotic, or suffering from personality disorders. Psychological theories have focused on these issues and have explored a wide range of factors.

One of the best known attempts to link criminality to personality is found in the work of Hans Eysenck whose personality tests measure extraversion, introversion, neuroticism and psychoticism. While most people fall in the mid range of these scales, extreme scores may be related to a propensity to criminality. Those with high extraversion scores tend to be outgoing, sociable, optimistic and impulsive. Those with a high neuroticism score tend to be anxious, moody and sensitive, and a high psychoticism score involves insensitivity, solitude, sensation seeking and lack of regard for danger. Those with high extrovert scores he argues are more difficult to condition, and a neurotic extrovert is the most difficult to condition (Eysenck 1977). Some studies have found clusters of high scores among delinquents, but this could be the result of going through the criminal justice process and being institutionalised. In general, there is a lack of empirical support for Eysenck's theories (Sanderson 1992; Williams 1991).

Other psychologists have looked for evidence of a link between criminality and mental illness. Some mental illnesses such as schizophrenia can lead to delusions and hallucinations which may make the affected person feel that they have a 'mission' to rid the world of particular groups of people such as prostitutes. These conditions are however extremely rare and there is no general link between schizophrenia and criminality (Williams 1991). Others have linked a particular form of murder, followed by the suicide of the murderer, to depressive illnesses. In such cases, the depressed person wishes to leave the world and may also feel a need to save their loved ones by taking them with them (West 1965). This again affects only a very small number of people and there is no evidence that depression is linked to criminality in general.

Criminals, especially those showing signs of apparently uncontrolled and bizarre violence, are often popularly described as psychopaths. As a scientific description, however, the condition of psychopathy has so far proved extremely difficult to establish, define and measure, with studies being restricted to institutionalised offenders. Some researchers have associated the psychopathic personality with an inability to form loving relationships, a lack of responsibility for actions, a failure to feel or admit guilt for one's actions and aggressiveness (see, for example, Sanderson 1992). However this can involve a circular argument – have these characteristics led to offenders being described and classified as psychopathic or do they genuinely distinguish one group of offenders from another? The fact that many so-called psychopaths who have been studied have already been institutionalised might suggest that these traits are a result of incarceration or labelling. Alternatively there may be many in the general population with similar traits who have never been involved, or at least known to have been involved, in criminal behaviour. One noted psychologist of crime has commented that psychopathy remains 'something of a puzzle' (Hollin 1989).

## The family

Individuals learn appropriate standards of behaviour from a number of other people. Much of this learning takes place within the family which is widely regarded as responsible for child rearing. The family is often blamed for crime committed by children and teenagers and rising rates of youth crime are often seen to be symptomatic of the breakdown of the family. The link between criminality and the family is shown by the results of interviews with almost 4,000 randomly selected inmates conducted for the first national survey of prisons in England and Wales (Home Office 1992).

In the survey convicted prisoners were asked, 'whether any other member of their family had been convicted of a criminal offence; 43 per cent said this had occurred, and 35 per cent said that someone in their family had been imprisoned.' (Home Office 1992: xii) This would encourage the view that there is a strong link between the family and criminal behaviour. Another factor relating crime to the family suggested by the same survey would be the link between crime and early removal of a person from the family into the care of the local authority. 'A quarter of prisoners (26 per cent) said they had at some time before the age of 16 been taken into local authority care. As many as 38 per cent of prisoners under 21 reported that they had such an experience. The comparable figure for the general population (whether under 21 or not) is 2 per cent.' (Home Office 1992: vii).

Many studies have therefore looked at which aspects of family life can be related to delinquency and crime. As with the search for the born criminal however it is difficult to assess how much of a person's upbringing is affected by the immediate family and how much by the social and environmental circumstances of that family.

Many studies have associated the likelihood of future delinquency with what is often described as 'poor child rearing behaviour', which includes a combination of factors involving discipline, attitudes and conflict (Farrington 1992). In a major study conducted by the Cambridge Institute of Criminology, 400 South London boys born in 1953 were followed throughout their development. This study found that delinquency was associated with the following family-related factors: harsh or erratic parental discipline; a cruel, passive or neglecting attitude; poor supervision; parental conflict (West and Farrington 1973; 1977).

Note here that despite popular arguments that lax discipline is related to delinquency, it is inconsistent discipline that is found to be more important. Parents who consistently apply either strict or lax discipline would appear likely to produce children with fewer problems than those whose discipline is erratic. Supervision of children is also an important factor. Wilson found that the likelihood of delinquency was less in families who knew where their children were and who took them to and from school (Wilson 1975). These factors are however strongly related to the wider environment. The Cambridge study found that delinquency was more prevalent in families with low incomes and amongst those living in run-down housing estates and Wilson found that delinquency was highest in what she defined as the most severely socially handicapped families (Wilson 1980).

Rising divorce rates and the growth in single parent families have also been popularly linked with delinquency. However, many children from families in which there has been divorce grow up with no adverse effects let alone turn to crime or delinquency. In addition, any effect of family break-down works along with other factors. For example, divorce and single parenthood are often associated with low income and housing problems, the stress of which may affect how well the parent is able to look after children.

Experiences within the family are therefore important factors with erratic supervision, parental neglect and conflict emerging as problems which may be related to delinquency. As one noted psychiatrist argues, 'socially deprived, unloving, erratic, inconsistent and careless parents tend to produce badly behaved boys' (West 1969: 197). It is also clear that the effect of the family is related to socio-economic circumstances. The effect of the family may be further limited the older the child becomes – after a certain age, families may have less control over their children as they become more influenced by their friends and associates. What sociologists call the peer group may then be a crucial factor, along with the culture in the surrounding neighbourhood. In addition, individuals coming from homes where there are obvious problems may be more likely to come into contact with formal agencies and be labelled as potential criminals.

The complex interplay between family and crime requires an awareness of biological and social influences at work. Dr Simon Wessely writing in *The Times* comments, 'Modern researchers no longer ask the question of nurture versus nature, but instead how nurture influences nature – what factors are involved in the pathways from birth to later criminality?' (*The Times*, 7 February 1995: 17).

## Control theories

The importance of supervision within the family directs attention to the significance of different kinds of control and a very simple argument is that crime may be related to a lack of control. Thus control theories argue that we would all be criminal if we were not in some way controlled. Learning what is considered to be right and wrong is in itself a form of control – as is being involved in a family, a job and other responsibilities. As we have already seen parental supervision and discipline may be linked to criminality, and crime is more likely to occur where there is an absence of some kind of surveillance. According to Hirschi, delinquency is more likely to occur where delinquents are less attached to families and others close to them, less committed to conventional behaviour, less involved in a conventional lifestyle and lack a strong belief in the need to obey (Hirschi 1969).

Control theories have had considerable influence. They raise the question of why people conform, a different focus to asking why they break the law, and one from which much can be learned. A well-known finding of many early criminological studies was that juvenile offenders stopped offending once they grew up, got married or found a job. In addition, some have argued that the greater controls exercised over girls within the family may be one reason why so few girls compared to boys turn to delinquency.

Like other theories however they may not fully explain many aspects of crime. Crime may be related to the absence of controls but this does not explain why some offenders commit some kinds of crime and others take up a different form. Crime is socially patterned and it may be too simplistic to view it as emerging from an absence of control. Socio-economic and individual factors may be needed to explain its variations.

## Crime and opportunity

Control theories strongly influenced the development of theories which focused on the situations in which crime occurs. Individuals it is argued make rational choices – to commit an offence or not. When faced with an opportunity to commit crime they may evaluate their chances of success, whether or not they are likely to be caught, and what their punishment might be. Whether or not a crime occurs depends therefore on the opportunities provided by the situation (see, for example, Clarke 1980). Faced with an open till in an empty shop, a potential thief is far more likely to steal the money than if the shop is crowded and has advertised the existence of video surveillance. Thus much crime is opportunistic, rather than being driven by individual pathologies or subcultural motivation.

This kind of approach has led, as will be seen in Chapter 11, to a wide range of policies aimed at crime prevention. In addition it prompted the widespread use of the victim survey to establish more precisely the kind of situations in which most crime occurs, and where risks of victimisation are highest.

Like many of the other theories we have looked at, these approaches also have limitations. If for example some crime is committed by individuals or groups who are determined or predisposed to commit an offence, they may be less deterred by crime prevention measures and may commit their crimes elsewhere. Therefore theories based on crime and opportunity may neglect the wider causes of crime.

## Labelling

One of the problems highlighted in relation to earlier approaches has been the extent to which some individuals may be labelled as potential criminals and are thus more likely to be caught. Another problem with some approaches is that they are based on a comparison between offenders and samples taken from the population at large who are assumed not to be criminal. As will be seen in Chapter 3 however, many offences are not detected and offenders are not prosecuted – therefore some of the so-called non-offending population may in fact have committed crimes.

The labelling perspective focuses on many of these questions. Actions or behaviour are not, as we have seen, intrinsically criminal – society defines which acts are against the criminal law. Those committing these acts are not defined as criminals until they have been caught and convicted. Thus to writers such as Becker, no behaviour is intrinsically criminal or deviant, these are labels applied by others (Becker 1963). An important distinction can also be made between primary and secondary deviance (Lemert 1967). Primary deviance refers to the initial act and secondary deviance follows initial labelling. Once a person is labelled as a thief or a delinquent, many consequences follow. They may feel stigmatised, cast out and may seek the company of other deviants. Stigma may make it difficult to return to a normal existence. They may be mistrusted by friends, treated with suspicion by their families and find it difficult to obtain legitimate employment. Some, labelled as troublesome, may react with hostility to those who have labelled them – leading to a confirmation of that label – a self-fulfilling prophecy.

The labelling approach has been enormously influential, and its practical implications extend to arguments to divert children and young persons from custody and formal criminal procedures. It is not however a full theory of crime as it does little to explain why people choose to commit deviant acts in the first place, but it has considerable significance for other approaches and for criminal justice policy.

## Social structure and subculture

Crime is seen by some sociologists as a sign of wider cultural problems or as a symptom of the effects of social and economic change. One of the earliest sociologists to look at crime in this way was Emile Durkheim. To him, social and economic changes following the industrial revolution had led to the decline of communities and religion which provided people with guidance about morality and standards of behaviour. Rapid change could lead, he argued, to the development of anomie, or normlessness, in which individuals lacked such guidance. In addition, the growth of materialism led to people developing what he called 'boundless aspirations' which could often not be met. These ideas were taken up and reformulated by the American sociologist, Robert Merton. In American society he argued, goals of material success predominated. These goals could be achieved by legitimate means such as hard work and educational achievement, but not all who work hard would achieve the goals. This strain could produce a state of normlessness or anomie, in which the norms of hard work are no longer relevant, especially to those at the bottom of the ladder (Merton 1938).

Merton outlined several ways in which people could adapt to this strain. While most continue to conform, others may adopt deviant adaptations. Thus *innovators* devise their own means to achieve the goals – stealing money instead of earning it for example. Ritualists abandon the goals while conforming to the rules and *retreatists*, such as drop outs, abandon both the goals and the means. *Rebels* reject both the goals and means and attempt to substitute their own. Many theories developed out of this anomie paradigm, and while its original formulation had many limitations, the view that crime can be interpreted as a 'solution' to the problems of blocked aspirations influenced many subsequent writers, particularly those looking at criminal and delinquent subcultures.

Subcultural theory, of which there are many different formulations, focuses on groups within which particular kinds of crime are seen as normal and where status may derive from delinquent or criminal activity. Many have a distinctive set of norms, values, language and dress and may include a career structure through which younger members graduate from less serious activities to more serious involvement in crime. Examples of such subcultures include groups of joyriders, young thieves and drugtakers. Subcultural theories basically are concerned with why subcultures emerge.

To some American writers, subcultures represented a collective solution to anomie. Richard Cloward and Lloyd Ohlin identified three main forms of delinquent subcultures – conflict subcultures based on gang violence, retreatist subcultures based on drugtaking or vagrancy and criminal subcultures based on theft (Cloward and Ohlin 1960). Participation in a particular kind of subculture was related to what they described as the structure of illegitimate opportunities of a particular neighbourhood. Thus in areas with an existing criminal subculture, young people could learn the 'know how' to engage in activities such as burglary or theft. Without this 'know how', and suitable outlets for stolen goods, such participation would be far less likely. It is also unlikely that young people could obtain drugs without an existing market in illegal drugs. In a slightly different formulation, Albert Cohen saw delinquency as arising from the failure of young lower class boys to measure up to society's middle class measuring rod (Cohen 1955). They reacted to this by rejecting the values of mainstream culture and forming what he described as an oppositional culture.

In Britain, where in the past young people had not on the whole been encouraged to aspire to middle class status, these models were more difficult to apply, and few examples of oppositional subcultures were recorded. With the development of youth culture and the social and economic changes of the post war era however youth subcultures could be seen as a solution to the problem of how to achieve the leisure goals of youth culture (Downes 1966). For some young people, failure at school produced a situation in which, faced with dead end jobs, delinquency became an alternative means of pursuing desirable leisure pursuits.

Later writers in a subcultural tradition argued that the decline of traditional industries had led to a situation where young people could not achieve, either in the terms of dominant cultural values or their own local culture, the culture of their parents. Phil Cohen related the rise of subcultures to the decline in traditional jobs, urban renewal and the break up of communities, which affected traditional working class values and aspirations. Subcultures did not replace these in any real sense but offered a 'magical' solution (Cohen 1979). Similarly the work of the Birmingham Centre for Cultural Studies interpreted subcultures such as skinheads or teddy boys as being attempts on the part of youth to find themselves a cultural space within a dominant culture which had no relevance to their situation (Hall and Jefferson 1976).

Delinquent subcultures can therefore be interpreted as providing an achievable, if criminal, aspiration for the young who have failed to achieve the many different goals presented by mainstream culture, local cultures and leisure goals transmitted through the media. This may be exacerbated where they face unemployment, giving them little stake in society. Thus for example, what is often described as joyriding, or within subcultures 'twoc-ing', (after the offence of taking a motor vehicle without the owner's consent), may spring from the emphasis in advertising and the media on the desirability of cars and driving. Few unemployed youths can afford these status symbols and may be tempted to steal them to give themselves an illusion of participation.

In some ways subcultural approaches provide almost too easy an explanation of many kinds of delinquency. If delinquent subcultures are so attractive, why do all lower class youth, presumably facing the same problems, not participate? One critic of early subcultural theories, David Matza, argued that they explained too much delinquency (Matza 1964). In addition the extent of subcultural participation may be less than often assumed. While there are many forms of subcultural delinquency as we have seen above much crime may be simply opportunist.

Nonetheless, subcultural theories raise important questions about the relationship between crime and social and economic change, and point out that to some offenders crime performs a positive function. In addition they point to the importance of the local structure of opportunities for participation in many criminal activities. Studies of drugtaking for example have found that drug subcultures are more likely to emerge in areas with a pre-existing drugs market and a history of subcultural involvement (Pearson 1987). Furthermore, in some areas drugtaking can give meaning to the lives of young people faced with continued unemployment. The activity of having to steal to obtain drugs, obtaining them and using them may provide an alternative occupation for these youth (Pearson 1987). In a recent study of 100 car thieves carried out for the Home Office, taking cars 'for the hell of it' emerged as a major factor (Light et al 1993). Many had been introduced to car crime by friends from their local neighbourhood from whom they had learnt the necessary skills. When asked why they had become involved in car crime, 31 per cent cited peer influence, 18 per cent cited boredom and a further 18 per cent cited a search for excitement. In some areas the thrill of outwitting the police and engaging in car chases may also become a major attraction of 'twoc-ing' (Campbell 1993).

## Critical and realist criminology

As seen above, the labelling approach criticised many theories for their focus on convicted offenders, on the grounds that law enforcers may be highly selective. This point is further taken up by theorists who see the criminal law and criminal justice process as a form of class domination – as outlined in Chapter 1. This group of theories, often known as critical or radical criminology, focus in particular on the role of the criminal law and its agents – the police and the courts. To marxists, criminal law is one of the means by which the ruling class exerts control over the lower classes, and thus the criminal law tends to criminalise 'lower class crime' and downplay the 'crimes of the powerful' – corporate and business crime.

Critical criminologists tend to focus on this criminalisation of aspects of lower class behaviour, and the use of the police and the courts to maintain the power and legitimacy of the ruling class. Moral panics – such as those about black muggers and rioters or football hooligans function, they argue, to emphasise the values of society by attributing crime to outsiders, crazed individuals and mindless morons. This in turn justifies the use of tougher law and order measures. This was seen particularly during the so-called 'law and order' crisis of the 1970s, where tougher responses to crime were seen as an example of the state's desire to maintain its legitimacy by scapegoating muggings widely perceived to have been carried out by black youth (Hall et al 1978).

Critical criminology raises important questions about the very definition of crime, and whose interests the criminal law and its agencies serve. It also raises questions about which offences and offenders receive the attention of the police and agencies of criminal justice. But presenting criminals as victims of the oppressive state has been criticised for ignoring the effects of crime and for elevating criminal acts into political gestures.

Thus those advocating a realist approach argue that crime really is a problem, and that its many forms require many different kinds of explanation. They further argue that to understand crime fully we need to recognise the 'square of crime' – the interplay between the state and its agencies, the offender, society and the victim (Lea and Young 1992).

To realists, a major factor underlying crime is relative deprivation. Many theories imply that crime is related to social deprivation. But not all socially deprived people turn to crime, and crime did not rise significantly during earlier depressions. There are some indications however that crime may rise as income differentials widen suggesting a more complex picture (Box 1987). Relative deprivation is likely to arise where groups have reasonable expectations of achievement in comparison to other groups but whose expectations have not been met. Thus they are deprived in relation to other groups to whom they feel they can justifiably compare themselves. This means that we should not look for simple equations between economic conditions, or unemployment and crime, but must look at the meaning of such conditions to those affected.

One way of doing this is to look at how unemployment affects individuals in different ways, only some of which might lead to crime. For example we would hardly expect those made redundant in their forties or fifties to turn to crime in any large numbers. Nor would we expect large numbers of unemployed women or indeed the idle rich to turn to burglary or robbery (Lea and Young 1992). Where the association is assumed to have an effect is amongst unemployed youth or amongst the offspring of those whose unemployment has caused financial, housing, family and other problems.

The young unemployed for example may quite simply have time on their hands and few legitimate pursuits readily available to them. They may be attracted to subcultures in which excitement, thrills or kicks can be got from participation in illegitimate pursuits. This may be further underlined by the absence of a control factor such as a job, a concerned parent or a mortgage – they may have little to gain by conformity. They may live in an area which has a reputation for delinquency, and where delinquency is normal. They may have few expectations of employment – Loveday for example points to rises in crime in areas containing large numbers of the 'never employed' (Loveday 1992). As Roger Graef comments, 'We want youth to believe in the system, and join it at the bottom with the promise of greater rewards on the way up. But they have no access to the ladder at all.' (Graef 1992: 257).

To others unemployment means a lower income and reliance on state benefits which may in turn give rise to family and housing problems. Parents coping with such stresses and strains may be less able to provide adequate care and supervision for their children. They may become labelled as problem families and their children, when they do get into trouble, may be more likely to be taken to court or into care. Finally, as critical criminologists would point out, the law and its enforcement may target the street crimes of the unemployed and thus identify them for greater criminalisation.

Some indication of the links between unemployment and crime are provided by a survey carried out by the Association of Chief Officers of Probation (*Guardian*, 8 January 1994: 1). This looked at 30,000 offenders across 30 of the 55 probation services. It found that only one in five offenders were in paid employment and suggests that 70 per cent of serious offences are being committed by people out of work. These percentages varied throughout the country with the proportion of unemployed being higher in the North – a high point of 83 per cent was recorded in Merseyside.

But unemployment can only be related to certain kinds of crime, and the relationship is assumed to exist amongst those for whom unemployment leads to other problems. It may therefore be a factor in many forms of property crime such as property theft, robberies, mugging or joyriding. The stress of unemployment and consequent feelings of failure may also lead to higher levels of domestic violence. But it can scarcely be related to the multitude of crimes which people commit in the workplace, to financial frauds, corruption or insider trading. Different approaches are needed to explore these kinds of crime.

## White collar crime

Many of the approaches to crime explored above focus on what is in effect a very narrow range of crime. Many other crimes are committed in the world of business and employment where employees abuse their occupational position to commit crimes. What is known as white collar crime is often ignored in public discussions of crime or law and order (Sutherland 1949; Croall 1992). Yet it can involve enormous sums of money and undermine the trust that people have in the institutions of business, commerce or government. Frauds often involve hundreds of thousands or millions of pounds, and much recent concern has surrounded the unlawful and unethical activities of public appointees, government ministers, MPs and many others. Often included in the category of white collar crime is organisational or corporate crime in which the offender is a corporate body and where the offence involves the breach of criminally enforced regulations to protect consumers, workers or the public from fraud or physical harm caused by a neglect of trading or safety regulations. Neglect of safety regulations for example can kill and injure workers, consumers or passengers as seen in recent cases such as the sinking of the Herald of Free Enterprise off Zeebrugge and a number of cases involving the death of workers in the Channel Tunnel.

This neglect of white collar crime may be partly because the offences involved are seen as less serious and threatening than murder, rape or robbery. They are often less public than other crimes, taking place in offices rather than on the streets. The relationship between victims and offenders is indirect and where breaches of safety regulations are involved, offenders have not intended to injure or kill their eventual victims. They often involve complex technological or financial transactions which are less easy to detect by either victims or enforcement agencies. For these reasons they are often not defined as serious crimes.

Many theories of criminal behaviour discussed so far in this chapter do not apply to white collar crime. It makes little sense to attribute major frauds such as those involved in BCCI to maternal deprivation, chromosomal or chemical deficiencies in the brain and few white collar offenders are suffering from poverty or adverse socio-economic circumstances. The tolerance of many white collar offences such as tax evasion or insider dealing means that offenders are less likely to be labelled as deviant or form oppositional subcultures, although many offences may be seen as perfectly acceptable within business subcultures.

Yet some of the above approaches can be applied to white collar crime. Embezzlement for example may be related to feelings of failure (Cressey 1986). Pressures for success in business can be severe and those who have not reached the top may experience relative deprivation. Businesses faced with bankruptcy may attempt to fiddle the books or burn down their premises in an attempt to survive. Others faced with financial pressures may prioritise profits at the expense of consumer protection or safety regulations.

Thus many industrial accidents can be attributed to the strain between the need to comply with safety regulations and the need to cut costs. Within organisations workers who feel that they are not being given a 'fair day's pay' may resort to a variety of what they see as justifiable fiddles to enhance their incomes (Mars 1982). And as with all kinds of crime, offenders are reliant on opportunities. Mars for example identifies some occupations as 'fiddle prone'.

Despite the adverse effects of white collar or corporate crime, as we shall see in later chapters, they are far less likely to be detected, prosecuted or severely sanctioned (Croall 1992). The reasons underlying this are extremely complex, however they do lend some support to the arguments of critical criminologists that the offences of the powerful are less severely dealt with than those of the powerless. In addition, the treatment of white collar crime, and the tolerance of the many activities it involves, further reveals the complexities of attempting to define crime.

## CONCLUSION

In this chapter we have identified the three interrelated elements that are vital to understand and explain crime; behaviour, rules and their enforcement. The legal conception of crime defined in terms of actus rea and mens rea focuses the issue onto the need of the criminal justice system to establish the blame or degree of blame with respect to behaviour either proscribed or required by the criminal law. Hence the importance of criminal defences such as self-defence or duress which might absolve a person of an act otherwise deemed criminal, and the mitigation statements put forward for those convicted in order to diminish their culpability for an offence.

Public perceptions of crime are not always confined by these legal considerations about criminal liability. Different groups within society may have very different conceptions of what activities the criminal law should proscribe and how it should assess blameworthiness. The public are likely to be influenced by the sources of information about crime such as the media, politicians, pressure and interest groups, policy makers and academic theorists.

Theories of crime, or a popular version of them, come to enter the public imagination and provide guides or cues to public debate about what is to be done about crime. The models of criminal justice discussed in Chapter 1 relate to these theories. The rehabilitative model for example is linked to the idea that offenders are in some way pathological. If for example, crime is the result of some identifiable problem in the individual offender, then the problem may be addressed by developing suitable forms of 'treatment'. In addition, research which sought to distinguish which factors could predict criminality could be used to assist sentencers in their assessment of the likely effects of alternative sentencing options – they could be used for prediction.

Sentencing policy could therefore be likened to a doctor's recommendations for treatment.

The promise of these theories was however not fulfilled. Crime cannot be easily traced to an offender's individual characteristics – making it difficult to devise appropriate treatment programmes. Furthermore, some research links criminality to factors outside the reach of sentencers. Not all football supporters are hooligans. Nevertheless it is obvious that football crowds in this country attract some young men looking for an opportunity for violent behaviour. To what extent male hormones or alcohol are contributory factors is not easily diagnosed. However, this does not mean nothing can be done. The sale and consumption of alcohol can be banned at a football ground, as can known offenders.

The labelling perspective has had a major impact on criminal justice polices. It suggested that intervention by criminal justice agencies can potentially increase the volume of crime and precipitate criminal careers. For many years, policies for young offenders have sought to divert children and young persons from the formal processes to avoid stigmatisation and labelling. In addition, harsh responses by the police may produce reactions on the part of some groups which may intensify problems. This may also be the case in public order situations where both the police and demonstrators may expect trouble from each other. Different agencies within the criminal justice process should therefore attempt not to exacerbate problems and be aware of the effects of their actions. These kinds of policies however may run counter to other models. The crime control model for example suggests that those who are guilty of a crime should be prosecuted and punished and the due process model requires that this should be done publicly and equally. Should some offenders therefore avoid such public trial and punishment? In addition the criminal justice process performs an important denunciatory role – which again requires that offenders be publicly held accountable for their offences. Labelling theory however suggests that such denunciation and punishment should not be such as to create outsiders or oppositional subcultures (Braithwaite 1989).

Some of the theories outlined in this chapter relate crime to the wider socio-economic context in which crime takes place. This raises a further set of questions. The criminal justice process deals primarily with individual offenders. It has no power over the economic system let alone the social structure. Yet the due process model requires that offenders are treated 'fairly'. This could pose problems for example in the sentencing of an offender claiming that offences had been brought about by the effects of unemployment. Should this be taken into account? If on the other hand it is the case that unemployment is related to crime it may also mean that the criminal justice process may be able to do little to reduce crime substantially. The causes of crime may quite simply lie outside its remit. Sentencers can scarcely provide jobs for offenders, remove them from a crime prone environment, or sentence them to marriage!

## Review Questions

1. How would you define a criminal?
2. List the ways in which the criminal law reflects a concern with blame-worthiness.
3. What are the main ways we come to hear about crime?
4. Which of the main theories of criminal behaviour do you think help to give an insight into the reasons offenders commit burglary, business fraud, vandalism or murder?

## Further Reading

Heidensohn F (1989) *Crime and Society*. London: Macmillan
Sanderson J (1992) *Criminology Textbook*. 3rd edn. London: HLT
Williams K (1991) *Textbook on Criminology*. London: Blackstone Press

# CHAPTER 3

# HOW MUCH CRIME?

Crime and its Impact
Home Office Statistics on Crime
British Crime Survey
Public and Police Influence on the Crime Statistics

## INTRODUCTION

In Chapter 2 it was seen how difficult it is to define and explain crime, and many difficulties also surround its measurement. Thus before an offence can be counted, behaviour must be defined as being against the criminal law and brought to the attention of a law enforcer. Chapter 2 also showed that as public tolerance of different activities changes, the criminal law itself can change. New crimes may be added to the statute book, increasing the total amount of crime. Technological and social change can also affect crime rates – if for example there are more cars on the road, there are more opportunities and temptations to steal them and more regulations concerning their use. The activities of law enforcement agencies can affect the volume and kind of crimes which are recorded. If the police associate certain areas with particular kinds of crime, they might pay more attention to these areas, thus producing more recorded crime.

Therefore criminal statistics must be interpreted with considerable caution. As we saw in Chapter 2 these statistics are often taken as a barometer of crime from which the media, politicians and the public shape their ideas about crime. This in turn affects criminal justice policy. It is important to realise however that these statistics are likely to be at considerable variance with the actual incidence of crime and that all attempts to calculate the crime figure are no more than estimates. Thus the Home Office *Digest 2: Information on the Criminal Justice System in England and Wales* 1993 comments that 'no-one knows the true extent of crime in this country'. (Home Office 1993: 7).

This chapter will explore in more detail the available information about crime and convicted offenders, and will look at how this is constructed and interpreted. It will start by looking at some general indications about the extent and impact of crime and at statistics on offences, convicted offenders and victims. The main sources of crime statistics will then be outlined along with an indication of what they can and cannot tell us about the amount of different kinds of crime. We will then look at how the actions of the police, the public and victims influence these statistics. We will examine the insights into the extent of crime provided by the British Crime Survey and other assessments of the amount and impact of crime.

## CRIME AND ITS IMPACT

There are a variety of ways of looking at the extent of crime and its impact including statistics based on police records, statistics derived from victim surveys such as the British Crime Survey, self report studies and estimates of the cost of crime.

In recent years the official statistics, based on police records, have charted a steady growth in recorded crime, illustrated in Figure 3.1. In the 12 months to June 1994, the police recorded 5.4 million offences in England and Wales. This compares with 2.5 million in 1980, 1.6 million in 1970, 0.5 million in 1950 and an annual recorded figure of 100,000 which was relatively stable between 1876 and 1920. But the population itself has grown and therefore it could be expected that crime would also rise. A less dramatic growth is indicated when population figures are taken into account. Methods of recording crime have also changed during the period that the table covers. Categories and definitions of crime have changed and new crimes have emerged. Furthermore, the Home Office has helped to promote more reliable and consistent data collection methods. Crime statistics may also be affected by the growth of the police – if there are more police to record and investigate crime, this will produce higher rates of recorded crime. Nonetheless, even when these factors are taken into account, the figures show a dramatic and sustained growth in recorded crime, tenfold since 1950, and they illustrate why crime has come to be seen as such a major social problem.

The total volume of crime known to the police is affected by many factors, not all of them directly related to actual increases in crime. Changes in the crime rate can be affected by wider changes in society as a whole. For example, mass car ownership in the 20th century has resulted in the creation of new offences, such as reckless or dangerous driving, and has also led to the extension of offences such as driving without a licence or insurance. Motor cars parked in streets have created many opportunities for theft, both of the cars themselves and of accessories such as radios and spare parts. In 1994, thefts of, and from, cars accounted for 27 per cent of all notifiable crimes recorded by the police.

Another way of looking at crime is to explore its impact on the public, on

**Fig 3.1** Crimes recorded by the police

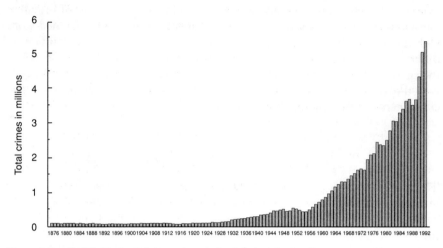

(Home Office (1993) *Digest 2: Information on the Criminal Justice System.*
London: HMSO: 8)

victims and on community life in general. All members of the public are
affected by crime. They pay for crime through taxes which pay for the criminal justice system. They also pay higher insurance premiums to protect
themselves from the financial losses incurred by property crimes. These
taxes may be higher to compensate for the large amount of tax frauds and
evasion. Prices in shops include an amount to take account of theft by cus-
tomers and employees.

Our daily lives are affected by the impact of and the fear of crime. Houses
must be locked and protected against potential burglars and many people are
scared to go to certain areas through fear of being mugged, raped or
assaulted. Valuable items are post-coded, car windows have numbers etched
on them, car breakdown services are informed of lone female drivers and
give them priority. Violent offences are most likely to have a psychological
impact on victims and also have consequences for the community and the
way people lead their lives. Many women avoid walking in the streets at
night – potentially reducing their freedom to participate in a variety of
leisure activities. The fear of crime may deter people from using public
transport and going to public places and can thus dramatically alter the quality of peoples' lives along with that of the community as a whole.

Individual victims may be affected in many ways. As we have seen, many
crimes involve property offences, such as those involving cars. While many
may be insured and may not lose financially, others are not. Financial losses
are exacerbated by the inconvenience and frustration involved in the immediate aftermath of an offence. To some, burglaries not only involve the loss
of goods but the feeling that their homes and privacy have been violated.

Victims of fraud may also experience these feelings (Levi and Pithouse 1992). In general, the extent of fraud and corruption in organisations can undermine the trust which people have in many public and private institutions (Croall 1992).

Another consequence of crime is its cost to the community and business interests. This is illustrated in a report, *Counting the Cost*, published by Crime Concern and the Thames Valley Crime Prevention Group in 1994. The report estimated that crime costs £24.5 billion a year. This estimate is based on government statistics, crime surveys and on the costs of lost and damaged property, policing, insurance and the cost of the criminal justice system. Thus in 1991/92 government expenditure was £9 billion and the cost of private security to companies, private individuals and public authorities was £1.6 billion. Burglary losses are set at £1 billion and theft losses at £1.9 billion including £775 million in stolen cars. Insurance companies estimate that arson accounts for £500 million annually and local authorities pay £500 million per year to deal with vandalism. The Confederation of British Industry and Crime Concern estimate that crime costs business £5–£10 billion per year – with losses of more than £3 billion in business fraud, £165 million per year on credit card frauds and £400 million a year through computer-based crime. While it is difficult to assess the accuracy of these or any such global figures they do illustrate the enormous financial costs of crime. Another way of assessing the impact of crime is by looking in more detail at the global figures and looking at some statistics on offences, offenders and victims. Statistics can be of considerable use and can often be contrasted with the images of crime presented in the media which were explored in Chapter 2. This section will look at some aspects of statistics in relation to offences, offenders and victims.

## Offences

Despite the prominence given to crimes involving sex and violence in the media and in popular discussion, 93 per cent of all recorded crime in England and Wales involves property offences, many of which are a result of theft of and from motor vehicles. In 1994, burglary accounted for 24 per cent of all notifiable offences recorded by the police, and theft other than that involving motor vehicles for a further 22 per cent.

Within the category of violent crime, minor wounding predominates, with serious wounding, including murders, consisting of only a tiny proportion of all recorded offences. This of course can be strongly influenced by decisions to report offences, but it is reasonable to suppose that serious woundings are more likely to be reported than trivial ones.

Homicide, a general category that covers the offences of murder, manslaughter and infanticide, attracts a lot of public attention. Many of the most notorious criminal incidents that enter public consciousness relate to unusual murders such as the killings by Ruth Ellis, the last woman to be hanged, the

Moors Murderers Ian Brady and Myra Hyndley, Peter Sutcliffe – the York-shire Ripper, and Frederick West, the Gloucester builder who committed suicide in prison in 1995 whilst awaiting trial for the murder of 12 people. Much public concern was aroused by the brutal killing of the two year-old James Bulger, murdered in Bootle on 12 February 1993 by two 10 year-old boys, Robert Thompson and Jon Venables.

In 1987 one incident in Hungerford accounted for 16 deaths. However, more typically homicide is a crime in which acquaintances and relatives rather than strangers kill each other and many homicides are the result of domestic disputes. In 1992, the principal suspect in 82 per cent of recorded homicides with a female victim was her spouse or other acquaintance. With male victims the figure was 61 per cent. Figure 3.2 shows the relationship and the method of killing.

## Offenders

Statistics give details of the age and gender of offenders found guilty of or cautioned for offences. Information from the Home Office Offenders Index (which contains the criminal histories of people convicted of standard list offences since 1963) was used in a cohort study to trace the criminal his-tories of males born in 1953. It showed that by the age of 30, 36 per cent had been convicted of one serious offence, that most first convictions occurred at the age of 17, and that a few offenders (6 per cent) accounted for nearly two-thirds of all crimes resulting in a conviction.

In general, statistics show that recorded crime is very much a young person's activity, with just under 46 per cent of known offenders in 1991 being under 21. One-fifth of offenders were aged under 17. It should also be borne in mind that many young offenders caught for the first time may not be formally cautioned, but are given an informal warning and that 'young offender crime' such as vandalism and criminal damage is considerably under-reported, which is largely confirmed in self report studies. The peak age for known offending is 18 for males and 15 for females.

A consistent feature of the statistics, not only in England and Wales but across Europe and America is that far fewer women are convicted of crime than men – 82 per cent of offenders in 1991 were male, a proportion which has changed little over the years. Female offenders also show a different pat-tern of offending being less involved in violent offences and proportionately more involved in theft.

In general most now accept that girls and women do commit fewer offences than boys and men. Girls are likely to be more subject to parental control than boys and while a certain amount of delinquent activity is 'nor-mal' for boys it is less so for girls, and girls would appear to be less likely to participate in the delinquent subcultures described in Chapter 2. In addition, women's lives tend to be more centred around domesticity and the home, giving them fewer opportunities to commit crime (see, for example,

**Fig 3.2** Murder victims

**Offences currently recorded as homicide by apparent method of killing and sex of victim**

ENGLAND AND WALES 1992
*622 Offences*

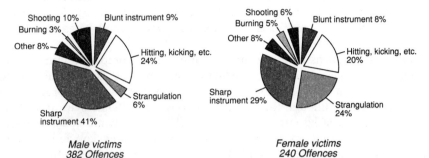

Male victims
382 Offences

Female victims
240 Offences

**Offences currently recorded as homicide by relationship of victim to principal suspect**

ENGLAND AND WALES 1992
*622 Offences*

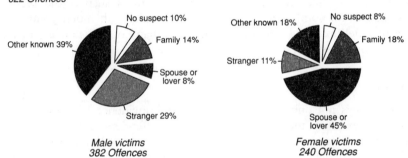

Male victims
382 Offences

Female victims
240 Offences

(Home Office (1993) *Criminal Statistics in England & Wales*. London: HMSO: 70)

Heidensohn 1985; 1994). The different pattern of female offending can also be explained by these factors – thus women's proportionately higher rates of shoplifting and credit card fraud could be explained by their propensity to be more concerned with shopping.

Statistics do not give breakdowns of offenders by ethnic groups and information on this matter is somewhat inconclusive, having been gathered by a number of different research studies using only partial information. Broadly speaking, figures indicate that black people tend to be arrested, convicted and imprisoned in higher proportions than would be expected from their overall proportion of the population, with Asians being under-represented (Smith 1994). However, these figures are extremely difficult to interpret and could be affected by a variety of factors. For example, black people tend to be more concentrated in areas where more street crime occurs, and compared to the white population, the black population has higher proportions of young people – who as we have seen, feature prominently as offenders. Thus it might be expected that higher proportions of black youth would appear as offenders although many argue that there is also discrimination against black people at different stages in the criminal justice process. Finally, black youth feature amongst those who might be considered to experience relative deprivation, as discrimination in relation to employment may mean that they are more disadvantaged than white youth (Lea and Young 1992).

These breakdowns may of course be affected by unreported crime. Fewer offences of domestic violence or white collar crime are likely to be reported or detected so it could be argued that males over 21 are under-represented in the statistics. Although the majority of convicted offenders are from lower socio-economic backgrounds, the relative absence of white collar offenders from reported crime means that we cannot necessarily conclude that the majority of offences are committed by lower class individuals. On the other hand, acts of vandalism are estimated to be one of the least reported offences. This might explain differences in interpretation of the current amount of youth crime. Some commentators claim that there is a decrease in crime amongst children and young persons. Others suspect the recorded crime figures on youth crime are far from reliable, with much youth crime being regarded as trivial, unreported and with many offenders being diverted from the formal system.

## Victims

Victim surveys not only tell us more about the incidence of crime, but also help us to examine the relationship between offenders and victims, which also corrects some media stereotypes about crime. Moral panics about crime in the mass media have led, it has been argued, to a widespread fear of crime, which exceeds the risk of actually being a victim. The first British Crime Survey in 1982, for example, found that a statistically average person aged over 16 could expect a robbery once every five centuries, an assault once every century, and a burglary once every 40 years.

But who is a statistically average person? Later locally based surveys such as the Islington Crime Survey, pointed out that the risks of victimisation are unevenly spread with those living in inner city areas being most at risk from burglary and car theft (Jones et al 1986; Walklate 1989). In addition young people, especially those who drink, are most at risk from assaults. Therefore a person's lifestyle may well affect the risk of victimisation. Young men are more likely to go out to pubs and are more at risk of becoming a victim of an assault.

The 1988 British Crime Survey took an additional sample – called a booster sample – of Afro-Caribbeans and Asians to obtain a more accurate picture of crime victimisation amongst ethnic minorities. This found that both of these groups had a higher than average chance of being a victim of theft. Asians were more likely to suffer from crimes with a racial motivation.

The report on the 1988 British Crime Survey found that some of the apparent ethnic variations were not necessarily related to ethnicity:

> In contrast, [to Asians] differential risks between Afro-Caribbeans and whites were more likely to be accounted for by differences other than ethnicity. After accounting for age, family composition and aspects to do with where they lived, the greater burglary risk among Afro-Caribbeans disappeared (a finding consistent with Tuck and Southgate's 1981 study). Personal characteristics (age, sex and marital status in particular) largely accounted for differences in assault rates between whites and Afro-Caribbeans. The same factors (as well as inner city residence and tenure) were important in explaining risks of contact thefts.
>
> (Mayhew, Elliot and Dowds 1989: 45)

It has been seen in Chapter 2 that the media tend to focus on sexual and violent offences and on the fear of crimes committed by strangers. Yet victim surveys show that women are more likely to be raped by acquaintances and intimates than by strangers, and both sexes are more likely to be murdered by family, friends, spouses or lovers rather than by a stranger. However, people who spend more time in pubs and clubs increase their chances of becoming a victim of a violent crime committed by a stranger.

We will now explore in more detail the kinds of information on which these sorts of estimates are based starting with the official government statistics on crime.

## HOME OFFICE STATISTICS ON CRIME

The government publishes many different statistics on crime and the criminal justice process. The main source of information provided by the Home Office is the publication *Criminal Statistics in England & Wales*. These statistics contain a wealth of information about the amount and kinds of offences dealt with by the police and the courts. They give details for example of the following:

- Numbers of offences reported to the police by the public, along with breakdowns of different categories of offences.
- Numbers of offences recorded by the police. This may differ from the numbers of offences reported to the police because the police, for reasons which will be explored below, may not record all offences reported to them.
- Proportions of offences 'cleared up' by the police. Not all offences reported to or recorded by the police will be attributed to a suspect. Thus the police may not clear up the crime.
- Numbers of offenders cautioned and convicted for offences, broken down by offence category, age and sex.
- Numbers of court proceedings and sentences – again broken down by offence category, age and sex.
- Increases and decreases in all of these categories.

71

More detailed information on specific offences such as different kinds of theft and fraud and less serious offences are given in the *Supplementary Criminal Statistics* which also show statistics by police area. A very useful summary of these statistics can be found in the *Criminal Justice Digest* which can be obtained from the Home Office, which also includes data from the British Crime Survey (see, for example, Home Office 1993).

The Home Office's Offender Index holds data on individuals convicted of serious offences. Computerised in 1991, the index adds nearly half a million new pieces of data a year. Each record includes a name with initials, gender, date of birth, ethnicity and, if known, a CRO (Criminal Records Office) number. Six million individual criminal histories are available to the police with information about offences and sentences.

Official statistics refer to many different categories of offences. The main statistics refer to notifiable offences recorded by the police. This covers most serious crimes including indictable offences which must be tried in the Crown Court, and others which can be tried in either the Crown Court or magistrates' courts. They also include some summary offences, which are less serious than indictable offences and are tried only in magistrates' courts. But few statistical details of summary offences are available. Statistical literature also refers to the category of grave offences. Broadly speaking, these are offences which attract a maximum sentence of life imprisonment and include homicide, serious wounding, rape, buggery, robbery, aggravated burglary and arson. Another way of classifying offences is 'Standard List' offences. These include all 'grave offences' along with violence against the person, sexual offences, burglary, theft and handling stolen goods, fraud and forgery, criminal damage (in excess of £20) and drug offences. They also include a variety of other offences including blackmail, kidnapping, offences against the state or public order, aiding and abetting an offender and firearms and public health offences.

The compilation and publication of criminal statistics involves considerable effort in bringing together data from many agencies including the 43 police forces and the resulting publication provides much detailed information about crime and the activities of the criminal justice agencies. The statistics could never be wholly accurate but, in any event, many offences are not included. They omit, for example, offences recorded by police forces outside the ambit of Home Office such as the British Transport Police, the Ministry of Defence Police and the UK Atomic Energy Authority Police. Many other offences which are known to agencies other than the police are not prosecuted, and do not appear in the Home Office statistics. Thus the Inland Revenue, Customs and Excise and Department of Social Security may deal with many offences which they do not prosecute, as do the many regulatory agencies involved with public health, pollution or trading standards offences. Many of these are summary offences and statistics are only available for numbers of convictions.

Other factors may affect what is counted and how offences are classified.

For example changing views of the seriousness of offences may affect their classification and whether or not they appear in the main statistics. Mike Maguire cites the example of offences of criminal damage of £20 or less. These were not counted before 1977 but their re-classification as notifiable offences immediately raised the total volume of crime by around 7 per cent (Maguire 1994).

In addition, as seen previously, many potential offences may not be defined as criminal or reported to the police. Some kinds of offences are less likely to come to the attention of the police than others including:

- Offences which are not readily detectable by the police or public. These include offences which take place in private, for example domestic violence, sexual offences and drug offences.
- Offences with no discernible victim, often called victimless crimes – for example prostitution, pornography, illegal gambling or drug abuse. These involve an exchange between consumers and suppliers of illegal commodities who are unlikely to report themselves to the police.
- Offences where victims are unaware that they have been a victim of a crime. Many frauds, for example, depend on victims not noticing that they have been defrauded. Other offences, such as the failure of businesses to comply with health, safety or environmental regulations, involve dangers which cannot be readily detected.

Many offences are therefore omitted from the statistics. Criminologists have long recognised that there is a large hidden or 'dark figure' of crime and that official crime rates reflect only those crimes reported to the police. Variations in crime rates therefore could be the result, not of differences between the real rates of offending, but of variations in reporting.

Even when crimes are reported to the police, they may not subsequently be recorded and counted as crimes 'known to the police'. In some cases the police may decide to take 'no further action' or decide that 'no crime' has been committed. This may happen, for example, where police are called to an incident such as a pub brawl and resolve it without arresting or charging someone, or where items are reported missing but it is unclear whether they are lost or stolen.

Statistics relating to offenders also have limitations. Clearly many offenders are never caught as their offences are invisible or not reported. In addition, the police only clear up a proportion of all crimes reported thus many offenders escape detection. Some crimes are easier to detect than others, which accounts for variations by offence in the clear-up rates given in the statistics. For example, many victims of assault know their assailant, leading to almost automatic clear up. If a fraud is discovered its perpetrator may be self-evident.

The Home Office *Criminal Justice Digest* (1993: 30) reports that only 26 per cent of offences recorded by the police were cleared up. Reassuringly, 95 per cent of homicides were cleared up, as were 75 per cent of violent and sexual offences. Less than a quarter of thefts, burglaries and robberies were cleared up. The proportion of offenders detected becomes even smaller when the large volume of unreported crimes is taken into account. Thus only a very small proportion of offenders are ever caught.

Not even all known suspects and offenders are subsequently brought to court as the police or the Crown Prosecution Service may decide not to proceed with a case (see Chapter 5). The police have discretion when dealing with a case and may decide to take no further action, to caution offenders rather than bring a formal charge, not proceed with the case because they consider they have insufficient evidence, or proceed with the case and pass the papers on to the Crown Prosecution Service.

In effect therefore official statistics tell us which crimes the public choose to report and how those crimes are dealt with by the police. The data produced by the police will tell us as much about the method of policing and the level of public concern about crime as it does about the amount of crime. The report on the first British Crime Survey commented that:

> Variations over time or place in recorded crime rates can reflect the processes by which the statistics are compiled as much as the condition they are intended to depict.

(Hough and Mayhew 1983)

This is illustrated in Figures 3.3 and 3.4 which show the sharp drop in numbers at each stage of the process. The British Crime Survey estimates that about two in 100 offences committed result in a criminal conviction. Variations occur between offences such as wounding where fourteen in 100 offences result in a caution or a conviction while for burglary the figure is three in 100 and one in 100 for vandalism.

Finally, the statistics may tell us about the numbers of different offences reported to the police, but little about how serious these offences are or the situations in which they occur. Many offence groups include vastly different kinds of offences. Thus categories of theft include very minor thefts along with serious ones, and frauds may involve very trifling sums or the millions of pounds involved in major frauds. In addition, as Maguire points out, a long-standing criticism of official statistics is that they cannot indicate changing patterns of crime – there may for example be changes in the kinds of typical thefts or robberies which are not reflected in broad classifications (Maguire 1994: 251). More information about these kinds of issues can be found in victim and self report studies, which will be described below.

## BRITISH CRIME SURVEY

One way of finding out more about crime is to ask the public what kinds of crime they have been the victims of and whether or not they have reported this to the police. This is done in what are called victim or crime surveys

**Fig 3.3** Attrition within the criminal justice system

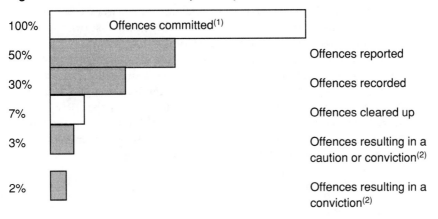

| | |
|---|---|
| 100% | Offences committed[1] |
| 50% | Offences reported |
| 30% | Offences recorded |
| 7% | Offences cleared up |
| 3% | Offences resulting in a caution or conviction[2] |
| 2% | Offences resulting in a conviction[2] |

(1)   Criminal damage; theft of a motor vehicle; theft from a motor vehicle (including attempts); bicycle theft; burglary; wounding; robbery; and theft from the person.
(2)   Estimates include additional findings of guilt at any court appearance and offences taken into consideration.

( Home Office (1993) *Digest 2: Information on the Criminal Justice System in England and Wales.* London: HMSO: 29)

**Fig 3.4** Attrition: Specific Offences

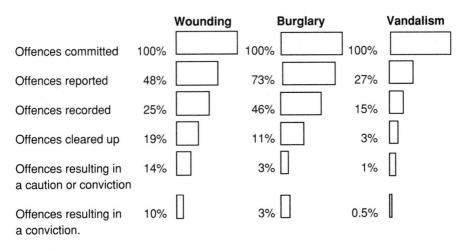

| | Wounding | Burglary | Vandalism |
|---|---|---|---|
| Offences committed | 100% | 100% | 100% |
| Offences reported | 48% | 73% | 27% |
| Offences recorded | 25% | 46% | 15% |
| Offences cleared up | 19% | 11% | 3% |
| Offences resulting in a caution or conviction | 14% | 3% | 1% |
| Offences resulting in a conviction. | 10% | 3% | 0.5% |

(Home Office (1993) *Digest 2: Information on the Criminal Justice System in England and Wales.* London: HMSO: 29) such as the British Crime Survey which was first carried out in 1982. The 1994 survey estimated that a total of 18 million crimes were committed in 1993 against individuals and their property, of which only just over a quarter are estimated to be recorded by the police (Home Office 1995).

This survey has become a regular feature of the criminological scene and further surveys were held in 1984, 1988, 1990, 1992 and 1994 and are likely to be conducted every two years in future. A random sample is used to select respondents. A core sample of 13,800 addresses in the 1988 sample led to 10,392 face-to-face interviews being completed, plus a booster sample of 1,349 from ethnic minority households. The survey asks members of the population how often they have been a victim of a specific offence in a specified time period. The scope of the questionnaire is extensive with 200 questions to elicit information on the following matters:

- what kinds of crime people have been victims of
- what proportions of these offences are reported to the police
- why some offences are not reported
- what kinds of crime people are most worried about.

This information can be compared with police statistics to ascertain the difference between crimes known to the police and those experienced by victims. This data can be charted over time to give a more accurate picture of crime trends. Thus the British Crime Survey estimates that the crime rate in the 1980s rose at a slower rate than that suggested by recorded police statistics. Between 1981 and 1991, for the sub-set of crimes covered by the British Crime Survey, the police recorded a 96 per cent increase in crime, in contrast to a 49 per cent increase reported in the survey. However, between 1991 and 1993, the British Crime Survey indicated an 18 per cent rise in crime compared with a 7 per cent increase recorded by the police, for comparable categories of crime (Home Office 1994).

In addition to the comparisons with police figures referred to above, the survey can give useful information about unreported crime. The 1988 survey found that the following proportions of offences were not reported to the police:

| | |
|---|---|
| Vandalism | 90% |
| Burglary with no loss | 84% |
| Wounding | 79% |
| Theft from motor vehicles | 70% |
| Burglary with loss | 27% |

The 1992 survey estimated that the numbers of crimes committed exceeded the numbers recorded by the police in the following proportions:

- twice as many domestic burglaries
- three times as many thefts from vehicles

- four times as many woundings
- seven times as many offences of vandalism
- eight times as many robberies and thefts from the person.

Crime surveys can also compare the difference between the public's fear of crime and their actual risk from different offences, along with figures relating to the risks of victimisation for different groups such as the young and ethnic minorities and how these risks vary by neighbourhood. The survey can thus capture information on aspects of crime which escape official attention and indicates the types of crime that give the public most concern. Numerically, crimes associated with motor vehicles, such as vandalism to a vehicle and theft of, or from, motor vehicles, account for more than a third of crime (34 per cent) according to the 1988 British Crime Survey. This does not however cause as much anxiety as other types of personal crime such as robbery and burglary which are less numerous.

While producing much valuable information, the British Crime Survey has important limitations. It only includes private households and therefore does not include crimes committed in organisations and businesses (such as shoplifting and pilfering from a workplace) and thus greatly underestimates the amount of theft committed. Many of the offences or incidents reported to the interviewers do not conform easily to legal classifications of crime and are therefore difficult to compare with police statistics. For example, if someone reports an assault, how is it to be classified? Respondents' information may be inaccurate. They may forget some incidents or exaggerate others. In some circumstances they may be unwilling to reveal offences to interviewers that cause them embarrassment. Respondents may misunderstand a question or the meaning of a word. Victim surveys cannot cover crimes of which victims are unaware, such as consumer fraud or those which have no direct victims, for example drug offences. Some groups, many of which may be at risk from crime, are under-represented as victim surveys are based on the electoral register. Crimes against children are not included as only those aged 16 and above are included in the sample. Others, such as the homeless, are unlikely to find their way onto the Electoral Register.

## Self report studies

Another way of attempting to find out more about crime is the self report study. These ask groups of the population what kinds of crime they have committed in a given period. These may be used along with victim surveys, and crime surveys often include both victim and self report questions. They have been used with schoolchildren to reveal large amounts of hidden delinquency, with respect to crimes such as vandalism and shoplifting. These kinds of surveys, whose use has grown recently, can illuminate some of the many questions posed by the limitations of official statistics. They can be used for example to test the often made links between sex, class and delinquency. Self report studies have tended to confirm that girls are far less likely to commit delinquent acts than boys, although they do report many more offences than appear in the statistics (Heidensohn 1985).

Self report studies have many limitations, not least of which is the problem that however carefully anonymity is assured, respondents may not be honest in their answers: some may exaggerate the amount and seriousness of crimes they have committed. In addition, they tend, like victim surveys, to reveal vast amounts of fairly trivial crime which would probably not have been the subject of formal proceedings in any event. Like victim surveys they may also be difficult to compare with official figures as respondents' descriptions of activities may not be the same as legally classified offences. Self report studies amongst adolescents are often carried out in schools, where researchers can find large numbers of young people in one place. This may not however be representative as school surveys will not include those who are truants or those in special establishments who may be the most likely to have committed offences (Williams 1991). In addition, because of their anonymity data cannot be independently checked against police records (Williams 1991).

Both victim and self report studies are nonetheless invaluable sources of information about many dimensions of crime and they fill in some of the gaps left by official statistics.

## PUBLIC AND POLICE INFLUENCE ON THE CRIME STATISTICS

As we have seen, official statistics are the result of actions and decisions of both the public and the police, which will be examined next.

### Public attitudes to reporting crime

In both Chapter 2 and in earlier sections of this chapter, it has been stressed that victims and the public play a key role in defining activities as crime and bringing these to the attention of formal agencies. In the British Crime Survey, respondents who have been victims of crime were asked, 'Did the police come to know about the matter? If no, why not?' Respondents were allowed to give multiple answers to this question so they could give more than one reason. Data from the 1984 survey shows that the most frequent reason (55 per cent) for not reporting a crime to the police was that they thought the crime was 'too trivial with no loss or damage'. Sixteen per cent thought the police would do nothing, and 7 per cent thought the police would not be interested. Ten per cent answered that it would be inappropriate to inform the police as they would deal with the matter themselves. Only 1 per cent cited fear of reprisal as a reason, and 2 per cent said it was inconvenient. Several factors might influence the decision to report a crime and the main ones are outlined below.

- *Awareness of victim status.* Quite simply, many victims are unaware of any offence having been committed against them. Citizens for example may be abstract or indirect victims of offences such as social security, tax or customs fraud. In more routine criminal cases the loss of property from an office or in a shop could be attributed to a misplaced or dropped wallet instead of a theft. In other cases, victims will not necessarily know that they have been a victim of a crime, for example a young child in an incest case or the elderly relative who is forgetful and bedridden whose savings are used without prior consent by relatives.

- *Crimes without victims.* As seen above, some conduct defined as criminal does not have a victim in the traditional sense of the word in that there is no obvious person who is suffering and likely to complain about the offence, even when there is awareness that a crime has been committed. Drug abuse, some sexual offences, gambling and prostitution are therefore less likely to be reported.

- *Public tolerance.* For a crime to be reported, a victim or member of the public must feel sufficiently aggrieved to consider it worthwhile reporting – it must be something that exceeds their limit of tolerance. As seen in Chapter 2, public tolerance changes over time, and varies in different areas and within different subcultures. Thus for example people who live in the country may have a very different view of what activities are considered serious enough to report to the police than those living in towns, who may be more used to noisy parties or minor thefts from cars. Young people often experiment with different kinds of controlled drugs like cannabis and may not regard this as a real crime.

- *Seriousness or triviality of the offence.* One of the most common reasons given by victims for not reporting an offence is that it was too trivial to bother with. This will obviously be affected by levels of tolerance, but it is clear that a number of petty thefts or minor assaults are seen as insufficiently troublesome to bother the police with. On the other hand serious offences are more likely to be reported, at least when victims are aware of them.

- *Lack of confidence in the police.* Some victims feel that even if they did report an offence the police would either not be able to solve it or would not pay much attention. Some crimes may be sufficiently trivial for them to realise that the police cannot deal with it. Where sections of the population hold hostile attitudes towards the police they are less likely to report crime to them.

- *No motive.* A victim or a witness may conclude they have nothing to gain personally by reporting a crime and may consider the loss of time involved as not worth the effort. This might be counteracted by compensation or insurance incentives, or by public spiritedness.

- *Fear of reprisals.* Some victims may not wish to report offences because they are afraid that offenders may take some form of reprisal. This might be particularly the case with organised crime, school bullying and street vandalism where the offenders are known to the victim.

- *Embarrassment.* In some cases victims may be too embarrassed to report offences – victims of fraud or sexual assault may feel that they might be seen to have precipitated the offence and feel ashamed. In other cases victims may themselves have been indulging in behaviour they want to keep secret – clients who have their money stolen by prostitutes for example may well choose not to report an offence. Companies who find that senior executives have been embezzling funds may fear the public embarrassment following trial and conviction and decide to sack the executives concerned rather than call in the police.
- *Fear of self-incrimination.* Theft or violence against users of illegal drugs or illegal immigrants means that the victim has a difficult choice of revealing their own illegal behaviour if they choose to report an incident to the police.
- *Sympathy for the victim.* Where the offender is known to a victim as a friend or relative the victim may be reluctant to report a criminal incident as they do not wish to get the person into trouble. This can even be the case in crimes involving strangers, for example when the victim feels sympathy for the destitute state of the thief and decides not to report a loss.

## Police influence on crime statistics

Crimes become 'known to the police' in two main ways. The vast majority of offences recorded by the police, about 90 per cent, are reported to the police by the public, the rest coming to their attention as they patrol the streets or carry out surveillance operations, as they might do to catch the suppliers of illegal drugs. It was pointed out above however that not all incidents reported to the police are recorded as crime. Furthermore, police priorities will be reflected in subsequent statistics as deployment of officers to cover one type of crime means that there are less to cover others. This will be discussed in more detail in Chapter 4, however it is important here to point out some of the ways in which variations in police practice affect the crime figures.

Different areas may have different rules regarding what should be recorded, which can affect local variations in crime rates. For example, the increase of 29 per cent in reported rape in 1985 by the Metropolitan Police did not necessarily represent an increase in the number of rapes or in the victim's readiness to report them, but reflected a change in police procedure in the recording of rapes. Policies of individual departments may produce apparent crime waves resulting from decisions to crack down, for example on street crime. Policy decisions by the chief constable will be reflected in the following year's criminal statistics, as arrest and summonses shift with the transfer of personnel from one type of work to another, for example, from the anti-burglary unit to the vice squad.

In other cases the police may decide that no crime has taken place. This might happen in cases of domestic violence where after the police have been called in, they calm the situation down and the victim does not wish any further action to be taken. In many public order incidents it is the police who decide whether or not to take any further action. In other cases, as in the example of a missing purse or bicycle, the incident form may be completed by writing 'no crime' and no further action is taken. The attitude of the victim is also crucial here – if victims are unlikely to press for further action in a relatively trivial case, then it will usually be dropped.

No further action may result in a variety of other situations. The police may know who committed an offence but not be able to prove it. Gathering evidence may be costly and time consuming, as in the case of financial frauds, and allocation of budgets may mean that the case is not pursued. Alternatively the offence may be regarded as too trivial to pursue. In other cases, it may be decided that it is not in the public's interests to proceed – the offender may be seriously ill, very young or very old and therefore unlikely to repeat the offence.

Statistics also record the number of offenders cautioned or convicted. The basis for cautioning decisions will be discussed in Chapter 5 but it is important to recognise that here, as elsewhere in the criminal process, the numbers going forward to the next stage are dependent on the policy and decisions of a preceding agency.

In addition, there is no standard method of recording crimes used by all the separate police forces around the country. The story in Figure 3.5, 'Secret of a One-Man "Crime Wave"', provides an example of the difficulties of interpreting the data in the case of multiple offences when the police decide to issue a summons for each breach of the criminal law.

Maguire also points out that there may be many different ways of counting an offence or series of offences (Maguire 1994). One offence may involve several offenders – is this to be counted as one offence or several? In other cases, a number of single offences may be counted as one or several. This could happen for example with a series of thefts of different items taking place in one location. Figures are also affected by how the police choose to classify an offence. While legal categories appear watertight, many offences may fall into several categories. When for example does an assault occasion actual or grievous bodily harm? The police may not have evidence to sustain one charge and therefore choose another.

An indication of how these many factors operate can be seen in comparisons between different areas. In 1981 Nottinghamshire had the highest recorded crime rate in the country, ahead of London, Liverpool, Manchester and Newcastle. In contrast, two of Nottingham's neighbouring counties, Leicester and Staffordshire, had a crime rate less than half that of Nottingham, as shown in Figure 3.6. A study by Farrington and Dowds in 1985 suggested an explanation for these differences. The British Crime Survey showed that there was indeed a higher crime rate in Nottinghamshire but there were other important factors, revealed by the greater number of

**Fig 3.5** Secret of a one-man 'crime wave'

**BY MICHAEL KERR**

---

Buried in the annual report of the Northern Constabulary – a litany of highland crime, including malicious mischief, false fire alarms, and offences under the Deer (Scotland) Act – lies a staggering statistic: traffic offences in the Shetland Islands apparently rose by more than 400 per cent last year – **from 500 in 1976 to a grim 2, 210.**

For a group of islands whose population is a mere 18,268, the figures seem to suggest some appalling sociological mutation.

The explanation is simpler, but no less bizarre. One man – an Irish lorry contractor called Darrall McKnight – has been summoned for what could be an international record of 1,380 alleged offences. Police in Shetland are still working on the formalities of this horrendous state of affairs.

McKnight, who also owns the Pig and Chicken restaurant near Belfast, had won a sub-contract to move rubble from a quarry on the island to a road construction site. At one point in the journey the lorries had to cross a public highway.

Lerwick police say that a constable making 'routine inquiries' discovered that McKnight's lorries did not have the appropriate operator's licence and that each time they crossed the highway they committed an offence.

Diligently he did his sums. He worked out how many times a day a single lorry crossed the road. He multiplied it by the number of lorries, and then multiplied it by the number of days they had been working on the contract. The grand total was 1,380.

Lerwick police listed each offence as a 'separate occurrence report' and sent the whole lot into the Procurator Fiscal for action. The procurator drafted an identical charge for each offence and then police carried the bundle of 1,380 summonses out to the construction site to confront McKnight.

There, however, they encountered Murphy's Law, whereby if anything can go wrong it will. McKnight had returned to Ireland. The police carried the unserved charges back to Lerwick.

Back in Belfast, McKnight was undaunted. 'They are just learning about traffic in the Shetlands,' he said last week. 'They are just like a lot of childish policemen trying to make it sound like a murder case.'

But the Shetland police remain determined to get their man. A spokesman said that since they could not serve the summonses in person they intended to send all 1,380 of the charges to the Pig and Chicken.

(*Sunday Times*, 23 April 1977)

---

recorded crimes originating from admissions to the police, usually after interviews with the police, (Figure 3.7), and the greater number of property offences recorded involving property of little value (Figure 3.8).

They conclude that police interviewing and recording practice was a major factor explaining the differences between the three Midland counties. If the same recording practices had been used, the authors wrote:

> the crime rate per 1,000 population would have been about 57 in Nottingham, 48 in Leicestershire, and 36 in Staffordshire, in comparison with the observed figures of 87, 44, and 40. It was estimated from the study of police records that the greater number of crimes originating in admissions, and crimes involving stolen property of little value, amounted to a difference in crime rate between Nottinghamshire and the other two counties of about 31 per 1,000 population.

(Farrington and Dowds 1985: 70)

**Fig 3.6** Crimes recorded by the police per 1,000 population

| Year | England and Wales | London | Liverpool | Notts. | Leics. | Staffs. |
|------|-------------------|--------|-----------|--------|--------|---------|
| 1981 | 60 | 88 | 87 | 90 | 45 | 42 |
| 1980 | 55 | 81 | 76 | 79 | 42 | 38 |
| 1979 | 52 | 77 | 71 | 75 | 36 | 38 |
| 1978 | 49 | 73 | 69 | 71 | 35 | 34 |
| 1977 | 50 | 73 | 76 | 76 | 35 | 32 |
| 1976 | 44 | 64 | 68 | 65 | 31 | 29 · |
| 1975 | 43 | 60 | 68 | 65 | 29 | 27 |

(Farrington D and Dowds E (1985) 'Disentangling Criminal Behaviour and Police Reaction' in Farrington D and Gunn J (eds) *Reactions to Crime: the Public, the Police, Courts and Prisons.* Chichester: Wiley: 42)

**Fig 3.7** How crimes were discovered

| | Notts. | | Leics. | | Staffs. | |
|---|---|---|---|---|---|---|
| Police, directly | 19 | (2.3) | 17 | (5.2) | 26 | (6.7) |
| Police, on admission | 211 | (25.4) | 14 | (4.3) | 30 | (7.7) |
| Public call at station | 143 | (17.2) | 103 | (31.3) | 108 | (27.7) |
| Public telephone call | 340 | (41.0) | 178 | (54.1) | 203 | (52.1) |
| Public call to patrol | 111 | (13.4) | 9 | (2.7) | 20 | (5.1) |
| Other | 6 | (0.7) | 8 | (2.4) | 3 | (0.8) |
| TOTAL | 830 | (100) | 329 | (100) | 390 | (100) |

Note: The 'other' category incudes burglar alarms, reports by letter, and the offender giving himself up.

(Farrington D and Dowds E (1985) 'Disentangling Criminal Behaviour and Police Reaction' in Farrington D and Gunn J (eds) *Reactions to Crime: the Public, the Police, Courts and Prisons.* Chichester: Wiley: 58)

**Fig 3.8** Values of stolen property

| | Notts. | | Leics. | | Staffs. | |
|---|---|---|---|---|---|---|
| £1 or less, nothing | 167 | (25.0) | 38 | (12.6) | 43 | (15.4) |
| £2–£10 | 154 | (23.1) | 50 | (16.6) | 57 | (20.4) |
| £11–£25 | 79 | (11.8) | 33 | (10.9) | 48 | (17.1) |
| £26–£50 | 67 | (10.0) | 51 | (16.9) | 35 | (12.5) |
| £51–£100 | 66 | (9.9) | 43 | (14.2) | 34 | (12.1) |
| £101–£250 | 67 | (10.0) | 37 | (12.3) | 26 | (9.3) |
| £251–£500 | 41 | (6.1) | 30 | (9.9) | 21 | (7.5) |
| Over £500 | 27 | (4.0) | 20 | (6.6) | 16 | (5.7) |
| TOTAL | 668 | (100) | 302 | (100) | 280 | (100) |

(Farrington D and Dowds E (1985) 'Disentangling Criminal Behaviour and Police Reaction' in Farrington D and Gunn J (eds) *Reactions to Crime: the Public, the Police, Courts and Prisons.* Chichester: Wiley: 59)

## CONCLUSION

We can see therefore that estimating the extent and impact of crime is extremely difficult and official statistics and crime surveys can only give a partial picture of the real extent of crime. In effect they may tell us more about what the public define as crime and what the police and other agencies choose to process. The above analysis of how these statistics are created has several implications for a consideration of criminal justice agencies and policy.

In the first place, it shows that the actions of the public and the police have an important impact on the crime figures. It is therefore important, in examining the role of criminal justice agencies, to also examine how they contribute to overall estimates of the extent of crime and how offenders are selected for subsequent stages. They reveal the considerable discretion which exists at all stages in the process. In addition, the public can also be affected by the images of crime portrayed in the media. If, for example, they learn that there has been an increase in a particular kind of crime, they may be more likely to report it. In addition, they may come to be more afraid of this kind of crime and take action to prevent it.

The analysis of crime figures also shows that public pressure and policy may be directed against only a very selective group of crimes, those which receive most attention in the media. Many crimes never reach the attention of the police and many more offenders remain undetected. Therefore those going through the criminal justice system may be a small and unrepresentative group of offenders. This raises important questions in relation to the role of criminal justice. How far can it seek to prevent crime, when it deals with only a proportion of those who commit it? A common response to a moral panic or a seeming spate of offences reported in the media is often to institute tougher penalties. However if so many offenders remain undetected, how effective are these strategies likely to be? Should the system not focus on attempting to catch more offenders rather than punishing the ones that are caught? How much can sentencing policy really affect the volume of crime? These considerations underlie the current emphasis on crime prevention which will be discussed in Chapter 11.

However, other views (explored in Chapter 9) stress that the impact on the volume of crime is not the only purpose of sentencing. From the 'just deserts' and denuncitory perspectives it is important to punish wrong-doers regardless of their numbers. Whatever is considered the main objective of sentencing, it must first be understood that it occurs at a late stage in the criminal justice system, and starts with the police as the gatekeepers of the system. The following chapter will analyse their work in more detail.

**Review Questions**

1. List the main factors which could account for an increase in crimes reported to the police in the last 40 years.

2. List offences which might be under-represented in the crime figures along with the reasons why they might be under-represented.
3. List some factors which might explain why men are convicted of more offences than women and young offenders are convicted of more offences than adults.
4. List the main reasons why victims might not report crimes to the police.
5. See also Appendix, Practical Exercises, Exercise No 1.


**Further Reading**

Bottomley K and Pease K (1986) *Crime and Punishment – Interpreting the Data*. Milton Keynes: Open University Press

Home Office (1993) *Digest 2: Information on the Criminal Justice System in England and Wales*. Barclay G. (ed). London: HMSO

Home Office (annually) *Criminal Statistics in England & Wales*. London: HMSO

Maguire M (1994) 'Crime Statistics, Patterns and Trends: Changing Perceptions and their Implications' Maguire M, Morgan R and Reiner R (eds) *The Oxford Handbook of Criminology*. Oxford: Clarendon Press.

Mayhew P, Elliot D and Dowds L (1989) *The 1988 British Crime Survey*. London: HMSO

# CHAPTER 4

# THE POLICE

The Role and Development of Policing
Organisation and accountability
Police Powers
Discretion in Police Work
Discrimination and Police Culture

## INTRODUCTION

Policing attracts much public interest. Police dramas and documentaries nightly fill up television schedules and detective fiction and crime stories regularly feature in publishers' bestseller lists. But these popular images are often very far from the reality of policing. Police dramas feature murder, violent and organised crime, and investigations involve following up clues, dramatic car chases and confrontations. In reality murders are rare, most crimes are solved because the victim identifies the perpetrator, and in the life of an average police officer car chases and violent encounters with suspects are, perhaps fortunately, rare.

There are other, less positive images of policing. In riots and demonstrations the police are seen in pitched battles with demonstrators and there have been allegations of planting evidence, 'fitting up' suspects and violence by the police. These different images illustrate some of the problems in defining the role of the police. Are they better described as a force or a service? Is it possible to talk about consensus policing or are the police essentially a paramilitary force waging a war against crime and disorder?

The conflicting demands of due process, crime control and bureaucratic efficiency strongly affect how the police are organised and evaluated. They are expected to find and bring to court those suspected of having committed an offence, but while doing so must stay within the law. They must have powers to investigate crime but the public must be able to proceed without undue interference. Policing must be cost effective, but is difficult to subject to measurement – how, for example, can due process be measured? Having more police on the beat may make the public feel happier, but it might be costly and have little effect on crime.

86

Other models of criminal justice are also relevant to policing. While a key role of the police is to ensure that offenders are brought to court and punished, many offenders, especially young offenders, may have a better chance of being rehabilitated if they are diverted from formal proceedings. Thus the police play a role in both rehabilitation and denunciation. The police also play a role in preventing crime. This might conflict with their role of bringing offenders to justice. For instance, should an officer who observes suspicious behaviour intervene to prevent a potential crime happening or await the outcome of events and act only if a crime is committed? To critics following the class domination model, the police are essentially an organisation protecting the interests of the propertied and powerful and function as an arm of the state.

Police policy therefore faces conflicting pressures, illustrated by the volume of recent legislation and reviews affecting virtually all aspects of policing. The Sheehy Report of 1993 dealt with managerial and organisational matters and the following Police and Magistrates' Courts Act 1994 had an extremely stormy passage. The Criminal Justice and Public Order Act 1994 brought in new police powers with regard to stopping and searching citizens. A Home Office Review, due to report in 1995, also raises key questions about the core functions of the police.

This chapter will examine many of these issues and explore the current organisation of policing in England and Wales. It will start by exploring the role and development of the police. It will then examine how the police are organised and how accountable they are. Legislation regulating how the police exercise their powers will be considered. As we have seen, the police have considerable discretion and how they exercise this will be explored along with a discussion of the extent to which this involves discrimination against any particular group. Finally, at a day-to-day level, policing is strongly affected by how officers themselves interpret their role and the conflicting pressures on their work. This involves looking at what has been described as the occupational culture of the police.

Other chapters will explore further aspects of policing. The police role in cautioning will be looked at in Chapter 5, community policing will be explored in greater depth in Chapter 11, and the likely implications of current reforms will be taken up in Chapter 12. Many discussions of the police automatically refer to the police in the public sector, but it is important also to recognise, as seen in Chapter 1, that there is a vast and growing private security sector, who are carrying out an increasing number of police tasks. The implications of this will be looked at in Chapter 12, while the focus of this chapter will be on the public police.

## THE ROLE AND DEVELOPMENT OF POLICING

Policing involves many different functions from patrolling and detection to traffic control, licensing and dealing with incidents which do not involve crime at all. This is well illustrated by a snapshot survey of police work in 1992. This was conducted during an eight-hour period from 8 pm on Friday, 7 February to 4 am on Saturday, 8 February 1992 and while Fridays are not typical of other days in the week, it shows the range of incidents which the police are expected to deal with.

## Public order snapshot

It was an ordinary winter's night, relatively mild for the time of year and uneventful as far as the general public and the media were concerned. In fact, as the public sat down to their breakfast that Saturday morning they would have had no idea what the police service had been doing on their behalf during the previous night.

During this eight-hour period, in fact, police officers responded to 20,932 separate incidents, that is 43 incidents every minute. 6,212 of these incidents (approximately 30%) were the result of 999 emergency calls which required an immediate response. There were four murders, seven rapes and 502 serious and indecent assaults, together with 112 cases of arson and 1,264 incidents of criminal damage to property. Robbery, burglary and car crime amounted to a further 3,045 separate incidents. 108 road traffic accidents involving personal injury included six fatalities. Minor assaults and drink-drive offences accounted for 1,548 incidents. 9,830 (47%) of the total incidents represented police attendance to matters not specifically identified but requiring advice and assistance.

In addition there were 4,458 incidents of public disorder ranging from 59 incidents of violent disorder and affray to almost 3,000 general disturbances in the streets. As a consequence of this 759 people were arrested, 30% of the total number arrested during the eight-hour period.

One of the most disturbing facts arising out of this survey is that, in this one short period, 54 police officers were assaulted whilst in the execution of their duty. In one area, three officers were injured whilst arresting a man for stabbing two other youths.

(Her Majesty's Chief Inspector of Constabulary *Annual Report for the Year 1991*, (1992) 22)

The many tasks carried out by the police are often divided into three distinct roles. In the first place the police are responsible for law enforcement, for investigating crime, arresting suspects and deciding whether or not to pass the case on to the Crown Prosecution Service. This reflects their key role as enforcers of the criminal law. They are also the guardians of the Queen's Peace and preserving law and order in society. This involves tasks such as patrolling the streets and monitoring public gatherings, football matches or demonstrations. Less obvious is a third, social service role, in which the police deal with an enormous number of tasks which do not involve crime such as traffic management and dealing with accidents, deaths and emergencies. Roger Graef estimates that, 'some 75 per cent of police time is spent on non-crime matters'. (Graef 1993). In practice, these roles are interrelated.

For example, not all incidents the police are called to can be clearly identi-fied as crime, public order or social service – they are incidents requiring some form of action. Imagine, for example, a situation in which officers are called to investigate complaints about noise and disturbance in a street. In this situation they will principally be concerned to calm the situation which might be achieved by their very presence or might involve making arrests. If they behave too aggressively however they might exacerbate the situation. In other circumstances they may proffer advice and help or refer parties to another agency. Thus in many situations, all three roles are combined.

In other situations these roles conflict. For example, during the miners' strike of 1984, groups of police officers were accused of violence, harass-ment and intimidation. Afterwards, the local police in mining towns, who had by and large not been involved in these incidents, complained that their ability to enforce the law was impeded by the hostility which had developed towards the police in general. Indeed the police vitally need the support of the public to enforce the criminal law. As we have seen, the public play a crucial role in reporting crime, and the majority of crimes are cleared up on the basis of public information. If, however, the public mistrust the police they will be less prepared to volunteer information.

The adversarial system creates further dilemmas. As seen in Chapter 1 this system does not seek to establish the truth, but requires that a case is proved beyond reasonable doubt through the provision of legally admissible evidence. Thus the test of success for the police becomes whether an investi-gation leads to a prosecution and finding of guilt. In some of the cases which have been labelled as 'miscarriages of justice' it would appear that the police tampered with evidence or unfairly gained confessions in order to provide evidence to support their view of the defendants' guilt. In other cases, vic-tims and witnesses may privately offer details of an incident but refuse to give evidence in public. In such cases the police may stop the investigation because they have no evidence that can be used in court, or seek other ways of collecting evidence. If no other source of evidence is available they face the possibility that a guilty person will escape justice. In high profile cases arousing public outrage, especially those involving terrorism, pressure to get a result may be sufficient to lead to the use of illegally obtained evidence.

The requirement for triable evidence may also lead to situations in which the police may need to wait for the crime to be committed instead of pre-venting it. This is illustrated in the story in Figure 4.1 from the USA. Timothy Ray was suspected of maiming and killing show jumping horses so that their owners could claim the insurance money. One wealthy show jump-ing figure, Barney Ward, was accused of having Ray kill four of his horses for an insurance payout of $570,000. The law enforcement agents from the Agricultural Department of the US government put the suspect, Timothy Ray, under surveillance so as to collect the evidence before they could arrest him.

**Fig 4.1** The death of Streetwise

> # Death in the Stables
> ## By Charles Laurence
>
> It was at a tournament in Gainsville, Florida, in February, 1991, that the cops were waiting for 'Ray' (the name used on the charge sheet). Tipped off by Miller, they followed him from bar and motel to paddock and show jumping ring. The tournament passed: a horse called Streetwise performed badly, as usual, and afterwards the police followed
>
> Ray back through the rain back to the stables from a bar. Ray, who was travelling with an associate, Harlow Arlie, loaded three horses, and then led Streetwise from his stall.
>
> The rain gave Ray the perfect cover. Instead of leading the trusting animal into the horse box, Ray held it by its halter in the yard, while the burly Arlie took up a crowbar and smashed it against the horse's right rear leg. The horse fell, bellowing and then rose, broke free and stumbled into a paddock where it fell again. The scene had shocked
>
> even Ray, but so far everything was going to plan. Ray called the vet, with the story that Streetwise had fallen in the rain and broken a leg. The vet called the insurance company hotline, and was given authority to put the horse down.
>
> Ray drove away with the three remaining horses, ready to collect his $5,000 fee, but ran straight into a roadblock which had been set up following the call of an Agricultural Department agent who had watched the whole performance from the top of a horsebox.

(*Daily Telegraph*, 13 August 1994: 1 Weekend Section)

## Development of policing

Before the 19th century, no one public organisation was responsible for policing and different functions were carried out by what Brogden describes as a hotch potch of different arrangements (Brogden et al 1988). Local boroughs employed constables and watchmen who were not very efficient. Many other policing functions were carried out privately – individual businesses hired men to protect property and landowners employed gamekeepers. Towards the end of the 18th century, the famous Fielding brothers, magistrates at Bow Street, set up and financed the Bow Street runners to catch thieves. Industrialisation brought large numbers of migrants into urban areas and led to fears that public safety would be threatened by the 'dangerous' classes. Early calls for an organised police force were however resisted as a publicly financed police organisation was seen as a threat to the liberty of the individual citizen.

Campaigners such as Sir Robert Peel continued to press for a more organised system and in 1829, the Metropolitan Police Improvement Act set up the Metropolitan Police Force. Initially this consisted of 1,000 officers controlled from No 4 Whitehall Place – backing on to Scotland Yard. Similar forces were set up in municipal corporations and counties and, following the County and Borough Police Act 1856, there were 239 forces operating in

England and Wales. These early police forces concentrated largely on patrolling the streets. In 1842, following two attempts on the life of Queen Victoria, a small detective branch was set up, consisting of two inspectors and six sergeants. By 1877 it had expanded to 250 men. A Fenian bombing campaign during the 1880s led to the formation of the Special Irish Branch, later to become the Special Branch, specialising in counteracting subversive political and industrial activity. As the police force grew and new technology became available, new specialist functions emerged. In 1901 the system of classifying fingerprints was introduced, and in 1910 the Metropolitan Police first caught a criminal using radio telegraphy. In 1920 the police acquired two motor vans – the birth of the flying squad. Women officers were introduced in 1919, although women, often police constables' wives, had been employed as 'matrons' to deal with female convicts and matters involving children. Until 1973, women were organised in a separate department and paid less than male officers. After 1973 the women's organisation was abolished and the force was integrated.

From their inception, the 'new police' were unpopular. The working classes saw them as a potentially oppressive force, popularly described as a 'plague of blue locusts', 'blue devils', or 'crushers'. The middle and upper classes saw a threat to their liberty from so called government spies. Gradually, however, opposition from both groups was overcome and the police gained legitimacy. According to Robert Reiner:

> By the 1950s policing by consent was achieved in Britain to the maximal degree it is ever attainable – the wholehearted approval of the majority of the population who do not experience the coercive exercise of police powers to any significant extent and de facto acceptance of the legitimacy of the institution by those who do.

> (Reiner 1992a: 60)

This success was due, according to Reiner, to the policies adopted by early commissioners which created the distinctive style of English policing. Crucial to these policies, devised in an attempt to secure the support of the public at large, was the emphasis on the independence of the police from any particular class or political influence.

Reiner identifies several key elements of these early strategies. In the first place, a quasi-military command structure incorporated elements of rank, authority and discipline. This bureaucratic organisation, which included training and a career structure to attract high quality recruits, distinguished the 'new' police from their disorganised and often corrupt forerunners. In addition the importance of upholding the rule of law was stressed, thus protecting citizens from any abuse of police powers. A policy of minimum force sought to allay fears of the working classes that the police would be unduly oppressive. This led to one of the most distinctive features of British policing – the absence of firearms in everyday duties and a reluctance to use paramilitary tactics more common in the US or many European countries. In addition, the police were to be non-partisan and impartial in their enforcement of the law, favouring the interests of neither one class nor the other. This impartiality was underlined by denying police officers the vote until 1887, and they are still not allowed to affiliate to political parties or have a trade union. The Police Federation represents police officers of the rank of constable (up to Chief Inspector) but they are not allowed to take industrial action.

The reluctance to expand the detective branch arose out of a deep-rooted suspicion of the plain clothes officer. Hostility was reduced as the new police gained a reputation for being relatively effective in preventing and detecting crime. Finally, argues Reiner, their legitimacy increased as a result of changes in society itself. By the 1950s there was less class conflict than before, the working classes had become more incorporated into society and were relatively homogenous – thus the public as a whole tended to have a shared conception of what they expected from the police.

By the 1950s, generally depicted as a golden age of consensus policing, the legitimacy of the police was established. This was symbolised by the popular Dixon of Dock Green television series which portrayed a friendly local bobby whose knowledge of his patch helped him to prevent crime, catch local villains, and help many members of the local community. Dixon was followed by very different TV heroes in such programmes as The Sweeney and the Professionals in the 1970s and 1980s, and the popular series of the early 1990s Between the Lines dealing with police discipline and complaints.

From the 1950s the legitimacy which the police had established was challenged on several fronts. The urban disturbances of 1981, which led to the Scarman Report, were in part attributed to the frequent use in multi-racial areas of stop and search powers. Increasing evidence emerged of cases where the police were found to have tampered with evidence, secured false confessions and abused their powers. Other complaints concerned how suspects were dealt with in custody. This raised the issue of how accountable the police were – both in terms of individual complaints and police policy. What happened to change the image of the police, in Reiner's words, from 'plods to pigs'? (Reiner 1992a: 77).

The key factors which led to increased legitimacy, according to Reiner, can also account for its decline. Revelations about corruption on the part of police officers during the 1960s and allegations about improper behaviour severely dented the image of the police as a disciplined force, showing that they could readily break the law in order to enforce it. The 1970s and 1980s saw the increasing use of riot shields and other modern hardware in the control of industrial disputes and urban unrest replacing the 'pushing and shoving' strategy used in demonstrations during the 1950s and 1960s. The accidental killing of innocent citizens by armed police officers attracted much criticism, especially from their traditional supporters, the middle classes. The traditional political impartiality of the police was also questioned during the general election of 1979, when they campaigned vigorously for stronger law and order policies. Finally, society itself had changed. Whereas during the so-called golden age, the working class was a more homogeneous community, by the 1980s it was increasingly fragmented and divided with the growth of unemployment, the increasingly multi-racial nature of urban communities, and the growth of what some describe as an underclass. This made it more difficult for the police to satisfy the now conflicting expectations about how areas should be policed.

Police relationships with the public were also affected by the consequences of changes in the nature and organisation of policing. Like any organisation the police face pressures for efficiency and must respond to changes in crime which may lead to the use of more sophisticated technology. These pressures also produced specialisation. This necessitated organisational changes which vitally affected relationships between the police and local communities.

A simple example of this is the effect of expansion in cars, traffic and car ownership. The increasing volume of cars on the roads necessitated the development of techniques of traffic control and the enforcement of road traffic legislation. Specialist traffic control using increasingly sophisticated technology followed. As car ownership spread, many groups, particularly the middle classes, previously unlikely to encounter the police in their law enforcement role became the subject of police attention. This on occasion provoked the response 'why don't you go out and catch real criminals?' Cars also became an essential tool in law enforcement and patrolling, and had a fundamental impact on the job of the police constable. The car chase has become a symbolic feature of policing in both popular imagery and police folklore. And of course cars, as well as increasing the mobility of criminals, have provided multiple opportunities for crime – from vandalism to serious car theft, ramraiding and joyriding: for some joyriders part of the thrill is the chase with the police.

Similar points could be made about other technological developments – computers have radically changed the nature of policing as have developments in communications. The beat officer of 40 years ago could not instantly call on the police computer, let alone the local station, to provide instant back-up. Information had to be gathered directly from the public. While undoubtedly these developments have increased the ability of the police to respond quickly to emergencies, to call for help, and to sift through large amounts of information, they have had important consequences for relations between the police and public, and for the basic role of the police officer.

This can be seen in contrasting the work of officers during the period of the so-called golden age of policing, when officers were allocated a beat and were responsible for patrolling it, often on foot. This meant that officers got to know the local community – they would make purchases from shopkeepers, visit local cafés and come into contact with many residents. The intelligence they gathered from these natural social contacts may have helped when they came to investigate a crime. Armed only with a truncheon and a whistle to call for help, the constable had to rely on his or her own wits to handle troublesome situations. Communication with the station was made through the police box and incidents had to be handled on the spot.

This form of policing was, however, inefficient. One officer could only cover a limited area, whereas two officers, in a car, receiving their information from a radio link with the station, could cover a much larger area and arrive at incidents much quicker. The lone officer on patrol is also unlikely to catch many criminals – no self-respecting burglar is going to break in when they see a constable walking down the road. The growth of many specialised functions also fundamentally changed the job of the basic constable on the beat, who became less involved in detecting crime and proportionately more involved with the more mundane elements of police work such as dealing with drunks, vagrants or handling minor local incidents.

This affected relationships between the police and the public. Whereas the old style beat officer encountered many members of the public while pounding the beat, officers in cars had less immediate contact. The public were less likely to know or have encountered these officers, and information tended to come from the police station rather than from the public. The ability to call instantly for back-up meant that officers were less reliant on their own personal skills to handle situations and the cars and radios in themselves became symbols of authority.

In addition, pressures for efficiency led to a stress on law enforcement as opposed to service or preventive roles – to the more readily measurable aspects of police work such as arrest rates, clear-up rates and response times – often described as fire brigade policing. This meant that other, less easily measurable tasks became seen as less significant. The 1970s and 1980s also saw the rise of what is often called paramilitary policing. A spate of urban disturbances and industrial disputes prompted the development of specialist squads trained to deal with riots and crowd control. These units, including the Special Patrol Group, were increasingly armed with the hardware used for disturbances in Ulster and abroad. Their tactics caused enormous controversy, especially during the miners' strike of 1984. Some were also used as a back-up for crime fighting initiatives, which involved the intensive use of stop and search powers. These kind of tactics were found by the Scarman Report to have been partly responsible for local resentments which contributed to the breakdown in relations between the police and public preceding the Brixton Disturbances of 1981.

All these factors illustrate the many tensions in the role of the police which has been questioned in recent years. Yet, despite the problems associated with modern police work, the police still enjoy widespread support amongst the population as a whole. Figure 4.2, taken from a Gallup Poll published in 1993 shows that, in comparison to other institutions, the police rank second to the armed forces in terms of public confidence.

**Fig 4.2** Confidence in public institutions

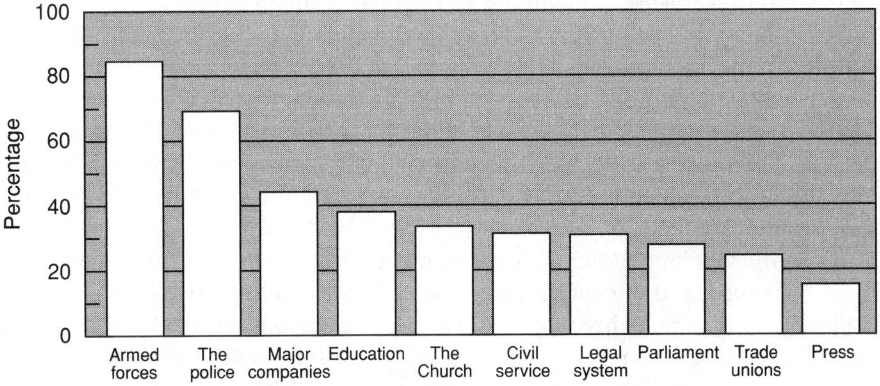

(Gallup Poll for *Daily Telegraph*, 22 February 1993)

## ORGANISATION AND ACCOUNTABILITY

Policing in England and Wales is carried out by 43 forces. In 1989/90 these forces employed an average of 126,204 police officers – a rise of 15 per cent since 1978/79. The number of civilian staff has also grown by 17 per cent in 10 years and expenditure on the police rose by 30 per cent between 1984/85 and 1988/89. The largest force is the Metropolitan Police with 28,135 officers in 1994, and the smallest is the City of London with only 789 officers. The size of individual forces reflects the size of the population and the demands of the area. The ratio of police to population is one officer to 257 in the Metropolitan Police District, whereas in the non-metropolitan counties the figure is one officer to 497.

Police officers are distributed between various ranks, a feature introduced to maintain discipline. The rank structure was felt by the Sheehy Report to contain, 'too many chiefs and not enough indians' and the number of ranks was reduced by the Police and Magistrates' Courts Act 1994. From 1 April 1995 the ranks of deputy chief constable and chief superintendent were abolished. Thus by 1995, the rank structure will be as follows:

**OUTSIDE LONDON**

Chief Constable

Assistant Chief Constable

**LONDON (MPD)**

Commissioner (MPD)
Deputy Commissioner (MPD)
Assistant Commissioner
Deputy, Assistant Commissioner
Commander

Superintendent
Chief Inspector
Inspector
Sergeant
Constable

Each force is divided into geographical areas or divisions with management and support services – including personnel, training and the inspectorate. Metropolitan Police District areas are headed by a Deputy Assistant Commissioner assisted by two Commanders. Each has its own headquarters and controls a number of support branches including dog sections, traffic patrols, area major incident teams, complaints sections, and child protection teams. There are also local crime squads, drug squads and robbery squads, depending on demand. Each area has patrol cars for rapid response, panda cars, traffic cars and motorcycles.

The Metropolitan Police have a number of specialist squads and departments including the central drugs squad, the central cheque squad, the stolen motor vehicle investigation squad, the serious and organised crime squad (the gangbusters), the central robbery squad (flying squad or colloquially 'the Sweeney'), the regional crime squad, the fraud squad, special branch, the anti-terrorist branch and the international criminal police organisation (Interpol). These squads can all call on specialist departments such as the forensic science laboratories, the fingerprint branch, the photographic branch and the national identification bureau.

Because of its size, the Metropolitan Police also has a number of specialist departments including the traffic police, the Thames division which patrols the River Thames 24 hours a day; the mounted branch which assists with traffic and crowd control; the air support unit which assists with traffic and crowd control along with the royalty and diplomatic protection department and the special escort group. Not all forces have such a large number of branches. Other responsibilities include public relations and the growing organisation around community policing which will be discussed in Chapter 11. Increasingly regional and national units have been established to combat crime such as the regional crime squad and the National Criminal Intelligence Service (NCIS) football unit. Before the riot at the England–Ireland match in Dublin in February 1995, the unit had targeted known troublemakers who were travelling to the game.

## Investigating crime

While it is important to understand the many functions of the police such as emergency services and traffic control they have a unique role in investigating crime. Apart from a few specialist agencies the police handle most crime investigation in this country. Thus most prosecutions depend on the routine information collected by uniform officers and the detective work of their non-uniformed colleagues in the criminal investigation departments, the CID.

Criminal investigations over the years have stimulated the development of technical and expert services such as forensic services. Today's police have access to computer information systems such as those storing details of all car registrations, and more recently they have employed psychological profiling in murder cases, such as that of Rachel Nickell on Wimbledon Common. The Royal Commission on Criminal Justice 1993 recommended a national database and wider powers for the police to require suspects to give DNA samples, similar to the powers they have with fingerprints. In 1994 the Home Office announced that Britain was to have the first such database in the world. This will not only assist crime investigation, but might also be a deterrent in that a person listed might abstain from committing further sexual crimes as the chances of being identified are increased.

The most widely accepted form of forensic evidence is the fingerprint test. The idea was developed by Edward Henry who noticed its use in 19th century India and the Metropolitan Police introduced it in 1901. Its use led to the conviction of two brothers – the Strattons – for murder in 1905. The assumption has been that no two sets of fingerprints are the same. The process of checking fingerprints is still done by trained observers who look for one of four distinctive characteristics in a fingerprint – split, lake, island or end of a ridge. The use of computers to check for fingerprints has not been possible because of the unreliability of the images yielded by the process. Fingerprinting until recently was widely regarded as foolproof and conclusive of guilt by police and juries. But doubt was raised about the ability of fingerprints to determine individual identity in the case of Neville Lee who was arrested, solely on the basis of a fingerprint left in blood in a lavatory cubicle after a brutal rape of an 11 year-old girl in Clumber Park near Worksop in August 1991. He was arrested by the Nottinghamshire police and detained in custody for six weeks before another sexual attack in the same park led to the arrest of a person who confessed to the rape that Lee had been accused of.

Forensic evidence, based on scientific procedure, provides valuable evidence for investigators and prosecutors in contrast to the unpredictability of human witnesses. But the faith in scientific evidence has been shown to be unjustified in dramatic cases such as the Birmingham Six convicted in 1975 for the murder of 21 people in 1974 after a bomb was left in a public house in the central shopping district. The test to show that the suspects had been handling explosives, crucial in convincing the police that they had got the right suspects, was later to prove unreliable with positive results also being given by innocuous substances such as soap.

The use of DNA profiling was also regarded as reliable as fingerprinting to check the unique characteristics of an individual. Developed by Dr Alec Jeffries, the technique is now used in rape cases around the world. The DNA technique involves comparing a number of bands in the suspect's DNA with those of the DNA from body fluid or tissue involved in the crime. A calculation is then made on the probabilities of another person having a similar match. But in two tests carried out on behalf of the Californian police authorities, the process revealed a positive misidentification of two separate people in two distinctive tests and undermined claims that the chances of two people having the same DNA profile was as high as one in 100,000.

## Who are the police accountable to?

A key issue in looking at police organisation is who they are answerable, or accountable, to. As we have seen, a major characteristic of the British police has been their supposed independence from direct political control. This can however lead to a situation in which they could be seen to have too much autonomy from both central government or local communities. At the same time over-control from the centre is often criticised as leading to centralisation and nationalisation, thereby reducing any influence of local communities. In addition, individuals must be protected from abuse of police powers. Theoretically, the police are accountable in a variety of ways. Outside London, local police authorities (LPAs) are responsible for a variety of functions, disciplinary and complaints procedures deal with individual matters, and the police are ultimately accountable to the law and the courts.

The Police Act 1964 set up what became known as a tripartite structure involving, outside London, chief constables, the Home Secretary and police authorities which were composed of two-thirds elected representatives from local councils and one-third justices of the peace. The Metropolitan Police area does not have a police authority and the Commissioner is directly answerable to the Home Secretary. By the 1990s these bodies were subject to much criticism. They were large, some having as many as 46 members, and their exact links with the local community were uncertain. Their powers were somewhat ambiguous. While they were, for example, responsible, under s 5(1) of the Police Act 1964, for 'the maintenance of an adequate and efficient police force for the area', exactly how they should do this was unclear. Two key roles were the appointment of a chief constable and approving the budget. The Home Secretary however approved the appointment of chief constables and in practice police authorities had little control over how budgets were spent or over police policy. While they could ask for a report from the chief constable, this could be refused if it would contain operational matters which it would not be in the public interest to disclose. In addition, as Mary Tuck points out, much policy was dictated by Home Office circulars and the police inspectorate. Indeed, she argues, the tripartite structure was effectively reduced to a bipartite one with the government and chief constables being responsible for more decisions and the authority for less (*Guardian*, 18 December 1993).

In a study by the Policy Studies Institute it was also found that policy developments such as crime prevention, crimes against women and children and the diversion of administrative tasks from uniformed officers to civilian employees was increasingly determined by central government and that local police authorities had little influence over developments (Jones and Newburn 1994). This study also found that police authorities took too narrow a view of their role, lacked relevant information and expertise and were too large and cumbersome to carry out effective discussion.

The Police and Magistrates' Court Bill, introduced in 1993, sought to change this structure. The government proposed that chief constables should be more responsible for budgets. Accordingly, the government should have more control over their appointment and they should be placed on fixed-term contracts. Other sections of the Bill proposed that the number of authorities should be reduced, forces merged, and that elected local authority councillors be replaced by Home Office nominees. These proposals faced vehement criticism not only from opposition parties but from the Police Federation and a number of former Home Secretaries in the House of Lords. The main focus of this opposition was the fear that the proposals would lead to greater central government control and an abandonment of local involvement.

Many of the original proposals had to be dropped, and the resulting Police and Magistrates' Courts Act contained the following changes. The size of police authorities was reduced to 17 members consisting of three magistrates, five independent nominees and nine locally elected councillors. A list of potential nominees would be submitted to the Home Secretary who would then choose from this list. The Chair will, however, not now be a direct nominee of the Home Secretary. From 1995 local police authorities would no longer be committees of local authorities but be free-standing authorities. Along with the chief constable they will develop a local policing plan with the chief constable being responsible for deciding on spending priorities within the context of this plan. In line with their new financial responsibilities, chief constables will be on performance related pay and short-term contracts. What Loveday sees as new style accountability involves the production of performance indicators and national league tables (Loveday 1994). In addition to local police plans there will also be National Police Objectives. The Act also enhances the Home Secretary's power to amalgamate police forces in future.

The effect of these changes is as yet unclear but the debates surrounding their introduction well illustrate the problems involved in police organisation. Clearly the police must be able to make key decisions about how to police their areas – but at the same time, local communities, through elected representatives, also feel that they should influence this policy. In addition, while the structure of police authorities does allow some, albeit limited local involvement, provisions in the Act further enhance the role of central government (Loveday 1994).

One way in which local communities may affect policing is through Police Consultative Committees (PCCs) set up after the Scarman Report and underpinned by the Police and Criminal Evidence Act 1984. These consist of members of the public, usually invited from a number of relevant organisations and a number of local officers. These committees have no power, and some see them as little more than talking shops. In addition, they tend to be drawn from a very small section of society, with few representatives from groups who are likely to suffer most from any abuse of police powers or from the adverse effects of policies (Morgan 1989).

## Legal accountability

The police are not above the law. They must operate within the same laws as the public and to rules specific to the police. The Police and Criminal Evidence Act 1984 (PACE) and the codes made under its authority, outlined below, are there to protect the citizen from the abuse of police powers. In order to convict a court must be sure that an offence has been committed and that the evidence to prove this is admissible. Thus the courts and the judiciary play a role in police accountability. Theoretically any known abuse of powers in the early stages could prevent a conviction being obtained.

Yet despite safeguards, courts do convict on illegally obtained evidence, if the judge and jury are convinced that it is reliable and relevant evidence. In court, in some cases the reality often is that it is a police officer's word against a defendant's. Given that the police are trained to present evidence in court they are likely to appear more credible witnesses, especially where they enjoy public confidence.

Aggrieved citizens can complain to the police force in question, and internal discipline within the police also protects the citizen. All complaints must be recorded and, if not dealt with informally, will be investigated under the auspices of the Police Complaints Authority. Complaints are investigated by an officer within the force, but if the complaint is serious or against a senior officer, an officer from another force will be appointed.

This structure has attracted criticism, particularly on the grounds that it is largely the police investigating themselves. This is justified on the basis that professionals such as the police, along with doctors and lawyers, are the only people with the necessary knowledge and expertise to investigate complaints. Nonetheless, the absence of an independent element in this procedure has attracted much criticism particularly since very few complaints are successful (Uglow 1988). Figures published by the Home Office show that of a total of 22,300 complaints, 750 or 2.1 per cent were substantiated (Home Office *Statistical Bulletin*, Issue 13/93, 6 June 1994). Seventy per cent were withdrawn or informally resolved and one-third were investigated. Of those investigated 7.2 per cent were substantiated. The largest number of complaints (28 per cent) were for neglect of duty. In addition, in 1993, 485 officers were the subject of proven disciplinary charges; 47 were dismissed and 55 were required to resign. While there is of course no way of assessing how many complaints are justifiable, figures such as these inevitably raise questions.

## POLICE POWERS

As we have seen, the exercise of police powers is subject to rules and guidelines, and the extent of police powers has occasioned considerable controversy since the inception of the 'new police'. On the one hand, the police clearly need powers to stop people on the street if they are suspected of a crime, to enter people's houses if they suspect that they are hiding stolen goods or firearms and to arrest people they suspect of a crime. They need to be able to interview suspects in the police station and may have to hold suspects in cells. On the other hand, individual citizens need to be able to carry on with their everyday lives without risking being stopped on the street, having their homes ransacked by the police and being arrested and taken to the police station. Suspects must be protected from torture, brutality and the extraction of false confessions. Legislation on police powers therefore must balance conflicting needs.

The Royal Commission on Criminal Procedure (RCCP) set up in 1978 found that the law on police powers was piecemeal and haphazard. Different provisions enabled the police to stop and search and powers of arrest were included in around 70 different statutes. In addition the Royal Commission felt that crime investigation should be separated from prosecution and accordingly recommended the setting up of a separate Crown Prosecution Service (discussed in Chapter 5). The subsequent Police and Criminal Evidence Act 1984 (PACE) sought to modernise and rationalise the law governing police powers and to reform aspects of the law relating to criminal evidence. One of its major innovations was to provide for the tape-recording of interviews in police stations. Other safeguards for suspects included provisions for the police to keep records on their dealings with suspects of stops, arrests and for those held in police custody. PACE, as it has become universally known, fundamentally changed many aspects of policing. Since PACE other changes have been introduced, mainly in the Criminal Justice and Public Order Act 1994. The major aspects of these Acts are outlined below.

Crucial to PACE are the codes of practice provided for in ss 66 and 67. Code A deals with powers of stop and search, Code B with the search of premises and the seizure of property and Code C with the detention, treatment and questioning of suspects. Code D deals with identification and Code E with the tape-recording of interviews. These codes contain notes for guidance on the exercise of powers and a breach of any provision can result in evidence being excluded. Thus breaches of a code can endanger a prosecution and become the basis for a complaint against the police. Also important is the requirement for written records. Custody and search records may be obtained by the defence – which is crucial where they wish to establish that there has been a breach which could lead to the exclusion of evidence.

Stop and search powers are dealt with in PACE, ss 1–7. A person or vehicle may be searched in a public place for stolen or prohibited articles when a constable has reasonable grounds for suspecting that they will find such an article. Prohibited articles include offensive weapons and articles which are made or adapted for use, or carried with the intention that they are to be used, in offences of theft, burglary, taking a motor vehicle or deception. Persons or vehicles can be detained for a search for such a period as is

101

reasonably required to permit the search to be carried out. Any person being searched must be notified that the person carrying out the search is a constable, and must be told the officer's name, police station, the object of the search and the grounds for proposing to make it. They must also be told that they are entitled to a copy of the search record which the constable is obliged to make.

The key phrase in this section is reasonable suspicion. Code A deals with what may or may not constitute reasonable grounds and what actions have

**Figure 4.3** Operation of certain police powers under PACE – England and Wales 1993

## USE OF STOP AND SEARCH POWERS

**Table A** Searches of persons or vehicles under s. 1 of the Police and Criminal Evidence Act 1984 and other legislation, and resultant arrests, by search and reason for arrest.

*Numbers*

| Year | Searches made by reason for search | | | | | | |
|------|------------------|--------|----------|-----------------------|-------------------|--------|---------|
| | *Stolen property* | *Drugs* | *Firearms* | *Offensive weapons* | *Going equipped* | *Other* | *Total* |
| 1986 | 48,000 | 32,500 | 1,450 | 6,900 | 10,700 | 10,700 | 109,800 |
| 1987 | 48,800 | 38,300 | 1,060 | 8,500 | 13,600 | 8,100 | 118,300 |
| 1988 | 61,000 | 50,100 | 1,200 | 10,400 | 17,900 | 9,100 | 149,600 |
| 1989 | 77,300 | 79,100 | 1,590 | 12,400 | 23,800 | 8,600 | 202,800 |
| 1990 | 97,100 | 97,800 | 1,770 | 14,900 | 35,500 | 10,000 | 256,900 |
| 1991 | 113,700 | 109,600 | 2,480 | 15,800 | 50,900 | 11,300 | 303,800 |
| 1992 | 127,400 | 124,400 | 2,740 | 18,600 | 63,900 | 14,700 | 351,700 |
| 1993 | 174,800 | 135,700 | 3,650 | 22,500 | 85,200 | 20,900 | 442,800 |

| Year | Arrests made by reason for arrest | | | | | | |
|------|------------------|--------|----------|-----------------------|-------------------|--------|---------|
| | *Stolen property* | *Drugs* | *Firearms* | *Offensive weapons* | *Going equipped* | *Other** | *Total* |
| 1986 | 7,400 | 6,200 | 147 | 1,340 | 1,590 | 2,230 | 18,900 |
| 1987 | 7,000 | 6,500 | 141 | 1,940 | 1,780 | 2,220 | 19,600 |
| 1988 | 7,500 | 9,100 | 182 | 2,130 | 2,000 | 2,770 | 23,700 |
| 1989 | 9,800 | 14,000 | 245 | 2,700 | 2,500 | 3,500 | 32,800 |
| 1990 | 12,000 | 16,000 | 275 | 3,060 | 3,490 | 4,470 | 39,200 |
| 1991 | 15,100 | 17,500 | 389 | 3,370 | 4,890 | 5,060 | 46,200 |
| 1992 | 15,800 | 18,100 | 340 | 3,420 | 5,530 | 5,540 | 48,700 |
| 1993 | 19,400 | 19,400 | 435 | 3,550 | 6,600 | 6,460 | 55,900 |

* Sample data from one force indicate that around 1 in 20 arrests categorised as 'other reason for arrest' were apparently due to behaviour of the person during or after the search. Around a third of the arrests shown under 'other reason for arrest' should have been categorised as arrests for one of the specific categories, mainly 'stolen property' or 'going equipped'.

(Home Office *Statistical Bulletin*, Issue 14/94, 24 June 1994: 3) to be carried out before and after a search. As will be seen below, however, these words are not easy to define and in practice leave room for considerable discretion and potential abuse. Figure 4.3 shows how these powers were used in 1993.

In 1993, the police recorded 442,800 stops and searches and 13 per cent of these resulted in an arrest; 3,560 road checks were recorded in 1993, eight times the number in 1992 due to increased activity by the City of London Police following the IRA bombings in the city. There were 459 persons detained in police custody for more than 24 hours and subsequently released without charge. There were 301 warrants of further detention, granted to extend detention beyond 36 hours. In 244 or 81 per cent of these cases, the person was subsequently charged. That same year, 41 persons were subject to an intimate search, a 42 per cent reduction when compared to 1992 (Home Office *Statistical Bulletin*, Issue 15/94, 24 June 1994).

Further provisions in relation to stop and search are contained in the Criminal Justice and Public Order Act 1994, which allows certain exceptions to the 'reasonable suspicion' provision. Under these provisions the police will have powers to act when senior officers believe incidents involving serious violence may take place or to prevent terrorism. These powers will last for up to 24 hours, but may be extended if serious violence does break out. While introduced to allow the police to prevent serious violence, many fear that the abandonment of reasonable suspicion might lead to some groups being unduly harassed.

Police powers of entry and search and seizure are dealt with in ss 8–23 PACE. Under s 8 magistrates may issue search warrants for relevant evidence where there are reasonable grounds to suspect that a serious arrestable offence has been committed. Some items are excluded including those subject to legal privilege such as communications between lawyer and client; excluded material which includes personal records held in confidence by, for example, a doctor and special procedure material which includes material acquired or created in the course of a trade, which is held subject to an express or implied undertaking to hold it in confidence.

Sections 24–33 of PACE deal with powers of arrest. First, the Act lays down the circumstances in which any person, including a police officer, store detective or ordinary person carrying out a citizen's arrest, can arrest a person. They may arrest anyone who is, or whom they reasonably suspect to be, committing an arrestable offence, and anyone who has committed or who can reasonably be suspected of having committed an arrestable offence. Additionally, only police officers can arrest someone they reasonably believe is about to commit an arrestable offence, or anyone they reasonably believe to be guilty of an arrestable offence.

An arrestable offence is one for which the penalty is fixed by law (for example murder), or which carries a sentence of five years' or more imprisonment or, as in the case of taking a vehicle without consent, is specifically made arrestable by statute. Further, the police have specific powers of arrest where a breach of bail occurs or is anticipated, for specific offences listed in PACE, and where the general arrest conditions are satisfied. The general arrest conditions allow the police to make an arrest for any offence in circumstances where without such a power, someone might be injured or it would be impossible to bring proceedings because of insufficient information or damage.

Although these provisions provide the police with wide powers, they are not limitless and any officer infringing them may be liable for civil or criminal proceedings or disciplinary action. Perhaps most importantly they risk losing an otherwise promising case as evidence obtained after a wrongful arrest may be excluded by the court. Where an arrest is improperly made the police may also be liable for damages to the arrested person.

PACE also consolidated provisions about the suspect's rights on arrest and at the police station. On arrest any person arrested on suspicion of committing a crime is entitled to be:

- told that they have been arrested and why
- arrested without excessive use of force
- cautioned
- taken to a designated police station for interview and not interviewed before arrival at the police station except in urgent cases.

At the police station PACE and the codes provide a comprehensive and detailed framework for the treatment of suspects and arrestees at the police station. Those in custody are the responsibility of the custody officer, a police officer not involved in the investigation. This officer is wholly responsible for all aspects of the period of custody, for any incidents which occur, and for the custody record. The Act provides a complex timetable for the review of detention before charge to ensure that arrested people are not kept in custody without charge for long periods.

On arrival at the police station the custody officer must ensure that anyone arrested is informed about their rights. These include, first, a right to inform someone that they have been arrested. Secondly, anyone arrested has the right to contact and consult a solicitor in private. If they do not wish to or cannot contact a solicitor, or do not have one, free advice is available from a duty solicitor who can be contacted round the clock. Thirdly, arrested persons have the right to have access to PACE and the codes. This is to a certain extent window dressing, as few arrested persons are likely to pore over the minutiae of the codes, but it is an important reminder to suspects and the police of their provisions.

Prior to 1995, throughout the period of arrest and interview suspects had the 'right to remain silent' and were reminded of this in a caution given on arrest, before any interview, and on charge. Thus they should have been advised that:

> You do not have to say anything unless you wish to do so but what you say may be given in evidence.

The right to silence was affected by the Criminal Justice and Public

Order Act 1994. This, contrary to some assertions, does not remove the right, but affects the use that can be made of silence in the trial. Before 1995 juries were told that they should not assume a defendant to be guilty because they failed to answer the accusation at the time of first being taxed with it. Under the 1994 Act, the jury will be told that they can, in certain circumstances, make 'adverse inferences' from silence.

The words of the caution needed to reflect the change. After much debate, in January 1995 the following new wording for the caution was prepared by the Home Office:

> You do not have to say anything. But it may harm your defence if you do not mention when questioned something which you later rely on in court. Anything you do say may be given in evidence.

Vulnerable groups are given additional protection in PACE, in that young people should not be interviewed in the absence of an 'appropriate adult', usually a parent or member of the social services. Similar provision protects the mentally ill, those who do not speak English fluently, and the deaf, who should have appropriate translators present at interview.

Interviews with suspects for any other than trivial offences must now be tape-recorded rather than the old system of 'contemporaneous notes', which were more susceptible to fabrication. Interviews should only be carried out at designated police stations, except when an interview is urgent, for example, to prevent someone being injured. The technology associated with tape-recording prevents any doctoring of tapes.

When an interview forms part of the evidence against a defendant, he or she is entitled to a balanced summary of the recording, and can demand a copy of the tape. Whilst the taping of interviews protects the accused, it may also prevent unfounded complaints against the police and allegations of false confessions.

Detailed provisions also regulate rest and meal breaks along with the conduct of identification techniques, such as identification parades, confrontation and video identification. Perhaps the most significant provisions relate to the continuing assessment of whether an arrested person can be charged or released. Whenever the custody officer decides that the investigating team have sufficient evidence to charge the suspect a charge must be laid and all interviews stopped. On charge the suspect must be released on police bail to attend a magistrates' court on a specified date, or brought if in police custody before a magistrates' court as soon as possible for the court to decide whether or not to remand the suspect on bail or in custody.

## DISCRETION IN POLICE WORK

The effectiveness of all these rules depends on how they are enforced and implemented on the street, in the police station and by the policies and priorities drawn up by chief constables. The police have considerable discretion at all stages of the criminal justice process – quite simply they cannot enforce all the laws all the time. To attempt anything approximating full law enforcement would result in extremely large numbers of police officers exercising surveillance over the population by means of video cameras and intensive patrolling. This would be extremely costly and would lead to what would be regarded as a police state. The police therefore have neither the numbers, resources nor technological expertise to enforce all laws fully. Thus law is selectively enforced and the police, particularly at the lower levels of the hierarchy, have high amounts of discretion.

Chief constables must determine the style of policing and priorities for their area within their given budget and national and local policing plans. Some may favour an emphasis on community policing, others may target particular offences. These general policies are implemented by areas and divisions who may also interpret policy in the light of what they see as the most pressing problems of their area. In the police station yet more discretionary decisions are involved. How suspects are dealt with, interrogated, and charged are all decisions made at this level along with decisions about cautioning or proceeding with charges. Police officers on the streets have discretion in deciding where to patrol, what to investigate, whether and how to intervene in incidents, or whether to stop and search members of the public. Unlike many other organisations, where those at the top exercise the greatest amounts of discretion, police officers on the street have to make difficult decisions on the spur of the moment. This is illustrated in comments made by the Commissioner of the Metropolitan Police, Sir Paul Condon, who in a speech in October 1993, said that many key decisions have to be taken by some of the most junior officers. He went on to say 'they are expected to be counsellors, negotiators, mediators, managers, advisers, experts, parental figures, law enforcers and humble servants, ready to make contentious decisions, some involving life or death'.

Of course priorities are not just about the deployment of police for street work. The whole range of police work has to be prioritised. Traffic flows in London are a top concern for most citizens yet only 600 officers in the Metropolitan Police are deployed full-time on traffic duties. Is this enough? In terms of crime work the Commissioner indicated the following top three priorities for 1994; terrorism, burglary and armed crimes. After a process of public consultation the Metropolitan Police identified the following three aspects of their work as the highest priorities for the public: provision of an emergency response service (999 calls); more visible street patrolling, even though this is unlikely to result in an increase in crime detection; and a decent crime investigation service with proper consideration being given to victims (comments made in a talk to the British Society of Criminology). There have now been many studies of aspects of police discretion exploring how decisions are made and how tasks are prioritised. Clearly the law constrains the use of discretion, but a variety of non-legal or extra-legal factors are also important, and there may well be a gap between the law in action and the law as described in books.

In general, while legal factors form a backcloth against which decisions must be made, the law is often ambiguous and requires interpretation – what situations for example amount to 'reasonably suspicious'? As seen in previous chapters, the police must judge when actions are to be defined as criminal. The immediate situation affects the way an incident will be dealt with. Outcomes may be affected by apparently trivial circumstances such as the weather, the officer's mood, or the time of day. For example, at the end of a long shift, an officer may not want to be delayed by the amount of paper work which could result from an arrest. Alternatively, on a wet cold night they might want to get back to the station and might even look out for people to arrest (Cain 1973). Many studies of police behaviour have found that a wide variety of factors affect how the police react to specific incidents such as drunken brawls, disturbances by youths or disputes between neighbours. Blitzes or purges may be made against particular offences as a result of public policy.

Whether a person is likely to be seen as 'suspicious' depends also on cultural cues. The police have a set of expectations about what kinds of people belong in a certain area, and when and in what circumstances one would expect to find them. Behavioural cues like walking slowly or quickly may also affect judgments of 'suspiciousness' – and these are also culturally determined. The local knowledge and experience of the officer is likely to be important here, as is the local police culture which defines certain areas and groups as representing trouble, and which also provides guidelines for appropriate responses.

Many studies of the exercise of police discretion have focused on street level discretion – perhaps because this aspect has been subject to so much criticism. It is also more visible and easier for researchers to investigate. Police policies and organisation, both national and local, also affect the use of discretion. They will determine the priorities and style of policing in any area and thus the areas and groups of the population that the police come into contact with. Policy is a crucial aspect of discretion, as it influences and informs other decisions. The sections which follow look at some of these decisions and illustrate the limitations of laws and guidelines.

**The decision to stop and search**

The significance of the words 'reasonable suspicion' in relation to stop and search powers has already been indicated. PACE codes state that this must not be based on someone's race or hairstyle, on the fact that they are members of a group or community that have a higher than average record of committing that type of offence, nor on the fact that they are known to have previous convictions for possession of an unlawful article. These guidelines however, like the law, are limited. Decisions to stop and search are made on

107

the spot, and rely on the individual officer's judgment of the situation. In deciding who to stop, officers are looking for something incongruous, something which doesn't fit (Dixon et al 1989). They are encouraged to learn, as part of their training, to identify such situations. This in turn implies a conception of normal – what does fit, which may depend on factors such as age, sex, race, behaviour, dress, time and place. These are impossible to capture by guidelines. In addition argues Dixon, laws such as PACE are limited because they view a stop as an isolated event with its own set of rules. Often, however, officers do not have any specific purpose in mind when they stop someone – they may be acting on a hunch, the reasons for which cannot be legally defined. Thus a decision to stop and subsequently to search is a process rather than an isolated event. Many studies have found that factors such as being 'known to the police' by virtue of previous convictions, or failing to show appropriate respect for the police officer's authority may constitute informal reasons for a stop or an arrest. A police sergeant in Dixon's study says:

> the bobby out on the street . . . doesn't appreciate what the rules are until he's back in here. He's got to make an instant decision; sometimes the rules and regulations go by the board and he uses his commonsense. Then he may find when he comes into the police station that he's done something he shouldn't have, or he's used a power that he didn't have. Then we have to sort of find a way round that . . . find him a power!

> (Dixon et al 1989)

## In the police station

PACE also deals with the exercise of police discretion in the police station, where individual suspects are interviewed and decisions are made about how to proceed with a case. As we have seen it introduced requirements for the taping of interviews and custody records. Nonetheless, in any job, ways are often found to circumvent formal rules, and informal practices may become the norm. Simon Holdaway, for example, in a study written before PACE, found that the police attempt to prevent those with power to challenge their actions (such as doctors or lawyers) from entering the 'back regions' of the station – the interview or interrogation rooms (Holdaway 1983). In addition, just as the rules and guidelines surrounding stop and search cannot fully reflect the social processes underlying encounters, recorded interviews cannot capture the 'reality' of conversations with suspects. They cannot, for example, control the informal interviews which police have with suspects outside the police station, in the car or in the cells (Leng et al 1992). Such conversations are not officially defined as interviews. In this way, deals such as charge bargains can be made which must not form part of formal interviews. In addition, in recorded interviews, the fear of the suspect and the attitude of the officer cannot be fully reproduced on tape. Thus even though confessions which are involuntary, or produced in oppressive circumstances, are inadmissible, these factors may still mean that tactics used by skilled and experienced officers may 'put words into' a suspect's mouth.

These considerations do not imply that the police currently act illegally – many practices are essentially a way around the constraints of law. To the police, obtaining confessions from, or prosecuting someone they 'know' to be guilty is part of their job. Nor does it mean that laws such as PACE are entirely without effect as they may severely curtail the more blatant abuses and indicate what behaviour is seen as appropriate.

# DISCRIMINATION AND POLICE CULTURE

## Discrimination

Residents of some areas may feel that they are being unfairly picked on if the police pay too much attention to them, whereas other groups may feel that the police neglect their problems. Thus women's groups may complain that the police pay insufficient attention to domestic disputes and complaints of rape, and some ethnic groups have complained that racial harassment has not been dealt with effectively. These allegations suggest that the police are discriminating – that is treating some complaints less seriously on the basis of either the gender or race of the complainants. In addition, throughout the 1970s and 1980s there were allegations that the police racially discriminated in stop and search and arrest decisions. It is difficult to find evidence supporting or rejecting such allegations. As the race of offenders is not collected in the criminal statistics, any research must be based on studies in individual areas. A number of studies have now been undertaken, however their findings require careful interpretation.

Some studies have found that in many, though not all, areas black people were stopped in higher proportions than white. For example research by the Policy Studies Institute in the Metropolitan Police area found that proportionately twice as many black males aged 15–24 were stopped as white youth (Smith and Gray 1985). Thus 8 per cent of black males aged between 15 and 24 were stopped in the year preceding the study compared with 5 per cent whites and 2 per cent Asians. Other studies have found that black youth are proportionately more likely to be arrested than other ethnic groups. After examining the statistics for arrests in the Metropolitan Police area, Monica Walker concludes that 'black people must have four and a half times the chance of being arrested for a burglary . . . (compared to white) . . . to account for their over representation'. (Walker 1987).

This does not necessarily mean that the police are dealing unfairly with black youth. Demographic factors may account for many of these differences. Higher proportions of the black population are younger, unemployed, come from lower class backgrounds and live in lower class areas – all characteristics associated with the likelihood of being stopped. Therefore we would expect a higher number of black youth to be stopped in proportion to white youth, especially where studies are carried out in large areas. Were the base of studies to be smaller, more homogenous areas amongst groups of similar social class backgrounds, living in the same area, the results might be different (see, for example, Walker 1987).

In a more recent study in Leeds, it was found that while overall blacks were stopped twice as much as whites, a more complex picture emerged when the characteristics of individual areas were taken into account (Jefferson et al 1992). Thus black people were disproportionately stopped in areas where the majority of residents were white, but in areas where the majority of residents were black, white people were stopped more often. This could, argue the authors, reflect patterns of home ownership – where any group predominates they are more likely to be home owners, whereas the minority population are more likely to be in rented accommodation and to live in parts of the areas more likely to attract police attention.

Research conducted by Simon Holdaway and the Policy Studies Institute (PSI) found that police officers did use derogatory language when describing black people, and that the 'canteen culture' contained many racist elements (Holdaway 1983; Smith and Gray 1985). A report of the Chief Inspector of the Constabulary cites unacceptable levels of prejudice and sexist and racist behaviour on the part of the police as a disincentive for both women and ethnic minority individuals to join the police (*Guardian*, 14 June 1994). But such attitudes do not necessarily lead to direct discrimination – which involves treating a group differently on the grounds of race. The PSI studies found little evidence of discriminatory decisions. What is more likely is that there may be indirect discrimination, which exists where the policies or practices of an institution are applied evenly, but have an unequal impact on different groups. Thus when the police prioritise lower class, high crime areas containing a large proportion of ethnic minority residents, more lower class and black people are inevitably subject to stops, searches or arrests. Wider social inequalities such as unemployment, poor housing conditions and family breakdown further compound the disadvantages of black youths as they enter the criminal justice system – as they may then be less likely to be cautioned or warned and more likely to be taken to court.

Nonetheless, the perception of inequality amongst black groups has had a number of effects. It may make black people more 'combative' in their attitude to the criminal justice process, which can affect relationships between the police and the black population. This may mean that the black population as a whole are less supportive of the police and less likely to co-operate. Lea and Young suggest that this can start a vicious circle. If the black community are less supportive, then the police may have to use more aggressive styles in black areas, leading to more use of stop and search tactics (Lea and Young 1984). This may create 'flashpoints' where a seemingly trivial incident may provoke a more widespread disturbance. These kinds of considerations led, during the 1980s, to the development of more community based styles of policing.

## Police culture

The informal rules which affect how the police behave in any particular incident or situation form part of what has been called the occupational culture of policing. Many occupations have associated cultures, within which members use a special language, and share a similar view of the world and their occupation. Anyone starting a job very quickly learns the distinction between how things should be done and how they really are done. These informal rules are learnt during what sociologists call occupational socialisation where a recruit learns the norms and values associated with the occupation. The expectations associated with the job and what constitutes success are part of such a culture as are attitudes about the role of the occupation. This is particularly the case where the occupation faces hostility or misunderstanding from the public – as may be the case with the police. In this case the culture may have a justifying role, justifying the job that members do.

In some occupations this culture is stronger than others – particularly where work spreads into other aspects of life and leisure. Policing is not a nine to five job from which officers can switch off when they leave the station. It makes heavy emotional demands on officers, involves high levels of stress and is a vocation as well as a job. A key aspect of policing is that it involves danger and on the beat the police face the ever present threat of physical harm. Violence against police officers has increased in recent years. The Annual Report of the Commissioner of the Metropolitan Police 1993 records that out of 28,000 officers, 12,000 were injured on duty, 3,000 were badly assaulted, 200 were stabbed or had broken bones and four were murdered. Police officers therefore need to be able to rely on each other often in life threatening situations. This makes for closer relationships between officers and a stronger culture than in many jobs.

The police must display authority in order to handle some situations, especially where large numbers of people are involved. Police can only 'handle' situations if the public respect the authority of the police. This may affect decisions about suspects to the extent that those who appear to challenge authority may be more likely to be stopped, arrested or charged. Authority is re-enforced by the symbols of the job – cars, radios and uniforms all signify the authority vested in the role of police officer (Holdaway 1983).

Police officers are also geographically and socially isolated. Policing involves shift work, therefore they are often working when others are enjoying their leisure time, they may not be able to undertake many leisure pursuits involving the general public and may find it difficult to maintain friendships with non-police officers. In some areas, the police may live in police accommodation. Police officers tend to mix socially with other officers and they may prefer to let their hair down where they are not observed by the public.

All these factors give rise to a strong occupational culture within the police, described by writers such as Holdaway, Reiner and Brogden (Reiner 1992a; Brogden et al 1988; Holdaway 1983). While it is impossible to make sweeping generalisations about this culture, certain themes appear to characterise police culture in Anglo-American societies.

Most studies emphasise that police officers feel that their job is important – they feel a sense of mission. They often see themselves as forming a 'thin blue line', protecting society from disorder. A key part of this mission is catching criminals, which attracts many to the job. Thus law enforcement tasks are described as 'real police work', making an implicit contrast with much hated desk or paper work, and reflecting an emphasis on action, seen most clearly in the imagery of the car chase. Car chases, according to Holdaway are often the subject of animated conversations in the dull moments in the canteen and they form an important part of the police folk lore. This may mean that the more mundane elements of policing are downgraded and seen as 'rubbish' rather than real police work. Nonetheless the emphasis on catching criminals is reflected in how the police are assessed – the clear up rates – and there is a great emphasis on the figures. Resolving a dispute without an arrest is less amenable to measurement and may be seen as less important.

There is an element of machismo within police culture with an emphasis on action and crime fighting. This, plus conservative views about gender relationships, affects their views towards women officers – who are treated protectively. Indeed attitudes about women officers demonstrate many elements of the police culture. Heidensohn for example found that a common objection to women officers is that they cannot handle 15 drunks. This implies, she argues, that a macho way of handling drunks is appropriate, rather than the more persuasive 'soft cop' image associated with women police (Heidensohn 1992).

Reiner also sees police culture as containing strong elements of conservatism (Reiner 1992). This does not imply that all police vote Conservative but that police tend to hold very traditional views about crime, the family, law and order and discipline. Indeed it would be surprising if they did not as they have chosen a job which involves upholding the law. These attitudes however may affect their judgments about the people they come into contact with most. It may also affect aspects of discrimination both in relation to the public, and within the force itself. The social isolation of the police further reinforces these beliefs.

Studies of police culture are important when police policy is considered. For example the view of real police work which is associated with the love of action may mean that many officers resist community policing styles, and the elements of machismo, racism and conservatism may affect how well women and ethnic officers can be integrated. The occupational culture may also affect the emphasis placed on crime control and due process. This is not to say that attitudes cannot change and it is important not to paint too static or simple a picture.

There is more than one approach to police work as many of the studies on policing show. For example, detectives may have a perspective and a culture very different from uniformed officers and may need to adopt very different styles to perform their job adequately (Hobbs 1991). Different stations within a particular area may have very different cultures, affected by the policy of the division (Foster 1989). Some officers may value their role within the community, whereas others may see themselves more as crime fighters. Rural policing may be very different from urban policing with rural police being more involved in all the tasks of the police simply because of the time it may take to call in the specialists from the town (Cain 1973). Those involved in public order duties, especially those in special patrols may also come to look forward to a 'piece of action' (Jefferson 1990).

## CONCLUSION

This chapter has shown how the police are organised and how different models may assess their role and function. It has also outlined the main laws governing police investigation along with how the police are made accountable. These rules and guidelines however provide only a backcloth against which the police operate on a day-to-day level, which is inevitably affected by their own perception of their job and how they interpret the many rules and guidelines. This is important for a number of reasons. Should the police for example, perceive their main role as one of crime control, then they may be tempted to neglect due process in the interests of making sure that those guilty of crime are brought to court and found guilty. They may, as we have seen, downgrade the service or preventive aspects of their role. Discussions of police policy must therefore recognise the significance of discretion in police work and the role of the police culture and its influence on police work.

This chapter also raises questions about the role of the police vital to our understanding of the criminal justice process as a whole. What is the main role of the police? Should they be responsible mainly for law enforcement or should they also seek to prevent crime, protect the public, consider the welfare as well as the prosecution of suspects and perform many other services for the community? Should their time be spent chiefly on crime related tasks while they pass other duties onto other agencies? And how might this affect their law enforcement role? One of the functions of the police not yet explored is their role in determining whether a suspect is prosecuted or diverted out of the criminal justice system. This will be taken up in Chapter 5.

**Review Questions**

1. Outline the range of tasks carried out by the police service.
2. What are the main ways in which the police are rendered accountable? How and why have these arrangements recently been changed?
3. Look at the way in which the police are portrayed in the media through police dramas, documentaries or news stories. How does this reflect the different roles of the police?
4. How does the law seek to protect the suspect from the abuse of police powers?
5. In what ways is the exercise of discretion affected by non-legal factors?

**Further Reading**

Brogden M, Jefferson T and Walklate S (1988) *Introducing Police Work.* London: Unwin Hyman

Reiner R (1992) *The Politics of the Police.* London: Harvester Wheatsheaf

Stephens M and Becker S (eds) (1994) *Police Force Police Service: Care and Control in Britain.* London: Macmillan

Uglow S (1988) *Policing Liberal Society.* Oxford: Oxford University Press

# CHAPTER 5

# PROSECUTION AND DIVERSION

Cautioning
Prosecution
Juvenile Justice
Mentally Disordered Offenders

## INTRODUCTION

Once the police are reasonably sure they have identified a suspect, they have several options. They may decide to take no further action at all, or they may give an informal warning. They may decide to issue a formal police caution or refer the case to some form of mediation. They may instead decide to pass the papers to the Crown Prosecution Service. Many criminal cases are therefore diverted from the criminal justice process without any public trial or hearing. The decision to prosecute is a vital one and we shall look at the rules and guidelines surrounding this decision, at the agencies responsible for it, and at the issues raised for criminal justice.

Prosecution and diversion raise many issues which can again be highlighted by looking at the different perspectives on criminal justice. Under a crime control approach for example, it is clearly important that guilty offenders are convicted and punished and the system would be seen to lack any deterrent potential if this does not happen. Principles of due process also require that the defendant should have the opportunity to be publicly tried and enabled to refute any allegations of guilt. In addition, the notion that all are equal before the law underlies the principle that justice should be seen to be done. Diversion of some at the expense of others might produce a situation where critics from a class domination perspective could argue that some groups of offenders enjoy advantages. In addition, it is important to proponents of a denunciatory approach that offenders ought to be publicly tried and punished for the system to perform its function of expressing society's disapproval of particular behaviour. Victims also may feel aggrieved if they

115

do not see those that have harmed them publicly held to account. If suspected offenders are diverted from the system it implies that the police and prosecutors are making essentially judicial decisions which should be made formally in the public forum of the criminal courts to ensure just deserts.

There are strong arguments that all suspects should be prosecuted (Gross 1979). Such an approach however would pose considerable problems. The process of prosecution and trial is costly. Police officers, prosecutors and the legal profession must collect evidence and produce and contest it in court, which also occupies the time and resources of court personnel. Diverting offenders from the formal process can therefore produce considerable savings and reduce delays. In addition, there may be many circumstances in which diversion is desirable. The labelling perspective outlined in Chapter 2 suggests, for example, that the stigmatising effects of public trial and punishment could propel some offenders into more crime. For young offenders particularly it may be desirable in the interests of rehabilitation to avoid prosecution and eventual punishment. Some offenders, such as the very young or the mentally disordered may be considered to be not fully responsible for their own actions, making trial and punishment inappropriate.

In recent years a number of policies have encouraged diversion although not as we shall see without some criticism. This chapter will focus on four main aspects of prosecution and diversion. It will first look at the considerations surrounding the cautioning of offenders. It will then explore the decision to prosecute, and describe the agency responsible for the majority of prosecutions, the Crown Prosecution Service (CPS), along with a brief account of the work of other agencies involved in prosecution. Further sections will explore the treatment of two groups for whom diversion is seen as more appropriate, young offenders and the mentally ill. The arrangements for these offenders are clearly distinguishable from other offenders and we will outline the options available to the court and in pre-trial stage to divert these offenders from punishment as well as prosecution.

## CAUTIONING

Before looking at formal cautions given in lieu of trial and sentence, it is important to recognise that some cases are diverted from the system with no formal action being taken. Whereas an official caution is recorded and can be referred to on subsequent appearances, cases which result in no further action (NFA) or an informal warning are not recorded. While precise numbers are not officially recorded, on the basis of research it has been estimated that as many as 25 per cent of known offenders are so dealt with (Sanders 1994). This proportion varies both between and within police areas – one survey for example found variations of zero to 24 per cent, with an average of 10.6 per cent, reflecting different police policies (Evans and Wilkinson 1990).

No further action may be taken in a variety of situations. An individual officer may do nothing because the matter is too trivial and making an 'issue' of it could create further problems out of proportion to the incident. In other cases there may be a formal reason why the police cannot proceed with a prosecution, for example, where they cannot provide sufficient evidence for the court, or where the offender is too young. In other situations they may feel that no useful purpose will be served by taking matters any further, particularly where offenders are elderly or mentally ill.

The officer may, instead of doing nothing, give an immediate informal caution or warning. This might happen with trivial offences, such as where an officer observes young people riding bicycles on the pavement, and issues a few words of warning (Evans and Wilkinson 1990). This is only appropriate in less serious matters and is completely within the discretion of the officer. In some offences involving the maintenance of vehicles, an officer can issue a Notice to Rectify advising the motorist to correct the defect within a number of days, to avoid prosecution. Only if this is not done will prosecution result. A further option is the formal warning, a system which operates in some areas where a written warning is given in lieu of prosecution after the suspect has been reported for a possible offence. These alternatives are used for a variety of minor infringements – road traffic matters and very minor public order matters being the most common.

No further action may also reflect the use by the police of what Sanders describes as speculative arrests, which might occur where the police arrest people to encourage them to give information (Sanders 1994). Arrest may in effect be a strategy to assist further investigation and may not be intended to lead to prosecution.

The most significant alternative to prosecution is the formal caution, which is used in a wide range of offences of varying seriousness. The issue of a police caution is a regulated and recorded procedure whereby a potential defendant admits guilt without evidence being fully gathered and is formally warned by a senior police officer 'not to do it again'. Cautions are recorded at the local Criminal Record Office, retained for three years and may be quoted in court in sentencing procedures. Although cautions are given most often to young defendants, including young adults, they are available for defendants of any age.

Because cautions can be referred to in court, and because they constitute a significant diversion from prosecution, the system is regulated. Thus a number of guidelines have been issued, including the Attorney General's guidelines entitled *Criteria for Prosecution* issued in 1984, and Home Office Circular 14 in February 1985 which encouraged the greater use of cautioning. In 1990 Home Office Circular 59 was issued to promote national standards for cautioning. The Code for Crown Prosecutors also gives guidance on the use of cautioning. In some circumstances chief constables issue internal guidelines indicating which offences are appropriate for a caution. The most important prerequisite for a caution is that the offender accepts guilt. In order for a caution to be administered the following conditions must be fulfilled:

- there must be sufficient evidence to warrant a prosecution;
- the offender must admit guilt;
- either the person being cautioned, or, in the case of a child or young person, the parent or appropriate adult, must consent to such a disposal after being warned that the caution may be cited in future court appearances.

A number of criteria guide the decision of whether to initiate a prosecution including the following:

- The nature and seriousness of the offence.
- The likely penalty if the offender was convicted by the court.
- The offender's age, personal circumstances and state of health.
- The offender's character and previous criminal history.
- The offender's attitude to the offence, including practical expressions of regret.
- The likely view of the victim.

The 1990 circular indicates that 'courts should only be used as a last resort, particularly for juveniles and young adults', and that where the criteria for cautioning are met there should be a 'presumption in favour of not prosecuting'. These guidelines however are not legally binding, leaving considerable scope for discretion and the operation of informal factors which produce considerable variation in practice. Thus one commentator points out that 'police cautioning is almost entirely a set of extra-legal practices' (Ashworth 1994a: 137).

Following these official encouragements to use cautions, there has been a considerable increase in their use. In 1991 cautioning rates for males and females aged 14–16 in England and Wales were 71 and 87 per cent respectively of those found guilty of or cautioned for indictable offences; for those aged 17–20 years the figures were 26 per cent and 45 per cent respectively. Thus girls are more likely to be cautioned than boys, and younger offenders more often than older. In 1992 cautioning rates showed an increase over 1991 for all age groups, but with the greatest rate of increase in the 17–20 age group suggesting that exhortations to use cautions for young adults have had some effect. In addition, throughout the 1980s the use of repeat cautioning, that is cautioning for a second or third time, also increased.

The 1990 standards were in part a response to the diversity in cautioning rates referred to above (see, for example, Evans and Wilkinson 1990; Ashworth 1994a). This variation can be seen in figures provided in the *Criminal Justice Digest*, which indicate that in 1991, 'The use of formal cautioning for indictable offences varies from 20 per cent of known offenders in South Wales to 45 per cent in Humberside.' (Home Office, 1993: 31). These variations, it comments, reflect the use of formal rather than informal cautioning.

118

They also reflect the high amount of discretion underlying these decisions. For example, guidelines do not specify precisely what account need be taken of particular factors and the police may use the decision to caution or prosecute in a way that accords with their working rules. Thus officers may simply feel that some offenders deserve prosecution, and cautions may avoid unnecessary paperwork. Indeed, while cautions should only be made where there is sufficient evidence to prosecute, Sanders points to research indicating that some suspects were cautioned because there was insufficient evidence to prosecute – thus a caution can be used to clear up a case which might otherwise not have been prosecuted (Sanders 1994). Thus, argues Sanders, the low visibility of cautioning can enable the police to use cautions as bargaining tools.

The exercise of discretion also raises issues of possible bias. As we have seen, girls are more likely to be cautioned than boys, although most research indicates that this reflects the tendency for girls to be first offenders and to have committed less serious offences (see Chapter 3 and Eaton 1986). Some differences have also been found in relation to race. One study found that white juveniles had a greater chance of being cautioned than black youth (Landau and Nathan 1983). A later study found that Asians were more likely to be cautioned than any other group while Afro-Caribbeans were less likely to receive a caution (Jefferson and Walker 1992).

As with the use of police powers, complex factors underlie these figures. Landau and Nathan, for example, conclude that while bias on the part of the police cannot be ruled out, much of the difference can be explained by the fact that more black youth had previous convictions, and came from what were seen as problem or one parent families. In addition we have already seen that offenders must plead guilty in order to receive a caution. Where there has been hostility between the black population and the police, the more combative attitude of black youth may mean that they are more likely to plead not guilty and go to trial (Jefferson and Walker 1992). Indeed some studies have found that more black people plead not guilty, and that more are acquitted (Walker 1987). The police in some areas may be more sensitive to such feelings, leading to changes in attitudes and policy.

There is also some concern that cautioning may have a built-in class bias. Many of the criteria relating to offenders' circumstances may unintentionally advantage better off offenders or young people from middle class homes. Ashworth indicates how the criterion concerning attitude to the offence may work in this way. This criterion includes consideration of whether the offender has made some practical demonstration of regret, such as an apology to a victim or an offer to put matters right, for example by voluntary compensation. Thus, he comments, 'wealthy offenders might be able to buy themselves out of prosecution by offering payments to their victims, whereas impecunious offenders cannot' (Ashworth 1994a: 138–139).

In addition, the regulatory agencies responsible for the prosecution of offences involving white collar or business offenders, such as the Inland

Revenue or local authority consumer protection departments, often follow a policy of not prosecuting offenders and extensively use both informal and written cautions. Indeed these agencies regularly caution offenders on many occasions before a prosecution is considered and the extent to which offenders have sought to rectify matters is part of this decision (see for example Croall 1992; Ashworth 1994a and below).

An important objection to the increased use of cautioning is that it might encourage persistent offending as children and young persons may be encouraged to offend on the basis that they will only be cautioned. On the other hand, as we have seen, a major argument in favour of cautioning is that it might prevent the development of a criminal career. Can these conflicting claims be evaluated?

The *Criminal Justice Digest* reports that 6 per cent of those aged over 20, and 19 per cent of those aged between 17 and 20 who were cautioned in 1985 were convicted within two years (Home Office 1993: 32). Whether this shows cautioning to be successful is of course debatable as we do not know what would have happened had these offenders been prosecuted. What these figures do indicate is that the vast majority of those cautioned were not subsequently convicted – and cautions appear no less effective than conviction and sentence (see, for example, Ashworth 1994a).

Another fear about the increased use of cautions is that it might increase the numbers of children and young persons with formal proceedings taken against them. Following the introduction of wider cautioning powers in the Children and Young Persons Act 1969, there was a steep rise in rates of cautioning and of the numbers of young offenders being cautioned or convicted. This rise may have reflected what is described as 'net widening' – in that the police may have been giving formal cautions to children and teenagers who would previously have been given informal warnings – thus involving more young offenders in the formal process. There is however little evidence that this effect continued into the 1980s where, as we have seen, many were dealt with by informal warnings or no further action.

The rights of both defendants and victims are also affected by cautions. A caution can only be given following an admission of guilt. This raises the question of the extent to which defendants may be under pressure to admit guilt which they otherwise deny in order to avoid the stress of a court appearance. The low visibility of cautions raises concerns about how far defendants' rights are observed at this stage, especially since a caution may have a bearing on subsequent sentence.

There may also be a conflict between the benefits of diversion and the interest of victims. When offenders are cautioned, victims are deprived of the opportunity to obtain compensation (Ashworth 1994a). While some areas have provisions for offering mediation between offenders and victims as a form of diversion, this practice, which will be discussed more fully in Chapter 11, is by no means widespread.

A final concern about cautions, which involve the police making quasi-

judicial decisions, is how accountable these powers are (Ashw
Better record-keeping and some provision for legal advice bef
guilt might answer some of these points, and the Royal Co
Criminal Justice of 1993 recommended that police cautioning
by statute. Others have suggested a role for the CPS in caution
(see, for example, Ashworth 1994a). This however would involve far-reaching changes in the respective roles of the police and the CPS.

Once the police have decided that a prosecution rather than any other
form of action is appropriate, the papers are referred to the CPS for consideration.

# PROSECUTION

The vast majority of prosecutions are undertaken by the CPS, but a number
of other agencies also have responsibility for undertaking criminal prosecutions. These include the agencies responsible for enforcing laws regulating
many aspects of business, trade and commerce. Their work will be outlined
following an examination of the CPS. Private individuals may also prosecute
but this only accounts for a very small number of prosecutions.

## The Crown Prosecution Service

Before the creation of the CPS in the 1980s, the police and the Director of
Public Prosecutions (DPP) were responsible for prosecution. The office of
the DPP was set up by the Prosecution of Offences Act 1879, and its task
was to institute, undertake or carry on criminal proceedings, and to give
advice and assistance to chief officers of police and other persons responsible
for the prosecution of offences. The DPP was responsible for prosecuting
cases of murder, along with those involving national security, public figures
and police officers.

The police were responsible for the prosecution of routine offences in
magistrates' courts, and there were 43 prosecution authorities in England
and Wales. They were advised by solicitors, who were either employed or
consulted by them, and who conducted more complex cases in the magistrates' courts. Cases in Crown Courts were conducted by barristers on
behalf of the police.

The police were therefore both investigators and prosecutors, a dual role
which caused considerable concern. It was argued for example that the crime
control function of investigation could clash with the interests of due process
in ensuring that prosecutions only be undertaken on the basis of sufficient
evidence. Thus a Royal Commission on Criminal Procedure, known as the
Phillips Commission, was set up in 1978 and reported in 1981. It pointed
out that there was no uniform system of prosecution in England and Wales,
and that there was a strong civil liberties case for an independent agency,

other than the police, to review and conduct the prosecution of criminal cases and to encourage consistency in prosecution. It also stressed that the roles of investigating crime, collecting evidence and arresting suspects were likely to interfere with the impartial review of a case and decisions about whether prosecution was necessary and likely to be successful. The dual responsibility for policing and prosecution could also lead to the abuse of the rights of the arrested person by the police, born out of an anxiety to convict those whom the police believed were guilty. There were also concerns from a efficiency viewpoint about the number of weak cases where the evidence was insufficient to lead to a conviction, being taken to court and then thrown out, which was both costly and time consuming.

Following a debate in the House of Commons and the Bonan Working Party whose report was published in August 1983, a White Paper proposed the setting up of a Crown Prosecution Service. The Prosecution of Offences Act 1985 established the CPS and specified its functions which included taking over the conduct of all criminal proceedings instituted by the police. As seen in Chapter 4, the introduction of the CPS was closely linked with the Police and Criminal Evidence Act 1984 (PACE).

The functions of the CPS are:

- to give pre-charge advice to the police and other law enforcement agencies on the admissibility of evidence;
- to review all cases in terms of whether there is sufficient evidence for a case to proceed and whether it is in the public interest;
- to oversee the progress of the case after the papers have been passed from the police;
- to conduct the prosecution of cases in the magistrates' courts;
- to instruct counsel on cases in the Crown Court;
- to liaise with other agencies in the criminal justice system.

The CPS therefore represents a single independent and nationwide authority for England and Wales. It is independent of the police and has the power to discontinue prosecutions. Unlike prosecution agencies in other jurisdictions it has no powers to institute proceedings or to direct the police to carry out any further investigations. Its introduction had substantial constitutional significance for a number of reasons. For the first time there was a single state prosecuting authority charged with making decisions of a quasi judicial nature which could ultimately affect the rights and liberties of the individual. It also created a new legal interest group directly linked to government. These lawyers, although civil servants, were expected to be independent of government control, though little was put in place to guarantee this, save the *Code for Crown Prosecutors* and the existing *Codes of Professional Conduct for the Legal Professions*.

The introduction of the CPS as a body with a duty to review cases at every stage of a prosecution inevitably caused problems. Some of these sprung from initial rivalry between the police and CPS and misunderstandings about their respective roles. The necessary bureaucratic changes also produced problems – major delays followed changes in the system for transmitting files to court and prioritising cases. The Royal Commission on Criminal Justice in 1993 commented that the service was hastily conceived and inadequately resourced. A report in 1990 by the Public Accounts Committee on a Review of the Crown Prosecution Service (House of Commons 1990) found that estimates of how much the system would cost were initially too low and that many problems were caused by understaffing and inadequate resourcing. This necessitated the use of private practitioners, although this declined as the system became established, and it is planned that this use will be reduced from nearly 30 per cent in 1991 to 10 per cent by early 1995 (CPS (1994) Annual Report 1993–94: 4).

The powers of the CPS to discontinue cases also caused friction with the police and frustration on the part of victims and courts. As we shall see below, the rate of cases discontinued continues to cause concern although one of the roles of the CPS was to reduce the number of trials aborted on evidential grounds. Other critics saw the CPS as a threat to civil liberties, as it intermingled judicial and executive functions. Some of these criticisms however emanated from the legal profession, who perceived a threat to their work from the growth of the CPS. As we have seen however private practitioners were initially used in magistrates' courts to conduct a substantial proportion of CPS cases.

## The organisation of the Crown Prosecution Service

The major responsibilities of the CPS are dealt with by 2,000 full-time lawyers who are all civil servants. Their role as civil servants is tempered by the Code for Crown Prosecutors and their professional ethics as lawyers – which provide, for example, that their first duty is to the court.

The head of the CPS is the Director of Public Prosecutions (the DPP). In 1992 Barbara Mills became the DPP. Below the DPP is a Deputy Director and Chief Crown Prosecutor, each of whom is responsible for one area. Originally the CPS was organised into 31 areas, subsequently reduced with effect from October 1993 to 13 areas, each headed by a Chief Crown Prosecutor. Area 12, which covers the whole of London, approximately coincides with the boundaries of the Metropolitan Police area and accounts for 25 per cent of the work of the CPS.

Each area is subdivided into a number of branches, totalling 111, each of which is headed by a Branch Crown Prosecutor. The branch is the main operational unit, and after reorganisation, branches work through teams responsible for cases throughout the prosecution process to ensure consistency and improve communication. Below the Branch Crown Prosecutor are other grades of lawyers and there are also 4,000 administrative and support staff.

Once an accused person has been charged or summoned the papers are forwarded to the appropriate branch of the CPS which deals with cases from the police station where the offence originates. On receipt of these papers the CPS is under a duty to review the case in accordance with two criteria involved in the decision to prosecute. These two criteria, which will be discussed in detail below, are (a) that there is sufficient evidence to continue the case and (b) that it is in the public interest to continue.

When the accused is brought to the magistrates' court in custody, the CPS normally receive the papers on the morning of the first hearing and are expected to represent the prosecution on adjournments and applications for bail. Once papers are received the CPS is entirely responsible for the conduct of the case. This includes deciding which charges should be proceeded with, what evidence is relevant and admissible and whether or not it is sufficient – in effect whether there is a reasonable prospect of success. It also includes assessing whether or not it is in the public interest to continue with the prosecution and, if so, ensuring that the case is prepared and ready for trial.

## The Code for Crown Prosecutors

The Code for Crown Prosecutors is a public statement of the guidelines to be applied to the decision on whether to prosecute an offender or not. In June 1994 the code was revised to simplify and clarify it. Two statements explain the CPS approach.

> One of the most important tasks of the CPS is its review function. This means that we consider the evidence supplied by the police, and any other relevant information, and make a decision . . . in accordance with . . . the Code. . . . At all times, we exercise an independent judgement about the case presented, on the basis of the tests set out in the Code. . .

> The decision to prosecute . . . is a serious step. Fair and effective prosecution is essential to the maintenance of law and order . . . a prosecution has serious implications for all involved – the victim, a witness and a defendant. The Crown Prosecution Service applies the Code . . . so that it can make fair and consistent decisions about prosecutions.

(CPS (1994) *Annual Report 1993–94*: 6)

The code is the cornerstone of the CPS's review and decision-making role and embodies the values and principles of the CPS. It was issued under s 10 of the Prosecution of Offences Act 1985 and reissued after a review in June 1994. It restates general principles concerning the fairness, objectivity and independence of the CPS, and gives guidance about their approach to cautions, charges, mode of trial and the acceptance of guilty pleas. The bulk of the code is concerned with the two tests involved in the decision to prosecute; the evidential sufficiency and the public interest test.

The evidential sufficiency test is applied first; if the case does not pass this test, no matter how serious, important, or publicly notorious, it will not go ahead. Only if the case passes the evidence test will the second test, public interest, be applied.

The purpose of the evidential test is twofold. First, on a financial and practical basis, there is no point in proceeding with a case which will inevitably be 'thrown out' by the court because there is not enough evidence. To proceed in such cases would be very wasteful of limited resources. Secondly, it follows the general principle underpinning the whole criminal justice system, that people should not be put at risk on insufficient evidence, and that the duty of providing sufficient evidence is always on the prosecution. Some might argue that in certain cases the high public interest in a prosecution – even if it is doomed to failure – overrides the lack of evidence: that it is important to air the matter, even the lack of evidence, in the public domain.

*Evidential test*

The CPS must be satisfied that there is a realistic prospect of conviction on the available evidence. The test must be applied in respect of each defendant and each charge. A realistic prospect of conviction means that – in the view of the CPS – the magistrates or jury, properly advised on the law, are more likely than not to convict. This involves considering the availability, admissibility and reliability of evidence. In reaching a view, the CPS must consider whether any of the available evidence:

- would be inadmissible as hearsay: if leave to admit evidence would be required, is it likely to be given?
- is likely to be excluded by the judge because it has been illegally obtained – for example by breaches of PACE and its codes?
- is confession evidence likely to be excluded because of a breach of s 76 PACE?
- emanates from witnesses who are legally incompetent (can not give evidence); are unwilling and cannot be compelled to give evidence; or who are children to whom special rules and considerations apply?

In considering reliability the CPS will consider:

- the defendant's age, understanding and intelligence
- whether the witness has a motive to lie or 'adapt' their evidence
- whether the witness has a relevant previous conviction
- if identification evidence is involved, whether the evidence is strong enough, bearing in mind the special difficulties in identification evidence.

*Public interest test*

This refers to criteria by which the CPS may, even after satisfying the evidential sufficiency criteria, decide not to proceed with a case. The use of the phrase public interest is somewhat misleading as what is deemed to be in the public interest involves no consultation with the public, but relates to notional standards encompassing concepts of 'fair play', whether a prosecution is 'worthwhile' and so on. Why this was called a public interest criteria is difficult to discern. Until the revised Code for Crown Prosecutors (CCP) was published in June 1994, the criteria indicated a series of points which favoured dropping the case against a defendant. It was assumed to be mainly in the defendant's interest not to proceed with a case, the only public benefit being to save money. It was also assumed that only certain cases needed to go forward for the public interest to be served. This assumption generated claims of unfairness and public disquiet from victims and public alike. Lord Shawcross, the Attorney General at the time, is quoted to justify this criteria:

> It has never been the rule in this Country – I hope it never will be – that suspected criminal offences must automatically be the subject of prosecution. Indeed the very first Regulations under which the Director of Public Prosecutions worked provided that he should . . . prosecute 'wherever it appears that the offence or the circumstances of its commission is or are of such a character that a prosecution in respect thereof is required in the public interest'. That is still the dominant consideration.
>
> (Shawcross 1951)

In 1994, for the first time, the criteria indicating which public interest criteria militate both in favour of and against prosecution were published. As a general rule more serious cases are less likely to be discontinued as the public interest militates towards prosecution of more serious offences, but the criteria must be applied in each case. The factors for and against prosecution must be weighed carefully. It is in this context that the greatest discretion lies, and where most concern or confusion is caused. Thus it is stated that the factors for and against prosecution are not exhaustive, must be considered where appropriate and that all factors do not apply in all cases. Prosecutors are specifically expected to consider the interests of the victim, of young offenders, the possibility of a police caution and guidelines for dealing with mentally disordered offenders. The criteria are summarised in Figure 5.1.

The criteria used by the CPS are broadly similar to those used in sentencing. In other words, the offences which will be perceived as less serious by a court, thus attracting the lowest sentence, are unikely to be prosecuted at all. This may have a number of implications for the criminal justice system. First, the 'bottom layer' of offences will be removed with the possible consequent down-grading of remaining incidents. Secondly, the CPS are applying a quasi-judicial function 'second-guessing' possible sentences. Thirdly, the public interest in the denunciatory effect of bringing a range of offences to court is ignored.

**Fig 5.1** Public interest criteria used by the CPS

---

**Factors militating against prosecution:**

- the likelihood of a small or nominal penalty
- the offence was committed as a result of a genuine mistake
- the loss or harm was minor and the result of a single incident, particularly if caused by misjudgment
- there has been a long delay since the offence – except where the offence is serious; the delay caused by the defendant; the offence has only just come to light or there has been a long investigation.
- a prosecution will adversely affect the *victim's* physical or mental health (having regard to the seriousness of offence)
- the *defendant* is elderly, or at the time of the offence suffering from significant mental or physical illness, unless the offence is serious or there is a possibility of repetition
- the defendant has put right the loss (but defendants should not be seen as 'buying' their way out of prosecution)
- details could be made public which in the public interest should not be revealed

**Factors militating in favour of prosecutions:**

- the likelihood of a significant sentence
- use of a weapon or violence threatened
- offence against a person serving the public (for example, a police officer or nurse)
- defendant committed the offence in a position of authority or trust
- defendant was the prime mover in the offence
- premeditation
- group offence
- victim particularly vulnerable, put in fear, or suffered personal attack, damage or disturbance
- offence motivated by racial, sexual, religious or political discrimination
- marked difference between ages (real or mental) of defendant and victim or element of corruption
- defendant has relevant previous convictions
- commission of offence whilst subject to court order
- likelihood of repetition
- widespread offence in area

---

(Adapted from: CPS (1994) *Annual Report 1993–94*. London: HMSO: 46)

The code also sets out guidelines in relation to what charges should be made – for example which offences a defendant should be charged with. This can on occasion cause disquiet, where, for example, it appears that a defendant is being charged with a lesser offence. Charges should therefore reflect the seriousness of the offence, give the court adequate sentencing powers, and enable the case to be presented clearly.

127

In August 1994, the first charging standards were published, resulting from co-operation between the CPS and police to encourage consistency and understanding between the two agencies and those dealing with the courts. The first standards related to an area where most confusion and inconsistency is likely – that of assaults:

- Common assault will be the appropriate charge where the injuries include no more than grazes, scratches, abrasions, bruises, swellings, 'black eye', or superficial cuts.
- Assault occasioning actual bodily harm (ABH) will be appropriate where there is loss of or breaking of a tooth, temporary loss of sensory functions, extensive bruising, displaced broken nose, minor fractures, minor cuts, or psychiatric injury more than fear.
- Examples of grievous bodily harm (GBH) are injury resulting in permanent disability, or more than minor, permanent visible disfigurement.

## The role and function of the Crown Prosecution Service

The introduction of the CPS radically changed the system of prosecution, altered the role of the police and created a new organisation. After nearly 10 years, can the effectiveness of these changes be assessed? This involves looking at the work of CPS and at how their relationship with the police has developed.

The initial problems occasioned by the introduction of the CPS have already been outlined, along with some reservations about their role. The initial problems led to attempts in Annual Reports to provide performance indicators of their work and more information on the outcome of cases. Statistics for 1991/92 indicate that:

- 1,571,175 cases were received from the police
- 71.9 per cent were heard (that is a decision on guilt was arrived at in the magistrates' court)
- 8.8 per cent were committed to Crown Court
- 11.8 per cent were discontinued – that is the CPS decided not to proceed with the prosecution.

(CPS (1994) *Annual Report 1993–94*: 27–28)

In the Crown Court, 91 per cent of cases in 1991/92 resulted in a conviction; 80 per cent as a result of a guilty plea and 11 per cent after a trial (CPS (1994) *Annual Report 1993–94*: 30). Of those resulting in acquittals, nearly three-quarters resulted from a full contested trial, whereas one-quarter resulted from a direction from the judge.

Statistics also indicate that the number of cases reaching courts is falling. Thus in 1993/94 the CPS dealt with 1,454,239 cases, representing a continuing drop in total cases received and finalised. This could reflect the activities of the police, who may be using more cautions, and who may be anticipating CPS views on whether a prosecution should be continued.

This latter point indicates the difficulties of using figures as means of assessing the effectiveness or otherwise of the CPS, and the need to consider their working relationships with the police. As we have seen, the police also consider the sufficiency of evidence and make decisions on whether to take any further action or to caution. In theory therefore the police should initially have sifted out cases which do not merit prosecution. Therefore, as Ashworth points out in relation to discontinuances on public interest grounds, these could either be interpreted as 'police failures' or 'CPS successes' (Ashworth 1994a: 182).

Thus the developing relationship between the police and the CPS, and the CPS and the courts are crucial factors underlying the figures. As Ashworth points out, it must be recognised that:

> prosecution decisions are taken not in a laboratory atmosphere but in a working context that brings the CPS into contact with the police, with victims, and with magistrates . . . any attempt to explain practical decision making must take account of the organisational and operational contexts in which the decisions tend to be made.
>
> (Ashworth 1994a: 193)

It is apparent, that while the CPS is independent of the police, they are reliant on police information. And, given that the police have already sifted out cases, the CPS may have a tendency to assume that cases passed to them merit prosecution. In addition, developing working relationships and shared assumptions about which cases should be prosecuted may result in a reluctance on the part of the CPS to go against police advice, thus reducing discontinuance rates. Some research conducted in the early days of the CPS was critical of this tendency, and pointed out that the police tended to provide information which would support their decision to prosecute (Leng et al 1992). Factors indicating public interest grounds, already considered by the police, and information about likely defences or mitigating factors which might reduce the sentence were unlikely to be provided.

In addition, the evidential sufficiency criteria essentially ask the CPS to predict the likely outcome of a case. This may change however as a case proceeds. Vital witnesses may refuse to give evidence, or new evidence may come to light. The CPS does not know in advance what the defence is likely to be. In addition, weak evidence may not always lead to a case being dropped, especially where defendants indicate at an early stage that they intend to plead guilty. Thus the CPS may feel that a weak case is worth proceeding with and one writer comments that 'it is the experience of prosecutors that weak cases commonly produce a guilty plea' (Leng et al 1992: 136). Other factors such as the attitude of local courts may also affect decisions in that prosecutors may second guess the likely attitude of the courts. This can produce local variations. The local CPS build up working relationships with the local police, who in turn may come to second guess the likely attitude of the prosecutor. Figures on discontinuances therefore may reflect the operation of these informal factors. The statistics on the number of cases that are dropped or subsequently acquitted could be taken to indicate a failure of the review process. But the reasons why cases are dropped may not, as seen above, be evident at the start of a case, and may only emerge during the trial (Sanders 1994).

Rising numbers of cases discontinued in the 1990s raised questions about the benefits of prosecution and diversion. In 1993, for example, a total of 193,000 cases were discontinued. If these figures are taken alongside the large numbers of cautions and the under-reporting of crime it means that fewer and fewer cases are being taken to court. This could be seen as reducing any deterrent, denunciatory or crime control potential of the criminal justice system. In addition, defendants who are repeatedly asked to attend court and then told that the case has been dropped may have a valid grievance: not least those who wished to clear their name positively in court. Such defendants do have the right to seek repayment of costs incurred by them – for many this, combined with the relief of having the case dropped, is sufficient. For others there remains a lingering grievance against 'the system'.

On the other hand, many cases are dropped in accordance with the criteria, because of a 'missing legal element', which indicates that they should never have been commenced at all (see Figure 5.2). As we have seen, official policy has encouraged diversion, and it is clearly stated that it is not in the interests of efficiency or public interest to prosecute all cases. The CPS was indeed intended to reduce the number of weak cases coming to court. Other critics have argued that the CPS does not discontinue enough cases on public interest grounds and is therefore not sufficiently independent of the police (Leng et al 1992).

More recent studies show that the CPS do discontinue cases on public interest grounds as well as on the grounds of evidential insufficiency. This can be seen in a recent survey of discontinued cases carried out by the CPS (Crown Prosecution Service Survey, January 1994) of 11,000 cases in November 1993. Prosecutors across the country were asked to record the reasons for discontinuance under four main headings: insufficient evidence, public interest, prosecution unable to proceed, and defendant producing documents in court for the first time. Forty-three per cent of cases dropped or discontinued were through the application of the 'insufficient evidence' criteria and 31 per cent through the application of the 'public interest' criteria. Forty-one per cent of all cases discontinued during the month of the survey were minor motoring offences. Figure 5.2 summarises the main reasons why cases were discontinued, and includes some examples. Figure 5.3 gives further details of those discontinued on public interest grounds.

The most common single factor leading to discontinuance on public interest grounds was that the defendant had been convicted or sentenced for other offences, and in a further 6 per cent the court was expected to impose

**Fig 5.2** CPS Discontinuance Survey

---

### RESULTS OF CPS DISCONTINUANCE SURVEY (NOVEMBER 1993)

**Insufficient evidence (43%)**

11% of the cases discontinued related to insufficient evidence about the identity of the accused. For example, a witness identified a man she said she had seen committing a burglary, but she had seen him in poor lighting and had not had a good view of him. There was no other evidence to link the man with the offence.

13% of the cases dropped due to insufficient evidence were dropped because there was a legal element missing. For example, a defendant was charged with theft of a car radio cassette even though there was no evidence that it was stolen.

**Prosecution unable to proceed (17%)**

13%  were because of a missing witness
2%   related to offences already taken into consideration
2%   case not ready and adjournments refused

**Defendants produced driving documents in court for the first time (9%)**

**Public interest (31%)**

---

(CPS (1994) *Annual Report 1993–94*. London: HMSO: 15–16)

only a nominal penalty, such as an absolute discharge. An example of staleness was a case where a defendant was summoned for having no driving licence, test certificate or insurance. The CPS did not receive the papers until almost 33 months after the offences were committed. Other examples include that of a woman charged with being drunk and disorderly and subsequently admitted to a psychiatric hospital. Consistent with the spirit of the Home Office Circular on Provision for Mentally Disordered Offenders the CPS decided that the wider public interest did not demand a prosecution. In another case, an 82 year old motorist collided with a parked car without causing injury. The motorist surrendered his licence to the Driver and Vehicle Licensing Agency so the CPS decided that it was no longer necessary to prosecute.

Other cases are not proceeded with or fail because of the non-attendance of witnesses. In a recent case William and Valerie Wicks were jailed in November 1994 for four weeks for contempt of court after refusing to give evidence against a person charged with causing grievous bodily harm to Mr Wicks. The attack on Mr Wicks was witnessed by his wife. (*Daily Telegraph,*

**Fig 5.3** Analysis of prosecutions discontinued in magistrates' courts on the grounds of public interest

Public interest reasons account for 31% of all cases discontinued in the survey by the CPS

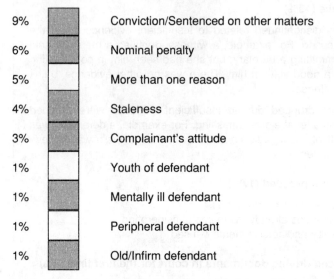

| | |
|---|---|
| 9% | Conviction/Sentenced on other matters |
| 6% | Nominal penalty |
| 5% | More than one reason |
| 4% | Staleness |
| 3% | Complainant's attitude |
| 1% | Youth of defendant |
| 1% | Mentally ill defendant |
| 1% | Peripheral defendant |
| 1% | Old/Infirm defendant |

In about 5% of cases more than one public interest factor applied.

(CPS (1994) *Annual Report 1993–94*. London: HMSO: 16)

19 November 1994: 6). In another case an expert witness went on holiday instead of giving evidence at a rape trial. The defendant was acquitted, and Dr Kusum Agrawal (the police doctor involved) was fined £3,000 by an Old Bailey judge. (*The Times*, 21 January 1995: 8).

A final issue to be raised is what role victims can or should play in the prosecution process. Recent attention to the victim in the criminal justice process lay behind the criteria that victims' interests should play a part. But to what extent does this conflict with other criterion? What, if any role, should victims play? If the victim does not wish to proceed with a case, and is unwilling to give evidence then the prosecution may be unsuccessful. Thus the victim's role in the provision of evidence may be crucial, as in the Wicks case referred to above. In addition, as with cautions, a failure to prosecute may deprive the victim of compensation, although some diversionary schemes provide for mediation between victim and offender (see Chapter 11). Any further role for the victim is problematic as it could be argued that to take the victim's attitude into account might conflict with any public interest there may be in prosecuting the offender to ensure that they are duly punished.

## Prosecution by regulatory agencies

While the CPS are responsible for the majority of prosecutions, it was pointed out above that many other agencies also undertake criminal prosecutions. These include local authority departments responsible for consumer protection and environmental health, the Health and Safety Executive, and agencies responsible for pollution. Taxation matters are the responsibility of the Customs and Excise and Inland Revenue departments, and many more government departments are responsible for investigating frauds and other offences involving business, trade and financial services. These include the Serious Fraud Office and the Department of Trade and Industry. It was seen in Chapter 3 that many of these offences are not included in the criminal statistics, and statistics on how many offences are prosecuted in relation to known offences are not generally available. Research into these agencies however indicates that they prosecute only a very small proportion of known offenders. It has already been seen that they use the caution extensively and prosecution is often seen as a last resort (see, for example, Croall 1992).

It is interesting to examine briefly how these agencies proceed, as their attitude to prosecution is very different. In his study of the origins of the factory inspectorate, established by the Factory Act 1833, which regulated the labour of children and young persons in mills and factories, W G Carson made the following observation:

> We . . . need to understand the social origins of an enforcement agency which, from its very inception, has not seen itself as being busy about the business of catching criminals. In adopting this historically explicable stance, the Factory Inspectorate has played its own inadvertent part in perpetuating a collective representation which portrays crime as being concentrated in circumscribed and morally peripheral segments of the community.
>
> (Carson 1974: 138)

Different attitudes to prosecution are strongly related to the perceived role and function of these agencies. Many see themselves not as industrial police officers with a primary duty to prosecute the guilty, but as agencies responsible for improving standards of business, trade or commerce by ensuring that businesses comply with regulations. Securing compliance is therefore seen as their primary aim, and prosecution is only one of many tools to achieve this. Therefore they tend to pursue what are often described as compliance strategies, which can be compared with a prosecution strategy (see, for example, Hawkins 1984; Croall 1992). Under a compliance strategy, the prevention of offences is seen as paramount, with education, advice and persuasion being seen as preferable to prosecution. Prosecution is likely to be seen by many agencies as costly and counter-productive, as it may lead to poor relationships between agencies and businesses.

Cost effectiveness underlies many of these strategies. In many areas prosecution involves high costs. Many offences in the world of business and finance are very complex, and investigation may involve gathering enormous amounts of evidence and interviewing many witnesses. Fraud trials for example can be lengthy and involve extremely complex evidence. The cost to the taxpayer for example of the first series of trials in the celebrated *Guinness* case was estimated at around £3 million (Croall 1992). Fraud trials are also seen as risky – the chances of conviction may be lessened by the complexity of the case and the ability of defendants to contest it. If there is a chance for the matter to be resolved without trial an out of court settlement becomes an attractive prospect. For local authority departments, if a prosecution is unsuccessful, they may have to bear the costs of prosecution themselves, thus reducing the resources they have for investigation.

In addition, many agencies have options other than doing nothing, cautioning and prosecuting. Some, like environmental health departments, may be able to grant or withhold licences from offending businesses, thus effectively threatening their viability. Others, like the Inland Revenue, can impose sanctions or fines without taking offenders to court. Yet others can disqualify those who need licences to operate, such as financial service employees. Many would argue that these powers constitute a greater deterrent than prosecution which may be followed by only a small fine.

Prosecution may only result if compliance is not forthcoming after a series of other measures. A prosecution may therefore reflect enforcers' attitudes that defendants are more blameworthy and deserve prosecution. In addition, the threat of prosecution may be used as a bargaining counter in persuading offenders to comply (Hawkins 1984). In some cases however these considerations can be overridden where for example there has been considerable public interest in a case and where prosecution may be considered necessary given the seriousness of the case. This may happen following major incidents in which there has been large scale pollution or where members of the public have been killed or injured.

A number of issues are raised by this brief outline of regulatory enforcement. While there may be considerable concern over high rates of discontinuances by the CPS, little public outcry is aroused by the low rates of prosecutions of many business offenders. This may be because as seen in Chapter 2, these offences are not so readily defined as crime. Nonetheless it could be argued that there is little equity in the treatment of different groups of offenders and that these differences amount to class bias, in that the CPS is likely to be dealing with primarily lower class offenders, and regulatory agencies with primarily middle class offenders (Sanders 1985). It also raises the question of the extent to which some offenders, by negotiating out of court settlements, rectifying matters and threatening an effective defence may be able effectively to buy themselves out of prosecution.

Another issue of interest is the role of the prosecution agency. Regulatory agencies play a major diversionary role, and in addition some have powers to sanction offenders. Some argue that this means that justice is being done in private rather than in a public hearing. To others, these powers represent an important and cost effective means of diverting offenders from the full process of trial and conviction and there have been suggestions that prosecution agencies such as the CPS should have similar powers. In Scotland, for example, there is a system known as the Prosecutor Fine, which the Royal Commission on Criminal Justice 1993 has recommended should be considered in England and Wales.

# JUVENILE JUSTICE

As seen above, young offenders are amongst those for whom cautioning and diversionary policies are seen as most appropriate. The law also makes provision for different treatment for children and young persons, reflecting differences in the degree to which young offenders can be held responsible for their own actions. Cases involving children and young persons are held in a special court, the youth court, and sentencing options are also different for children, young offenders and young adult offenders. This section will look firstly at the different legal arrangements regarding the culpability of younger offenders and the current system for dealing with them.

## Age and criminal responsibility

The law distinguishes between different age groups in an effort to recognise differences in maturity and understanding. Section 107 of the Children and Young Persons Act 1933 (CYPA 1933) defines a child as a person under the age of 14 and a young person as someone who has attained the age of 14 years and is under 18. The term young offender, not defined by statute, is often used to describe persons aged between 15 and 20, whilst the term young adult is sometimes used to mean an offender aged 18–20.

Children under 10 years of age are deemed by the law to be incapable of telling right from wrong and therefore incapable of doing wrong – in legal terms *doli incapax*. As they are not regarded as responsible they can therefore not be found guilty of or punished for any crime as they cannot be regarded as blameworthy. A child under this age committing a crime can however be placed in care or under supervision by the Family Court as they are seen to be in need of help, not punishment. The age at which a child is automatically regarded as not reponsible for criminal acts varies across jurisdictions; in Scotland it is eight, in Finland it is 15.

One special rule relating to the criminal responsibility of young people was recently altered by statute. The Sexual Offences Act 1994 removed the legal presumption that boys under 14 were incapable – at law – of committing rape, or any offence involving sexual intercourse. The lower age for liability for rape is now 10, as for other offences.

Apart from legal liability for a crime, the age of an offender will also affect where and how the young person is dealt with in the criminal justice system.

## Welfare or punishment

It has been accepted for many years that special procedures are needed to deal with young offenders, and a series of different arrangements have developed. These reflect conflicting views over how such offenders should be dealt with. In general, two broad approaches can be contrasted. On the one hand what is often described as a welfare approach seeks to protect children and young persons from the potential stigma of a criminal prosecution and encourages courts to take the welfare of the child or young person into account at all stages. Under this approach, diversion is encouraged and prosecution should be a last resort, and when taken to court, special procedures should protect young people from the harshness of a criminal trial and ensuing punishment. The rehabilitative approach was of particular relevance for young offenders who were seen to be potentially more likely to respond to measures involving help, treatment, discipline and education. On the other hand, many of these measures have been criticised as too soft, as insufficiently deterrent or punitive, and have attracted recurrent calls for tougher measures.

The range of measures therefore has tended to reflect a mixture of approaches, and recent very serious incidents involving young offenders have renewed these conflicts. When the toddler James Bulger was abducted and murdered in Liverpool by two children in 1993, a shocked public was exposed to the views of the experts, whose opinions ranged from the call for more treatment to the demand for the punishment of the offenders. In addition, it was seen in Chapter 1 that the Criminal Justice and Public Order Act 1994 was introduced amidst concerns about increasing rates of offending by the young and introduced a number of tougher measures. Recent publicity given to cases where young offenders have been sent to holiday camps or abroad as part of their sentences has attracted criticisms that offending youngsters should not be given advantages not enjoyed by their law abiding counterparts (see also Chapter 11).

Before the 19th century juvenile offenders were treated in the same way as adults and could be sent to adult prisons, hanged or transported. Throughout the 19th century however, there was a gradual development of measures specifically directed at young offenders, influenced by arguments that juveniles could be 'saved' and rehabilitated. This led to the development of special institutions such as reformatories, whose very name indicated an emphasis on reform through education and training.

The Children Act 1908 set up the juvenile court and formally separated cases involving juveniles from adult courts. It also abolished the use of imprisonment for juveniles. A mixture of welfare and punitive philosophies can be seen in the comment of the minister responsible for introducing this Act, Herbert Samuel, who stated that the 'courts should be the agencies for the rescue as well as the punishment of juveniles' (cited in Gelsthorpe and Morris 1994: 951). Other institutions for juveniles also reflected a welfare

136

and punishment approach – special institutions were set up as part of the prison system, the first being in Borstal in Kent. The Borstal system, as it came to be known, emphasised a mixture of discipline and training. Some Borstals stressed education, being strongly imbued with the values and traditions of English public school education, and later some adopted a therapeutic approach (see, for example, Hood 1965).

Further moves towards a more welfare based approach included the Children and Young Person Act 1933 which established a special panel of magistrates to deal with juvenile offenders and stipulated that the court should have regard to the welfare of the child. In addition the court could act in the place of parents, *in loco parentis*, and take such steps as necessary to ensure that the welfare of the child was being met (see, for example, Gelsthorpe and Morris 1994). In 1948 local authorities were enabled to take into care children considered to be 'in need of care and protection'. The same year however saw the introduction of detention centres and attendance centres which reflected a more punitive approach (Morris and Giller 1987). Detention centres were institutions in which young offenders could be sentenced to a short period of custody, in a regime intended to be tough and disciplinary. Much emphasis was laid on physical education although there were also elements of education and training. Attendance centre orders required juveniles to attend a centre, run mainly by the police, for a number of hours per week, often on a Saturday afternoon. They aimed to deprive delinquents of their leisure time and were often used in an attempt to take football hooligans off the terraces. Discipline was a key feature of early attendance centres which mixed elements of physical education with more practical pursuits.

The argument that there is little point in punishing juveniles whose delinquency may be related to family or other problems continued to influence policy. Some went so far as to suggest that juveniles should be removed from the criminal justice system entirely, and dealt with by a family council or tribunal which would deal with all children with family or social problems. These proposals were resisted. However, such ideas strongly affected the next important piece of legislation dealing with young offenders, the Children and Young Persons Act 1969 (CYPA 1969). This Act, often seen as representing the peak of the welfare approach, was based on a mixture of welfare and diversionary policies and made several radical and controversial changes (Morris and Giller 1987).

It stressed the benefits of diversionary policies, and one of its aims was that all offenders under 14 should be dealt with through care and protection proceedings rather than the juvenile court. The police were encouraged to use cautions for juvenile offenders and only refer them to court following consultation with the social services. The expanding role of the social worker was also reflected in provisions for care orders, which, after being given by magistrates were to be implemented by social workers. Social workers rather than magistrates therefore would make the key decision as to whether the young person would be sent to a residential institution or left at home. Community homes, which were to house all children in care whether or not they had committed an offence, replaced the approved schools which dealt only with delinquents. It was also intended to phase out Borstals and detention centres and to replace them with a sentence of intermediate treatment – again run by social services.

In the event, many sections of the CYPA 1969 were never implemented and it attracted considerable controversy and opposition amongst observers of and practitioners involved in the system. Magistrates for example felt that too much power had been lost to social workers and that they were powerless to determine what might happen to an offender. Rising rates of juvenile crime attracted criticisms that the system was too soft and was unable to cope with serious juvenile offenders.

Diversion increased in the years following the CYPA 1969 with an enormous rise in numbers cautioned by the Juvenile Liaison Bureaux set up by the police. In the 1980s there was a growing recognition of the limitations of custodial or institutional treatment. Not only was such treatment costly – with detention in some institutions costing more than boarding schools – but the vast majority of juveniles coming out of such institutions went on to re-offend. Recidivism rates for detention centres, for example, were as high as 80 per cent. Many also argued that institutions for juveniles acted like schools of crime where offenders perpetuated a delinquent or criminal sub-culture. Concern was also aroused by evidence of violence and bullying within institutions. Treatment in the community therefore was seen as being preferable and as no less effective in terms of re-conviction rates.

The CJA 1982 introduced criteria to restrict the use of care and custodial orders and introduced requirements for juveniles to be legally represented. Custodial orders were only to be made in cases where it could be established that the offender had failed to respond to non-custodial measures, where a custodial sentence was seen as necessary for the protection of the public or where the offence was serious. Borstals were abolished, removing any element of indeterminacy from the system. Up until then, offenders had been sentenced to a period of Borstal training, with the date of release of up to three years to be decided by those running the system. Borstal was replaced by a fixed-term youth custody order and the Act also abolished the use of imprisonment for offenders under the age of 21. Different sentences were then introduced and abolished with bewildering speed. From 1983 a determinate sentence of youth custody was introduced for offenders aged 15 and under 21, with a maximum sentence for those aged under 17 of 12 months. A sentence of custody for life was introduced as the equivalent to life imprisonment when the offender was aged 17 and under 21. Detention sentence orders for males were changed so that the usual sentence ranged from 21 days to four months instead of three to six months. The CJA 1988 abolished the detention sentence order and youth custody. The new term for youth custody was to be detention in a young offender institution.

**Fig 5.4** Number of younger males sentenced for indictable offences in 1982 and 1992

|  | *1982* | *1992* |
| --- | --- | --- |
| Number of males sentenced |  |  |
| Aged 10 and under 14 | 13,600 | 2,300 |
| Aged 14 and under 17 | 59,200 | 15,900 |
| Aged 17 and under 21 | 120,000 | 74,300 |

(Home Office (1993) *Criminal Statistics in England & Wales 1992.* London: HMSO: 160–2)

Diversionary policies continued throughout the 1980s with a series of Home Office circulars stressing that prosecution should be used as a last resort for young offenders. There was also encouragement for the greater use of informal warnings instead of cautioning to avoid net widening (Gelsthorpe and Morris 1994). The use of cautions for second and third offences was encouraged along with the development in some areas of caution plus schemes, which incorporate a caution with some form of supervised activity in the community. As we have seen however, this extension of diversion was criticised on the grounds that persistent offenders were not being sufficiently deterred and the public was being insufficiently protected. The decline in numbers of young offenders appearing in court, shown in Figure 5.4, was in part produced by these policies.

The sustained policy of making less use of custody is reflected in the fall in the number of males aged 17 and under 21 sentenced for an indictable offence given a sentence of immediate custody from 22,100 in 1982 to 10,900 in 1992. The number of males aged 14 and under 17 sentenced to custody fell from a peak of 7,100 in 1982 to 1,400 in 1992 (*Criminal Statistics, England & Wales* 1992: 142). Over the same 10-year period the use of supervision orders for males aged 10 and under 14 sentenced for indictable offences dropped from 2,700 in 1982 to 400 in 1992. Figure 10.3 shows the number of young offenders in custody on 30 June 1992.

This drop in the rate of custody may be attributed to many factors, including an increasing use of intermediate treatment orders, and a toughening up of the image of community sentences, stressing their punitive element and focusing more on the offence than on the needs of the child or young person (Allen 1991; Gelsthorpe and Morris 1994). The use of the care order declined and was eventually abolished. Another trend in justice policy for young offenders was to stress the responsibility of parents and provisions were introduced to fine or bind over parents.

Criticisms of these policies along with concerns about persistent young offenders led to the setting up of new secure units for offenders aged from 12 to 14 in the CJPOA 1994. It is planned to set up five units, each holding 40 young offenders. The new secure training order will last between six months and two years with half the time spent in the secure training unit, the other half under supervision in the community. The units are to be run by private organisations, rather than by local authorities. Commenting on the draft rules for these centres, which focus on discipline rather than training or education, Frances Crook, director of the Howard League for Penal Reform said:

> Overall, the proposed rules for the secure training centres are founded on principles of punishment and cost cutting. The routine will be spartan, the atmosphere bleak, and the ethos that of retribution . . .
>
> The secure training centres will throw out frightened and bitter children, estranged from families and suspicious of adults. It is inevitable that they will commit more crimes.
>
> (*Guardian*, 20 June 1994: 11)

Whether these fears will be realised, and whether there will be a reversal in the trends to divert young people from both prosecution and custody remains to be seen. The final section of this chapter outlines the current provisions for young offenders.

## Youth courts

Youth courts were set up by the CJA 1991 and replaced and extended the jurisdiction of the old juvenile courts. They now deal with the majority of offenders between 10 and 17, although some younger offenders may be dealt with in the Crown Court. The situations in which this occurs are as follows:

- where defendants are charged with homicide (murder or manslaughter) they must be sent to the Crown Court for trial (s 53(1) CYPA 1933);
- defendants aged 14–17 or more, when charged with other grave crimes – defined as any offence which carries a maximum term of imprisonment of 14 or more years, plus indecent assault on women and dangerous driving – may be sent to the Crown Court for trial when the court of first appearance decides that if convicted, they should be given a longer sentence than the magistrates can give (s 53(2) CYPA 1933);
- young defendants may be dealt with in an adult court if charged in association with another defendant, aged over 18, when both are to be dealt with in the adult court.

They may also be referred to the Crown Court for sentence. Guidelines from the Court of Appeal indicate that where, in the case of an adult, the sentence for the offence would be two or more years' imprisonment, it is appropriate for the youth court to refuse jurisdiction and commit the defendant to the Crown Court for trial.

The youth court has more informal procedures than adult courts, and special rules protect young people from publicity and contact with older defendants. Members of the public are not allowed to be present at a youth court hearing, and although members of the press are allowed to attend, they may not publish any information which can identify a young defendant. The CYPA 1933 empowers the court to restrict any reporting of cases revealing the name, address or school of a defendant or containing any particulars which could lead to the identification of any child or young person concerned in proceedings. This provision applies to witnesses as well as defendants, and may be applied in the adult court. A youth court may not be held in a courtroom that has been used in the preceding hour, or will be used within the next hour, for adult proceedings. This minimises the risk of young people coming into contact with adult offenders or members of the public. Most courts hold youth court hearings on a different day, or in a different part of the building, from the adult court. For defendants under 16 the court must require a parent or guardian to attend also. For those over 16 the court may require the parent or guardian to attend. Where a child or young person is in the care of the local authority, a local authority representative can be required to attend.

In Inner London, magistrates are appointed directly to the Youth Court Panel. In other areas a youth court panel is made up of magistrates especially chosen from the bench because of their special knowledge of, or interest in, young people. Because of this interest many magistrates sit in both the youth court and the Family Proceedings Court which deals with care proceedings. The bench dealing with a youth court hearing will be composed of two or more (usually three) members of the Youth Court Panel. A stipendiary usually sits with lay magistrates. The bench should contain at least one male and one female. A single-sex bench or trial by a stipendiary sitting alone is only permissible in the youth court in emergencies, where it is not possible to adjourn.

Magistrates have a wide discretion in the youth court but are guided by s 44 CYPA 1933 which states that every court shall have regard for the welfare of the child or young person and, where proper, take steps to remove him or her from undesirable surroundings and ensure that adequate provision is made for training and education.

## Sentencing in the youth court

Before sentence is passed, the offender, either individually, or through a lawyer, parent or guardian must be allowed to make representations and the court has to consider all available material concerning the offender, his or her background, education and medical history. It is usual to have reports from social or probation services, and often a school report.

The sentences applicable to a young offender vary according to the court in which they are being sentenced. Very often, where a conviction is recorded in an adult court, a young offender will be remitted to the youth court for sentence. Like adult offenders, young offenders can be given absolute or conditional discharges and compensation orders. Some special

141

provisions relate to the sentencing of young offenders:

- *Fine.* The maximum fine payable by an offender under the age of 14 is £250, and for an offender aged 14 to 17 is £1,000. Where the offender is under 16 the court is under a duty to order that compensation is paid by the parent or guardian unless they cannot be found and it would unreasonable for them to be ordered to pay. For offenders over 16, magistrates have discretion to make such an order.

- *Parental recognisance.* The court may, with the consent of the parent or guardian, order them to enter into a recognisance to take and exercise proper control of an offender under 16. The parent then promises to pay a specified sum (up to £1,000) if they fail to do so.

- *Attendance centre order.* This sentence is only available for offences punishable with imprisonment in the case of an adult. The offender must not have received previous detention. The attendance centre must be reasonably accessible to the offender. The maximum attendance is 12 hours if the offender is under 14. The maximum is 24 hours for under 16s and 36 hours for 16–17s.

- *Supervision order.* This is the equivalent of probation for young offenders and must not be longer than three years. An order may impose conditions of residence or intermediate treatment, either at the direction of the court or an appointed supervisor. A night restriction order can also be imposed ordering the supervisee to stay in a specified place for up to 10 hours per night. The restrictions can not be imposed for more than a total of 30 days and cannot continue over a period longer than three months.

- *Community service.* This is available for offenders aged 16 and over, in the same terms as for an adult.

- *Secure training order.* From early 1995, younger offenders with previous convictions may be sentenced to secure training orders, introduced under the Criminal Justice and Public Order Act 1994. These orders may be between six months and two years.

- *Detention in a young offender institution.* Young offenders are not sentenced to imprisonment, but to detention in a young offender institution, which deals with incarcerated offenders between 15 and 21. There are restrictions on the length of sentence that can be imposed on different age groups. In contrast to adult offenders, there is a minimum term of custody for young offenders to discourage courts ordering a few days in order to give offenders 'a taste of custody' where the offence itself does not merit incarceration. The minimum term for detention in a young offender institution is two months and the maximum period is 24 months for 15–17 year olds. The youth court's maximum sentence is six months for one offence with an aggregate of 12 months for two or more.

- *Secure accommodation.* This is usually in a local authority residential home and is available for those aged 10 to 14 convicted of very serious crimes as they are not able under the law to be sent to young offender institutions.

As we have seen some young offenders are dealt with in adult courts. When a young person appears for sentence in the Crown Court, the court has similar sentencing options and additionally has powers to impose a sentence of 24 months' detention in a young offender institution – increased by the CJPOA 1994 – and there is a minimum period of incarceration of 21 days for those aged 18 to 21. The Crown Court may also impose a sentence of extended detention under s 53 CYPA 1933 of up to the maximum for an adult for the offence, including life detention during Her Majesty's Pleasure for offenders aged 10 to 17 convicted of murder. It is not possible to suspend a sentence of detention in a young offender institution.

It can be seen from the above that different notions of responsibility and the desire to divert and rehabilitate young offenders affects the treatment of children and young persons. The final part of this chapter will look at the treatment of another group requiring special consideration, the mentally disordered offender.


## MENTALLY DISORDERED OFFENDERS

Like children and young persons, there are strong arguments for diverting mentally disordered offenders from the criminal justice system before trial and before punishment. As Peay comments in respect of the mentally disordered offender, 'diversion and treatment are paramount' (Peay 1994: 1119). At the same time however, mentally disordered offenders may constitute a danger to themselves and others and may arouse fears on the part of the public. In order to protect the public therefore, it may be seen as necessary to commit them to hospital, or, if this is not possible, to some form of containment, even where their offences are not so serious as to merit a prison sentence. Thus due process may conflict with a protectionist stance which raises issues concerning the rights of mentally disordered offenders.

Our approach to the mentally disordered offender, as it is with the younger offender, is affected by notions of responsibility. The criminal law, as we have seen, depends by and large on the concept of a 'guilty mind' to create criminal liability which forms the basis of criminal punishment. It is important to recognise that the mental state of the defendant is considered at three stages in the criminal justice process. In the first place, there is the issue of whether someone is culpable for an act committed while they were suffering from some kind of mental disorder. A second question arises in establishing whether a person is mentally fit and able to undergo a trial. Finally, there is an issue as to whether someone who was mentally disordered at the time of the offence, or has subsequently become mentally disordered, can or should be punished.

## Responsibility for the offence

The criminal courts do not regard a person as culpable or blameworthy for an offence who is deemed 'not guilty by reason of insanity', or where the court accepts the statutory defence of diminished responsibility, or the state known as automatism is established.

*Insanity* is governed by the M'Naghten Rules, formulated after the trial in 1843 of Daniel M'Naghten who, suffering from a delusion that he should kill the then prime minister, Sir Robert Peel, killed his secretary by mistake. The rules provide that a defendant is not guilty by reason of insanity if 'he was labouring under a defect of reason because of a disease of the mind so that he did not know the nature and quality of his act, or if he did know it, did not know it was wrong'. If found not guilty by reason of insanity, the court may make a hospital order, a guardianship order, a supervision and treatment order or an absolute discharge. There is a right of appeal against such a verdict.

This definition has caused many difficulties, principally surrounding what is to be counted as a disease of the mind. For example in the case of *Sullivan* in 1984 it was held that a minor epileptic seizure fell within the definition of insanity. In addition, courts have distinguished between defects of reason caused by internal factors such as medical conditions which can only give rise to an insanity defence or verdict and external factors such as a blow to the head or medication which can give rise to a non-insane automatism defence.

*Automatism* describes a condition where a person is not strictly in control of his or her actions. If a criminal act is not voluntary there is no actus reus. Where automatism is caused by something deemed to be a disease of the mind the verdict should be not guilty by reason of insanity. If the automatism is caused by any other reason, for example, an injury, the defendant should be acquitted. As described above, there has been much unease about the line between non-insane and insane automatism, first because of the possible stigma attached and, secondly, because of the consequent disposal.

*Diminished responsibility* is a special defence to murder and is defined in s 2 of the Homicide Act 1957, under which a person who kills or is a party to the killing of another, cannot be convicted of murder if found to be 'suffering from such an abnormality of mind as substantially impaired his mental responsibility for his acts or omissions'. The abnormality in question may arise from arrested or retarded development, an inherent cause or disease or injury. The onus of proving such an abnormality is expressly placed on the defence. Diminished responsibility is only a defence to murder and if the actus reus is established the accused using such a defence will be found guilty of manslaughter instead. Diminished responsibility is therefore a partial defence, which reduces the culpability of the defendant and avoids the mandatory life sentence.

Before reaching a trial, defendants may be found unfit to plead. It is inherent in a criminal trial that a defendant is fit to plead – that a defendant knows and understands any charges and is able to instruct a lawyer. A defendant is held to be unfit to plead if he or she is either physically or mentally incapable of instructing legal advisers, following the proceedings or objecting to jurors.

The procedure of establishing fitness to plead is governed by the Criminal Procedure (Insanity) Act 1964 as amended by the Criminal Procedure (Insanity and Unfitness to Plead) Act 1991, which provide that the issue can be addressed by the court at any time up to the beginning of the defence case. Unfitness must be determined on the evidence of two or more doctors. If found unfit, the trial proceeds to establish whether or not the defendant has committed the actus reus – this is to avoid a mentally ill person being sentenced without proof of an offence. If the defendant is found fit to plead, the trial is carried on in the normal way, and any issues of mental disorder are raised in defence or mitigation. In cases where defendants are found to be both unfit to plead and have committed the actus reus, the court may make a hospital or guardianship order, a supervision order or impose an absolute discharge.

## Orders available to the courts for mentally disordered offenders

The courts have a number of options in dealing with mentally disordered offenders. These raise the issue of the rights of mentally disordered offenders, who may find themselves being deprived of their liberty for longer periods of time than if they were not mentally disordered, arising from the inevitable tension between the desire of the court to protect the public and the rights of offenders. In addition, diagnosing what form of mental disorder an offender is suffering from is not always straightforward, as is assessing how amenable the condition is to treatment. There are four types of mental incapacity defined in s 1 of the Mental Health Act 1983.

*Mental disorder* is defined as 'mental illness, arrested or incomplete development of mind, psychopathic disorder and any other disorder or disability of mind'. More specifically, *mental impairment* is defined as 'a state of arrested or incomplete development of mind (not amounting to severe mental impairment) which includes significant impairment of intelligence and social functioning and is associated with abnormally aggressive or seriously irresponsible conduct on the part of the person concerned'. *Severe mental impairment* is defined as 'a state of arrested or incomplete development of the mind which includes severe impairment of intelligence and social functioning and is associated with abnormally aggressive or seriously irresponsible conduct on the part of the person concerned'. A *psychopathic disorder* is defined as 'a persistent disorder or disability of mind (whether or not including significant impairment of intelligence) which results in abnormally aggressive or seriously irresponsible conduct on the part of the person concerned'.

The main options for the court when dealing with a mentally disordered offender are outlined below.

- Supervision or probation with treatment if the court is satisfied on the evidence of an approved medical practitioner that the mental condition of the offender requires and may be susceptible to treatment but that the condition does not warrant a full hospital order.
- Mental health hospital or guardianship orders can be made if the court is satisfied first that the defendant is suffering from:

  (1)   a mental illness
  (2)   a psychopathic disorder
  (3)   mental impairment
  (4)   severe mental impairment (see definitions above);

  and, secondly, that either the condition makes it appropriate for detention in a hospital for treatment (which, in the case of a psychopathic disorder and mental impairment is likely to improve the condition) or the offender is 16 or over and the condition warrants a guardianship order and the court feels such an order is the most suitable disposal.

  A hospital order lapses after six months but can be renewed and the detainee can be discharged at any time by the hospital managers or the medical officer responsible for the case. For a hospital order to be made the condition must be treatable – which is not required for a guardianship order. The order lasts initially for one year but is renewable. Hospital or guardianship orders cannot be made by an adult magistrates' court on a young person under 18. Both Crown Courts and magistrates' courts can make interim hospital orders on the evidence of two registered medical practitioners initially for up to 12 weeks but this may be renewed for periods of up to 28 days at a time for a maximum of six months.

- An order under s 37(3) of the Mental Health Act 1983: where a person has been charged and the court would have power on conviction to make a hospital or guardianship order, the court may, if satisfied that the accused did the act, make such an order without a conviction. This section does away with the requirement for a finding that the actus reus was accompanied by the requisite mens rea.

- Restriction order under s 41 of the Mental Health Act 1983: this power is not available to magistrates and can only be exercised by the Crown Court. The order provides for detention for a defined or indefinite period, so that the offender cannot be discharged from hospital without the permission of the Secretary of State or the Mental Health Review Tribunal. It may be imposed where it is felt necessary to impose such an order to protect the public from serious harm taking into account the nature of the offence, the history of the offender and the risk of future offending.

Where magistrates, taking the same considerations into account, feel that a restriction order is necessary, they may commit the offender to the Crown Court.

In 1993, 1,031 restricted patients were admitted to hospital: 60 per cent of all restricted patients detained in hospital were diagnosed as having mental illness. A further 18 per cent were considered to have a psychopathic disorder and 6 per cent had some form of mental impairment. These figures reflect those of earlier years (Home Office *Statistical Bulletin*, Issue 1/95: 1, 4]).

While few would dispute that it is desirable to divert mentally disordered offenders from the criminal justice process or refer them for treatment rather than punishment, there are some concerns about the provisions outlined above. Particularly problematic is the definition of different kinds of mental disorder. These definitions are somewhat narrow and may not accord with psychiatric diagnoses. The definition of psychopathy has raised special problems, as there is little agreement over what kind of underlying condition produces the behaviour which amounts to its definition. In essence, argues Peay, it is 'a legal category defined by persistently violent behaviour', rather than being a clearly defined mental disorder (Peay 1994: 1146).

Other problems arise from the current treatment of mentally abnormal offenders. The definitions of mental disorder may exclude some offenders, such as those affected by drug addiction, alcoholism or sexual offenders, who are in need of treatment and who may cause problems when placed in prison.

In addition, diagnosis and treatment may be inexact. A person's mental condition may change and indeed be affected by the process of being arrested or institutionalised, making predictions of whether and how the condition will respond to treatment extremely problematic. It is difficult therefore to state with any certainty how long a mentally disordered offender should be held in hospital. Given the fear that released offenders may re-offend this may lead to longer periods of hospitalisation than would be merited either by considerations of the offence or the needs of the offender for treatment.

However, recent tragedies have shown these fears are not imagined; fears which have been exacerbated by the current policy of treating mentally disordered offenders in the community. In December 1992 Jonathan Zito, a musician aged 27, was waiting for an underground train at Finsbury Park Station in London when he was stabbed in the face and killed by Christopher Clunis, a diagnosed schizophrenic. Clunis had a long history of violence which included stabbing a person in the neck. He had been released from prison to a mental hospital from which he had been discharged in 1992.

A report from the Royal College of Psychiatrists (17 August 1994) revealed in a survey of an 18-month period from July 1992 to December

147

1993, that 34 people were killed by newly released mental patients. William Boyd of the Royal Edinburgh Hospital investigated 22 of the 34 killings and discovered that all the perpetrators had been in the care of psychiatric services in the 12 months preceding the killings. Of the 22, 17 had histories of violence. Fifteen of the killings were committed by men, most of whom had been diagnosed as schizophrenic or paranoid psychotic. Nine of the 15 men had convictions for violent behaviour. The seven women in the study were mostly suffering from depression and six of them killed their own children.

Cases like these clearly cause public concern and in 1995 a new supervised discharge order was proposed to make it easier to return a mental patient to hospital if they refused, on release, to continue with their medication. It must nevertheless be recognised that only a small proportion of offenders are considered to be mentally disordered, that the vast majority of mentally disordered people do not commit crime,.

## CONCLUSION

In this chapter we have examined the pre-trial decisions by which some offenders are diverted out of the criminal justice system. Some are diverted because of their status either as young offenders or because they are mentally disordered; others are diverted because of decisions made by the police and the CPS. Many of the issues involved in these decisions and the policy that drives them have their roots in our concepts of criminal responsibility. Diversion also demonstrates the conflict in goals of the criminal justice system: to treat all equally before the law, to provide a cost-effective system, and to ensure judicial decisions are made openly, fairly and even-handedly.

It is for example clearly cheaper and less wasteful of resources to divert offenders who for various reasons might not be convicted, or if convicted would receive only a nominal penalty or some form of treatment rather than punishment. It may even be seen as desirable in the interests of equity and efficiency to allow prosecutors greater powers to impose sanctions for some offences without taking offenders to court. To prosecute all offenders uses up valuable resources which might be better used for the investigation and prevention of crime.

At the same time however, this means that justice is being done in private rather than in public, which in turn means that it is less publicly accountable and that equal treatment cannot be guaranteed. Diverted defendants have less chance to dispute fully allegations, and treatment programmes which may seem more desirable than punishment may involve more control than punishment. In addition as we have seen it may be in the public interest to see offenders publicly tried and punished as well as giving victims the chance to obtain compensation and the satisfaction of seeing justice being done. Another consideration from a crime control perspective is the potential threat to the public of dangerous offenders, be they sometimes young or mentally ill, being released back into the community. Many of these considerations also affect pre-trial processes. The next chapter describes the procedures they will go through before they reach the final stage.

## Review questions

1. Identify the main considerations underlying the decision to caution or prosecute and relate these to the models of criminal justice.
2. What criteria do the Crown Prosecution Service use in deciding whether to continue with a prosecution? What reasons are given for discontinuing prosecutions?
3. (a) What are the main options available to the youth court in respect of different age groups of young offenders?
   (b) Look for some recent public statements about the treatment of young offenders. How do these reflect different views of dealing with young offenders?
4. (a) What are the four types of mental incapacity defined in s 1 of the Mental Health Act 1983?
   (b) What are the main orders available to the courts in respect of the mentally ill?

## Further reading

Ashworth A et al (1992) *The Youth Court*. Winchester: Waterside Press
Ashworth A (1994) *The Criminal Process*. Oxford: Clarendon Press.
Gelsthorpe L and Morris A (1994) 'Juvenile Justice 1945–1992' in Maguire M, Morgan R and Reiner R (eds) *The Oxford Handbook of Criminology* Oxford: Clarendon Press: 949–996.
Peay J (1994) 'Mentally Disordered Offenders' in Maguire M, Morgan R and Reiner R (eds) *The Oxford Handbook of Criminology*: Oxford: Clarendon Press: 1119–1140.

# CHAPTER 6

# CRIMINAL COURTS AND PRE-TRIAL PROCEDURE

Magistrates' courts and the Crown Court
Rights of the Defendant in Court
Bail, Custody or Summons
Mode of Trial Decision

## INTRODUCTION

After a decision has been made to prosecute there are various stages that have to be gone through before an eventual conviction or acquittal. Criminal cases are dealt with in either magistrates' courts or the Crown Court. Nearly all start in the magistrates' court, and before a full trial or hearing the magistrates may have to decide whether or not the accused is to be held in custody while awaiting trial. In some cases the accused has to decide whether to have the case heard by magistrates or before a judge and jury. As with the decision to prosecute or caution, many issues are involved with conflicting pressures between the goals of due process, crime control and cost efficiency.

In a trial the defendant, according to the principles of due process, is presumed innocent until proven guilty. Yet many of the decisions made before a trial appear to pre-judge its outcome. Defendants, for example, can be placed in custody without a finding of guilt, to ensure that they appear to answer the case against them or to protect the public. Crime control interests, therefore, may require that the defendant's liberty is restricted before they have been convicted. Other procedures seek to ensure that defendants' interests are protected, particularly in respect of their rights to legal representation, to a jury trial and to not being tried on insufficient evidence. In addition, the organisation of criminal proceedings seeks, by including lay persons in both the magistracy and the jury, to involve representatives of the community as well as professionals and experts. As we have seen in previous chapters however, due process may be lengthy and expensive and pressures

150

for efficiency have led to many changes in these procedures. This has led to fears, particularly from a class domination perspective, that too much power lies with the police and other professionals and that defendants' rights are being eroded.

This chapter will first describe the functions and organisation of different courts and how cases are classified. It will then look at how the system seeks to protect the rights of individual suspects and defendants and provides for their legal representation. It will then go on to consider crucial pre-trial processes which include the decision whether to remand on bail or in custody, transfer proceedings and the mode of trial decision before going on to examine the process of establishing guilt in Chapter 7.

## MAGISTRATES' COURTS AND THE CROWN COURT

Different courts in the English legal system deal with different kinds of cases and proceedings. We are concerned with criminal cases which are generally contrasted with civil cases. In criminal cases, a prosecution is conducted on behalf of the state or the Crown, though occasionally privately, against a defendant in order to establish whether or not that defendant is guilty of a crime. Guilt may be proved by a verdict following a trial or accepted after a guilty plea, following which a conviction is recorded. This will normally be followed by a form of punishment referred to as a sentence.

Civil cases in contrast are mainly concerned with the settlement of disputes between two or more parties, often involving arguments over such matters as rent, boundaries, contracts, negligence, family disputes on the break up of marriage and inheritance. In civil cases a plaintiff sues another person – called the defendant – with a view to obtaining a judgment. A judgment may result in the court ordering the defendant to pay money as damages to compensate the plaintiff. Alternatively the court may issue an order or injunction requiring the defendant to do or to refrain from doing something. In other cases the court may make a declaration, or change the status of an individual – for example by granting a divorce.

Civil or criminal courts deal with these different types of cases. The county court can only deal with civil cases – it has only civil jurisdiction. Other courts, for example the High Court and magistrates' courts, have jurisdiction in both civil and criminal matters. Magistrates' jurisdiction over civil law matters is limited to licensing matters and family proceedings.

An individual case may be dealt with in different courts at different stages. Nearly all criminal cases start in the magistrates' court and some, as will be seen below, are then passed to the Crown Court. Other cases may be heard by different courts because one or other party has appealed against the decision of the first court. Courts are therefore classified not only on the basis of the type of matter they deal with, but also in accordance with their jurisdiction to hear cases 'at first instance' or on appeal. Two criminal courts, magistrates' courts and the Crown Court, deal with trials – they therefore have first instance criminal jurisdiction. These courts will now be explored in more detail. We shall start with the magistrates, those voluntary workhorses of the system along with stipendiary magistrates, and then go on to examine proceedings in the Crown Court, before the thoroughbreds of the process, the judges.

## Magistrates' courts

If you visit a magistrates' court, which are all open to the public except when dealing with family matters or children, you will find that between 9.45 am and 10 am, when business normally starts, the lobby of a typical urban court resembles a station ticket office during the rush hour. Defendants are looking for their name on lists pinned to the wall and lawyers and probation officers are seeking out their clients. Ushers and clerks are attempting to impose order by checking lists to see which defendants have arrived. Victims, witnesses, reporters and the interested public are also attempting to find out what is happening, which is not always immediately evident. To the uninitiated the high turnover of defendants making short appearances may give an impression of confusion and of nothing being achieved.

Only very trivial cases can be dealt with on the defendant's first appearance. Most defendants are making their second or third trip to the court after an adjournment. They are therefore appearing at different stages of the pre-trial and trial process; some for remand or bail hearings, others to enter a plea or decide whether a case is to be heard in the magistrates' court or in the Crown Court. Other defendants will be returning for a summary trial to take place. Even that may not be the end of the matter as proceedings may be adjourned again to await a pre-sentence report before a sentencing decision. The average number of adjournments per case rose from two in 1986 to 2.5 by 1991, and in 1991, an average of 18 weeks elapsed between the date of the offence and the completion of proceedings for indictable offences dealt with in magistrates' courts (Home Office 1993: 35).

A magistrates' court is presided over either by lay magistrates, who are also known as justices of the peace (hence JP), who usually sit as a bench of three, or by a stipendiary magistrate sitting alone. Lay magistrates are advised on matters of law by a legally qualified clerk. A senior magistrate chairs the bench and speaks on its behalf but all three magistrates have equal power. As we have seen, a special panel of magistrates sit in the youth court.

In a summary trial, magistrates decide on guilt in cases where the defendant contests guilt, that is pleads not guilty. A contested case will involve a trial, which in a magistrates' court is known as a summary trial. Most defendants do not deny guilt, that is they plead guilty, and are sentenced by the magistrates as are those who have been found guilty following a trial. Nearly all criminal cases start in the magistrates' court and most, approximately 93 per cent, end there.

The justices' clerk is responsible for the administration of the court, and for the legal advice given to justices. The clerk should advise magistrates on legal matters only, which includes guidance on the powers of sentence, but should never seek to influence them on questions of fact, such as whether they believe a witness, nor on the actual sentence to impose.

Stipendiary magistrates sit in larger urban courts and have exactly the same powers as lay magistrates. They sit alone and can exercise all their powers alone. They are paid, and are professional lawyers with a number of years' experience as a barrister or solicitor. In 1992 there were 76 stipendiaries, 10 of whom were women.

Lay magistrates are unpaid, sit part time, and are not required to be legally qualified, though they undergo introductory and continuing training. On 1 January 1995 there were 30,008 lay magistrates in the 550 petty sessional divisions in England and Wales. Magistrates are appointed by local panels which include experienced magistrates, under the jurisdiction and direction of the Lord Chancellor. Individuals may put their own name forward for appointment, others are nominated by existing magistrates, charitable bodies, political parties, trade unions or other organisations. Suitable candidates are then interviewed by the appointments panel who are concerned to appoint magistrates who as far as possible represent a cross-section of the community. They therefore attempt to balance the bench in terms of sex, age, political affiliation, ethnic origin, and background.

The overriding consideration for appointment is that the candidate is suitable in terms of integrity and local standing. Thus anyone who is an undischarged bankrupt or has a conviction for a serious offence or a number of minor offences is unlikely to be appointed. Certain categories of people employed in enforcing the law are ineligible to apply, even when retired. This includes police officers, members of the special constabulary, traffic wardens, civilians working for the police and members of the armed forces.

An applicant will not be appointed to a petty sessional division if he or she has a mother, father, son, daughter, brother or sister who is a police officer, special constable, traffic warden or JP in that district. No one may be appointed with a close relative who works for the Crown Prosecution Service or the magistrates' courts in that district, or is a retired police officer, traffic warden or a special constable. You cannot apply to be a JP in a specific petty sessional division if you are a Member of Parliament, are adopted as a political candidate, or are a full-time political agent in that petty sessional division.

All of these restrictions are based on the need to keep those who adjudicate on the law separate from those who make or investigate it. A key feature of criminal justice in England and Wales is that magistrates are generally lay, as opposed to professional or expert. They are therefore clearly distinct from other participants in the adversarial system such as the police, prosecution or defence and from other professionals such as probation officers. The magistracy is therefore independent of any other interest, and its members are there to represent the wider community.

The constitution of the magistracy has occasioned some criticism. It has been argued, for example, that it makes little sense for such vital roles as the adjudication of guilt and the sentencing of the offender to be carried out by amateurs, who cannot be expected to appreciate the finer points of criminal liability, let alone the complexities involved in making sentencing decisions. It could therefore be argued that criminal justice should be in the hands of full-time professionals.

On the other hand, leaving these decisions in the hands of professionals and experts could be seen as leaving too much power in the hands of experts, power which the involvement of lay persons in the system can check. Magistrates themselves clearly value their independence and argue that their experience and commonsense are valuable assets in making the system work (see, for example, Parker et al 1989). Sentencing they feel is not a task for experts, but is more akin to an art. Magistrates also tend to resent any attempts to curtail their powers, by, for example, standardising court procedures and sentencing practice. Some magistrates resigned at the time of the introduction of the unit fine in the Criminal Justice Act 1991 because they felt that this reduced their discretion.

Others are critical of the composition of the magistracy on the grounds that they are not elected and are not representative of the general population. The magistracy is often perceived to be dominated by middle class, middle aged white professional groups. In 1992, 45 per cent of lay magistrates were women and 2 per cent were from ethnic minorities. Thus women are well represented, although ethnic minority numbers are lower than their proportion in the population. Critics have also focused on the social class profile of magistrates. Recent figures on the class composition of magistrates are hard to come by, but it is likely that the middle classes are over-represented for the following reasons.

Being a magistrate takes up a considerable amount of time. Many people are not able to leave young children, the office, the schoolroom or the factory floor for extended periods. This inevitably means that some groups, such as middle class housewives or the relatively affluent self-employed are over-represented and others, such as manual workers are under-represented. Also the latter are less likely to be proposed, or to be seen as having 'local standing' – a point which also militates against the appointment of the unemployed, the young and recently settled members of ethnic minorities.

The issue of representativeness is not, however, easy to resolve. What would a more representative magistracy achieve and just what, or who, should it represent? A representative magistracy on the grounds of demographic characteristics alone may not make different decisions in relation to either guilt or sentencing than the current magistracy. Women magistrates appear no more sympathetic, for example, to female offenders, who often come from very different socio-economic circumstances (see, for example, Eaton 1986), and there is also little evidence of any direct bias on the grounds of social status in respect of business offenders (see, for example, Croall 1991).

154

Should magistrates in some way represent the views of the community? Should they be elected? In California judges have to go through an election or re-confirmation process. This means that they must campaign for office as if a politician. This could itself be seen as undesirable as the magistracy should be free from political commitments – they are supposed to make decisions on behalf of the whole community, not just those who vote for them. Should the magistracy be selected on the basis that they represent the views of the population on punishment? Representativeness in terms of community values could, for example, see a magistracy in which a large proportion would welcome the restoration of capital punishment. A 1993 survey of social attitudes confirms previous findings from opinion polls in that 74 per cent of respondents thought that for some crimes, the death penalty was appropriate (Jowell 1994: 78).

The magistracy represents a lay element in the system which means that the public, albeit a somewhat selected group, play a part in the administration of justice and sentencing. A professional magistracy, which as we have seen would place more power in the hands of professionals would also be unrepresentative in terms of social class.

## The Crown Court

The Crown Court is presided over by a judge. Usually this will be a circuit judge, a full-time judge appointed by the Lord Chancellor from the ranks of barristers and solicitors to the circuit bench. In 1992, 471 circuit judges sat at 90 Crown Court Centres. Other judges are known as recorders or assistant recorders. These are part-time judges drawn from barristers and solicitors of a number of years' standing. A High Court judge presides over the most serious criminal cases. The role of the Crown Court judge is explained in Chapter 7.

The Crown Court system was introduced by legislation in 1971 and replaced the older system of assizes and petty sessions. Technically there is one Crown Court in England and Wales sitting at a number of locations or Crown Court Centres. Although the Crown Court has a limited civil jurisdiction on appeals, the vast majority of its work is on criminal matters. It is a first instance court which deals with more serious matters than the magistrates' court and also hears appeals against conviction or sentence from the magistrates' court.

Criminal cases come to the Crown Court in three main ways. Some have been previously sent to the Crown Court for trial from the magistrates' court. These may not always lead to trials, as defendants may change their mind at the last minute and plead guilty. Other cases have been sent on from the magistrates' court for sentence and yet others involve appeals against decisions of guilt or sentence at the magistrates' court.

The Crown Court, High Court and Court of Appeal all have appellate jurisdiction which means the right to hear an appeal. Most appeals against conviction and sentence from the Crown Court go to the Court of Appeal, Criminal Division. A few appeals on points of law will go to the High Court which is divided into Divisions and it is the Queen's Bench Division which deals with appeals on criminal matters. The Court of Appeal has a wider appellate jurisdiction hearing both criminal and civil matters, and the Criminal Division of the Court of Appeal is the usual venue for appeals from the Crown Court. An appeal from the Court of Appeal goes to the House of Lords, which is the highest domestic appeal court. In certain cases there is an appeal to the European Court of Justice.

The number of cases dealt with in the magistrates' courts and the Crown Court is given in Figures 6.1 and 6.2. Figure 6.1 shows the total number of hearings, that is decisions on guilt or not; the cases not continued by the CPS; and the number of committals or transfers to the Crown Court. Figure 6.2 shows the Crown Court caseload in the three years from 1991 to 1993 and indicates the number of cases committed for trial from the magistrates' courts. It also gives the number of appeals that were sent to the Crown Court, either against conviction or sentence, and the number of cases sent to the Crown Court from the magistrates' court for sentencing.

## The jurisdiction of magistrates' courts and the Crown Court

Jurisdiction for criminal cases, that is where cases can be tried, is determined by a number of factors. The first is the type of offence. Criminal offences are divided into three categories as follows:

- summary offences
- offences triable on indictment only
- offences triable either way, ie summarily or on indictment.

The latter two categories are referred to as indictable offences. Cases triable only on indictment must be tried at the Crown Court. An indictment is the formal document used in a Crown Court trial setting out the charges against the defendant. The magistrates' court has power to hear summary offences and offences that are triable either way where a decision has been made to try them summarily, that is in the magistrates' court. In 1993, 1.96 million offences were prosecuted, of which:

- 479,000 were indictable
- 581,000 were summary non-motoring
- 897,000 were summary motoring.

The time and place at which the alleged offence was committed can also affect where it is heard. Magistrates' courts can only try offences committed in their area and normally proceedings must be started within six months of the commission of the offence. Indictable offences may be tried in any Crown Court and there is generally no time limit for the commencement of proceedings.

**Fig 6.1** Magistrates' courts: number of completed cases

|  | 1991–92 | % | 1992–93 | % | 1993–94 | % |
|---|---|---|---|---|---|---|
| Hearings | 1,058,747 | 71.9 | 1,010,363 | 70.5 | **941,053** | **69.5** |
| Discontinuances | 174,411 | 11.8 | 193,774 | 13.5 | **168,707** | **12.5** |
| Committals | 129,667 | 8.8 | 112,082 | 7.8 | **102,549** | **7.5** |
| Other disposals | 110,275 | 7.5 | 117,639 | 8.2 | **142,687** | **10.9** |
| TOTAL | 1,473,100 | | 1,433,858 | | **1,354,996** | |

Other disposals: this includes cases in which the defendant was bound over to keep the peace without a trial and committal hearings at the end of which the defendant is discharged. It also includes cases in which the prosecution cannot proceed, perhaps as a result of the death of the defendant, or because the defendant cannot be traced, or because the case has been adjourned indefinitely. There was a fall in the number of prosecutions discontinued, from 193,774 (13.5% of completed cases) in 1992–93 to 168,707 (12.5%) in 1993–94. We believe that this reflects the introduction of national Practice Standards for the timeliness and content of police files, which has reduced the number of weak cases referred to the Service.

(CPS (1994) *Annual Report 1993–94*. London: HMSO: 28)

**Fig 6.2** Crown court caseload 1991–93

**CASE CATEGORIES IN THE CROWN COURT**

|  | 1991–92 | % | 1992–93 | % | 1993–94 | % |
|---|---|---|---|---|---|---|
| Committed for trial | 119,170 | 82.6 | 108,310 | 81.8 | **91,748** | **80.1** |
| Appeals | 14,729 | 10.2 | 15,828 | 11.9 | **18,124** | **15.9** |
| Committed for sentence | 10,427 | 7.2 | 8,239 | 6.3 | **4,603** | **4.0** |
| TOTAL | 144,326 | | 132,377 | | **114,475** | |

(CPS (1994) *Annual Report 1993–94*. London: HMSO: 26)

## Classification of offences: summary and indictable

Summary offences are comparatively less serious crimes. Most motoring offences are summary, including driving with excess alcohol, but there is a wide variety of other summary offences, including common assault, assaulting a police officer, and taking a motor vehicle without the owner's consent. All summary offences are made so by statute.

Generally speaking, the maximum penalty for a summary offence is six months' imprisonment or a £5,000 fine or both, but many summary offences carry much lower maximum penalties, and many are not imprisonable at all. The maximum financial penalties are determined in accordance with a range of levels established by Parliament. Level one offences currently carry a maximum fine of £200 and level 5 offences carry a maximum fine of £5,000. The offence of being drunk and disorderly for example is a level 3 offence. These five levels were introduced by the Criminal Justice Act 1982 and they mean that as inflation erodes the value of money, fine maxima can be simply adjusted by legislation altering the value of the levels.

Offences triable only on indictment are very serious matters, including murder, rape, blackmail, robbery, and wounding with intent. For those convicted of murder the only sentence available to the court is life imprisonment. Maximum penalties for other offences are laid down by statute and may include a discretionary life sentence or a simple term of years. For example, 14 years is the maximum custodial penalty for blackmail and burglary of a dwelling, while 10 years is the maximum for burglary of a non-dwelling. Financial penalties for offences tried on indictment have no limit but fines are rarely imposed for such serious offences.

Triable either way (TEW) offences include theft, burglary, assault occasioning actual bodily harm, and unlawful wounding. This category covers many offences where the offence's relative seriousness can vary tremendously depending on the facts. Theft, for example, includes stealing a bottle of milk from a doorstep, shoplifting and stealing from an employer. The seriousness of these matters is affected by the value of the theft and all the circumstances surrounding it, including the relationship between thief and victim.

Criminal damage is another offence where the circumstances can vary tremendously. The offence is committed when someone knowingly or recklessly inflicts damage on the property of another person and it is generally a TEW offence. However, in criminal damage cases not involving threat to life or arson and where the value of the damage inflicted is £2,000 or less, the charge is regarded as summary with a maximum penalty of three months' custody or a £2,500 fine. When the value of the damage is over £2,000 the offence remains triable either way. Under the Criminal Justice and Public Order Act 1994, this limit is increased to £5,000, but the principle is retained.

Successive acts have attempted to reduce the numbers of TEW offences, in part to reduce costs and to spread the work more efficiently between the courts. During the discussion of the Criminal Law Bill 1977 proposals were made to change the classification of some offences including criminal damage and theft. These changes were criticised on the grounds that they reduced the defendant's right to a trial by jury. In respect of theft, it was felt that anyone threatened with a conviction for dishonesty must retain this right, however trivial the offence. Proposals for changing the classification of offences were made by the 1993 Royal Commission.

An offence which was reclassified in response to changing legislative and public perceptions of seriousness was taking a vehicle without the owner's consent, an offence under s 12 of the Theft Act 1968. This, in its original form, was a TEW offence. In the Criminal Justice Act 1988 it, along with

**Fig 6.3** Number of offenders in the magistrates' court 1980 and 1992

**PERSONS PROCEEDED AGAINST AT MAGISTRATES' COURTS BY TYPE OF OFFENCE AND HOW DEALT WITH PRIOR TO FIRST APPEARANCE**

| | Number of persons proceeded against (in thousands) | | |
|---|---|---|---|
| | *1980* | *1988** | *1992** |
| Indictable offences | | | |
| Summoned | 136 [24%] | 109 [19%] | 78 [13%] |
| Arrested and bailed | 364 [63%] | 391 [67%] | 422 [73%] |
| Arrested and held in custody | 74 [13%] | 81 [14%] | 79 [14%] |
| TOTAL | 574 [100%] | 582 [100%] | 580 [100%] |
| Summary offences: non-motoring | | | |
| Summoned | 271 [58%] | 364 [72%] | 438 [76%] |
| Arrested and bailed | 165 [35%] | 124 [25%] | 121 [21%] |
| Arrested and held in custody | 31 [7%] | 15 [3%] | 18 [3%] |
| TOTAL | 467 [100%] | 503 [100%] | 578 [100%] |
| Summary motoring offences | | | |
| Summoned | 1,334 [99%] | 733 [89%] | 865 [88%] |
| Arrested and bailed | 15 [1%] | 85 [10%] | 106 [11%] |
| Arrested and held in custody | 2 [–] | 6 [1%] | 8 [1%] |
| TOTAL | 1,351 [100%] | 823 [100%] | 979 [100%] |
| All offences | | | |
| Summoned | 1,741 [73%] | 1,205 [63%] | 1,382 [65%] |
| Arrested and bailed | 544 [23%] | 600 [31%] | 649 [30%] |
| Arrested and held in custody | 106 [4%] | 102 [5%] | 106 [5%] |
| TOTAL | 2,391 [100%] | 1,908 [100%] | 2,137 [100%] |

* The data given is as presented by the Home Office. The totals and subtotals have in some cases been adjusted by them because of the quality of the data received.

(Home Office (1989) *Criminal Statistics, England & Wales 1988*. London: HMSO: 175 and Home Office (1993) *Criminal Statistics, England & Wales 1992*. London: HMSO: 186)

common assault and driving whilst disqualified, became triable in summary proceedings only. The early 1990s saw an increase in public concern about offences involving a number of widely reported incidents where such cars were used to commit robberies, or resulted in the deaths of the drivers or bystanders. Vivid newspaper reports about ramraiders and twoc-ers fuelled political disquiet. In response Parliament created a new indictable offence, 'Aggravated Vehicle-Taking', to cover the situation in which a car, taken without the owner's consent, was involved in an accident or crime.

As we shall see below with TEW offences a decision has to be made as to where the case will be tried. Before looking at these pre-trial decisions how-ever, we will first examine what rights the defendant has in court along with the arrangements for legal aid for criminal cases. Figure 6.3 shows the total number of offenders dealt with in the magistrates' courts between 1980 and

1992, which showed a decline in the numbers over this period with a rise in 1992 when about 2.03 million persons were proceeded against in magistrates' courts (Home Office 1993: 124).

# RIGHTS OF THE DEFENDANT IN COURT

A person suspected, arrested, prosecuted or convicted of an offence has rights under the law at each stage of the criminal justice system. These are there to protect the suspect or defendant against the greater power of the state as embodied by the police, the courts and the prison system, and are a key feature of the due process model. As seen in Chapter 1, the most important protection for the citizen is that no official is above the law and that all officials are accountable for their actions regardless of their rank. It was also seen in Chapter 4 how laws relating to police powers seek to balance the interests of the citizen with those of efficient law enforcement. Along with this general principle established by the rule of law, the citizen has specifically defined rights at each stage of the system. Many of these arise from the key principle that the prosecution must prove beyond reasonable doubt that the accused person is guilty of a crime and that it is not the duty of the suspect to help them to prove guilt.

## First appearance at court

Having been charged by the police, an arrested person now becomes a defendant and is entitled to certain rights even before the case is heard. These include the following:

- To know the nature and brief details of any charges.
- The opportunity to be legally represented by a solicitor or barrister.
- An entitlement to unconditional bail except where there are reasons for not granting bail, described below.
- If remanded in custody defendants are entitled to apply again for bail on their next appearance if their circumstances have changed.
- To jury trial in TEW cases.
- To advance disclosure of the evidence in any TEW offence.
- Not to disclose their defence before trial except in the case of alibi or expert evidence.
- To see unused prosecution evidence before Crown Court trial and be notified of witnesses interviewed by the prosecution but not called. The prosecution has a general duty to give the defence information of use to them.

## During the trial

Defendants have the right to a fair trial in which they are entitled to challenge any evidence or witness used in the case against them. They are also entitled to call witnesses and evidence on their own behalf to counter the accusations of the prosecution. The defendant should expect to be found not guilty unless the case has been proved beyond reasonable doubt. The defendant should be assured that the usual established procedure for trial applies to him or her. In particular they have the following rights:

- To seek legal representation, and to have it free if the criteria on merit and means are fulfilled (see below).
- To have the assistance of a Mackenzie friend (someone to assist them if they are unrepresented).
- To challenge any number of jurors, if they have a good reason (ie cause).
- Not to give evidence.
- Not to have previous convictions mentioned during the trial stage except in unusual and well-defined circumstances.
- To insist that, if acquitted, their fingerprints and photographs be destroyed.
- To argue that the prosecution has not made out a case to answer.

## Legal aid and the duty solicitor scheme

For many defendants the key to their protection is the assistance of someone who understands the issues and the legal system. This section will briefly outline a defendant's rights to legal representation. Where defendants have insufficient resources to pay for their own lawyer, they are entitled, under certain circumstances, to assistance by means of legal aid. This is provided in a variety of ways. Much legal aid is means tested, which means that its availability is dependent on the financial circumstances of the defendant. An assessment is made of the disposable income and capital of the defendant, on the basis of which a calculation is made as to how much legal aid will be granted and how much the defendant must contribute to legal costs.

The Green Form Scheme allows defendants to obtain preliminary advice and to ascertain whether they may need or be entitled to full legal aid. This scheme is also means tested, and is available to those who, after allowable deductions, are left with a weekly disposable income of less than a specified amount: in 1995 the amount was £70.

PACE 1984 provided for a legal advice scheme, available 24 hours per day, for those being questioned by the police whether under arrest or attending voluntarily at the police station. The interviewee may seek free advice from the duty solicitor. This is most important during out of office hours, especially as the police station will have access to the duty solicitor's home phone number.

161

Most magistrates' courts are covered by a free duty solicitor court scheme. On arrival at a court defendants can seek advice from a nominated solicitor from a locally appointed panel. This solicitor can represent the client on simple matters such as bail applications and pleas in mitigation after a guilty plea. If more extensive representation is needed the solicitor may apply for the case to be adjourned for full legal aid to be applied for. The court duty solicitor scheme does not cover road traffic matters and other minor incidents.

Assistance by representation in court is provided for under s 21 of the Legal Aid Act 1988 and is means tested on a sliding scale with contributions on the basis of income. Legal aid is always available, subject to means, in the following circumstances:

- where the defendant is committed for trial for murder
- where the prosecution is appealing to the House of Lords
- in the magistrates' court where the defendant is in custody or is likely to be remanded in custody.

Otherwise legal aid is available where it is seen to be desirable in the interests of justice and is subject to a means test. In 1995 a disposable income of less than £45 per week after allowable deductions will entitle the defendant to full legal aid. If legal aid is refused there are rights of review. In determining whether legal aid should be granted the clerk of the court will consider whether the case involves any of the following:

- a possible loss of liberty, livelihood or reputation
- a substantial question of law
- a defendant whose command of English is poor or who is hampered by physical or mental infirmity
- the tracing and interviewing of witnesses
- interests of persons other than the defendant are at stake.

Many aspects of the current provisions have been criticised and are under review. There has been a tendency to restrict the availability of full legal aid, much driven by the high costs of the system. In 1991, for example, the total cost of the legal aid service was £684 million according to a report by the National Audit Office (*The Administration of Legal Aid in England and Wales* HC 90 (1991–92) HMSO). In that year 446,000 people received legal aid to contest a criminal case. As a result of spiralling costs the government has consistently sought to reduce eligibility for legal aid and to reduce the amount it pays to the legal profession to administer the system. Thus in 1992, Lord Mackay, the Lord Chancellor, announced that a ceiling was to be put on available funds and that only those whose need was greatest should receive legal aid. In addition the fees paid to defence lawyers would also be reduced (Burton 1994).

In 1994, changes to the income limits were introduced and defendants with over £45 per week disposable income must contribute towards the costs of a case. In addition anyone with capital assets of over £3,000 must contribute the excess towards legal fees: these limits may act as a disincentive to seeking legal aid. When they were announced the Lord Chief Justice, Lord Taylor, commented that, 'a large band in our community will become ineligible for legal aid and will have no access to the courts unless they are willing to appear without a lawyer' (quoted in Burton 1994: 1491).

In addition, the government has altered the way legal aid fees are calculated for solicitors for legal aid work which in itself may be a disincentive for some solicitors to accept legal aid work. The provision of legal aid is a further example of how pressures for cost clearly conflict with the interests of due process. This will also be seen when we consider the issues underlying many of the pre-trial processes explored below, starting with decisions regarding remanding a defendant on bail or in custody.

## BAIL, CUSTODY OR SUMMONS

The court process starts with the attendance of the defendant. Most will have been summonsed, normally by post, as is the case for example with minor motoring offences. Some will have been arrested and may have been held overnight in police custody, or released on police bail to attend court. Yet others may have been remanded in custody and arrive from a prison. Cases are not normally heard on their first appearance and most are adjourned. This is necessary to allow both the prosecution and the defendant time to prepare their case, to seek legal or other expert advice or to contact witnesses.

Both the police and the courts can make decisions about holding an accused person in custody prior to conviction. The police must decide whether to release arrested persons or to detain them in police custody. In 1991 the police arrested and detained in custody 6 per cent of those who were prosecuted. They released on bail a further 32 per cent. Most (62 per cent) of those prosecuted were summonsed (Home Office 1993a: 34). Following their first appearance in the magistrates' court, defendants may be released to await trial or may be remanded on bail or in custody by the magistrates. Similar decisions have to be made by the judge if the case goes to trial in the Crown Court. In 1991, 22 per cent of offenders prosecuted were granted bail by the magistrates, 3 per cent were remanded in custody and 75 per cent were released with no conditions (Home Office 1993a: 34).

Less serious cases will simply be adjourned and defendants notified of the date of the next hearing. In more serious cases however defendants will be remanded, either on bail or in custody. Remands can only be for a fixed period of time, and remand length varies in relation to whether or not the accused is held in custody. There are fixed limits to the length of time that a person can be detained by the police at a police station and by the magistrates when remanding an offender in custody.

As seen in Chapter 4, PACE governs police powers in relation to detention without charge. Under a strict timetable, a suspect may only be held for questioning for a limited time before being charged. If the time limit is reached the suspect must be charged or released. PACE also provides that once a suspect has been charged they may be released by the police on unconditional bail to attend the magistrates' court at a specified time. The police may be unwilling to release defendants on bail because they fear further offences will be committed or witnesses interfered with. In other cases the police may use bail as a bargaining tool to secure a plea of guilty (Sanders 1994). Suspects must be brought before a magistrates' court as soon as possible, for the decision on bail or custody to be made. Under the Criminal Justice and Public Order Act 1994 however the police will be able to impose conditions of bail which will prevent the necessity of referring the matter to court when a simple condition would meet their concerns.

Defendants may be detained initially for 24 hours. If, in the opinion of the police, the offence is a 'serious arrestable offence', then the period of detention by the police may be extended for a further 12 hours on the authorisation of a senior officer of superintendent rank or above. After 36 hours accused persons must be presented at a magistrates' court, who may return them to police custody for a further 36 hours. After this time they must again be returned to the court, when the magistrates may decide on a further period of remand. The maximum total period of remand without charge in police custody is 96 hours. Thereafter the suspect must be charged or released. After charge, further decisions on remand in custody or bail are made by the court and if remanded in custody, the accused will be held in a remand wing or centre in a prison service establishment.

Unconvicted defendants may not be initially remanded in custody by magistrates for more than eight days at a time. They may be remanded for up to 28 days, however, if they have been previously remanded in custody for the same offence and are present in court. A convicted defendant can be remanded in custody for up to three weeks for reports. In order to prevent repeated custodial remands, custody time limits were introduced following the creation of the Crown Prosecution Service. These provide a maximum time limit for proceedings where the defendant is in custody. When the limit is reached, leave to extend the period must be applied for or the defendant must be given bail. Under the Prosecution of Offences (Custody Time Limits) Regulations 1987 the limits are 70 days between first appearance and summary trial or committal proceedings, unless the decision to have summary trial is reached earlier than 56 days in which case the limit is 56 days. The maximum period for holding a defendant in custody between committal to the Crown Court and trial is 112 days.

## Bail

The operation of the bail system in England and Wales is governed by the Bail Act 1976. If a person accused, convicted or under arrest for an offence is granted bail, they are released under a duty to attend court or the police station at a given time.

Bail may be granted subject to certain conditions, which aim to ensure that the defendant appears for the next hearing. The court may ask for a *surety*, someone who will pledge to pay an amount of money set by the court should the defendant not turn up, or may require a *security* – the deposit of a sum of money. In other circumstances, the court may require that the accused lodge their passport with the police to ensure that they do not flee the country, or the court may decide to restrict defendants' movements. Other conditions typically involve reporting to a police station, curfew orders and refraining from contacting witnesses or victims.

Those who are granted bail must appear at the time and place specified, which they will be given written details of. If they do not surrender to custody, they are guilty of an offence, except when they are prevented from so doing because of, for example, an accident. A warrant may be issued for their arrest and if found guilty of the offence of failing to attend they risk a fine of up to £5,000 from the magistrates' court or up to three months' imprisonment. The police may also arrest someone on bail if they have reasonable grounds for believing that any conditions are not being met or that the accused is unlikely to surrender.

## Criteria for bail

The criteria for granting and refusing bail are also dealt with by the Bail Act 1976. In general there is a presumption in favour of bail for unconvicted defendants but there are some important exceptions. Bail need not be granted where there are 'substantial grounds' for believing that the accused would fail to surrender, commit an offence, interfere with witnesses or otherwise obstruct justice. In these circumstances, the court may take account of the nature and seriousness of the offence and the probable sentence along with the character, antecedents, associations and community ties of the defendant. They will also consider the defendant's record in respect of bail in previous proceedings and the strength of the evidence. The magistrates may decide in the case of the defendant with a history of offences associated with drinking in public houses to ban the defendant from entering a public house as a condition of bail. A defendant charged with violence against a specific individual may be ordered not to approach or communicate with the victim.

The courts need not grant bail when the magistrates think the accused should be kept in custody for his or her own protection, where they are already serving a prison sentence or where there has been insufficient time to obtain information. Another exception is where the person has been accused of murder, manslaughter, rape, attempted murder or attempted rape. If the court grants bail in such cases, the reasons for its decision have to be included in the bail record.

As a result of increasing concern about the possibility of dangerous offenders being released on bail, the Bail Amendment Act 1993 gave the Crown Prosecution Service limited rights to appeal against a bail decision made in a magistrates' court. In addition the Criminal Justice and Public Order Act 1994 aims to ensure automatic remand in custody with no opportunity for bail for those charged with murder, manslaughter or rape who have been convicted previously of those offences. The case of Andrew Hagans in 1992 highlighted the public disquiet caused by releasing convicted violent offenders charged with another serious violent offence.

Andrew Hagans was released from prison in July 1991. He was 25 years old, and had 28 convictions, mainly for violent and sexual offences. At the age of 15 he was placed under supervision after holding three women at knifepoint and indecently assaulting them. A year later he was again placed under supervision for three years for burglary with intent to rape. On 4 August 1991, three weeks after release from prison, he was arrested and charged with raping a woman in Cheltenham. After a week on remand in jail he was given bail by the magistrates' court, despite strong opposition from the police. The condition of his bail was that he lived in a bail hostel and did not go to Cheltenham. Sixteen days later Hagans was in Gloucester where he raped and murdered 23 year-old Anna McGurk. In June 1992 he was jailed for life at Bristol Crown Court.

When bail is refused the court must consider whether it ought to be granted on subsequent occasions. This does not mean that the accused can make repeated applications on the same grounds. After bail has been refused for any of the stated reasons, other than insufficient information, only one further bail application is usually allowed and the court does not have to hear further applications unless there has been a change in circumstances. A remand in custody on the basis that there is insufficient information is not a refusal of bail as such and does not count as a bail application so that the accused may still make two applications.

Some concern has been expressed about the length of adjournments, especially where defendants are remanded in custody. This clearly causes immense stress to defendants, let alone the cost to the taxpayer. In addition, those remanded in custody and subsequently acquitted are not entitled to any compensation. For defendants remanded in custody throughout their proceedings, the average time spent in custody was six and a half weeks in 1992 (Home Office *Statistical Bulletin*, 32/93, December 1993).

The issues underlying the granting of bail again illustrate the conflicting models of, and pressures on, the criminal justice system. As we have seen, there is an assumption that a defendant, who has not yet been proven guilty or sentenced by the court, should have a right to bail. Placing defendants, who may yet be found not guilty, in custody involves depriving possibly innocent persons of their liberty, disrupting their lives and possibly endangering their employment opportunities. The high cost of custodial remands also causes concern. In Autumn 1991, remand and unsentenced prisoners constituted 21 per cent of the average daily prison population. The weekly cost per inmate in local prisons and remand centres, where most of those remanded in custody are held, was £437 per inmate in 1991/92 (Prison Service 1993: 80).

On the other hand, it is important from the point of view of due process, just deserts, crime control and denunciation that those who are suspected of a crime appear in court to be tried and sentenced. In 1991, 7 per cent of defendants given bail by the police failed to appear for their court hearing along with 7 per cent of those granted bail in the magistrates' court and 9 per cent of those granted bail by judges in the Crown Court (Home Office 1993a: 2). Remands in custody are also necessary from a crime control perspective as the public require protection from offenders who may commit further offences while awaiting trial.

This can be seen in the concerns voiced in 1994 about the numbers of so-called bail bandits: offenders, mainly young offenders, who continue to commit crimes while on bail. The full extent of this problem is difficult to assess. A recent Home Office study suggested that around 10 per cent of those on bail commit offences, and that as many as 16 per cent of burglaries are committed while offenders are on bail (Morgan 1992).

Evidence from local police forces suggests not only higher figures, but that the pattern of offending while on bail varies as is indicated in this summary by Nick Cohen, the Home Affairs correspondent of the *Independent*.

> The Northumbria Survey, which was monitored by the University of Newcastle, was based on an examination of 3,960 people arrested in North Tyneside in 1989. It found that 23 per cent of all arrests were of people who were on bail for other offences. Bailed defendants committed 40.1 per cent of detected crimes in the area, and about half the detected burglary and motor offences . . .
>
> A study by the Metropolitan Police earlier this year estimated that only 16 per cent of crimes were committed by defendants on bail.
>
> (*Independent*, 17 September 1991: 6)

In July 1991 the Avon and Somerset Police issued the results of a survey which found that between 24 and 39 per cent of crimes committed in the county were committed by offenders on bail (Cohen, *Independent*, 4 September 1991: 6). These figures must also be treated with caution, it may be for example that the offences of those granted bail are easier to detect as the individuals concerned are watched more closely. In addition, police figures include offences taken into consideration (TIC), whereby offenders admit to many offences at the one time to avoid separate proceedings for each (Morgan 1992). Whether or not fears of excessive numbers of offences committed by those on bail are justified, they led to the provisions in the Criminal Justice and Public Order Act 1994 to remove the right to bail for a person charged with a further indictable offence while on bail.

Remanding defendants in custody raises important issues concerning civil liberties. Around 14–15 per cent of untried prisoners are subsequently acquitted or not proceeded against, and a further third will not receive custodial sentences (Morgan and Jones 1992). In a letter to *The Times*, Stephen Shaw, Director of the Prison Reform Trust, wrote:

> Some 40 per cent of those who are remanded in custody are eventually found not guilty or are given a non-custodial sentence. Clearly there are individuals who could, and should, have been granted bail.
>
> (*The Times*, 17 September 1991)

This argument reflects a view that some defendants are being unfairly dealt with – especially those who are eventually acquitted. It could be argued that depriving a person of their liberty before trial amounts to the police or the courts pre-judging guilt. On the other hand however, as we have seen, conflicting arguments surround the granting of bail. If a person has been accused of a very serious offence, the interests of public protection require that they should be prevented from committing a further offence. If they should re-offend, the public might well query why they were released back into the community. Also, as argued above, due process is not well served if defendants abscond and do not appear to answer any charges.

The other part of the argument concerns those who, having been remanded in custody, are subsequently given non-custodial sentences. Yet the principles underlying bail or custody decisions are different from factors shaping sentencing decisions. Remand in custody is not a punishment for an offence not yet proved, it is a preventative measure; to prevent further offending, interfering with witnesses or evidence or absconding. In the case of remand, as we have seen, public protection may be a paramount interest, and full information about the risk posed to the public by a defendant may not be available. Defendants may, before sentencing, provide sufficient mitigation to limit their culpability by giving information which may not be available at the time of the decision on remand.

Time spent in prison on bail will be deducted from any eventual sentence. Furthermore, the fact that a defendant has had a 'taste of prison' may be a factor militating against a custodial sentence. This is certainly an argument much used by defence counsel. On the other hand, it would not justify the use of such a 'taste of prison' as a tactic by magistrates to deter the offender before guilt has been proven. This again illustrates how difficult it is to examine any one stage of the criminal justice process in isolation from other stages. While theoretically separate, decisions on remands in custody and sentencing are necessarily interrelated.

A further criticism of bail decisions is that there may be inconsistencies in the application of the criteria. It has been found, for example, that benches refuse bail in varying proportions (Morgan and Jones 1992). This immediately raises the issue of inconsistencies between benches and discrimination in relation to remand. It is often argued, for example, that there is a tendency to remand in custody when the defendant has no fixed abode and the criteria specifically refer to community ties. This may clearly disadvantage the homeless.

While remand prisoners enjoy certain privileges compared to sentenced prisoners, there is considerable evidence that conditions in remand prisons can be severe – thus adding to the stress and frustration of those awaiting trial and sentence (Morgan and Jones 1992). However, although remand prisons and centres are amongst the most overcrowded, they do allow more freedom and they are usually nearer the defendants' home as they are often in urban areas. This may explain the finding of a survey asking defendants why they opted for trial at a Crown Court, in which 24 per cent responded that they wished to serve part of an expected sentence on remand (see Figure 6.5). So despite the poorer conditions found in many remand wings, the extra privileges of being on remand and the proximity to where they lived were an inducement for those who expected to be found guilty. Yet again we see how decisions which are theoretically separate are interdependent and how informal considerations influence these decisions.

Whether or not it is felt that too many, or too few defendants are granted bail, it is clear that the decision whether to remand on bail or in custody is a crucial one, both for individual defendants and for the system as a whole. Accordingly a number of initiatives have been suggested to assist magistrates in their assessment of which offenders are most suitable for bail. These include the use of information schemes which aim to provide more information about defendants on their first appearance. Bail can be denied if, at an early state of the proceedings, there is insufficient information to make a decision. This may happen when the individual refuses to give a name and address, or where the court doubts the reliability of the information given. In these cases bail information experiments have proved successful in enabling the courts to make decisions based on reliable and accurate information. Bail support schemes, involving a mixture of advice, counselling and surveillance, have also been suggested to cut down the numbers remanded in custody awaiting trial.

Bail hostels, run by the probation service, are available in some areas, providing accommodation for defendants awaiting trial. This provides a fixed address suitable for those of no fixed abode or where 'home' accommodation is considered to be related to the offending. Hostels provide a measure of freedom mixed with some supervision and enable those remanded to attend work. Many have argued for the provision of more of these hostels. In 1991, for example, there were only 559 places available in such hostels in England and Wales with an additional 1,782 in joint probation and bail hostels (cited in Ashworth 1994a).

We can see from this discussion of bail that not only do the conflicting pressures on criminal justice operate on pre-trial proceedings, but also that one stage cannot be treated in isolation from others. Whether or not the accused is remanded in custody or on bail is only one of many decisions taken before trial and magistrates also deal with cases that have moved further on in the process. One crucial decision with triable either way offences is the mode of trial decision.

## MODE OF TRIAL DECISIONS

In triable either way (TEW) cases a decision has to be made about which court will hear the case, a procedure known as the mode of trial decision. In 1993/94, 78 per cent of cases sent to the Crown Court for trial were for TEW cases. Magistrates must decide if they think the case is suitable for summary trial. This involves considering its seriousness, complexity and their limited sentencing powers. If they decide that they are prepared to hear the case the defendant's views are sought. Currently, the defendant has the right to a trial before a judge and jury at the Crown Court.

A defendant may prefer to be tried at a magistrates' court if the magistrates accept jurisdiction. Although, as will be seen below, the prosecution's view on the appropriate venue of trial may influence the magistrates' decision, they have no power to insist on jury trial except when the prosecution is being carried out by the Attorney General, Solicitor General or Director of Public Prosecutions.

Before the mode of trial decision is made, defendants have the right to advance disclosure of the evidence against them. This provision, introduced by the Magistrates' Courts (Advance Information) Rules 1985, is designed to ensure that defendants can make an informed decision, not only about the mode of trial, but also about how to plead – which may in turn affect the mode of trial decision. Thus the rules provide that for any TEW offence, the prosecution must, on request, provide the accused with either a copy or a summary of the written statements and documents upon which they propose to rely. The only exception to this is where it might lead to intimidation of witnesses or interference with the course of justice. This rule only applies to TEW cases but often the Crown Prosecution Service disclose statements voluntarily in summary cases also.

Currently the defence are not obliged to disclose their case in advance, save in respect of an alibi, but the Royal Commission on Criminal Justice 1993 recommended that in certain circumstances the defence should be disclosed. Whether this recommendation becomes law remains to be seen, but if so, it will represent a significant change in procedure.

The court must be satisfied that accused persons are aware of their right to know the evidence against them before making a decision on the mode of trial. Once advance disclosure has taken place, or the defendant indicates that they do not wish to take advantage of this right, the court hears representations from both sides as to the suitable mode of trial. First, the prosecution outlines the basic allegations, particularly those relevant to the seriousness of the particular case. It is assumed for the purpose of mode of

**Fig 6.4** Mode of trial decisions

### CROWN COURT: SOURCE OF CASES

|  | *1991–2* | *%* | *1992–93* | *%* | *1993–4* | *%* |
|---|---|---|---|---|---|---|
| Magistrates' direction | 61,867 | 51.9 | 54,738 | 50.5 | 46,954 | 51.2 |
| Defendants' elections | 35,584 | 29.9 | 32,865 | 30.4 | 25,249 | 27.5 |
| Indictable only | 21,719 | 18.2 | 20,707 | 19.1 | 19,545 | 21.3 |
| TOTAL | 119,170 | | 108,310 | | 91,748 | |

(CPS (1994) *Annual Report 1993–94*. London: HMSO: 29)

trial decisions that the prosecution's allegations are correct. The prosecutor will then give a view on the appropriate venue, bearing in mind a number of criteria (see below s 19 of the Magistrates' Courts Act 1980), the major one being whether the magistrates' powers of punishment will be sufficient if the defendant is convicted. Their maximum sentence is six months in custody or a maximum fine of £5,000 for one offence, with an overall maximum of 12 months' custody for two or more TEW offences tried together.

The defence may then make representations. If a defendant elects for trial by jury no representations need be made because the ultimate decision is the defendant's. They may however wish to urge magistrates to accept jurisdiction, when the prosecution are suggesting otherwise. Figure 6.4 shows the number of TEW cases between 1991/94 where the defendants elected, and the magistrates directed, a case to go to the Crown Court.

Having heard representations, and after asking for any further information that they require, the court must decide whether the case is suitable for them to deal with. Magistrates must consider, by virtue of s 19 of the Magistrates' Courts Act 1980:

- the nature of the case
- the seriousness of the offence
- the magistrates' powers of punishment (including compensation)
- other circumstances making one venue more suitable than the other
- the representations of prosecution and defendant.

National Mode of Trial Guidelines were issued in October 1990 and amended in January 1995 to give guidance to magistrates on the mode of trial decision and to encourage them to commit fewer cases to the Crown Court for trial. These list the factors that should be considered in mode of trial decisions in general and give particular guidance in respect of the most common offences. General guidance includes the following:

- the decision should never be on grounds of convenience or expediency
- a difficult question of law or fact should be dealt with on indictment
- subject to the defendant's consent, the presumption is in favour of summary trial.

They also list specific factors that may make a case not suitable for summary trial, the overriding factor being the magistrates' powers of punishment. For example, for offences of violence that are TEW (s 20 and s 47 Offences Against the Person Act 1861), the guidance states that summary trial should take place unless one or more of the following features are present:

- use of a weapon of a kind likely to cause serious injury
- a weapon is used and serious injury is caused
- more than minor injury is caused by headbutting, kicking, or similar forms of assault
- serious violence is caused to someone working with the public, for example taxi driver, publican, police officer
- a particularly vulnerable victim, for example very young or elderly
- the offence has a clear racial motivation.

Appropriate guidelines are given for other offences. It is important to note that any previous convictions are not put before the court at this stage. If the bench decides it is not suitable for summary trial the case will go to the Crown Court for trial. The view of the accused is not then sought – as it is not relevant. As the right to jury trial is seen as a cornerstone of the criminal justice system, it is important that defendants are aware of their rights in order to make an informed choice. The mode of trial procedure is therefore mandatory, and if any part is omitted, subsequent proceedings will be void.

If the bench decides that the case is suitable for summary trial the accused will be given a choice. The clerk explains to the defendant that the magistrates are willing to hear the case. The court clerk will say to the defendant:

> You have a right to be tried at the Crown Court by a judge and jury, but should be aware that if you are found guilty or plead guilty you may be committed to the Crown Court later for sentence if, on hearing more about the facts of the case, you and your background, the magistrates feel that their own powers of punishment are inadequate.

The defendant is then asked where he or she wishes to be tried, and must indicate a choice: magistrates' court or Crown Court. If the magistrates or defendant decide on jury trial, no plea is taken. If the defendant wishes to be tried in the magistrates' court, then a plea (guilty or not guilty) will be taken to the charges. If the plea is guilty the matter can then proceed to sentence, although in some cases a pre-sentence report will be requested from the probation service. If the defendant pleads not guilty, the case will usually be adjourned for trial. If the defendant elects or the magistrates choose jury trial the case will be adjourned for proceedings to transfer the case to the Crown Court for trial which will be described below.

Defendants' choice may be influenced by a number of factors, and 70 per cent of defendants who opt for jury trial do so on the advice of their lawyer. Research carried out for the Home Office indicates some of these factors (Hedderman and Moxon 1992). Almost a third of defendants thought opting

172

**Fig 6.5** Reasons defendants and solicitors gave for preferring Crown Court trial

| Reason | Defendants % | Solicitors % |
|---|---|---|
| Better chance of acquittal | 69 | 81 |
| Magistrates on the side of the police | 62 | 70 |
| Lighter sentence | 59 | 38 |
| To get more information about the prosecution case | 48 | 45 |
| Would be sent to Crown Court for sentence | 42 | 40 |
| More likely to get bail | 36 | 11 |
| Crown court quicker | 34 | 6 |
| Delay start of trial | 28 | 19 |
| Co-defendant wanted Crown Court | 26 | 19 |
| To serve part of sentence on remand | 24 | not asked |
| Easier to get legal aid | 19 | 4 |

(Hedderman and Moxon (1992) *Magistrates' Court or Crown Court? Mode of Trial and Sentencing Decisions.* Home Office Research Study No 125. London: HMSO: 20)

for Crown Court would delay the trial, whilst just over a third thought it would be quicker. Rather unusually, 59 per cent of respondents in the survey thought that they would receive a lower sentence in the Crown Court, a perception which does not reflect the sentencing powers of the two courts. It may reflect a tendency for the Crown Court to give sentences at the lower end of their spectrum for TEW offences. And as seen above, almost a quarter of defendants were influenced by the consideration that they would, by delaying the trial, spend longer in remand prisons.

The most common reason given was the increased chance of acquittal (see Figure 6.5). It is generally believed that juries are more likely to acquit than magistrates, and there is some justification for this view as the acquittal rates in the Crown Court have been found to be higher than in magistrates' courts (Vennard 1985). It is also generally believed that magistrates' courts tend to accept police evidence more readily (Ashworth 1994a). It may be therefore that defendants are encouraged to elect jury trial whenever the case against them is not very strong. However, the study also found that 70 per cent of those defendants who elected trial at the Crown Court pleaded guilty to all charges on the day of the trial. These late plea changes involve enormous costs and inconvenience and will be discussed in Chapter 7.

The cost of a Crown Court trial far exceeds that of a summary trial. In 1988/89 for example, the average cost of a contested case in a magistrates' court was £295, compared with £3,100 at the Crown Court. It is perhaps unsurprising therefore, that on the grounds of cost effectiveness there have been successive attempts to reduce the number of TEW cases. As we have seen the national guidelines were introduced in an effort to encourage summary trial. These concerns were in part based on an increase in the proportion of TEW cases sent to Crown Court for trial. Between 1969 and 1989 this proportion rose from 11 to 22 per cent. This trend was caused both by magistrates sending more cases to Crown Court and more defendants electing to go to trial before judge and jury. In 1990, magistrates directed 64 per cent of TEW cases to the Crown Court, even though when a conviction followed, half the defendants received sentences that could have been imposed by the magistrates. Clearly many of these cases could have been dealt with by magistrates.

There is some evidence that the Mode of Trial Guidelines have had some effect. The number of cases received by the Crown Court fell during 1993/94 by 8.3 per cent compared with the previous year, while completed cases fell by 13.2 per cent, a fall which the Crown Prosecution Service attribute to closer compliance with these guidelines. In addition, the fall reflects the fact that since October 1992 defendants aged 17 years have been tried in the youth court, and no longer have the right to choose Crown Court trial (CPS 1994: 27).

The mode of trial decision was also looked at by the 1993 Royal Commission which concluded :

> We believe that the procedure for determining mode of trial should be changed in order to secure a more rational division of either way cases between the magistrates' court and the Crown Court . . . We recommend that, where the CPS and the defendant agree that the case is suitable for summary trial, it should proceed to trial in a magistrates' court without further ado. Similarly a case should go to the Crown Court for trial if both prosecution and defence agree that it should be tried on indictment. We see no reason why the courts should be concerned with mode of trial where the prosecution and defence both agree . . . Where, however, the defence do not agree with the CPS's proposal on which court should try the case, the matter should be referred to the magistrates for a decision as happens now under section 19 of the Magistrates' Courts Act.
>
> We do not think that the defendant should be able to choose their court of trial solely on the basis that they think that they will get a fairer hearing at one level than the other. Magistrates' courts conduct over 93 per cent of all criminal cases and should be trusted to try cases fairly. Aggrieved defendants have in any case a right of appeal by way of a complete rehearing of the evidence by a judge and two magistrates at the Crown Court. Nor in our view should the defendant be able to choose the mode of trial which they think will offer them a better chance of acquittal any more than they should be able to choose the judge who think will give them the most lenient sentence.
>
> (Royal Commission on Criminal Justice 1993: 87–88)

## Committal or transfer proceedings

The procedures concerned with sending a case from the magistrates' court to the Crown Court for trial have been known as committal proceedings. In

1995 they will be replaced by transfer proceedings. The Criminal Justice and Public Order Act 1994 provided for the abolition of committal proceedings following considerable debate over whether they really served the purpose that they were designed for. They were intended as a filtering procedure to ensure that cases did not go to the Crown Court when there was insufficient evidence for a defendant to stand trial. In reality, however, few cases were examined thoroughly by the court and the filtering role is now undertaken by the Crown Prosecution Service.

Committal proceedings took one of two forms. First, there was a procedure called variously new-style, short or paper committals or committal without consideration of the evidence, introduced in the Magistrates' Courts Act 1980. Secondly, old-style or full committals or committal after consideration of the evidence are properly referred to as s 6(1) committals. Old-style committals provided a mechanism for hearing the prosecution evidence, and an opportunity for the defence to challenge it.

Short or s 6(2) committals were designed to streamline the cumbersome procedures whereby all the evidence had to be orally presented to and recorded by the court even when all parties agreed that there was a case to answer. This shorter procedure involved handing in written statements and could be used when defendants were legally represented, accepted that there was sufficient evidence against them and did not want to challenge the evidence. It is important to realise that this did not mean that the evidence was accepted in any way by the defence, but merely that the defence accepted that there was sufficient evidence on which a jury might convict if convinced by the evidence. Nor was the defence prevented from challenging this evidence later.

Where the sufficiency of evidence was in doubt, or the defence wished to challenge it, or the defendant was not legally represented then a full committal took place. The court then was responsible for safeguarding defendants' interests by ensuring that they were not sent for trial on the basis of insufficient evidence.

Representations to the Royal Commission on Criminal Justice 1993 highlighted unsatisfactory aspects of both types of committals. First, the procedures instituted to protect defendants from being tried unnecessarily had failed as cases still went to the Crown Court only to be dismissed or abandoned as a result of insufficient evidence. Secondly, it was recognised that full committal proceedings caused stress for witnesses – in effect requiring them to give evidence twice. The Commission therefore recommended that both forms of committal proceedings should be abolished. It did nonetheless recognise concerns that there should be a procedure to obviate situations where the prosecution had an inadequate case and recommended that new procedures be instituted to allow such cases to be weeded out.

The Royal Commission stated:

> We accordingly recommend that, where the defendant makes a submission of no case to answer, it be considered on the papers, although the defence should be

able to advance oral argument in support of the submission and the prosecution should be able to reply. Witnesses should not be called: the right place to test their evidence is the trial itself. We do not accept that they should be required in effect to give their evidence twice over. Quite apart from the time and trouble wasted by unnecessary duplication, we agree that there is a significant risk that some of them will feel so intimidated on the first occasion that they will be unable to give their evidence at the trial satisfactorily or perhaps at all. We believe that a hearing on the papers would be sufficient to enable the court to prevent from proceeding to trial cases too weak to deserve it.

(Royal Commission on Criminal Justice 1993: 90)

## CONCLUSION

It can be seen from the above discussions that many important processes precede a full trial or hearing, and that complex issues are involved in pre-trial procedures. We have also seen the interdependency between different stages of the process. Although very different considerations and rules surround decisions to grant bail and the sentencing decision – in practice what happens at one stage affects the later stage. A remand in custody may affect the eventual sentence and become part of defendants' calculations on mode of trial or plea decisions (see Chapter 7). Thus some have expressed concern that defendants may feel pressured into pleading guilty to hasten proceedings and prevent a long remand period, and for the same reasons may choose to have their case heard in the magistrates' court. On the other hand defendants may attempt to play the system and choose to be tried in the Crown Court only to enter a plea of guilty at the beginning of the trial.

These processes show the conflict between the different goals and models of criminal justice, and further illustrate how difficult it is in practice to balance these competing pressures. The due process model stresses the rights of the defendant throughout the process. Yet the crime control model requires that those who are suspected of crime be brought to court, convicted and punished. Due process requires procedures to assure that defendants are able to take advantage of their rights. Any erosion of defendants' rights places more power in the hands of the police and professional experts and may have serious implications for underprivileged defendants. Similarly, erosions of the right to legal aid deprive some defendants of the opportunity to resist such power.

As seen above, the issues raised by bail or custodial remands are particularly difficult to resolve. It is clearly in the interests of due process that citizens are not deprived of their liberty until proven guilty. On the other hand, there is understandable concern that dangerous offenders may be allowed to return to the community and that many property offences may be committed while offenders are on bail. Crime control and prevention aims nonetheless conflict with due process. The cost of keeping offenders in

176

custody is high, and bureaucratic and financial pressures also indicate that remands in custody should be kept to a minimum and that court adjournment periods should be kept as short as possible. Many of these issues are also seen in Chapter 7, which deals with the processes by which guilt or not is established.

## Review questions

1. What are the advantages and disadvantages of having lay people make the decision on the guilt of the defendant?
2. What factors should be taken into account when a decision is made to grant a defendant bail?
3. List the three categories of criminal offences dealt with by the courts and which of them requires a mode of final decision?
4. What factors should the magistrate take into account when they make a model of final decision?

## Further reading

Ashworth A (1994) *The Criminal Process*. Oxford: Clarendon Press

Sanders A and Young R (1994) *Criminal Justice*. London: Butterworths

Sprack (1992) *Emmins on Criminal Procedure*. 5th edn. London: Blackstone Press

Zander M (1992) *The Police and Criminal Evidence Act 1984*. 3rd edn. London: Sweet & Maxwell

# CHAPTER 7

# ESTABLISHING GUILT

Role of the Trial
Participants in the Trial
Trial Procedure and Evidence
Plea and Sentence Negotiations

## INTRODUCTION

Court proceedings are the most public manifestation of the criminal justice process, the arena in which justice is very literally 'seen to be done'. This is especially true of the trial, generally assumed to be the stage in the process where the defendant has his or her day in court and the opportunity to assert innocence. The trial is a vital part of the adversarial system, and as we have seen the right to trial by one's peers, represented by the jury system, is seen as a fundamental protection for the defendant against the power of the state. In the trial the defendant is presumed innocent until proven guilty beyond reasonable doubt. Rules of evidence, which seem technical and abstract, embody the principles of due process, and are there to protect the defendant from unfair or unsuitable allegations. In addition the trial plays a key role in denunciation and just deserts – it is the arena in which society expresses its moral disapproval of wrongdoing and it is important in the interests of justice that all guilty persons are publicly tried.

As we have seen however only a minority of defendants exercise their right to a full trial, with many being diverted before prosecution and yet more pleading guilty. Indeed only a very small minority of defendants contest their guilt. Nevertheless the court system is still subject to delays and is very costly. The system operates with only a small number of defendants pleading not guilty and going to a full trial. Is there a pressure on defendants and officials in the system to speed up the process? Are defendants pressurised into pleading guilty? Are defendants aware of their rights and of the protection offered to them by rules of evidence? One commentator from the USA has argued that the pressures of crime control and cost effectiveness may lead to what is in essence a presumption of guilt, whereby defendants are processed through the system like cars on an assembly line (Blumberg 1967).

178

Although so few defendants exercise their right to a trial, it is nonetheless regarded as the epitome of the adversarial process. This chapter will begin by looking in more depth at the role and function of the trial and at its participants. In Chapter 5 we looked at the role and function of magistrates in summary trials. In this chapter we will look at barristers, judges and juries – the major participants in the trial in the Crown Court. In criminal courts in England and Wales the guilt of the defendant is in most cases determined by representatives of the public: lay magistrates or the jury. In addition we will outline the various arguments for and against the retention of the jury. We will then examine the rules of evidence and procedure which aim to ensure that defendants are dealt with fairly. As we have seen in previous chapters however, the practical impact of all rules and procedures is subject to how they are applied by court personnel and how they are affected by informal processes and working cultures. These will be explored before finally inquiring into the implications for concepts of justice of the idea of plea and sentence negotiation; another topic which clearly illustrates the problems of balancing the due process and just deserts models of criminal justice with those of bureaucratic efficiency and crime control.

## ROLE OF THE TRIAL

A Crown Court trial has some of the appearance of a theatrical performance with costumes, ceremony, dramatic setting and seating for an audience. These dramatic qualities are also evident in the cross-examination of witnesses to see who will play their part well, and the speeches of counsel to win the sympathy of the jury. They play out their roles in line with the adversarial principles of the trial. The prosecution and defence counsel present their arguments before a judge whose role is to ensure a fair trial, and the jury, who must decide on the guilt, or not, of the defendant. The real life drama of the trial lies in its public examination of and formal adjudication upon matters of human weakness and wickedness.

At a more prosaic level the trial seeks to establish the guilt, or otherwise, of the accused. Whether a trial takes place in the magistrates' court or the Crown Court, the key issues are the same and relate to the principle of the presumption of innocence and the application of the adversarial approach to justice. In a summary trial the magistrates determine the facts, including guilt or innocence, apply the law and, if appropriate, determine sentence. In a Crown Court the jury determine the facts whilst the judge alone is concerned with sentence.

At the trial stage a presumption is made that the defendant is innocent, and it is the duty of prosecution to try to establish guilt, thus the trial is based on the principle that the burden of proof is on the prosecution. The prosecution must provide evidence to establish the defendant's guilt 'beyond reasonable doubt'. If the jury or magistrates suspect a person has committed a crime, they should not convict unless convinced that the evidence clearly demonstrates guilt beyond reasonable doubt. It was seen in Chapter 1 that in an adversarial system a trial does not set out to establish the truth but whether there is sufficient evidence to establish that the accused is guilty of the offence. Hence, the trial is the quality control mechanism to try to ensure that only the demonstrably guilty are convicted and punished. Of course in the end this is a matter of human judgment and it does not guarantee that the jury or JPs will not make mistakes but the legal principle influencing the procedure of the trial is that a person is innocent unless and until proved guilty by a verdict of the court. If acquitted, does that mean the defendant is – in reality – innocent?

According to Lord Donaldson, Master of the Rolls from 1982 to 1992, this does not follow. In a letter to *The Times* he wrote:

> A 'guilty' verdict means that in the view of the jury the accused undoubtedly committed the offence. It is not only the innocent who are entitled to a 'not guilty' verdict. They are joined and, in my experience, are heavily outnumbered by the almost certainly guilty. This is as it should be because, as every law student is taught, it is far better that ten guilty men go free than that one innocent man be convicted.
>
> (*The Times*, 19 August 1994: 17)

Thus a jury might well suspect from what they have heard that the person has committed a crime but they cannot be certain beyond reasonable doubt. They must therefore find the accused not guilty. Everyone is innocent until proven guilty in legal doctrine but this does not always reflect commonsense notions of responsibility for a crime. In Scotland, besides guilty and not guilty there is a third possible verdict of 'not proven'. A 'not proven' decision by a jury does not result in any punishment and means the prosecution may not reopen the case, but it might more accurately reflect the opinion of the jury on the evidence.

Rules of procedure and evidence have developed to try to ensure that only the guilty are convicted, and they take account of and reflect our adversarial system. Some rules seek to prevent the jury being misled or unfairly prejudiced by information which is not strictly relevant to the question of whether the defendant committed the offence in question. Thus rumour or gossip about the defendant or evidence of the defendant's character is not normally allowed as evidence. Anyone who has been involved in the case or who knows witnesses or the defendant can therefore not sit on a jury. Other rules reflect our increasing understanding about human memory and observation and therefore limit or prevent the admission of certain types of evidence. In criminal cases it has for long been recognised that there is a need to limit the extent to which defendants' confessions can be used in evidence against them. Out of court confessions are in principle admissible – why would a defendant say something against his or her own interests unless it was true? Rules are necessary however to protect those who might have been induced by the police into making confessions. Section 76 of PACE provides criteria

**Fig 7.1** Crown Court cases

## CROWN COURT: NUMBER OF COMPLETED CASES

|  | 1991–92 | % | 1992–93 | % | 1993–4 | % |
|---|---|---|---|---|---|---|
| Trials* | 105,596 | 88.9 | 95,576 | 88.2 | 81,290 | 88.6 |
| Cases not proceeded with | 8,316 | 7.0 | 8,761 | 8.1 | 6,938 | 7.6 |
| Bind overs | 2,722 | 2.3 | 2,317 | 2.1 | 1,581 | 1.7 |
| Other disposals | 2,159 | 1.8 | 1,656 | 1.6 | 1,985 | 2.1 |
| TOTAL | 118,793 | | 108,310 | | 91,794 | |

\* Note:  Trials refers to the numbers designated for trial after proceedings in the magistrates' courts.

(CPS (1994) *Annual Report 1993–94*. London: HMSO: 29)

which must be met before a confession can be adduced in evidence. For example, Keith Hall was acquitted of murder after the judge ruled that a confession he made to a police officer was inadmissible according to legal rules to ensure that confessions are not obtained as a result of pressure (*The Times*, 11 March 1994).

Strict rules of procedure also determine the order the proceedings should follow and determine how and when evidence can be presented and challenged. This means that trials are formal proceedings which use legal rather than everyday language, which can often be confusing for the lay participant or observer. This however ensures that the proceedings are regulated and that only the right kind of evidence is brought to the court. It also ensures that the defence have the opportunity to challenge evidence and witnesses in a systematic way.

Figure 7.1 shows the number of cases resolved by the Crown Court. The figures for trials relate to those designated for trial, whatever the subsequent plea. As seen in Chapter 6, many defendants, having reached Crown Court, enter a plea of guilty. Cases not proceeded with account for some 7.6 per cent of the total. Cases are not proceeded with for a variety of reasons – it was seen in Chapter 5 for example that the CPS have a continuing duty to review the case. Cases not proceeded with include the following situations. A defendant may already have been dealt with by the Crown Court for other offences, or it may be found that the defendant has a serious medical condition. In other cases, witnesses may fail to attend to give evidence, or the CPS may feel that the evidence is not sufficient to proceed. In these latter cases, no evidence is offered by the CPS and the judge will order a formal verdict of not guilty. In Figure 7.1 the numbers of 'other disposals' refer to situations where defendants fail to appear for trial, have died, or have been found unfit to plead as a result of mental illness. Bind overs refer to cases where, without trial, the defendant is bound over to keep the peace. Data on the outcome of trials is shown in Figure 7.2.

181

**Fig 7.2** Crown Court: case results

|  | 1991–92 | % | 1992–93 | % | 1993–94 | % |
|---|---|---|---|---|---|---|
| Guilty pleas | 86,838 | 80.4 | 77,075 | 79.0 | 64,206 | 77.0 |
| Convictions after trial | 11,580 | 10.7 | 11,324 | 11.6 | 10,987 | 13.2 |
| Acquittals | 9,643 | 8.9 | 9,182 | 9.4 | 8,199 | 9.8 |
| TOTAL | 108,061 | | 97,581 | | 83,392 | |

(CPS (1994) *Annual Report 1993–94*. London: HMSO: 30)

## PARTICIPANTS IN THE TRIAL

### Role of the prosecutor

The prosecutor's duty is to present the evidence fairly, and to seek a conviction on the most serious offence warranted by the evidence. Their role is not to seek a conviction at all costs: they should prosecute not persecute. As seen in Chapter 5, the Code for Crown Prosecutors also indicates that the prosecution must have an eye to the public interest which includes, 'consideration of inter alia, financial matters – the cost to the public purse in prosecuting'.

Lawyers are bound by codes of conduct, which provide that they must never knowingly mislead the courts. Barristers and solicitors are deemed to be officers of the court, and must assist the court in the administration of justice. Although these general rules apply equally to the defence, the prosecution is charged, in furtherance of the concept of fairness, to disclose information that might be of assistance to the defence. This includes details of previous convictions of prosecution witnesses and unused witness statements. Judith Ward's conviction for terrorist offences was overturned by the Court of Appeal in June 1992. In this case witness statements obtained by the prosecution which undermined their case had not been made available to the defence. The Court of Appeal vehemently underlined the principle that the defence is entitled not only to information that the prosecution intend to use in the trial but also to any information collected by the police in the process of investigating a case which may assist the defence.

### Role of the defence lawyer

The role of the defence lawyer is influenced by the fact that the prosecution must prove the case, and the defence need – strictly – do nothing. The defence has no duty to disclose information on the nature of the defence, save where an alibi is relied on or expert evidence is to be called. However under new provisions introduced by the Criminal Justice and Public Order Act 1994, the court may draw inferences from the defendant's failure to disclose information about their defence.

Defence counsel must represent the defendant fearlessly, without regard to his or her own view of the case or his or her own interests. This latter point is reflected in the so-called cab-rank principle, which demands that a barrister must always represent a client when asked, provided the barrister is not otherwise engaged, practices in the relevant court and is offered a suitable fee. This means that defendants with unpopular beliefs and those accused of even the most unpleasant crimes will be represented.

The overriding duty of counsel or a solicitor is to the court. In the Crown Court both sides will normally be represented by barristers, known as counsel, as only recently have rights of audience been given in the Crown Court to certain solicitors. In the magistrates' court solicitors or barristers may appear.

## The role of the judge

The role of magistrates as triers of facts and sentencers is discussed in Chapter 6. In Crown Court procedure, the content and style of a trial are different to take account of the split in functions between those who decide on the guilt of the offender – the jury, and the person who decides on the sentence – the judge. In the Crown Court, the presence of, and separation of functions between judge and jury creates the need for special procedures and rules. Before these are considered in relation to the trial, we should put the trial process into the context of the judge's overall work, described below by the Lord Chief Justice:

What do judges do?

Many people believe that when judges sit in the morning from 10.30 to 1 pm and in the afternoon from 2 to 4.30 pm, they have a very cushy life. First of all, as any juror would confirm, sitting in court for 5 hours in the day is very exhausting in itself. It cannot be compared to attending an office or other workplace for 5 hours. Time in court requires concentrated attention on the evidence and the submissions. There is no scope for day-dreaming, telephone calls, cups of coffee, badinage with a fellow employee or even visits to the lavatory. But on top of that, what the public see of a judge's work between 10.30 and 4.30 is only the tip of the iceberg. He has to read all the papers and consult any legal authorities before coming into court. He also has to deal with paper applications, and find time to write reserved judgments. Most judges have in addition a number of extra-mural commitments, for example, Presiding Judges on the Circuits have much administrative work to do, others as members of the Parole Board, the Judicial Studies Board, Area Committees of Court Users and there are many other commitments.

(Lord Taylor 1993)

Court proceedings are the most visible part of judges' duties. In a trial the role of the judge is to direct the jury on the law, determine questions of the admissibility of evidence, determine sentence if the defendant is found guilty and generally to be 'in charge' of the proceedings. For trials to be regarded as fair it is important that judges are regarded as independent and not subservient to political or other interests. Lord Taylor also explains the importance of the independence of the judiciary.

> To maintain not only the fact of judicial independence but its appearance, judges have to be cautious in their social activities and must avoid politics. The result of all this care to guard judicial independence is that litigants can be confident the judge will try their case on its merit and as the judicial oath requires: Without fear of favour, affection or ill-will.
>
> (Lord Taylor 1993)

During the trial the judge's function is to direct the jury on the law. The jury must accept these directions, but any views the judge has or expresses on the facts can be disregarded by the jury. The judge is entitled to comment on the facts, and a very important part of the judge's role is to help the jury assess the relevance of evidence, and to marshal what is often a large body of material into some order. It is often very difficult therefore to gauge when the judge oversteps the line and begins to usurp the jury's function by determining or appearing to determine issues of fact. If, however, the judge does exceed his or her function convicted defendants may use this as a ground for appeal.

The judge's influence is paramount in a case where some evidence may be excluded as inadmissible. Where there is a legal dispute, it is a matter for the judge alone after argument from counsel to exclude evidence.

The most common formulation of the judge's general discretion is that evidence may be excluded where it is 'more prejudicial than probative'. This means that the judge may refuse to allow evidence to be put before the jury where its prejudicial effect outweighs its value as evidence. In addition to this general discretion the judge has discretion under s 78 of the Police and Criminal Evidence Act 1984 to exclude evidence whose admission would be unfair in all the circumstances, including the manner in which the evidence was obtained. This section is often relied upon or in cases involving breaches of the codes of practice under PACE (see Chapter 4).

## Juries

In the Crown Court, the body charged with determining guilt or not is the jury. Defended by some as the bastion of democracy, castigated by others as an unwieldy anachronism that allows miscarriages of justice to take place, the jury has been part of the criminal justice system in one form or another since the 12th century. Juries are currently composed of 12 men and women drawn from the register of electors for the area in which the trial is to take place. The qualification for jury service is now laid down in the Juries Act 1974. To be eligible for jury service a person must be:

- between 18 and 70
- ordinarily resident in the UK for at least five years since the age of 13

- not ineligible
- not disqualified.

Members of the judiciary and legal profession, the clergy and the mentally disordered are ineligible. Disqualified categories of persons include anyone who has received a custodial sentence of more than five years or a life sentence, those who have been sentenced to probation within the last five years, or to community service or imprisonment within the last 10 years. Added to this list of those debarred from jury service under the CJPOA 1994 are those on police or court bail. Other categories have a right to be excused jury service if they so wish, including the medical profession, armed forces, MPs and those over 65. Although all other persons called for jury service are expected to attend, and can be prosecuted for failing to do so, it is also possible to apply to be excused on grounds either that the potential juror is connected with the facts of the case or the people involved, or because jury service will cause personal hardship. Many categories, such as sole traders, or those responsible for the care of young children find even a two-week stint, the usual period, of jury service impossible. On application to the court, they are normally allowed to be excused or to defer jury service.

Each Crown Court Centre summons more jurors than they need for the start of each trial. This group of people form the jury panel, from which 12 are selected. Selection is done in the court of trial by the random selection of names. The 12 selected will then try the case unless any of them are challenged by prosecution or defence or asked to stand by for the prosecution. This may be done if a juror is known to someone involved in the case or appears unable to understand the proceedings, by virtue of mental disability or language difficulties. Jurors who may be biased can be challenged also, but as there is no normal power of jury vetting, by either side, it is unlikely that prejudices would be known. There is no power to create specifically a racial or gender balance, or indeed imbalance, on a jury, other than by the random selection process itself. There is a limited power of jury checking in cases involving national security, terrorism, or where there is reason to believe that disqualified persons are present on the panel.

Once jurors have been called and not challenged, they take the jury oath and a place in the jury box. The complete jury is then charged with returning a verdict on the charge or charges in the indictment. A jury is of course only required when the defendant pleads not guilty, so a plea is taken before the empanelling of the jury. Once the jury is sworn in the trial can begin.

In a criminal trial the function of the jury is to determine the facts of the case, including the most significant fact – whether the defendant is guilty of the charge on the basis of evidence. The jury will be told by the judge that it is their duty to seek to arrive at a unanimous verdict. Majority verdicts have been possible since 1967, but are only acceptable when the jury have been deliberating for a long period (at least two hours in straightforward cases, longer if the issues are complex) and have been directed by the judge that a majority verdict (a verdict of at least 10) is acceptable. The judge will stress however, that though prepared to accept a majority view, the jurors should still strive to achieve unanimity. When a majority verdict of guilty is accepted, the foreman is asked to announce the number comprising the majority and minority (10–2 or 11–1). When the verdict is not guilty, no information is sought about the distribution of views amongst the jury. In Scotland the jury consists of 15 people and a simple majority verdict is acceptable.

In England and Wales if at least 10 of the jury are unable to agree and there seems no prospect of agreement the judge will discharge the jury from giving a verdict. If the defendant has been convicted on other matters, the charge may be allowed to lie on the file or the prosecution may decide not to proceed. Normally, however, the defendant will be retried at a later date by a different jury. The judge may or may not be the same.

Proceedings within the jury room are entirely privileged. Jurors are forbidden to discuss the case or their deliberations with anyone else, for fear of distorting the trial process. If they do they may be charged as being in contempt of court. The Royal Commission on Criminal Justice 1993 has however recommended that the Contempt of Court Act 1981 be amended so that properly authorised research can be carried out into the way juries reach their verdicts. The secrecy of jury deliberations also has the result that alleged irregularities in the jury's discussions can not be a ground for appeal. Misconduct by the jury or a jury member outside the confines of the jury room can however be a ground for appeal. If the problem is discovered during the trial, it can be a reason for the judge to discharge the juror, or the whole jury. An example of where this might happen is when information inadvertently falls into the jury's hands about previous convictions of the defendant, where such matters were not admissible in the trial.

Figure 7.2 above shows the outcome of cases heard in the Crown Court in recent years, in terms of the number of guilty pleas, convictions after trial, and acquittals. Ninety per cent of all cases resulted in a conviction. Figure 7.3 shows, over a three-year period, the number of defendants acquitted by the jury after full trial, and the number acquitted at the direction of the judge at the end of the prosecution case because the prosecution had failed to make out a case. These judge directed acquittals accounted for 2.5 per cent of all cases resulting in a conviction or acquitted in the Crown Court in 1993–4.

**Fig 7.3** Reasons for aquittals in the Crown Court

|  | 1991–92 | % | 1992–93 | % | 1993–94 | % |
|---|---|---|---|---|---|---|
| Acquittals after trial | 7,111 | 73.7 | 6,785 | 73.9 | 6,074 | 74.1 |
| Judge directed acquittals | 2,532 | 26.3 | 2,397 | 26.1 | 2,125 | 25.9 |
| TOTAL | 9,643 |  | 9,182 |  | 8,199 |  |

(CPS (1994) *Annual Report 1993–94*. London: HMSO: 30)

Research carried out for the Royal Commission on Criminal Justice 1993 considered the reasons for ordered acquittals (before the trial begins) and directed acquittals (after the commencement of trial). Of the sample of 100 acquittals examined, 45 were found to be unavoidable – arising due to unforeseen problems. Fifty-five were probably foreseeable and at least 15 should have been foreseen before the committal stage. This means that the CPS review procedure, intended to reveal weak cases is failing to 'weed out' a sufficient number of cases (Block et al 1992).

The CPS conduct for example, in prosecuting Colin Stagg for the murder of 23-year old Rachel Nickell on Wimbledon Common in July 1992, drew adverse criticism from the trial judge (Mr Justice Ognall) in September 1994 for proceeding without sufficient 'proper' evidence. The police investigators knew a person fitting Stagg's description, and identified as him by an eye-witness in an identity parade, was on the Common at the time of the murder. Psychological profiling had further persuaded the police that they had the 'right person' so they used a female undercover officer to feign a relationship with Stagg. It was to her that Stagg claimed in a letter to have committed a murder, in response to her boast that she was a psycho-sexual murderess who could not love anyone who was not the same. The judge stopped the trial on the basis that there was insufficient evidence before the jury were asked to decide on Stagg's guilt or not.

The use of juries has been the subject of conflicting views amongst lawyers, politicians and the public at large. Some of the arguments in favour of and against juries are set out in Figure 7.4.

The arguments in favour of the jury involve fundamental principles developed over the centuries. The right to a trial by jury involves the right to be tried by one's peers. It is therefore essential to this principle that jury members be chosen from a random selection of the population. In this way lay members of the public are involved in justice. Fears of oppressive laws and governments also underlie the argument that juries can affect the law itself. In so called 'equity' verdicts juries have acquitted on the grounds that they do not think that the law is right even where the accused has quite clearly committed the act. This was apparently the situation in 1986 when Clive Ponting was prosecuted under the Official Secrets Act and acquitted by the jury despite a clear directive by the judge that he had no defence. Jurors may not wish to see the defendant receive a harsher punishment than they feel is deserved – juries during the 1950s, for example, often acquitted drivers accused of manslaughter. Because of this, a new offence of causing death by reckless or dangerous driving was introduced in 1956. On the other hand juries are costly and slow down the process of justice. In a complex society ensuring trial by a random sample of one's peers can also raise difficult issues. Should minority groups for example be able to ensure that a sample of their group is on the jury? This however would go against the principle of random selection. Another problem is that some crimes have become more complex – especially frauds, where trials are lengthy and the

**Fig 7.4** Debate on the jury

---

### REASONS FOR RETAINING THE JURY

Juries represent a cross-section of the population and the accused is tried by his or her peers.

Juries enable the public's view of the criminal justice system to be reflected.

Juries ensure that unpopular or 'unjust' laws cannot be enforced.

There is no acceptable alternative.

The jury system is the cornerstone of our criminal trial process.

### REASONS AGAINST RETAINING THE JURY

Juries are not representative of society as a whole.

Juries are not able to handle complex issues particularly in fraud trials.

Juries are subject to prejudice and irrationality.

Jurors are not treated with consideration, and are expected to perform a difficult important function in uncomfortable surroundings and without preparation.

Juries prolong the length and therefore the cost of trials.

Juries acquit the guilty.

Juries convict the innocent.

Juries are too ready to believe the prosecution evidence.

Juries are reluctant to believe the police.

---

ability of the jury to follow often complex financial evidence has been questioned. Yet frauds inevitably involve complex issues and judges themselves are not necessarily financially qualified. There is a danger that the jury has become a scapegoat for other failings in the prosecution of serious frauds (see, for example, Levi 1987).

Other arguments are extremely difficult to assess, particularly in relation to whether or not juries are likely to be swayed by eloquent arguments and produce 'perverse' verdicts. As no research on real life juries has been permitted it is difficult to produce firm evidence. The only research possible has been with either mock or shadow juries. The former consisted of a jury randomly chosen from the public who watched films of trials. Shadow juries watch the trial as a real jury and proceed to act as a jury. In general these studies found that juries did proceed in a rational manner, rarely disagreed over verdicts and that shadow juries tended to agree with the real jury (McCabe 1988). It can readily be objected that these juries were not dealing with real life cases and were knowingly participating in a research activity – both of which might affect their discussions.

Another method is to question participants in the trial about how they viewed the verdict. Here, a slightly different picture emerges. Baldwin and McConville (1979) found that out of 114 acquittals, judges expressed satisfaction in 70 and dissatisfaction in 41 cases. In many of the latter there appeared to be some reasonable explanation of the result, such as a weakness in the prosecution case. It is normally the trial judge who criticises the jury for being perverse and yet one of the main arguments for the jury is that they are there to counterbalance the judge. Thus can there ever be a perverse acquittal? Lord Devlin argued, 'perversity is just a lawyer's word for a jury which applies its own standards instead of those recommended by lawyers' (Blackstone Lecture 1978 cited in Harman and Griffith 1979).

Some have advocated the abolition of the jury; replacing the jury with lay assessors, or allowing the judge to decide not only on the law, but also on guilt and innocence. Others fear the power which would be placed in the hands of legal 'experts' were the jury to be substantially altered. The Royal Commission on Criminal Justice 1993 did not recommend the abolition of juries.

Having identified some of the participants, we will now examine the principles and procedures to be followed in the trial, which as we have seen are guided by the due process model, and affected by – or created for – the adversarial system in England and Wales.

## TRIAL PROCEDURE AND EVIDENCE

Visitors to courts are often surprised by the significance attached to, and the time taken by, matters of procedure. This may be particularly noticeable at the pre-trial stage, but may loom large also at the trial stage. Procedure can have immense significance for the outcome of a trial and, even where it does not directly affect the outcome, a knowledge of the structure and format of legal procedure is necessary to understand the context and significance of criminal proceedings. Rules of evidence, which are in part procedural and in part substantive legal rules, very often play a decisive role. The significance of procedural rules is partly practical – cases should finish within a reasonable time and impose a recognisable pattern on the trial process. Procedural rules are also affected by jurisprudential considerations, such as the need to seek justice by the even-handed application of rules. The system has its critics and currently there is much legal and public debate over whether changes in the procedure of criminal trials could remedy perceived shortcomings. The adversarial system, in which two opposing sides contest the evidence, also affects the procedure of the trial.

The main stages in procedure will be outlined below, but it is important to note that, as indicated above, there are some differences between the magistrates' court and the Crown Court. The differences in procedure between magistrates' courts and the Crown Court reflect a functional difference: while juries are not trained in any way for their role, even lay magistrates have considerable training and, of course, regular experience on the bench.

The structure of a trial in the magistrates' court highlights the adversarial nature of the trial process, with magistrates acting as independent arbiters, not investigators involved at first hand in the proceedings. Whether the offence is only triable summarily, or a decision has been made to try a triable either way offence summarily, the first stage is that the charges are read to the accused, and the defendant then pleads guilty or not guilty to each charge.

Where the defendant pleads not guilty, the prosecution outline their case and call evidence in support of it. After the prosecution evidence has been called and challenged if desired by the defence, the defence will call the evidence in support of its case. At the end the defence will make a closing speech, putting any argument on the facts and the law to the magistrates. The prosecution may reply on matters of law. When all the evidence has been heard, and all arguments made, the magistrates will reach a verdict.

Where a lay bench is sitting, they will usually retire to discuss their views. Where there is a disagreement, the majority view prevails, but normally magistrates will try to come to a unanimous decision. Whether the decision is unanimous or by a majority the verdict is announced without explanation. If the verdict is guilty the accused is said to have been convicted and will then be sentenced to some form of punishment, even if it is only a token form such as an absolute or conditional discharge. If the verdict is not guilty the accused is acquitted.

When a defendant decides to enter a plea of guilty, the prosecution outlines the facts and information is provided on the background of the offender. The defence can make a plea in mitigation and then the court proceeds to sentence, often after an adjournment in more serious cases to receive a pre-sentence report (PSR) from the probation service.

Trials in the Crown Court have a similar format to trial in the magistrates' court, but some differences reflect the presence of the jury as the fact-finding body, and of the judge as the arbiter of legal issues and procedure such as the admissibility of evidence. The most significant differences are that both prosecution and defence make closing speeches after all the evidence, and that the judge will thereafter sum up to the jury. In the summing-up the judge will direct the jury on the law and remind them of the evidence. The jury will then retire to consider their verdict and return to court to deliver it when they have agreed.

The format and structure of the trial process is affected by the rules of procedure. The content is affected by the rules of evidence, discussed below.

## Evidence

As we have seen, defendants can only be convicted on the basis of evidence. A criminal trial is founded on the presentation of admissible evidence with a view to persuading the tribunal of fact, that is the magistrates or the jury, of the soundness or otherwise of the prosecution's case. A trial determines whether or not the defendant is guilty as charged on the basis of evidence. Rules of evidence determine what must be proved, what can and cannot be used as evidence, along with who must prove the issues and to what standard. These rules will be referred to later, but it is important first to consider what is meant by the word evidence.

> Evidence is any material which tends to persuade the court of the truth or probability of some fact asserted before it.
>
> (Murphy 1992: 1)

Evidence can take many forms: oral testimony of witnesses, documentary evidence and real evidence such as exhibits of items to be displayed in court, for example, a murder weapon, fingerprints and forensic items. Rules relating to the admissibility of evidence mean that much material is not admissible.

The law of evidence is concerned with the rules governing these issues. It is a body of procedural or adjectival law, in contrast with what is termed substantive law – for example the law of crime or contract. It should not be thought that rules of evidence constitute a dry body of regulations unrelated to the social context of law – the development of evidential rules over the years has reflected social and moral concerns with the protection of the defendant, the delimitation of police powers and notions of justice as well as purely theoretical legal concepts. Fears that evidence may be unreliable or concocted have strongly influenced the development of the law of evidence – the hearsay rule in particular has developed to minimise the danger of unreliable evidence. This rule has been continuously refined especially in relation to confessions because of concerns over methods of police interrogation. In addition as mentioned above, many rules develop out of fears that the jury might be unfairly prejudiced against the defendant.

Evidence should not be confused with proof. Evidence is the means by which some fact is proved or disproved or rendered more or less likely. Neither should be confused with truth as we have already seen the court aims to establish guilt beyond reasonable doubt in the light of the evidence presented at the trial.

When considering evidence, three basic principles need to be considered: relevancy, admissibility, and weight. The relevancy of a piece of evidence is determined largely as a matter of commonsense but tempered by legal rules for the protection of defendants. Nothing can be admitted in evidence unless it is relevant to a matter before the court. But some relevant evidence may be inadmissible because of a procedural rule. Such evidence is often excluded to protect the defendant or to prevent the jury being misled. For example, previous conduct of the accused is usually deemed irrelevant to the current charge. This means that a jury or magistrates will not normally be told about any previous convictions of the defendant – at least not unless and until the defendant is found guilty.

The weight or cogency of evidence is not normally related to its admissibility, but to its reliability or credibility – how persuasive it is likely to be. A jury or magistrates, when assessing the weight to be attached to evidence of a witness in court, may, for instance, consider whether they believed the witness, whether the witness's memory was likely to be reliable, whether the witness had a reason to fabricate the evidence, or to misinterpret an incident. They are thus assessing the weight to be attached to that evidence. Similarly where two witnesses give conflicting evidence, the jury will need to assess the weight to be attached to each witness in order to determine whether they prefer one witness to the other. Oral witnesses may often give a version which contradicts documentary evidence – the jury will need to consider whether the documentary evidence is preferable to the oral evidence, which might be affected by how well the witness can remember an event which might have involved traumatic circumstances.

As we have seen, the criminal law determines that in order to prove theft, it must be established that the defendant:

> dishonestly appropriated property belonging to another with the intention of permanently depriving that other of it.

If Mrs Smith is charged with stealing a frozen chicken from a supermarket, the prosecution must prove that Mrs Smith (and not someone else) is guilty as described above. The prosecution may be able to bring evidence from a store detective that Mrs Smith was seen taking the chicken from the display and hiding it inside her coat, and leaving the supermarket without paying for it.

In the absence of a credible explanation the prosecution, if the above evidence is believed, will be able to show an appropriation of property (the chicken) belonging to the supermarket. What of dishonesty? That can be assumed or inferred from the action: who hides a frozen chicken in their coat if they are not dishonest? What of intention to permanently deprive? Again this can be inferred from the conduct.

The criminal law defines what must be proved; the law of evidence determines how that can be done, with rules concerning the admissibility of evidence and the burden and standard of proof. The defendant need do nothing, and is not compelled to give evidence or indeed to defend him or herself. The defence may simply say, in effect, to the prosecution, 'Prove it'. This reflects the principle outlined above that the burden of proof lies with the prosecution with the standard of proof being that it is proved beyond reasonable doubt. This means that the triers of fact – magistrates in the magistrates' court, the jury in the Crown Court – must be satisfied of guilt to that standard. Although the precise formulation of the standard may be varied, by for instance the use of the phrase 'satisfied so you are sure', the famous time-honoured formulation 'beyond reasonable doubt' is still that most favoured in the courts. The rules concerning the burden and standard of proof are the most significant of all rules of evidence.

These two concepts must be examined closely as they underpin any criminal trial and set the parameters for determination of guilt. The phrase 'burden of proof' indicates where the onus of proving a case lies. In a criminal case as we have seen this burden lies with the prosecution. The only exceptions are where the defendant is seeking to rely on insanity as a defence, or where statute expressly or impliedly puts the burden on the defendant. The fact that the prosecution has to prove its case – and every element of it – is reflected throughout the trial process. That the defendant is 'innocent until proven guilty' is the popular statement of the rule and the right for the defendant to remain silent during and before the trial is a natural concomitant of it.

However, certain statutes explicitly place the burden of proof on the defendant. Perhaps the clearest example of this is where someone is charged with not having a licence, for example a driving or shotgun licence. The relevant statute places the burden of proof to disprove the allegation on the defendant, who must show the court that he or she did have a licence. The rationale for this is that it is a matter specifically within the defendant's own knowledge, and also because it is much easier to prove a positive than a negative.

The CJPOA 1994 creates – in the view of some people – a significant inroad into the principle that the prosecution must always prove its case and the defendant need do nothing. When the relevant section of the Act is in force, the jury or magistrate may draw such inferences as they wish from any failure on the part of the defendant to give evidence in court or a failure to answer allegations at other stages in the proceedings. Currently, no inferences of guilt should be drawn from silence. This change has occasioned criticisms that the Act effectively erodes the 'right to silence'.

## Presentation of evidence

These are rules governing the order in which witnesses are called and evidence produced. The prosecution starts the proceedings and the defence responds, or decides not to respond to the prosecution case. After outlining the case, the prosecution calls the prosecution witnesses, in the order that enables the case to be presented most coherently. The defence are then entitled to call witnesses but need not do so. If the defendant is to give evidence they will appear before any other defence witnesses. Each witness will be asked questions initially by the counsel who has called them. They may then be cross-examined by the opposing side, to elicit inconsistencies or weaknesses, and may also be re-examined by the original questioner. Although as has been stated above, evidence can be in documentary or real form, the most common type of evidence is oral evidence given in the witness box and referred to as testimony. Most of the discussion below refers to testimony. In order to appreciate the process by which evidence is advanced, we will first examine the course of evidence and consider how the trial process takes place.

In the course of producing evidence, each side must be aware of what evidence is inadmissible. The scope of this book does not allow for a comprehensive discussion of all the principles involved, but a brief explanation of two of the most significant areas of inadmissible evidence will be provided. These are hearsay evidence and evidence relating to the bad character of the defendant. These are common kinds of contested evidence and they also arouse public confusion and criticism.

The hearsay rules come into effect when a witness states in court what someone told them. The rules are applied when a witness refers to a statement, comment or opinion made by another person. The reason for the hearsay rule is because unlike the person in the witness box, the originator of the statement is not available to be cross-examined on the accuracy of the statement. While it may be permitted to establish that this comment was made by someone else, it would be hearsay and therefore inadmissible if the purpose of repeating the statement was to seek to show that the original comment was a true statement. For example, if a witness gives evidence that they had been orally threatened by another person, they can repeat the words to show that they were said, whereas repeating the words to indicate that the threats were true would constitute hearsay. The distinction can be a fine one, as illustrated in the following recent case.

In an important case decided by the House of Lords in 1992 (*R v Kearley*) the defendant was charged with possession of certain drugs with intent to supply. Possession of the drugs was not strictly in dispute but the quantities were insufficient to suggest – without more evidence – the intent to supply. If the more serious offence was to be proved further evidence was needed. At the trial the police gave evidence that a number of people had called at the defendant's house during a police drugs investigation, and that the callers appeared to be requesting the supply of illegal drugs. The police officers gave evidence of visits and telephone calls but could not call the visitors as witnesses. The issue which eventually went to the House of Lords was whether the evidence of the police officers should have been excluded as hearsay. The majority in the House of Lords held that the evidence of the police officers had been wrongly admitted as the police officers' evidence was given in order to show, by implication, that the visitors were calling to seek drugs, and that therefore the owner of the house was in the business of supplying drugs. The evidence was thus held to be hearsay and inadmissible.

In criminal cases, hearsay evidence is usually inadmissible. An important exception relates to confession or admissions of guilt made out of court. It has long been recognised that as confessions constitute very powerful evidence against any defendant, the desire on the part of the police to obtain this evidence may result in defendants being pressured into making false confessions. There is also a growing awareness that some people do confess when they are in fact innocent. A series of measures therefore protect defendants. PACE provides that confessions will only be admissible if the prosecution can show that they were not obtained by oppression, or in consequence of anything said or done that would render a confession unreliable (s 76). The onus is on the prosecution to show that the confession was obtained properly before it can be admitted in evidence. If the way in which the confession was obtained is called into question, the prosecution must establish beyond reasonable doubt that it was not obtained in contravention of the Act. Breaches of the codes of practice under PACE are often relied on in arguments based on the potential unreliability of a confession.

In the case of *R v Paris and Abdullah* in 1992, the defendants were being interviewed by the police about the murder of a prostitute in Cardiff. One defendant denied being involved over 300 times before confessing. The Court of Appeal ruled that the confession should have been excluded because it was obtained by using oppressive methods. It also castigated both the police officers for their manner of interview and the accused's legal representative who had been present at the interviews and allowed it to continue.

The bad character of the defendant, and in particular, information relating to previous convictions, is not normally admissible as part of the prosecution case, so the jury would not know, for example, in a rape case, if the defendant has been convicted of previous rapes. This is because it is thought that knowledge of previous criminal history would unfairly prejudice the jury against the defendant. Having committed a previous offence does not necessarily mean the defendant is guilty of the present one – the law deems the previous matter irrelevant to proof of the current one.

There are exceptions, however, with regard to the admissibility of previous convictions. The first concerns what is known rather inaccurately as the 'similar fact' rule where it would fly in the face of commonsense to disregard previous matters. This could happen in cases where, for example, previous convictions are cited because they show that the same individual was responsible for a series of assaults or where previous matters show a distinctive pattern.

The difficulties inherent in this rule are demonstrated by the case of *R v Kevin Johnson* in 1994. The case turned on the identity of a masked intruder who had burgled, robbed and attempted to rape a woman. The victim and her boyfriend identified the voice of the defendant on tape as that of their attacker. The trial judge allowed evidence to be given of the defendant's two previous convictions for rape. In all the three cases reference was made to the rapist's 'gentleness' – thus the judge took the view that the previous convictions for rape could be put before the jury. The Court of Appeal held that the judge had erred in allowing the information of previous convictions to be used in evidence.

The second exception is where the defendant makes his or her own character an issue by asserting that he or she is of 'good character'. Thirdly, if a defendant attacks the character of a prosecution witness or a deceased victim, or gives evidence against a co-accused, he or she can be cross-examined about his or her own character, including previous convictions. But this third exception only arises if the defendant actually gives evidence. This exception, embodied in the Criminal Evidence Act 1898, was enacted as part of a fundamental change in the law. Until that time, defendants were not able to give evidence in their own defence as it was felt that such evidence was so obviously biased that it was of no value. When the law was changed allowing defendants to be witnesses, they were also protected by the prohibition on questions about previous convictions, as it was felt that this would be too prejudicial. In order, however, that the defendant should not shelter too easily behind this protection, a 'tit-for-tat' rule was included whereby defendants are safe unless they try to mislead the court about themselves or to malign prosecution witnesses.

The effect of hearing about the previous convictions of the defendant is well-illustrated by the case of *R v Bills* (set out in Figure 7.5) where it appears that the jury's minds were changed after hearing the defendant's previous convictions. This led to the unusual situation – and subsequent appeal – described.

## LAY PERCEPTIONS OF COURT PROCEEDINGS

It is clear from the above that the rules surrounding court proceedings, based on adversarial principles, aim to protect the innocent from unfair conviction. The due process model underpins the formulation of these rules. But what is their effect in reality? While in theory the onus of proof is on the prosecution, and defendants should be treated equally and fairly, many observers of courtroom proceedings have found that these aims are difficult to achieve. In the day-to-day operation of a court, it may be all too easy to assume that the police rarely make mistakes and that those who find themselves in the position of being accused are more than likely to be guilty. This is especially so where such large numbers actually plead guilty. Indeed to plead not guilty can be a high risk strategy as it may involve challenging the statements and credibility of victims and witnesses, in effect saying that they are either mistaken or are lying. In these circumstances, if found guilty, it makes it more difficult to provide strong mitigation at the time of sentence – after all it is difficult to say on the one hand that 'I didn't do it', and to subsequently argue that, 'I'm terribly sorry and won't ever do it again'.

The complexities of procedural rules may indeed mean that the courtroom is an alien environment to lay observers, jury members, witnesses and defendants. Court proceedings are highly structured and those most aware of the rules, the police, court personnel and lawyers are all familiar with the rules and the language in which proceedings are conducted. The defendant on the other hand may not understand these rules and needs to be guided through them by legal representatives or court personnel. Some argue that court proceedings can be likened to a game of bridge – with the experts as regular players and the defendant as the dummy player (Carlen 1976).

Defendants, for example, may simply want to tell the court their story in

196

**Fig 7.5** Jury's change of mind

# Jury changed verdict after hearing antecedents

## Regina v Bills

Before Lord Justice Russell, Mr Justice Hooper [Judgement February 17]

Although there was no fixed rule of principal or of law that once the jury had been allowed to reconsider their verdicts, it could not be considered safe for them to reconsider when they had heard evidence of the defendant's previous convictions.

The Court of Appeal, Criminal Division, so held in allowing the appeal of Adrian Mark Bills against his conviction in April 1994 at Wolverhampton Crown Court (Judge Malcolm Ward and a jury) of wounding with intent to do grievous harm, contrary to section 18 of the Offences Against the Person Act 1861, for which he was sentenced to three and a half years imprisonment.

Mr Patrick Darby, assigned by the registrar of Criminal Appeals, for the appellant; Mr Michael H.J. Grey for the Crown.

LORD JUSTICE RUSSELL, giving the judgement of the court, said that the defendant had been charged with an offence of wounding with intent to cause grievous harm, contrary to section 18 of the 1861 Act, but the jury had acquitted him of that offence and had convicted him of the lesser offence of unlawful wounding, contrary to section 20 of the 1861 Act.

After the trial judge had accepted that verdict, and while the jury remained in the jury box, prosecuting counsel dealt with the defendant's previous convictions which included other offences of violence such as assault occasioning actual bodily harm and robbery. The jury were then discharged. What happened thereafter was unique in the experience of the court.

It appeared that immediately upon leaving court a juror spoke to the court usher and told him that the jury foreman had given the wrong verdict. The judge was informed. He decided to reconvene the jury and invited them to explain themselves. They indicated that the wrong verdict had been returned. The judge clarified the three possible verdicts and the unanimous altered verdict of guilty of the more serious offence was given and recorded.

It seemed to their Lordships that the original verdict was plain and unequivocal and they were abundantly satisfied that no adequate explanation had been put forward as to the jury's change of mind. It could not be gainsaid that the jury had heard material which they had no right to hear, namely the previous convictions of the defendant.

Wherever the truth lay, that course of action had led to a verdict which was unsafe and unsatisfactory and the appropriate course would be to reinstate the jury's original verdict of guilty of the section 20 offence and to alter the sentence to one of 30 months.

Solicitors: CPS, Midlands.

(*The Times*, 1 March 1995 © Times Newspaper Limited, 1995)

commonsense language. This may not conform to the rules and order of the court proceedings. The events may be complex, and commonsense perceptions of guilt or innocence are often different from the precise legal concepts of mens rea or actus reus. In telling their story defendants may try to use inadmissible or irrelevant evidence – some may even give indications of their own bad character, by referring to previous encounters with the police or courts. In addition, only some kinds of questions are allowed and proceedings must follow the order laid down by the court. For example, at the start of the proceedings defendants are asked how they will plead. Some defendants assume that this is their chance to begin their story and they may reply to the question by saying, 'Well . . . I did it . . . but . . .' as a preamble to arguing that they didn't mean any harm, or that 'it just happened'. The defendant may then go on to challenge the word of the police or prosecution witnesses often in commonsense language and unrelated to the evidence. For example they may argue that they were 'picked on' unfairly, or that the police had 'no right' to be where they were. Very often they will be stopped from dealing with legal irrelevancies, thus disrupting the flow of their story. This is more likely to happen to defendants who attempt to conduct their own case (see, for example, Carlen 1976; Croall 1989).

Even where defendants are represented, as most are except in the most trivial cases, they may still feel left out of the proceedings. They may only see their lawyer for a few minutes before the case and fail to appreciate what the lawyer is trying to do. Many plead guilty on the advice of their lawyer – yet in commonsense terms legal representatives are expected to be on the same side as the defendant. Questions may be asked about the defendant's personal circumstances to provide mitigation, yet the defendant may fail to see their relevance. In addition, the defendant is often discussed as if he or she weren't there, and may fail to understand the meaning of the proceedings. In some cases it is apparent that the defence solicitor or counsel has not spent much time with the defendant and has to keep interrupting the flow of the proceedings to check the defendant's current address or earnings.

In September 1994 the General Council of the Bar made suggestions to change the Bar Code of Conduct to include a rule that counsel should always see their client before the day of trial in any contested matter. This suggestion no doubt surprised many who would have expected such consultations to take place in every case.

Some defendants may feel that they have not had a chance to give their side of the story. The following comments from two defendants in a study of magistrates' courts by Bottoms and McLean illustrate this:

> I felt awful; I was in a daze most of the time . . .

> The police statement of the facts . . . gave completely the wrong impression. But I wasn't given a proper chance to explain – I was so amazed at what the police said that I couldn't say anything.

(Bottoms and McClean 1978: 135)

Thus while the rules of evidence are quite clearly there to protect the defendant, they can, in some circumstances, do this at the expense of distancing the defendant from the proceedings. Some argue that this underlines the power relationships inherent in the trial – symbolically demonstrated by the spatial positions of the participants. Judges and magistrates are spatially separated from the rest of court – often on a raised platform or segregated bench – indicating their authority. The defendant on the other hand is segregated and 'in the dock'. The spatial segregation serves to underline the position of the defendant as supplicant. Indeed one sociologist has described the trial as a degradation ceremony (Garfinkel 1956).

The remorse expected by the court from those convicted, and the recital of the defendant's personal circumstances in court, can be viewed in commonsense terms as humiliating. To avoid this some defendants would prefer to admit guilt or lie about their guilt to minimise the shame of a court appearance. However, not all defendants respond to the court in the same way, and it is possible to identify a number of different typical demeanours amongst defendants: the remorseful, the inadequate, the bemused and overwhelmed, the unemotive professional criminal, the arrogant, the angry, the innocent, and the manipulative who knows 'how to play the game'.

'Playing the game' includes demonstrating expected levels of respect for the court, judged by such factors as dress, demeanour or respectful speech. This may well advantage the better-off defendant who is more likely to present him or herself as a respectful, well-dressed and responsible citizen. Wearing scruffy clothes, slouching, swaggering or chewing gum or using insolent language are all attitudes which may attract negative responses from magistrates and juries. One study, for example, found that magistrates paid considerable attention to demeanour and felt that they could judge the character of defendants (Parker et al 1989). While this may appear trivial, it underlines the fact that demeanour, speech and body language are an important part of the way in which defendants may be assessed. Demeanour can be indicative of a defendant's respect for the proceedings in particular and hence the rule of law in general. But this has implications for the impartiality of justice. Different groups in society may have different cultural standards of dress and respectful behaviour. Some defendants may be disadvantaged by different interpretations of body language and their responses to questions. What might appear to be shifty to some might in fact be a symptom of shyness or fear to others.

The subjective experiences of the trial process by defendants, victims and witnesses may be compounded by the somewhat confusing hustle and bustle in an average lower court, where those administering the system may be anxious to bring proceedings to a speedy conclusion, thus exacerbating the confusion. Victims in particular confirm the view that the experience of giving evidence and being cross-examined can be particularly confusing and upsetting (see Chapter 11). In recognition of this the victims of sexual attacks and of blackmail are protected by being granted anonymity when they give evidence. In 1984 the Criminal Law Revision Committee recommended that in rape cases the defendants should also be granted anonymity unless and until found guilty. This was not accepted. Recently calls have again been made for the introduction of such a provision after Surrey police officer Michael Seear was acquitted in February 1995 of raping a fellow officer at a New Year's Eve party.

In this chapter we have outlined the participants in the trial and the principles and procedures to be followed in the trial, consistent with the due process model of criminal justice. In the final section we will examine another issue affecting the actual outcome of this procedure in terms of the defendant's readiness to plead guilty and not exercise his or her right to trial. The realisation that the overwhelming majority of defendants plead guilty without a trial, in the context of the adversarial system where the onus is on the prosecution to prove guilt, suggests that other factors are at work influencing the guilty plea decision. The bureaucratic model of justice focuses on the need to understand the way the courts deal with such a large number of cases, approximately 100,000 a year in the Crown Court. One answer is the inducement to defendants to plead guilty in return for a more certain or more lenient outcome.

## PLEA AND SENTENCE NEGOTIATIONS

One of the most important decisions facing a defendant is whether to plead guilty or not. As we have seen, few defendants exercise their right to a trial. While it might be assumed that the vast majority of defendants are guilty, the decision to plead guilty may be affected by many considerations. In some situations, for example, defendants may feel that while they have committed the act in question, and are therefore 'technically' guilty, they did not intend the outcome – therefore there is no mens rea. Or they may know they didn't do it but feel that it is only their word against the police. They may be further persuaded that to persist in a plea of not guilty would protract the case and that if they plead guilty they will be able to have the matter dealt with immediately, thus avoiding the cost to the public purse of a trial and avoiding embarrassment to themselves, victims and witnesses. They may also be persuaded that they are likely to get a lighter sentence if they plead not guilty. The Court of Appeal has indicated that a discount of between a quarter and a third is appropriate for those who plead guilty and statutory force is given to the concept of reducing sentences for a guilty plea in the CJPOA 1994. Thus a plea of guilty may follow a process of bargaining or negotiation involving the defendant, possibly along with his or her legal representative, the prosecution, and in some cases the judge.

The term plea bargaining is used to describe negotiations that may take place between prosecution and defence before, or in the early stages of a trial. The phrase derives from the American process where it is a regular feature of trials. Albert Alschuler comments that:

> Plea bargaining appears in all common law jurisdictions. Nevertheless, the practice seems most intense in those nations whose trial procedures are most elaborate. For example, plea bargaining seems more firmly entrenched in the United States than in Canada – and more frequent and more intense in Canada

than in the United Kingdom, New Zealand and Australia. (On the European Continent, simpler trial procedures apparently have made plea bargaining unnecessary in most serious cases, although Italy has exuberantly embraced the practice and, especially in cases of white-collar crime, Germany has begun bargaining sub rosa.)

(Alschuler 1992)

An offender may agree to plead guilty to an offence because of a promise that more serious charges will be dropped, or because the sentence will be less severe. This is unlikely to occur when either the defendant is convinced of his or her innocence or the prosecutor is confident in the strength of evidence. For offenders who know the weight of evidence is against them, pleading not guilty until the last moment to take advantage of the one-third discount for guilty pleas, means that a longer period of time can be spent on remand and there is always the hope that the longer the delay witnesses might die, become ill, move abroad or that evidence might get lost. Hence, the decision on plea is linked to the decision on mode of trial.

The importance of appreciating the interdependence of different stages in the criminal justice system is highlighted in this extract from an editorial in *The Times*.

Pressure put on a defendant to plead guilty, especially if the pressure is from a judge, will almost always lead to a successful appeal. The Court of Appeal has made this clear often enough for it to be standard doctrine in every English criminal trial. This is the reason plea bargaining is not accepted practice in the English courts. In America, practice is wholly different. Such bargaining usually includes a formal offer from the judge of a reduced sentence, and sometimes a reduction in the seriousness of the charge, if the defendant pleads guilty.

English law is too fastidious about such oiling of the gears of justice. A form of plea bargaining already happens, though surreptitiously. In many a barristers' robing room before the trial, defence counsel has hinted to prosecuting counsel that an adjustment in the charge downwards, say from grievous bodily harm to actual bodily harm, might result in a change of plea, to the benefit of swift justice. This cannot be admitted; and as a result the justice is rougher and not as transparent as it ought to be.

Plea bargaining should be legitimised. With suitable safeguards it would increase rather than reduce the accuracy of the criminal justice system and make it cheaper and more efficient. The strongest argument for plea bargaining comes from regular practitioners in the criminal courts. They say that what professional criminals most want to know, before a trial, is what punishment is likely. Dreading the uncertainty of sentencing and the risk of exceptional severity, the defendant often pleads not guilty on the off-chance of an acquittal. It is not a strictly rational choice, but nor is a life of crime.

(*The Times*, 2 July 1992)

The editorial makes a clear link between the defendant's decision on plea and mode of trial. This was confirmed in the research by Hedderman and Moxon (1992) on mode of trial decisions. The Hedderman and Moxon study found that in their survey of convicted offenders, 40 per cent originally pleaded not guilty to all charges at the magistrates' court but that figure fell to 12 per cent by the time the final plea was taken. The reason given by 51 per cent of respondents for the change of plea was that they expected some charges to be dropped or reduced, resulting in a lighter sentence. A further 22 per cent claimed there was no chance of their not guilty plea succeeding.

In England and Wales there is currently no systematic plea bargaining but two separate situations may arise where negotiation takes place. The first is better described as charge bargaining, where the defence may offer a plea of guilty to one offence in exchange for a more serious charge being dropped. For example, dangerous driving gets reduced to careless driving, murder is reduced to manslaughter, rape becomes indecent assault.

It is a matter for the prosecution to decide whether to accept a plea of guilty to a lesser charge, or to some counts on the indictment and to take no action on the others. In coming to a decision, the public interest in the prosecution of offences must be weighed against the public interest in minimising expense. Account will be taken of the overall seriousness of the matters charged, the strength of the evidence and the likelihood of conviction. There is a tendency in some areas, though it is diminishing as a result of the CPS charging guidelines, to overcharge in any event. In such circumstances the negotiations do no more than restore appropriate charges. Although it is a matter for the prosecution, if the trial has already started it is normal for the prosecution counsel to explain a decision to accept certain pleas to the judge. The judge is entitled to comment and even to express disapproval of the proposed course but is not able to prevent the counsel's course of action. Naturally, however, it is rare for the judge's view to be disregarded.

The second situation is where a judge gives an indication of the likely sentence. This is better referred to as the sentence canvass. Whilst it is obviously an advantage to all parties that all are aware of the range of sentence that the judge has in mind if the defendant is convicted so that appropriate advice can be given, this too may be seen as putting pressure on the defendant. Guidelines have therefore been laid down by the Court of Appeal stressing that the judge should never indicate that a lesser sentence will be imposed if the defendant pleads guilty. It is however accepted that defendants are entitled to a discount on the length of a custodial sentence if they enter a guilty plea early in the proceedings, which can be taken as an indication of remorse: this is formalised in the CJPOA 1994.

What is not approved of is an indication that a contested trial, if lost, will result in a custodial sentence but a guilty plea will mean a non-custodial one. What the judge may say is that the sentence will be of a particular order, whatever the plea. This may therefore encourage a guilty defendant to accept guilt, knowing the likely sentence, rather than gamble on being acquitted after a contested hearing, through fear of an unknown sentence. The guidelines emphasise that although counsel must be able robustly to

**Fig 7.6** Sentence discount for guilty plea is not a right

## No discount for guilty plea Regina v R (a Juvenile)

Before Lord Lane, Lord Chief Justice, Mr Justice Kennedy and Mr Justice Jowitt

[Judgment January 14]

The granting of credit for a plea of guilty was not to be taken as an inflexible rule. Some offences were so serious that the public interest required imposition of a maximum sentence despite guilty pleas.

The Court of Appeal so stated when giving judgment dismissing an appeal by R, a juvenile aged 15, against sentences imposed at Durham Crown Court by Mr Recorder S Spencer, QC, where he had been committed for sentence to be dealt with under sections 37 and 56 of the Criminal Justice Act 1967, on pleas of guilty to two charges of taking a conveyance without authority, allowing himself to be carried in a motor vehicle knowing it had been taken without the owner's consent, reckless driving and driving uninsured.

For reckless driving he was sentenced to nine months detention in a young offender institution, ordered to run consecutive to three months detention on each of the other offences, except uninsured driving for which no separate penalty was imposed.

He was disqualified for holding a driving licence for two years.

Mr Jamie R Adam, assigned by the Registrar of Criminal Appeals, for the appellant.

MR JUSTICE JOWITT, giving the judgment of the court, said that the appellant unlocked and took a car parked at Teesside Airport and two days later took a high performance car from its garage in South Tyneside.

He was seen driving that car soon after 4 am on July 5, 1991 on a Sunderland housing estate and was pursued by a police patrol car. Then, on the appellant's part, there was driving of the most appalling recklessness.

He drove through red traffic lights at speeds in excess of 80 mph, reached speeds of 100 mph and drove the wrong way round a roundabout. When the car finally came to a halt, he ran off, pursued by police.

He was on bail when he committed his final offence of being carried in the vehicle which he knew had been taken without consent. He had a history of failing to respond to non-custodial sentences and was unable or unwilling to respond to them.

The reckless driving offence was too serious to allow of any but a custodial sentence. Had he been 21 or over, an immediate custodial sentence would have been inevitable.

Their Lordships took the view also that, having regard to the offence of reckless driving even without his history of offences, a custodial sentence was necessary to safeguard the public from serious harm by the appellant.

The only live point in the appeal was that, although the appellant pleaded guilty, he received the maximum custodial sentence: 12 months for a juvenile. It was submitted that meant he was given no credit for his pleas of guilty.

The first and foremost answer to that submission was that, although in most cases, the court would give credit for a plea of guilty, the public interest dictated that was not to be seen as an 'inflexible rule'.

There were cases in which, despite the plea of guilty, the offences were of such seriousness, the more so when it was so prevalent in a locality as the instant offence was and potentially highly dangerous to life and limb, the public interest required the imposition of the maximum sentence.

If ever there was such a case the present was it. That point alone was sufficient to dispose of the appeal which was dismissed.

(Law Report, *The Times*, 16 January 1992, Court of Appeal)

advise a client to plead guilty if all the evidence points to guilt, they should not persuade a client to plead guilty when the defendant insists on pleading not guilty.

## Court of Appeal decisions on plea negotiation

Two-thirds of appeals to the Court of Appeal (Criminal Division) are against sentence rather than against conviction. In some of these appeals the argument is based on the claim that insufficient discount was given by the sentencing judge for a plea of guilty by the defendant. Although normally a third or a quarter discount is given, the Court of Appeal in 1992 established that this was not an absolute or automatic right (*R v R* (a Juvenile) (1992)). The reasons for this are explained in the extract in Figure 7.6. In *R v McGill* (1965) the Court of Appeal said that it was wrong to add on an additional length of sentence if a defendant had contested a case, but it was correct to give credit and so reduce the sentence length when a defendant had pleaded guilty and had shown remorse.

In *R v Behman* (1967) the trial judge made a statement that the defendant's plea of not guilty had led to an increase in sentence. This was wrong. In *R v de Haan* (1968) the Court of Appeal took the view that: 'It is undoubtedly right that a confession of guilt should tell in favour of an accused person and that it is clearly in the public interest.' The appeal against sentence by de Haan led to a sentence of four and a half years being reduced to three years. The Court of Appeal held that the judge had given insufficient allowance for the plea of guilty.

The case of *R v Turner* (1970) highlighted – not for the first time – some of the dangers of advising on plea. The defendant, Turner, had reluctantly pleaded guilty to a charge of theft after strong advice from his counsel. The Court of Appeal set out four rules:

- Counsel must be completely free to give the accused the best advice, albeit in strong terms. This will often include advice that a plea of guilty, showing an element of remorse, is a mitigating factor which may well enable the court to give a lesser sentence than would otherwise be the case.
- The accused, having considered counsel's advice, must have complete freedom of choice whether to plead guilty or not guilty.
- There must be freedom of access between both counsel for the prosecution and the defence and the judge. Any discussion must be between judge and counsel for both sides. It is desirable that such discussions should be in open court, but it is sometimes necessary that they should be in the judge's room: for example, counsel may by way of mitigation wish to tell the judge that the accused had not long to live, is suffering, maybe from cancer, of which he should remain ignorant. Again counsel on both sides may wish to discuss with the judge whether it would be proper, in a particular case, for the prosecution to accept a plea to a lesser offence.

- Subject to one single exception the judge should never indicate the sentence likely to be imposed. Under the exception it is permissible for a judge, if he or she feels able to do so, to indicate that, whatever the accused's plea may be, the sentence will or will not take a particular form. A statement by the judge that, on a plea of guilty, he would impose one sentence, but that, on a conviction following a plea of not guilty, he would impose a severer sentence is one which should never be made.

In *R v Pitman* (1991) the Court of Appeal again drew attention to the difficulties of visits to the judge to discuss sentence. Such visits should only take place if there is no alternative and should be recorded by the shorthand writer.

## Advantages and disadvantages of plea bargaining

The issue of plea bargaining yet again reveals the tension between due process, just deserts and bureaucratic considerations. While undoubtedly most participants, including defendants, benefit from plea bargaining or negotiation as it saves time and money, and may reduce the eventual sentence, the system goes against the principle that people should be charged and sentenced for what they did, rather than for what they are able to negotiate. Because of the link between sentence discount and remorse the defendant has to make a difficult decision. Maintaining innocence may involve the defence in trying to discredit the veracity or character of the witnesses and the victim. Afterwards it is difficult to appear remorseful and contrite if found guilty.

With plea bargaining the state is spared the expense of a contested trial and the defendant, by accepting responsibility for a lesser charge, escapes being at risk of conviction of the greater. Plea bargaining saves police time as detectives do not have to attend the trial as witnesses. Staging a trial involves solicitors, barristers and the CPS in preparing their case in readiness for a trial. Plea bargaining also reduces the uncertainty of outcome associated with the trial process for both the defendant and prosecutor. It assures the defendant that the likely penalty is not going to be too draconian, and it ensures a conviction for the prosecutor and police.

It can mean that the victim or witnesses in a trial are spared from an embarrassing public performance and the subsequent publicity. In 1986 the Court of Appeal in *R v Billam*, commented with regard to sentencing in rape cases:

> The extra distress which giving evidence can cause to a victim means that a plea of guilty, perhaps more so than in other cases, should normally result in some reduction from what would otherwise be the appropriate sentence. The amount of such reduction will of course depend on all the circumstances, including the likelihood of a finding of not guilty had the matter been contested.

**Fig 7.7**  Judge comments on dropped charges

# Rape Decision 'Means Justice Not Done'
### By Craig Seton,

A judge said yesterday he had no confidence that justice had been done after charges of rape or attempted rape were dropped against four men who subjected two teenage girls to a sexual attack.

Mr Justice McCullough, sitting at Birmingham Crown Court, imposed a fine of £250 on Iftikhar Ahmed, aged 17, who pleaded guilty to indecent assault after a charge of rape was withdrawn. But the judge told Ahmed, of Sparkhill, Birmingham:

'Had you stood trial, as I think you should, of being an accessory to the rape of one of the girls and you had been convicted by a jury, you would have lost your liberty for a number of years'.

The court was told that two of the other three men were alleged to have confessed to rape in Cannon Hill Park, Birmingham, last year in interviews with police. The judge said the prosecution had decided to accept lesser pleas because some evidence was unsatisfactory.

'I am not saying that these men were guilty of the offences for which they were not tried, but I have no confidence that justice

has been done', he said.

Mahboo Khan, aged 18, from Balsall Heath, Birmingham, was sentenced to 27 months' youth custody after admitting attempted rape: a charge of rape and indecent assault were withdrawn. Nahim Ashad, aged 18, of Moseley, Birmingham, received 12 months' youth custody after admitting indecent assault; two charges of attempted rape were withdrawn. Razak Malik, 21, of Sparkhill, Birmingham pleaded guilty to indecent assault after an attempted rape charge was dropped. He was given a three-month jail sentence, suspended for a year.

(*The Times*, 2 February 1989 © Times Supplements Limited, 1989)

The sentencing discount, while it may be perfectly fair for sentencers to reward those who show signs of remorse by accepting their guilt, unintentionally disadvantages those who exercise their right to a trial. In addition it may run counter to the principles of just deserts – as defendants may be sentenced not for the offence they have committed, but for the offence that they have pleaded guilty to. Justice may not be done as in some cases the innocent agree to plea guilty. Also worrying to the public and victims is the number of criminals who may be convicted and sentenced for lesser crimes than they committed. This can cause outrage to the public, the victim and the investigating police who collected the evidence. This concern prompted the comments in Figure 7.7 of a trial judge on dropped charges in a rape case.

## CONCLUSION

This chapter has reviewed many aspects of the trial, looking at its participants and at the rules surrounding evidence and procedure. It is clear that while the trial is central to the due process model, many factors affect its outcome. The problems of reconciling the many goals of the criminal justice system are clearly seen in respect of plea negotiation. Few dispute that this greatly reduces the costs of the system and that in many cases it is advantageous for all concerned; indeed the consequent reduction in trials may ensure the system can function. Yet its popularity undermines many other goals of the system. It is, for example, in the interests of justice that offenders are punished for what they have done rather than what they are prepared to plead guilty to. A denunciation model would require that punishment should reflect society's disapproval of criminal acts – not reward them.

These matters are not easy to resolve, as seen in the continuing controversy over matters such as the right to silence, the admissibility of evidence and plea negotiation. In general, pressures for cost effectiveness may well conflict with those for crime control, just deserts and due process. When we add to this considerations which are more relevant to sentencing decisions, such as denunciation, rehabilitation and deterrence, the situation becomes even more complex. These sentencing decisions and policies will be the subject of Chapter 8.

## Review questions

Write short notes on the following:
1. Does the trial in England and Wales establish the innocence of the defendant?
2. How do the rules of evidence and procedure affect the trial process? Why do such rules exist?
3. What is meant by the terms 'burden' and 'standard of proof'?
4. Is there an acceptable alternative to the jury system?
5. How would the different models of criminal justice respond to the issue of plea bargaining?

## Further reading

Ashworth A (1994) *The Criminal Process*. Oxford: Clarendon Press
Murphy (1993) *A Practical Approach to Evidence*. London: Blackstone
Sanders A and Young R (1994) *Criminal Justice*. London: Butterworths

# CHAPTER 8

# SENTENCING PROCESS AND PROCEDURE

Aims of sentencing
Types of sentences
Sentencing Procedure
Factors Influencing Sentencing Decisions
Structuring Sentencing Decisions

## INTRODUCTION

Sentencing is a key function of the criminal justice process and involves many different and often conflicting considerations. The models of criminal justice explored in previous chapters indicate some of the issues to be addressed by an exploration of sentencing decisions and policy. Should sentences aim to rehabilitate the individual offender or to protect society from the risk posed by particular offenders? Should sentencing perform a broader role of expressing the community's condemnation of particular kinds of crime as the denunciation model indicates and if this is so, how fair to individual offenders might such policies be? Can or should the criminal justice process attempt to reduce crime, either by devising sentences aimed at individual offenders or at potential offenders in the general population? Can any criminal justice system reasonably aim to do all of these things or should the role of sentences be a more restricted one? As with other aspects of the process, a balance must be sought between the often conflicting pressures of different goals.

In this chapter we will focus on sentencing decisions and the mechanisms and procedures which affect the sentencing process. We start by examining the multiple aims of sentencing which affect the choice of sentence: a choice increasingly curtailed by statutory and other considerations. The Criminal Justice Act 1991 (CJA 1991) set out to impose a coherent theoretical approach to sentencing. The implications of this Act, along with other legislation are considered when we examine the types of sentence available to the

208

courts and the criteria and procedure for their imposition. The philosophical underpinnings of the CJA 1991 will be examined in Chapter 9.

We will look at the range and pattern of sentences given by the courts and the influence of statutory criteria, magistrates' guidelines and Court of Appeal decisions. The next section will examine overt and other less obvious influences on sentencing decisions, some of which have caused concern on the grounds of bias or inconsistency. Many suggestions have been made to limit inconsistencies and increasingly emphasis has been placed, especially in the magistrates' court, on a rational – perhaps rigid – approach to sentencing in order to ensure that relevant issues are considered appropriately.

## AIMS OF SENTENCING

In 1993 nearly 1.5 million offenders were sentenced by the criminal courts in England and Wales and 5.7 million fixed penalty notices were issued for motoring offences. To discover more about why all these people were sentenced in the way that they were, we need firstly to distinguish between the aims of sentencing, the justification for sentences and the distribution of sentences.

The *aim* of sentencing is the purpose or objective that the sentencer or policy maker is seeking to achieve. Does the sentence aim to rehabilitate or deter an individual offender or merely to mark the offence in some way? The *justification* for sentencing involves considering why the aims are desirable, especially where sentences aim at some beneficial consequences. The justification for sentencing policy may be that it can reduce crime, prevent private vengeance, or mark unacceptable behaviour. The *distribution* of punishment allows us to examine who is punished, and how they are – or should be – punished. Should the convicted criminal in a particular case be executed, locked away or made to pay a penalty? How long should they be locked away for? How much should they be required to pay if freed?

Usually a sentence involves some form of *punishment,* and a key feature distinguishing criminal from other branches of law is that it involves the state imposing a punishment on an offender. Such punishment however must follow a finding of guilt under the procedures of due process. This distinguishes state punishment from private vengeance. One definition of punishment in this context is provided by H L A Hart (1968).

- Punishment must involve pain or other consequences normally considered unpleasant.
- It must be for an offence against legal rules.
- It must be of an actual or supposed offender for an offence.
- It must be intentionally administered by human beings other than an offender.

209

- It must be imposed and administered by an authority constituted by a legal system against which the offence is committed.

Through punishment it is often hoped to achieve one or more sentencing aims, often described as theories of sentencing. Six main theories are found in most jurisdictions, although the balance between different theories varies according to the prevailing sentencing policy of any individual system, which may place a greater emphasis on one aim or on a particular combination. The six theories are retribution, incapacitation, rehabilitation, deterrence, denunciation and restitution.

These theories affect what the sentencer hopes to achieve by a sentence and what considerations should be taken into account. Thus if the aim is to rehabilitate, the needs of the offender must be considered; if to protect the community through incapacitating dangerous offenders, the risk of future danger must be calculated. If the aim is to deter, an evaluation of what will make an impact on those considering criminal acts in the future must be made; if to denounce, the moral expectation of the community must be signalled; if to seek retribution, the right balance must be found between the seriousness of offence and severity of sanction.

The theories can be distinguished in terms of what they wish to achieve. Three of the objectives are sometimes described as offender-instrumental in that they aim to affect the future behaviour of individual offenders. Rehabilitation aims to change future behaviour through counselling, treatment and training. Deterrence aims to make the potential offender think again through the anticipation of future sanctions. Incapacitation seeks to restrain offenders physically to make it impossible for them to re-offend. However, the impact on the offender is just one aspect of sentencing, for there is another audience: the public and its desire to see criminals punished and to be protected from physical injury and loss of personal property. This is reflected in the aims of retribution, denunciation and incapacitation. Restitution also seeks directly or indirectly to recompense the victim for the harm suffered.

Thus sentences may be individualised, that is based on a consideration of their impact on individual offenders. This means that the circumstances of the offender and the risk they pose must be taken into account. On the other hand, sentences may be based primarily on the seriousness of the offence in that they aim to reflect public disapproval or attempt to punish in proportion to the seriousness of the offence. In addition, it is often seen as desirable that sentences should be concerned with justice for, and fairness to, individual offenders, as implied by the due process model. Thus if different sentences are given for similar offences to offenders with similar circumstances and background, they could be seen as unjust or unfair. This is known as sentencing disparity, and is more likely to happen, according to Andrew Ashworth, when the sentencer can draw on any one or any combination of the six theories to justify a decision. Different sentencers may have different aims and different conceptions of distribution, producing little consistency of approach. Therefore, unless a priority is established and agreed, individualised sentences will lead to disparities. Ashworth argues that 'unless decisions of principle are taken on priorities among two or more sentencing aims, the resultant uncertainty would be a recipe for disparity.' (von Hirsch and Ashworth 1993: 258).

Turning penal aims into sentencing policy is not however easy, especially as most jurisdictions attempt to combine elements of the six theories so that sentencing policy simultaneously seeks to 'denounce the wrongful, deter the calculating, incapacitate the incorrigible, rehabilitate the wayward, recompense the victim and punish only the culpable'. (Davies, 1989: 6).

In addition, different theories may be more influential at different times and the shifting balance between them is apparent not only in England and Wales but in other jurisdictions. These shifting penal paradigms will be examined in detail in Chapter 9. It is helpful however, when exploring the influences on sentencing aims and practice, to look at policy pronouncements on these issues. In the 1990 White Paper *Crime, Justice and Protecting the Public*, which led to the CJA 1991, the following balance between objectives was articulated:

> The first objective for all sentences is the denunciation of and retribution for the crime. Depending on the offence and the offender, the sentence may also aim to achieve public protection, reparation and reform of the offender, preferably in the community. This approach points to sentencing policies which are more firmly based on the seriousness of the offence, and just deserts for the offender.
>
> (Home Office 1990a: 6)

Although regarding the two goals of denunciation and retribution as primary, the statement makes it clear that they are not the exclusive aims of sentencing and it also refers to public protection, reparation and reform of the offender (Home Office 1990a: 6). Note the absence of a reference to deterrence. Sentencing however is not just a matter of philosophical, criminological or legal principles. The CJA 1991 was passed following a period of unparalleled deliberation and planning. Yet it was subject to amendments after only six months of operation in the CJA 1993. This demonstrates that sentencing is not merely a matter of scientifically calibrating the tariff, as was attempted with unit fines, but must also inspire public confidence. The history of sentencing policy is a history of changing emphases on the six sentencing goals which we will now examine in turn.

## Retribution

As we have seen, many theories see the purpose of sentencing as to reduce crime or change offenders' behaviour or attitudes. Retributionists do not use this rationale. The purpose of retribution is to seek vengeance upon a blameworthy person because they have committed a wrongful act. While some

211

versions of retributive theory sought to justify punishment by talk of redressing the moral balance or atonement for wrongs committed, the more straightforward versions merely state that some acts are wrong and deserve to be punished, thus punishment is an end in itself.

This theory is sometimes referred to as an 'eye-for-an-eye', but if taken literally this would require the duplication of the offence as the punishment. Thus proponents of capital punishment use the phrase 'a life for a life'. However, punishment based on the literal duplication of the crime could be seen as unethical, especially where the crime was a particularly cruel murder. It is also impractical for most other crimes. For instance, what would be the eye-for-an-eye for offences such as burglary or handling stolen goods? Even more problematic would be deciding what punishment should be given to a serial killer, a rapist or a child molester. The eye-for-an-eye is more helpful as a metaphor to suggest that there should be some balance between the wrong done by the offender and the pain inflicted on that offender in the form of a punishment, popularly expressed as 'let the punishment fit the crime'.

In a retributive approach the calculation of punishment depends on two factors. First, culpability or blameworthiness. Retributionists insist that only blameworthy offenders should be punished. Therefore as seen in Chapter 5, children and the mentally ill are absolved of blame for their criminal conduct and need not be punished. We have also seen that a crucial issue in criminal liability is not only the actus reus but the mens rea. Thus before conviction for murder, the court must establish whether the defendant is blameworthy, or in a case of self-defence, acted in an acceptable way and is therefore not culpable of murder. Also, as we saw in Chapter 2, different defences and mitigating factors are used to absolve the defendant, or reduce the level of culpability.

Once culpability is established the retributionist will look at the seriousness of the offence to determine the deserved penalty. In this respect retributive theory refers to commensurate punishment, a concept not used so much today because it implies a notion of equivalence. The term proportionate sentence is preferred because this suggests that offences and penalties can be ranged from more to less severe without any suggestion that there can be an exact measurement of equivalence. Thus what is generally referred to as a tariff of penalties is notionally arranged in order of severity. There is no assumption however that they are somehow equivalent to the harm done by the offender.

## Incapacitation or public protection

We have already seen how considerations of public protection influence all stages of the criminal justice process. These underlie the aim of incapacitation, the purpose of which is to impose a physical restriction on offenders which makes it impossible or reduces the opportunities for them to re-offend. The most common way of incapacitating offenders is through long periods of imprisonment justified on the grounds that they prevent persistent or serious offenders from re-offending. Thus the Prevention of Crime Act 1908 introduced a new measure of preventive detention to deal with 'habitual criminals' who made a career from crime. Section 10 of the 1908 Act allowed an addition of five to 10 years' detention on top of the original sentence for the current offence. The term applied to those who were persistently leading a life of crime and had three convictions since the age of 16. The extended sentence which replaced preventive detention in the CJA 1967, the discretionary life sentence and the retention in the CJA 1991 of discretionary parole for offenders sentenced for over four years in custody were similarly justified in terms of public protection.

There are other ways of incapacitating offenders. Disqualification of drivers convicted of serious motoring offences aims to stop them driving and company directors convicted of serious fraud and other business offenders may also be incapacitated by disqualifications or by withdrawing licences which make it impossible for them to carry on in business. More recent 'high tech' forms of incapacitation, including electronic surveillance by the use of electronic tags and curfew orders, have an incapacitative element. Most controversial has been the use of medical means of incapacitation including the sterilisation of persistent sexual offenders. The common justification for these approaches is that they prevent a future offence from being committed and thereby protect the public.

In the USA, public protection was the justification given for the 'three strikes and you are out' policy of incapacitation of those criminals convicted of three felonies. In 1994 in some US jurisdictions legislation was introduced to make a mandatory prison term applicable after the third similar offence – whatever the mitigation.

Incapacitation and retribution are often contrasted in terms of sentencing aims and effects. Retribution relates to punishment for the wrong done, whereas incapacitation relates to the prevention of future wrong where exceeding any notion of proportionate sentencing is justified on the grounds that the offender is a continuing risk. The contrast is often articulated as 'deservedness versus dangerousness' (von Hirsch 1986), and both ideas are given as criteria for imprisonment in the CJA 1991. One of the major problems with incapacitation lies in how offenders are selected for extended periods of imprisonment or other forms of incapacitation. As this involves longer and more severe sentences than would be considered appropriate by other theories, it raises issues not only of fairness, but of how accurate predictions of the risk of further offending are likely to be.

## Rehabilitation

We have seen in previous chapters how the rehabilitative model affects not only the sentencing process but permeates the entire criminal justice process.

As a sentencing goal, rehabilitation is concerned with the future behaviour of an offender and aims to reduce the likelihood of future re-offending. Thus the use of welfare and treatment strategies targeted at individual offenders. The justification for this is that if successful, fewer people will be future victims of offences committed by these offenders.

As seen in Chapter 2, in the 1960s the emergent social sciences appeared to hold out the hope that crime could be reduced humanely. It was believed that through the application of science the causes of crime, which was seen as a kind of illness, could be diagnosed and treated. Criminals therefore were in need of treatment rather than punishment. Rehabilitative sentences therefore must consider the needs of the offender rather than issues of morality, the seriousness of the offence or criminal responsibility. Thus sentences with a rehabilitative aim may be very different from those indicated by other approaches. Rehabilitation could justify a longer sentence than the seriousness of the offence might suggest to allow for a programme of treatment to be carried out, or alternatively might suggest treatment outside institutions although this would mean less protection for the public. Rehabilitative ideals have strongly influenced penal policy in many jurisdictions and led to the development of social work and psychiatry in the penal system and of special institutions to cater for offenders considered to be in need of psychiatric help. The claims for rehabilitation are now much more modest for reasons which will be explored in Chapter 9.

Rehabilitation thus necessitates a sentencing policy that allows for the sentence to fit the individual rather than the offence. To this end, rehabilitative sentencing policies require the following:

- Monitoring and classification: pre-sentence reports are required by the courts to assess needs prior to sentencing and constant monitoring is required during a sentence to establish progress.
- Individualisation: a flexible range of sanctions and resources should be available so as to be able to respond to the individual needs of each offender in the hope of changing their future behaviour. Some offenders will need counselling with regard to drug dependency: others will need social skills training.
- Indeterminacy: if the offender has committed a sufficiently serious offence, or is deemed a danger to the public, institutional containment in prisons or hospitals might be necessary. However, rehabilitative and treatment needs mean that the length of such incarceration should be flexible, to allow for the response of the offender, now classified as an inmate, client or patient, to a treatment programme. Thus sentences may be indeterminate, where the amount of time is not fixed at the time of sentence but is dependent on the progress of treatment.

## Deterrence

The object of deterrence is to reduce the likelihood of crimes being committed in the future by the threat of punishment. It is based on the assumption that offenders, fearing punishment, will refrain from criminal behaviour. Deterrent policies may be aimed at individual offenders, thus we talk of individual deterrence, or it may aim to affect the behaviour of others who may be contemplating committing a crime, known as general deterrence. Deterrence is used in everyday life – it is, for example, the theory underpinning a threat issued to encourage people to comply with rules or refrain from infringing them, and is a principle well known to most parents: 'if you do that again I will . . . (threat), or you won't . . . (reward)'.

Deterrence, like rehabilitation and incapacitation, aims to reduce the likelihood of an offence being committed in the future. Thus they are described as 'consequentialist' theories as the focus is on the consequences of sentencing. Deterrent theory is not concerned with issues of fairness and justice but with the question of effectiveness. Does it work? This question can be looked at theoretically and empirically.

At a theoretical level the theory makes certain assumptions. It assumes that before engaging in criminal acts criminals calculate how unpleasant a sentence might be. This involves three other assumptions. First, that crimes occur as a result of individuals exercising free will and acting out of choice. Secondly, that these individuals consider the consequences of their acts. Thirdly, that the potential criminal regards the potential sentence as undesirable.

Objections might be made that many criminal acts do not match these assumptions. In particular, the most serious crimes such as homicide are not usually carried out after calculation, but result from anger, fear or a momentary loss of control. Other, and possibly most, offenders do not expect to be caught – so the likely sentence is far from their thoughts. Some serious crimes may be affected – offenders may for example think about the repercussions when deciding whether to use a weapon in a robbery. At the other end of the offending scale, in road traffic matters, deterrence has apparently had some effect. Sir Paul Condon, the Metropolitan Police Commissioner, is reported as commenting that 'fatalities on stretches of roads in West London are down by one-third since the introduction of law-enforcement cameras'. (Condon 1994).

Although as we have seen deterrence is not currently given much credence in the 1990 White Paper, Court of Appeal judges use it to justify sentencing decisions. In May 1993 the Court of Appeal reduced a 12 months' custodial sentence for Nicholas Decino to 10 months. Mr Decino had a 10 months' suspended sentence for burglary and possession of drugs activated after he was convicted of theft from a telephone kiosk. The Court of Appeal thought this was so serious as to justify a prison term but made it run concurrently so that the total term would be 10, not 12 months. Lord Justice Beldam explained the sentence of the court:

. . . this was the kind of offence which was capable of depriving members of the public of the use of the public telephone which, to many people, was a lifeline. Of necessity telephone boxes were left unprotected. It was a matter of public policy to deter thefts from such boxes.

(Law Report, *The Times*, 10 May 1993)

## Denunciation

The denunciation model stresses the role of the criminal justice system in publicly expressing society's condemnation. Thus sentences can be used to underline the community's outrage at the particular offence and crime in general. Denunciation is concerned with the impact of the sentence on the community and how this in turn affects the demarcation of the moral boundaries of society. Thus by identifying what behaviour is unacceptable, societies define themselves.

Under denunciation theory, sentencing is an act of official disapproval and social censure. It shares with retribution a focus on the morality of the act, but unlike retribution it looks beyond what should happen to the offender and examines the impact of a sentence on the community. It thus brings to centre stage issues of morality and how community perceptions of crime and punishment may conflict with those of the state and the law.

> The impact of punishment is not a private matter between offender and victim, for it also involves the community's expectations about appropriate standards of behaviour . . . The criminal provides us with a living example of our moral boundaries: by our outrage we come to recognise our shared fears, rules of communal living and mutual interdependency. We collectively define what sort of people we are by denouncing the type of people we are not.
>
> (Davies 1993: 15)

Thus one of the key functions of sentencing is to portray, however impressionistically, the public's mood about unacceptable behaviour, and to represent a collective expression of right and wrong in response to offensive behaviour. Judges, in passing sentence, sketch the official portrait of public morality but the community's response to sentencing decisions provides the fine detail. Sentencing decisions are on some occasions unpopular and judicial pronouncements are criticised as too avant garde or too dated.

This can be seen in cases where sentencing decisions have become the focus of public debate about the society we live in as they draw attention to the offence committed and the response. Of course, not all sentencing decisions evoke a moral debate; many, if not most, go unnoticed. However, occasionally sentences receive considerable publicity and criticisms of their appropriateness. In more routine cases the audience for the moral drama may only be the jury, victim and witnesses or their neighbours, friends and relatives. The message they receive may be distorted by their limited understanding of criminal procedure and law. But they will form an impression of the state of public morality, which while affecting only them directly, will influence their perception of the type of community they live in.

Everyday morality is constructed, in part, in this way. In a more individualistic and pluralistic society, the attempt to express the community's view becomes more difficult but even more important as an effort to identify commonly-held expectations about how we should behave towards each other. If unacceptable behaviour is not acknowledged and assumed morality is not reinforced by the courts, it might be concluded that there is no shared definition of unacceptable behaviour. This could enhance individualistic responses to crime and break down collective expectations, thus creating unpredictability and uncertainty and undermining the basis of citizenship. It is also likely to encourage people to take action themselves against crime by, for example, acts of vigilantism. This latter point has led to recent suggestions that there is possibly a further aim of sentencing – to maintain law and order and prevent such private responses to crime. We will look at vigilante response to crime in Chapter 11.

## Restitution or reparation

Increasing concern with the interests of victims has led to a growth of interest in reparation and restitution which aim to compensate the victim of crime, either specifically or symbolically, usually through a financial payment or services provided. Thus an offender can be ordered to make financial compensation to individual victims, or to symbolically pay back society or the state for the harm done. Experimental reparation schemes have involved bringing offenders and victims together to attempt not only reparation, but also conciliation. Outside the sentencing sphere, the Criminal Injuries Compensation Scheme provides a government fund whereby the state rather than the offender compensates the victim for harm done by violent crime. This however may be more akin to a state based insurance scheme: it is not a sentence, though it seeks to make reparation. These measures will be further explored in Chapter 11.

The potential effect of reparation is greatest perhaps with property crime and in circumstances where victims are willing to participate and offenders can make some kind of meaningful reparation. Their application is less appropriate in cases of serious violent crime, where it is unlikely that the offender can make any meaningful reparation. A symbolic form of reparation underlies other sentencing options, thus it can be argued that there is a notion of reparation in community service orders, in that the offender is in some way giving something back to the community.

Having looked at the theories underlying sentencing, we will now outline the main sentences available to the courts and, in general terms, ask which of the sentencing aims may be fulfilled by them.

# TYPES OF SENTENCES

Four main categories of sentence: discharges, financial penalties, community sentences and custodial sentences are available to the courts. All are available to both magistrates' courts and the Crown Court but the magistrates' court has an upper limit for financial and custodial sentences. In addition the court may bind over a defendant, defer sentence or impose a range of ancillary orders.

## Discharges

There are two main forms of discharge. An absolute discharge in effect means that although the conviction is recorded, nothing will happen to the offender. A conditional discharge means that if for the duration of the order, a specified period of up to three years, the offender is not found guilty of any other offence, they will receive no punishment. If, however, during the period of the discharge, they are sentenced by a court for another offence, they may be sentenced not only for the new matter, but also for the offence for which they were originally discharged. Under the Powers of the Criminal Courts Act 1973 a court may impose a conditional or absolute discharge where it is of the opinion it is 'inexpedient to inflict punishment'.

A discharge is thus a sentence that does not seek to punish. The main sentencing aim that would appear relevant therefore is denunciation – merely acknowledging that an offence has been committed – but in the circumstances it is accepted that is unnecessary to punish. The conditional discharge also has a deterrent purpose: 'Do this again and you will be punished.'

## Financial penalties

A fine is the most common penalty, and is the most likely result for summary offences and many triable either way (TEW) offences heard in the magistrates' court. Where a case is sentenced in the magistrates' court the maximum fine is governed by the statutory maximum for that offence, described as levels one (maximum £200) to five (maximum £5,000). Most TEW offences are governed by the overall magistrates' court maximum, currently £5,000 for adult offenders. In the Crown Court fines are 'at large', which means there are no limits. Fines must be assessed in relation to the seriousness of the offence, and it has long been a principle of sentencing that the level of fine imposed on an individual should take into account the offender's means – a calculation of a defendant's disposable income, involving a calculation based on regular income and necessary expenditure.

Compensation must be considered by a court when dealing with a case that has resulted in personal injury, or property damage. It can be ordered instead of, or in addition to, another order (Powers of the Criminal Courts

Act 1973 as amended). If the court fails to order compensation in such circumstances, it must state its reasons. If a compensation order is made, it means that the offender should pay a stated amount to the person harmed by the offence. A compensation order is the prime reparative disposal.

Costs are also frequently ordered against offenders and may represent a substantial part of the financial effect of a court order. Costs may be awarded against any convicted offender, but rank after compensation and fines in order of payment: if the offender's means are insufficient to meet all three, compensation to the victim takes priority.

## Community penalties

The following are community sentences: probation order, community service order, combination order, curfew order, supervision order, or attendance centre order. The combination and curfew orders were introduced by the CJA 1991.

The criteria for the imposition of a community sentence were laid down by the CJA 1991, later, as we have seen, amended by the CJA 1993. Consequently a community sentence can only be imposed if the offence or offences are serious enough to warrant its imposition, if the combination of orders is suitable for the offender, and the restriction on liberty of the offender is commensurate with the seriousness of offending. In most cases the offender must also consent to an order. A pre-sentence report must be obtained before assessing whether or not the offender is suitable for an order when any of the following are being considered: combination order, community service order or a probation or supervision order with additional requirements. The 1991 Act also contains a requirement that the reasons for giving such an order, and the precise effect of it should be explained in ordinary language.

In addition to the general criteria laid down by the CJA 1991, individual sentences are considered appropriate in different situations. A probation order is available for an offender of 16 or over where the court feels such an order is desirable to rehabilitate the offender, to protect the public or prevent offences. Thus the specific aims that the court is seeking are clearly stated. Orders must be for a specified period, from six months to three years, and can be combined with a financial or other community order except a community service order. Under the Act, a probation order with additional requirements may be made such as an order of residence, an order to engage in certain activities such as attendance at anger management or impaired driver groups or desist from others, or to attend a probation centre. Extra requirements may be imposed for sex offenders or those in need of treatment for alcohol or drug abuse or mental illness. Probation orders are still seen as primarily rehabilitative, although the 1991 Act sought to redefine all community sentences as punitive. The implications of this will be discussed in Chapter 11.

A community service order (CSO) requires the offender to do unpaid work for the community for a specified number of hours, ranging from a minimum of 40 hours to a maximum of 240, over a period of a year. It is available for offenders aged 16 and over convicted of any imprisonable offence. The offender must consent to an order and the court must be satisfied that they are suitable. The court may hear from a probation officer as to the offender's suitability and must be satisfied that work is available. A CSO satisfies simultaneously many penal objectives. It includes a symbolic element of reparation, if not to the individual victim, then at least to the community. It also involves denunciation particularly if the imposition of the sentence is followed by a visible performance of the work, and the restriction on liberty is intended to have a punitive impact so as to deter and punish offenders. Others point to the rehabilitative effect of doing valuable work for the community.

A combination order is a new disposal introduced by the CJA 1991, available for offenders who are 16 or over, where the offence is imprisonable and the court feels that such an order is in the interests of rehabilitation or of protecting the public or preventing offences. A combination order combines probation of 12 months to three years with community service of 40–100 hours.

The courts approach to a breach of the terms of any community order or of the commission of further offences during the period of an order was rationalised by the CJA 1993. For failure to comply with the terms of an order the offender can be ordered to pay up to £1,000 fine or to perform up to 60 hours of a CSO. If the offender already has a CSO, the total hours must not exceed the maximum applicable. The court may revoke the community sentence and impose a different penalty for the original offence. For offenders under 21, an attendance centre order may be made. If the offender wilfully and persistently refuses to comply with the order, this may be taken as refusing consent to it and the court can impose a custodial sentence. For the commission of a further offence the order can be revoked and the offender dealt with in some other way. The order can also be revoked and dealt with in some other way for good progress.

Sentencers also have various ancillary orders available, including orders allowing the confiscation of the proceeds of crime, the forfeit of money or property associated with offences and the destruction of items such as weapons or drugs. Other penalties relating specifically to motoring offences are worthy of note: the imposition of penalty points and disqualification from driving. Advertising campaigns, particularly over the Christmas period focus on the potential harm caused by driving with excess alcohol, to enhance the denunciatory effect and stress the impact of the penalty, ie disqualification from driving, highlighting the deterrent element of the sentence.

## Custodial sentences

As a result of successive legislative efforts to reduce the numbers of offenders receiving prison sentences, a prison sentence (which includes the suspended sentence) may only be passed where one of the following criteria is satisfied:

- The offence is so serious that only a custodial sentence is justified.
- The offence is one of sex or violence and only a custodial sentence is sufficient to protect the public.
- The offender has failed to consent to a community sentence, where consent is required.

A custodial sentence of up to two years may be suspended for between one and two years, but only if there are exceptional grounds to do so. Commonplace grounds such as the youth of the offender will not justify suspension of the sentence. Suspended sentences are in any event not available for offenders who will serve their sentences in a young offender institution.

A life sentence is the most severe penalty available. It is a mandatory sentence for those found guilty of murder, and thus the judge has no choice. It is also a discretionary maximum sentence for those convicted of serious indictable crimes such as manslaughter, arson, rape, robbery, aggravated burglary, causing grievous bodily harm, wounding with intent, supplying class A drugs and kidnapping. Under the Firearms Act 1968 crimes of assault, theft, arson and resisting arrest carry a maximum sentence of a life sentence if the offender is carrying a gun.

Custodial sentences can be justified by most of the major theories of sentencing. A prison sentence can be seen as a deterrent and it is still commonplace to argue that prisons should be austere places which should not provide comforts not generally unavailable outside. The forbidding nature of prisons also underlines society's disapproval of inmates. The essential punishment involved in imprisonment is the deprivation of a person's liberty, and thus a prison sentence can be retributive, with the length of a sentence being determined by the seriousness of the offence. Prisons also take offenders out of society and thus protect the public and as we have seen, they are the main form of incapacitative sentence. And as will be seen in Chapters 9 and 10, a major influence on penal policy and on the development of prison regimes throughout the 20th century has been the belief that offenders can be rehabilitated while in prison.

## Distribution of sentences

Of 1,427,000 offenders sentenced in 1993, 307,000 were sentenced for indictable crimes. The type of sentence they received is indicated in Figure 8.1.

In order to interpret these figures we need to explore some of the factors

**Fig 8.1** Offenders sentenced for indictable offences by type of court and sentence, 1991

| Type of sentence | Magistrates' Court % | Crown Court % |
| --- | --- | --- |
| Discharge | 25.8 | 6.2 |
| Fine | 41.4 | 5.4 |
| Community based | 24.1 | 34.2 |
| Suspended sentence | 0.4 | 2.8 |
| Immediate custody | 5.8 | 49.1 |
| Other | 2.5 | 2.3 |

(Home Office *Statistical Bulletin*, Issue 19/94, 20 July 1994, Table 7.1)

which affect these numbers and what if any trends can be discerned. As we shall see, sentencing policy has developed in response to a number of perceived problems and the CJA of 1991 and 1993 sought in various ways to affect the pattern of sentences. In part this was a response to concern over the wide disparities in sentencing produced by the individualisation of sentencing and inconsistencies between sentencers in how they interpreted the different aims of sentencing. Thus an influential study of 30 randomly selected magistrates' courts, published in 1979, revealed that the use of custody varied from 5 per cent to 23 per cent and the use of fines from 46 to 76 per cent. These differences could not be explained by significant differences in either the kinds of offences dealt with or the background of offenders (Tarling and Weatheritt 1979). In Crown Courts the use of custody also varies across the country for offenders of all ages. Thus in 1991, 47.7 per cent of young adults in East Anglia were given custodial sentences compared with 30.9 per cent in the South West. The highest rate for the use of custody for adult offenders convicted of indictable offences was 52.5 per cent in East Anglia, compared with the lowest rate of 40 per cent in Yorkshire and Humberside (Home Office 1993: 51). Many of the procedures and limitations on sentencing discretion to be examined next are a response to the concern caused by these kinds of figures.

## Impact of the Criminal Justice Acts 1991 and 1993

As we have seen, there have been dramatic shifts in sentencing policy in the early 1990s, which have strongly affected the use of different kinds of sentences. Thus the sentencing reforms of the 1991 Act came into force on 1 October 1992, including the statutory restraints on the use of custody, constraints on the sentencing of offenders convicted of multiple offences and the s 29 provision instructing sentencers to ignore previous convictions and sentences, except in narrowly defined circumstances, and the new and supposedly more demanding community penalties such as the combination order.

In the first four months until January 1993 the prison population fell, the proportionate use of fines for indictable cases sentenced in magistrates' courts rose and the proportionate use of those given a sentence of immediate custody for indictable offences fell. This is shown below:

Prison population 30 September 1992     45,835
Prison population 31 January 1993      41,561

Percentage use of fines for indictable offences all courts.

January to September 1992               42%
October to December 1992                45%

Percentage use of custody for all ages sentenced for indictable offences

January to September 1992               15.7%
October to December 1992                11.6%

(Cavadino 1994: 5)

Thus the immediate impact of the CJA 1991 seems to have been a drop in the numbers and proportions of offenders sentenced to imprisonment and a consequent increase in other sentences. As we have seen changes to the 1991 provisions were made by the CJA 1993. Even before the CJA 1993 was implemented, a shift of mood among judges, magistrates and the government was apparent. This was reflected in the increasing use of custody and the subsequent rise in the prison population, commencing during February 1993, as shown below:

Prison population 31 January 1993       41,561
Prison population 28 February 1993      42,882
Prison population 31 March 1993         43,195
Prison population 30 April 1993         43,391
Prison population 31 May 1993           43,585

By 30 September 1993 – only one year after the CJA 1991, an Act that sought to reduce the prison population – the prison population stood at 46,211, compared to the figure of 45,835 a year earlier. A more dramatic contrast is apparent if we compare the figures after the first three months of operation of the Act when the population stood at 40,606 on New Year's Eve, 1992 rising to 45,214 exactly one year later. Since 1993, the prison population has risen steadily and in October 1994 reached 50,000 (Prison Service Press Statement, 14 October 1994).

According to Home Office research based on a sample of courts, this rise was most apparent among offenders found guilty of property offences and those with high numbers of previous convictions (Home Office *Statistical Bulletin*, Issue 20/94, 20 July 1994). This research also shows changes in the proportionate use of other sentences. Thus the use of fines by magistrates' courts rose following the CJA 1991, but fell in the last three months of 1993. The use of community sentences also rose following the 1991 Act, particularly in the Crown Court but fell again in the latter part of 1993. Before we examine the influences on the types of sentences imposed by the courts we will outline sentencing procedure.

# SENTENCING PROCEDURE

Between the determination of guilt and decision on sentence there are various stages to go through, including a hearing of the mitigation the defendant may wish to offer in an attempt to reduce the severity of the sentence. Only in the most serious and the most trivial of cases will sentencing be carried out immediately after the decision on guilt. There is as we have seen a mandatory life sentence in cases of murder, and for many petty offences a discharge or small fine is likely and can be imposed immediately.

If the sentence follows a trial, the facts will have been presented. If there has been a guilty plea, the facts must be presented to the court by the prosecution. Occasionally there may be a dispute over the facts which affect the plea; for example the defendant may admit to an assault with fists, but deny kicking the victim. If the dispute is likely to affect the sentence, the sentencer must either sentence on the basis of the facts most favourable to the defence, or there must be what is called a 'Newton' hearing. This is like a mini-trial, where evidence is taken, but only on the specific issue involved.

The defendant may ask for offences to be taken into consideration (TICs). This means that the court takes them into consideration when sentencing, though there has been no formal conviction. This procedure is often used where a number of related offences have been committed, but the police may have been unable to prosecute them successfully, for example, where the defendant has confessed to a number of thefts from cars, or several cheque frauds. They may also form part of the plea negotiations discussed in Chapter 7.

The court will then be informed about the defendant's previous convictions, if any, and about any breaches of existing orders. As we have seen, one of the most controversial sections of the CJA 1991 was the restriction in s 29 on the extent to which the court could take account of previous convictions. Critics of this provision argued that it prevented the court from treating a repeated offender any more severely than a first offender. It was repealed by the CJA 1993 and courts may now again take into account previous offending and responses to previous sentences, which could have affected the rates of custodial and other sentences outlined above.

The defendant, personally or through an advocate, may then put forward any mitigation in respect of the offence or their own circumstances. This is known as making a plea in mitigation, and is the opportunity for the defence to put the offending behaviour into the best possible light in order to gain the lightest sentence. This is the point at which financial information may be also given to the court. Financial details are relevant not only to show why a defendant may have committed an offence, but also because the court must take the means of the offender into account when imposing a financial penalty. Apart from specific matters, such as the fact that the defendant only took a small part in the offence, mitigating factors include the fact that the defendant pleaded guilty, especially if the guilty plea was entered early, and that they were of previous good character, that is have no previous convictions. Defence counsel may argue, for example, that in some way the offender was pressured into committing the offence by financial or family problems. They may argue that while they have admitted the offence and can offer no defence that nonetheless they did not intend the harm done and that the offence occurred almost by accident, with no planning or forethought. This is especially the case where the offence is one of strict liability which does not require intent, or where the offence has involved an omission to do something. Thus defendants may claim that they simply forgot to renew a licence, but had always intended to do it or that they forgot to tell the Inland Revenue about their earnings from a part-time job. Others may claim that they didn't anticipate driving home after going to the pub. As seen in Chapter 2, these mitigating factors attempt to reduce the culpability of the offender and thus seek to influence the eventual sentence.

Before proceeding to sentence the court may require further information about the offender's circumstances, including their physical or mental health. In many cases before the Crown Courts and in the more serious cases in magistrates' courts a pre-sentence report is required. For adults, this is provided by the probation service and its preparation typically involves an adjournment of three weeks. The report contains information considered relevant by the probation officer and may cover such matters as home life, medical, psychiatric details, criminal background and schooling or employment. In addition it may consider the possible sentences and the likely impact of such sentences on the offender. Thus before sentencing the judge or magistrates will hear from the convicted person's defence counsel to remind the court of any mitigating circumstance and will also consider the pre-sentence report. This double exposure of mitigation before sentence has led to the criticism that it focuses too heavily on the circumstances, background and personality of the convicted person and insufficiently on the offence. The introduction at this stage of a victim impact statement has been suggested to provide a more balanced hearing for the purpose of sentence.

## FACTORS INFLUENCING SENTENCING DECISIONS

Many factors influence sentencers' decisions. In respect of a particular case, the judge or magistrate must consider how serious the particular offence is in relation to other similar offences and assess whether or not the offence had any particular mitigating or aggravating factors. For example, if the offence has involved harm to a particularly vulnerable group such as the elderly this would be an aggravating factor, whereas absence of direct physical harm to a victim is more likely to be seen as a mitigating factor. And as seen above, the defendant may provide information about mitigating factors. Sentencers are also likely to take into account the previous convictions and record of an offender, any recommendations in the pre-sentence report and plea negotiations are obviously directed towards reducing the sentence.

Sentencing is not done in a legislative or policy vacuum. First, there are the statutory requirements. We have a mandatory life sentence in the case of murder. All offences have statutory maximum sentences such as 14 years for burglary of a domestic dwelling, even though this maximum is rarely, if ever, used. It provides an indication however of Parliament's view of the seriousness of the offence and so helps to set the sentencing tariff. There are a few minimum sentences such as the two-year disqualification for those convicted of causing death by dangerous driving under the Road Traffic Act 1988. Offenders convicted of excess alcohol while driving receive a minimum period of 12 months' disqualification.

Statutes can prohibit some sentences so that children under 14 years must not be sent to prison. They can also limit sentencing powers by providing statutory criteria for the use of certain powers such as custody. The three statutory criteria for the use of imprisonment are set out in the CJA 1991 with respect to adults and described earlier in this chapter. The sentencing powers of magistrates are further curtailed by legislation which limits their ability to send a person to prison and imposes maxima on the fines they can give.

Other jurisdictions use legislation to indicate more precisely the power of sentences. In California the 1976 Uniform Determinate Sentencing Act specified the prison terms that a judge could give with respect to each criminal offence. Thus at that time, although subsequently amended upwards, the sentence for rape would be three, four or five years. The judge would choose which of these three terms to give depending on the aggravating and mitigating factors of the case. The middle term would be used in typical cases. Thus a system of presumptive, or expected, sentences was established and these sentences were determinate, that is fixed in length by statute.

In the magistrates' courts, sentencing decisions have increasingly been influenced by guidelines issued by the Magistrates' Association, an example of which is illustrated in Figure 8.2. These were originally issued in the 1970s in respect of motoring offences in an effort to curb complaints of inconsistency between benches. These had some success, especially for offences which could be easily compared – thus a speeding offence on the M1 is very similar to a speeding offence on the M25. Their use, after consultation with the Justices Clerks' Association and the Lord Chancellor's Department, was extended in 1989 to most offences dealt with in the magistrates' courts. More guidelines were issued to clarify the implementation of the CJA 1991 and reflected not only the framework of that Act but also the move towards more structured decision making discussed in the next section of this chapter. The guidelines were reissued in 1993 to reflect the changes in the CJA 1993 and in particular the abolition of unit fines.

As can be seen, the guidelines currently provide an 'entry point', that is the most likely sentence, for the most common offences in magistrates'

226

**Fig 8.2** Magistrates' Association Sentencing Guidelines, September 1993

| Burglary (Dwelling) | Theft Act 1968 s 9<br>Triable either way - see Mode of Trial Guidelines<br>Penalty: Level 5 and/or 6 months |
|---|---|

| ENTRY POINT  | CUSTODY |
|---|---|

 **CONSIDER THE SERIOUSNESS OF THE OFFENCE**

eg.
- Offence committed on bail
- Deliberately frightening occupants
- Group offence
- Night time
- Professional operation
- Soiling, ransacking, damage
- Previous convictions and failures to respond to previous sentences, if relevant

eg.
- Day time
- Low value
- No damage or disturbance
- No forcible entry

*IS IT SO SERIOUS THAT ONLY CUSTODY IS APPROPRIATE?*
*IS IT SERIOUS ENOUGH FOR A COMMUNITY PENALTY?*
*IS COMPENSATION, DISCHARGE OR FINE APPROPRIATE?*

**CONSIDER OFFENDER MITIGATION**

eg.
- Guilty plea: *for a timely guilty plea allow a discount of about a third*
- Age, health (physical or mental)
- Co-operation with the police
- Voluntary compensation
- Remorse

**DECIDE YOUR SENTENCE**

Compare your decision with the entry point - **CUSTODY** - and check your reasons if you have reached a different sentence

*NB. COMPENSATION - Give reasons if not awarding compensation*
*NB. FINES - If imposing a fine, remember to increase or decrease the amount according to the financial circumstances of the offender*

227

**Fig 8.2** Magistrates' Association Sentencing Guidelines, September 1993 (cont'd)

| Assault — Actual Bodily Harm | Offences Against the Person Act 1861 s 47<br>Triable either way - see Mode of Trial Guidelines<br>Penalty: Level 5 and/or 6 months |
|---|---|

| ENTRY POINT  | COMMUNITY PENALTY |
|---|---|

 **CONSIDER THE SERIOUSNESS OF THE OFFENCE**

eg.
- Offence committed on bail
- Deliberate kicking
- Extensive injuries
- Group action
- Offender in position of authority
- Premeditated
- Victim particularly vulnerable
- Victim serving public
- Weapon
- Previous convictions and failures to respond to previous sentences, if relevant

eg.
- Impulsive action
- Minor injury
- Provocation

> *IS IT SERIOUS ENOUGH FOR A COMMUNITY PENALTY?*
> *IS COMPENSATION, DISCHARGE OR FINE APPROPRIATE, OR*
> *IS IT SO SERIOUS THAT ONLY CUSTODY IS APPROPRIATE?*

**CONSIDER OFFENDER MITIGATION**

eg.
- Guilty plea: *for a timely guilty plea allow a discount of about a third*
- Age, health (physical or mental)
- Co-operation with the police
- Voluntary compensation
- Remorse

**DECIDE YOUR SENTENCE**

Compare your decision with the entry point - **COMMUNITY PENALTY** - and check your reasons if you have reached a different sentence

*NB. COMPENSATION - Give reasons if not awarding compensation*
*NB. FINES - If imposing a fine, remember to increase or decrease the amount according to the financial circumstances of the offender*

**Fig 8.2** Magistrates' Association Sentencing Guidelines, September 1993 (cont'd)

| Affray | Public Order Act 1986 s 3<br>Triable either way - see Mode of Trial Guidelines<br>Penalty: Level 5 and/or 6 months |
|---|---|

| ENTRY POINT ➤ | COMMUNITY PENALTY |
|---|---|

**(+)    CONSIDER THE SERIOUSNESS OF THE OFFENCE    (−)**

eg.

Offence committed on bail
Busy public place
Group action
People put in fear
Vulnerable victim(s)
Previous convictions and failures to respond
to previous sentences, if relevant

eg.

Single offender

> *IS IT SERIOUS ENOUGH FOR A COMMUNITY PENALTY?*
> *IS COMPENSATION, DISCHARGE OR FINE APPROPRIATE, OR*
> *IS IT SO SERIOUS THAT ONLY CUSTODY IS APPROPRIATE?*

**CONSIDER OFFENDER MITIGATION**

eg.

Guilty plea: *for a timely guilty plea allow a discount of about a third*
Age, health (physical or mental)
Co-operation with the police
Voluntary compensation
Remorse

**DECIDE YOUR SENTENCE**

Compare your decision with the entry point - **COMMUNITY PENALTY** - and check your
reasons if you have reached a different sentence

*NB. COMPENSATION - Give reasons if not awarding compensation*
*NB. FINES - If imposing a fine, remember to increase or decrease the amount according to the*
*financial circumstances of the offender*

courts. They also contain a list of factors that make a 'typical offence' more or less serious. Although the guidelines will inevitably lead to greater consistency, their influence can be a source of concern when sentencers feel unable to give a sentence they think to be appropriate in an individual case. The concern is that the guidelines, which are merely advisory, become the basis of original tariff.

A major influence on sentences in the Crown Courts in England and Wales is the appeal system. In 1907 the Court of Criminal Appeal was established to promote some degree of judicial self-regulation. Renamed the Court of Appeal, this deals with appeals from the Crown Court against conviction and sentence. Most appeals are however against sentence. In 1991, 6,340 offenders appealed to the Court of Appeal (Criminal Division); 4,630 appealed against their sentence, 777 against their conviction and sentence and 933 against conviction. (*Statistical Bulletin* Home Office Issue 13/93, 29 April 1993: Table 10).

In the 1980s the Court of Appeal gave guidance to sentencers with a series of guideline cases. These include *Bibi* in 1980 on the use of custody, *Maguire* in 1982 on burglary offences, *Aramah* in 1983 on drug dealing, *Roberts* in 1982 and *Billam* in 1986 on rape and *Barrick* in 1985 on theft.

The Court of Appeal sentencing guidelines play a decisive part in fixing the appropriate tariff for an offence. Guideline cases are those where the appeal court has taken the opportunity to lay down detailed guidance to assist courts in sentencing. For example in 1986 in *Billam*, the Lord Chief Justice made both a general statement of principle: that rape should be followed by a custodial sentence, and laid down a list of aggravating features which would call for a longer sentence than the norm, which he set at five years. Similarly in the case of *Barrick*, which involved theft in breach of trust, for example from an employer, guidelines as to the length of a custodial sentence were given in terms both of the amount stolen, and the degree of trust broken. In the case of *Aramah*, and subsequent cases, guidelines were set out in terms of street value and class of drugs imported or supplied.

While these cases are an important and influential guide for lower courts in sentencing – and indeed for defendants and those advising them as to the likely sentence in a given case – they have limitations. First, the Court of Appeal can only respond to cases brought before it: therefore no systematic approach to offences or a certain range of offence can be made. Secondly, the cases that come before the Court of Appeal have until recently been a result of appeals against sentence on behalf of the defence.

The prosecution has only limited rights to appeal against unduly lenient sentences by virtue of the changes made in s 36 of the Criminal Justice Act 1988. This allowed the Attorney General the right to refer to the Court of Appeal sentences that seem unduly lenient. This system of reference was not an automatic right for the prosecution to appeal routinely on sentences. It applies to sentences for those convicted of offences that are triable only on indictment, so that it does not apply to TEW offences. Despite this system of reference on unduly lenient sentences, the Court of Appeal tends to be concerned with lengthy custodial terms, as defendants receiving community sentences are not likely to appeal. It is comparatively rare therefore for short custodial or non-custodial sentences to be considered. Other measures may thus be necessary to develop a more systematic approach to sentencing which will be discussed later in this chapter.

All these are relatively open and identifiable influences on sentencing. As with any other discretionary process however, informal factors also play a role. As we have seen, sentences may be directed towards different aims and many different considerations affect the decision. How therefore do sentencers approach individual decisions?

In a detailed review of sentencing decisions in the Court of Appeal, David Thomas identifies a twofold sentencing process. In the first, or primary sentencing decision, judges decide on the basis of the individual case whether a 'tariff' sentence, primarily a retributive deterrent sentence is appropriate, or whether the sentence should be individualised – that is based primarily on rehabilitative grounds (Thomas 1979). Individualised sentences may also be based on incapacitative and deterrent considerations with respect to the individual offender before the court, and will depend on an assessment of the likelihood of their re-offending and the danger they may be to the public. The secondary decision is which sentence will be imposed. Factors affecting the primary decision include both the personal characteristics of the defendant such as age, sex and previous history along with relevant personal circumstances and the seriousness of the offence. Where sentences are individualised it is extremely difficult to discern whether or not they are consistent as so many factors may affect the individual case (Thomas 1979).

Sentencers themselves may have their own individual approach, or philosophy, based on a mixture of the theories of sentencing outlined above. They may also be affected by the attitudes and opinions prevailing on their own bench. In a study of disparities in sentencing motoring offenders, Hood found that many could be accounted for by local bench cultures. Thus within individual benches, sentencing norms evolved which could be affected by local considerations producing local variations (Hood 1972). These local 'bench cultures' may affect the perception both of offences and offenders and underlie sentencing disparities. Thus some studies have found that some courts consistently impose more severe sentences, while others sentence more leniently (see, for example, Parker et al 1989). This combination of sentencers' individual philosophies and bench cultures may also become a filter through which information about offences and offenders is received. Thus some magistrates and judges are known by participants in the system to be tougher on some kinds of offences than others, which may lead to attempts to put cases in front of selected benches or judges. Parker and his colleagues also found that some benches paid more attention to school reports than probation officers' reports, believing that probation officers could be too soft on offenders, whereas school reports told them more about work habits and discipline (Parker et al 1989). They also found that magistrates, who regarded sentencing as an 'art form' felt that they could judge many aspects of defendants' character from their general demeanour and bearing in the court. These attitudes were also reflected in a belief in the necessity to judge each case on its own merits, an approach which underlay magistrates' resistance to any attempts to reduce their discretion. This investigation was carried out before the CJA 1991 and it is not clear whether vestiges of that approach will survive the Act.

All these influences undoubtedly contribute to the variations found throughout the country which have caused so much concern. They may also, arguably, produce disparities not only when individual offenders are compared but when groups of offenders are compared. There has been criticism for example about the fairness of sentencing policy in relation to women and ethnic minorities. Unit fines attempted to tackle unfairness on the grounds of income, while concerns about the treatment of both unemployed and white collar offenders raise issues of how far socio-economic status affects sentencing decisions. The next section will look briefly at these issues.

## Race and sentencing

According to Home Office figures, in June 1993 black men formed 10.8 per cent of the male prison population, whereas black men of all nationalities formed 1.9 per cent of the resident population of England and Wales (*Statistical Bulletin*, Home Office Issue 21/94, 11 August 1994). The over-representation of black females is even greater; however, differences disappear when only UK nationals are considered, as a higher proportion of black females in prison are foreign nationals – often imprisoned for illegally importing drugs. South Asian males are also over-represented in the prison population with other ethnic groups being under-represented, such as the Chinese and Bangladeshi population. This over-representation or under-representation in the prison population does not in itself necessarily indicate any prejudice or discrimination on the part of sentencers although it has caused much concern particularly throughout the 1980s. It is enormously difficult to interpret these figures as studies which have attempted to discern whether there is any 'race factor' in sentencing have produced conflicting results. As we have seen in respect of earlier stages in the process, many other factors may account for this over-representation, indeed earlier stages of the process may affect sentencing outcomes. The legal and procedural factors which affect sentencing may account for many of the differences. Thus sentences are affected by the nature of the offence, the characteristics of individual offenders and whether or not defendants have pleaded guilty. We have already seen, for example, that more black offenders elect for Crown Court trial and plead not guilty. This means that if convicted they would receive

232

harsher sentences because they do not benefit from a discount for a guilty plea.

Early studies of sentencing found little evidence of any substantial amounts of discrimination, which would be indicated if, when all other factors were taken into account, there were significant differences between the sentencing of different groups of offenders. These studies however involved small groups and could not control for all possible variations. More detailed investigations have found that where larger numbers of factors are taken into account there may be what Hudson describes as a 'residual' race factor (Hudson 1989). In the most detailed study to date carried out in a sample of Crown Court Centres, differences between groups were found to be greater in some courts than others (Hood 1992). An attempt was made to estimate the size of any 'race effect' and Hood concludes:

> . . . about 80 per cent of the difference between the proportion of black males in the general population and their proportion among those serving prison sentences, can be accounted for by the greater number of black offenders who appeared for sentence in the Crown Court and by the nature and circumstances of the crimes they were convicted of. The remaining 20 per cent could be attributed to their subsequent different treatment by the courts: one-third of this (7%) to more being sentenced to custody than expected and two-thirds (13%) to more pleading not guilty and to the consequent longer sentences imposed.
>
> (Hood 1992: 203)

Some of this he argues, could be associated with bias on the part of individual judges. Differences between the treatment of black and white male defendants were found mainly amongst those over 21 and in relation to black defendants who were unemployed. As well as receiving more and longer custodial sentences, black defendants were less likely to be given probation orders. Similarly detailed studies are not available for magistrates' courts although one commentator argues on the basis of studies carried out so far that the extent of any racial discrimination in sentencing is considerably less in magistrates' than in the Crown Court (Smith 1994).

## Sentencing women

Women are generally assumed to be sentenced more leniently than men, often attributed to a 'chivalrous' attitude on the part of sentencers who may assume that a woman's crime is more likely to be related to mental illness or medical problems, and be reluctant to send women to prison, especially where they have children. On the other hand, some argue that women may be more harshly dealt with by the courts, as women who have offended may be seen as 'doubly deviant' – deviant as offenders and deviant as women.

A recent Home Office study looked at these issues (Hedderman and Hough 1994) and reported that:

- Women are far less likely than men to receive a custodial sentence for virtually all indictable offences except drugs.

- When women do receive prison sentences these tend to be shorter than men's.
- One of the reasons for this is that women are less likely to be dealt with at the Crown Court.
- Women are less likely to receive prison sentences irrespective of the number of previous offences.

These figures they argue 'call into question claims that the criminal justice system is systematically more severe towards women than men. If anything, the evidence points to more lenient treatment of women.' However, they also point out that differences may emerge within offence categories and their figures do not look at the individual characteristics of women and men sentenced.

This latter point is particularly important as it is very difficult to compare directly sentences given to men and women because the pattern of their offences is so very different that it is difficult to compare like with like (Eaton 1986). In general, the more lenient pattern can be attributed to the fact that women commit less serious offences and have fewer previous convictions. However, some have discerned a tendency for some women, particularly those who are divorced or single parent families, to be given more severe sentences than other women (Farrington and Morris 1983) . This might indicate the effect of more indirect forms of differentiation, reflecting notions of the 'ideal' woman, related to family and domestic considerations. Thus Eaton found that courts tended to look carefully at female offenders' family and domestic situations. Where a woman was seen to be capable of looking after her children and her husband was available to support her, the courts may be more lenient (Eaton 1986).

Women are also less likely to receive community service orders and the use of fines for women declined during the 1980s (Heidensohn 1994). This may reflect the socio-economic circumstances of some female offenders. It may, for example, be more difficult to fine a single parent and some community penalties may not be well suited to female offenders. For example, community service orders require the offender to spend a certain number of hours working – which may be difficult for women with children, and the common emphasis on manual labour may also make them appear less appropriate for women. There have accordingly been a number of efforts in some areas to devise more appropriate community service placements for women (Carlen 1990).

In respect of the sentencing of women it is perhaps less important to ask whether they are sentenced more leniently or harshly than to consider the differential impact of sentences on men and women in different circumstances. These considerations reveal that issues of justice are hard to resolve. It may well be reasonable for sentencers to refrain from sending women to prison to avoid adverse effects on their children, but this is scarcely fair on fathers and their families. On the other hand, women may feel unjustly dealt with if their family and social circumstances are part of an adverse judgment of the court.

## Socio-economic status

The effects of both gender and ethnicity may also be related to the socio-economic circumstances of offenders. Thus it is more likely to be women in adverse socio-economic circumstances who end up in prison and, as seen above, many black offenders are unemployed. Thus the potential effect of socio-economic status on sentencing must be explored.

This can be seen in the situation of the unemployed, which provides a clear example of indirect and 'unintentional' discrimination. It is routinely stated in mitigation for offenders that they are in employment and that imprisonment would lead to the loss of such employment. Such employment is generally regarded as being a sign of good character (Cavadino and Dignan 1992).

It would appear eminently sensible for sentencers to take into account the possible effect of loss of job on offenders let alone their families. However, this means that the unemployed, having less to lose, may be more likely to end up in prison. It is also more difficult to fine unemployed offenders.

The situation of the unemployed offender contrasts starkly with that of the middle class and particularly the white collar offender. Many such offenders, for example, may plead in mitigation that they have much to lose – that a prison sentence would harm their innocent families and they might lose their house and their 'standing' in the community. Again, while it may be fair to take such factors into account, it may discriminate, albeit unintentionally, against offenders who have little to lose, let alone any 'standing' in the community (see, for example, Croall 1992; Levi 1989). Few studies have however found that social status or class alone affects sentencing outcomes. Indeed, judges, concerned to be seen to be fair, may be conscious of any likely partiality on the grounds of class. Thus Mr Justice Henry, on refusing leave to appeal against a £5 million fine levied on one of the Guinness defendants commented that:

> punishments are after all intended to be punitive and the court must ensure that a man's wealth and power does not put him beyond punishment.
>
> (*Guardian*, 3 October 1990. Quoted in Croall 1992: 119)

At the same time however, few offenders could pay a massive fine and the ability of wealthier offenders to pay both large fines and substantial compensation may make a financial penalty more likely. In addition they are better able to employ legal representation which may affect how they present their case. Other factors may operate to reduce the severity of sentences for white collar offenders. The absence of direct victimisation in many white collar offences and in some the apparent lack of intent may also lead to less severe sentences (Croall 1992).

On a more general level, lower class offenders may appear in court to be less likely cases for sympathy. As indicated above, sentencers may make judgments based on the demeanour and bearing of offenders and look for evidence of character, remorse and an acceptance of the courts' authority. Decisions earlier in the criminal justice process may also demonstrate a differential approach where the police may be more likely to caution middle class youths – a decision which may reflect home circumstances and the employment of parents (Cavadino and Dignan 1992).

Taken together, consideration of the effects of ethnicity, gender and socio-economic status on sentencing decisions reveals how difficult it is to determine whether any discrimination exists on the part of sentencers. Nonetheless at the end of the criminal justice process there are differences in the proportions of some groups of offenders who receive different sentences. These raise important questions about the calculation of 'just deserts', which will be discussed in Chapter 9.

## STRUCTURING SENTENCING DECISIONS

We can see from the above that a variety of factors directly and indirectly influence sentencing decisions, many of which have been associated with disparities. Concerns over these issues reflect two different goals in respect of sentencing policy:

- the need for consistency so that justice is even handed
- the need for flexibility so that sentences can be matched to the individual circumstances of the case.

These concerns have generated a desire to achieve a more consistent approach to sentencing without creating too much of a straight-jacket. There have accordingly been various attempts to encourage a structured approach to sentencing decisions.

The 1990 White Paper which preceded the CJA 1991 pointed out that 'there is still too much uncertainty and little guidance about the principles which should govern sentencing... The Government is therefore proposing a new and more coherent statutory framework for sentencing.' (Home Office 1990a: 1) The paper goes on to argue that 'to achieve a more coherent and comprehensive consistency of approach in sentencing, a new framework is needed for the use of custodial, community and financial penalties.' (Home Office 1990a: 5). The CJA 1991 sought to provide a firm basis for such consistency. Magistrates' training has increasingly focused on a structured approach following a systematic path to the sentence, ensuring that factors are considered at the appropriate point of the sentence as illustrated in the Magistrates' Association guidelines shown in Figure 8.2 above. These show how seriousness is first assessed, including mitigation concerning the offence, and a provisional sentence arrived at. Thereafter offender mitigation is considered, the bench determining whether the provisional sentence should be reduced.

A number of initiatives have been introduced with the aim of achieving a more consistent or structured approach. The Judicial Studies Board is now responsible for collecting and disseminating statistics and for arranging Judges' Conferences and training sessions on sentencing. As already mentioned initiatives from the Magistrates' Association led to the development of guidelines to both the approach to sentencing and the actual sentences.

Another suggestion aimed at achieving greater consistency is to establish a sentencing council or commission. This would be a body comprised of a variety of criminal justice personnel and experts, who would produce ceilings or bandings for different offences along with articulating the principles to be used in calculating the precise sentence to be given. It would also consider how to deal with persistent or multiple offenders (Ashworth 1989). This has been popular in some states in the USA and Figure 8.3 shows the Minnesota sentencing grid to show how sentences are arrived at in that state. The two axes of the grid represent the main factors of seriousness of offence and the offender's previous criminal history. The bold line represents the in/out, or custody or not, presumption set out by the sentencing commission. Below the line incarceration is presumed, above it the judge may substitute a community penalty. But if they decide to give custodial sentence above or below the line, the range of sentences is set out for all categories of crime except for first degree murder.

Sentencing commissions are another initiative introduced in recent years in several states in the USA as well as for sentencing in the federal courts. Michael Tonry, writing for the National Institute of Justice, commented in 1987:

> The Minnesota and Washington experiences suggest that the combination of sentencing commissions and presumptive guidelines is a viable approach for achieving consistent and coherent jurisdiction-wide sentencing policies. However, the experiences in Maine, New York, Pennsylvania, and South Carolina counsel that the sentencing commission approach won't necessarily succeed. Six jurisdictions are too few to support any but the most tentative generalizations about success and failure. Still, it is clear that most local legal and political cultures shape the environments in which the commissions work. Minnesota and Washington, for example, are both relatively homogeneous states with reform traditions. In neither state were criminal justice issues highly politicized. New York and Pennsylvania, by contrast, are heterogeneous states in which criminal justice issues are highly politicized and law-and-order sentiment is powerful. In some states, especially where trial judges are elected, judges may vigorously resist efforts to limit their discretion. Perhaps the only generalization that can be offered concerning political and legal culture is that the potential and the effectiveness of a sentencing commission will depend on how it addresses and accommodates constraints imposed by the local culture.
>
> (Tonry 1987: 59)

It seems therefore that the legal and political culture of the jurisdiction

**Fig 8.3** Minnesota sentencing grid

## STRUCTURING CRIMINAL SENTENCES

### Presumptive Sentence Lengths in Months

| SEVERITY LEVELS OF CONVICTION OFFENSE | | CRIMINAL HISTORY SCORE | | | | | | |
|---|---|---|---|---|---|---|---|---|
| | | 0 | 1 | 2 | 3 | 4 | 5 | 6 or more |
| Unauthorized use of motor vehicle Possession of marijuana | I | 12* | 12* | 12* | 15 | 18 | 21 | 24 23-25 |
| Theft-related crimes ($150–$2,500) Sale of marijuana | II | 12* | 12* | 14 | 17 | 20 | 23 | 27 25-29 |
| Theft crimes ($150–$2,500) | III | 12* | 13 | 16 | 19 | 22 21-23 | 27 25-29 | 32 30-34 |
| Burglary – felony intent Receiving stolen goods ($150–$2,500) | IV | 12* | 15 | 18 | 21 | 25 24-26 | 32 30-34 | 41 37-45 |
| Simple robbery | V | 18 | 23 | 27 | 30 29-31 | 38 36-40 | 46 43-49 | 54 50-58 |
| Assault, second degree | VI | 21 | 26 | 30 | 34 33-35 | 44 42-46 | 54 50-58 | 65 60-70 |
| Aggravated robbery | VII | 24 23-25 | 32 30-34 | 41 38-44 | 49 45-53 | 65 60-70 | 81 75-87 | 97 90-104 |
| Assault, first-degree Criminal sexual conduct, first-degree | VIII | 43 41-45 | 54 50-58 | 65 60-70 | 76 71-81 | 95 89-101 | 113 106-120 | 132 124-140 |
| Murder, third-degree | IX | 97 94-100 | 119 116-122 | 127 124-130 | 149 143-155 | 176 168-184 | 205 195-215 | 230 218-242 |
| Murder, second-degree | X | 116 111-121 | 140 133-147 | 162 153-171 | 203 192-214 | 243 231-255 | 284 270-298 | 324 309-339 |

\* One year and one day

Note:   Italicised numbers within the grid denote the range within which a judge may sentence without the sentence being deemed a departure. First-degree murder is excluded from the guidelines by law and continues to have a mandatory life sentence.

contributes to the success or failure of such an approach. This point was reflected in the UK in the consultation leading up to the CJA 1991 when the idea of a sentencing council was rejected. John Patten, the junior minister at the Home Office in 1991, identified the traditions of the criminal justice system as a reason why he thought the idea of a sentencing council would not work in England and Wales. In a letter to *The Times* he wrote:

Sentencing councils are the most fashionable nostrum these days for how much that advice (on sentencing) might be formalised. There seems to be almost as many recipes as there are cooks, producing councils, commissions or whatever; they vary in how much guidance or instruction should be given to the courts on sentencing and by whom it should be given.

At the end of this road stands Minnesota in the United States. There, I am told, the local sentencing commission has produced tight numerical guidelines for prison sentences, which have taken the form of a 'sentencing grid'. Two axes determine the presumptive sentence. Along one side are the offence categories and along the other categories of 'criminal history'. So the ultimate sentence really depends on where the points along each axis occupied by the offender meet in the middle...

Those who ponder sentencing councils must not ignore that which is already in place, potentially providing so much of what they want to see, but in a way that works with the *grain of the criminal justice traditions* in this country. For there is a fast developing framework for judges and magistrates.

In no particular order, first, there is the coherent statutory framework for sentencing in the new criminal justice bill, as we do not think that Parliament has said enough about the principles that govern sentencing decisions. Second, there is the power for the Attorney-General to refer cases to the Court of Appeal, where sentences are allegedly over-lenient. Third, the powerful effect of guideline judgments with the Court of Appeal is self-evident. Last, the work of the Judicial Studies Board seems to be of ever-increasing importance in training and guiding the sentencers in their work.

(The Times, 5 February 1991. Emphasis added)

Whether a sentencing commission would help to achieve greater consistency is difficult to assess. While it might produce greater consistency it clearly goes against the notion of judicial independence which is firmly entrenched in the system of England and Wales. It might also be criticised on the grounds that it would be a centralised and bureaucratic system and places yet more decisions in the hands of unaccountable experts.

## CONCLUSION

This chapter has indicated the many issues involved in sentencing decisions. In the first place, the different theories of punishment embody the different aims which sentencers may take into account. The present range of sentences available to the court reflect these different aims, and many sentences may be directed to achieve a combination of these aims. Before the CJA 1991 and other reforms attempted to impose greater consistency in sentencing policy, sentencers could in effect choose between a range of different sentences in what has been described as a 'cafeteria' approach (Ashworth 1989). The tradition of judicial independence and the tendency of both magistrates and judges to judge each case on its merits may produce the disparities which have caused so much concern. As Ashworth comments 'unstructured discretion leaves leeway to the personal preferences of the judge, and if the concept of the "rule of law" has any stable meaning, it must exclude such preferences' (Ashworth 1994b: 852).

As we have seen therefore there have been a variety of attempts to encourage a more consistent approach to sentencing, including the use of statutory criteria, voluntary guidelines and Court of Appeal guideline cases. The CJA 1991 also attempted to introduce a more coherent approach and went further than much previous legislation to spell out the priority to be given to the various sentencing aims. It indicates the primacy of retribution, denunciation incapacitation and to a lesser extent restitution, in the light of a declining faith in rehabilitation or deterrence having any substantial effect on individual offender's propensity to re-offend. This clearly reflects a changing emphasis on the different aims of sentences. The reasons for this shift in emphasis will be explored in more depth in Chapter 9 along with the philosophy underpinning the CJA 1991.

## Review questions

1. Contrast the six major theories of punishment in terms of:
   (a) What they seek to achieve.
   (b) Which are concerned primarily with the impact of the sentence on the offender before the court rather than the impact on the public at large?
   (c) Which aim to reduce crime in the future?
   (d) If the judge or magistrates wish to achieve two objectives with the same sentence, which of the theories are compatible and which are not?
2. What are the main sentences available to the court? How can they be related to each of the major aims?
3. List the major factors which will influence sentencers in reaching a sentencing decision. Which factors are likely to produce disparity?
4. What are the main arguments underlying attempts to achieve a more structured approach to sentencing? How is this achieved in England and Wales?
5. See Exercise Nos 4 and 5 on sentencing in the Appendix below.

## Further reading

Ashworth A (1992) *Sentencing and Penal Policy*. 2nd edn. London: Weidenfeld & Nicolson

Ashworth A (1994) 'Sentencing' in Maguire M, Morgan R and Reiner R (eds) *The Oxford Handbook of Criminology*. Oxford: Clarendon Press: 819–860

Cavadino P and Dignan J (1992) *The Penal System: An Introduction*. London: Sage

Walker N (1985) *Sentencing: Theory, Law and Practice*. London: Butterworths

# CHAPTER 9

# PUNISHMENT PHILOSOPHIES AND SHIFTING PENAL PARADIGMS

The Era of Rehabilitation
The Justice Approach
The Prison Reductionists
Criminal Justice Act 1991
Sentencing for Whom?

## INTRODUCTION

We saw in Chapter 8 that policy makers, judges and magistrates have sought to find a balance between the six major theories of sentencing, and the 20th century has seen a change in the emphasis given to these goals. This chapter will focus on these shifting penal paradigms, that is ways of thinking about the causes and consequences of crime and how we should respond to them. The beginning of the century witnessed a growth in what was seen as a modern or progressive approach which believed that punishment could be replaced with treatment and welfare stratagems to cure criminals through a rehabilitative approach. This was to give way to the back-to-justice approach of the late 1960s as disenchantment with the rehabilitative model set in.

At the same time there was pressure to reduce the use of imprisonment by what came to be called the prison reductionists. Thus a number of academic and pressure groups argued that prisons were over used and counter-productive and had little impact on the criminal ways of inmates. These ideas were influential particularly in the context of the increasing financial costs of building and running prisons. Thus policy makers sought to devise non-custodial sentencing options as alternatives to imprisonment. However these lacked credibility amongst sentencers as being insufficiently punitive and not a real alternative to prison. In the search for new non-custodial sanctions it became necessary that they should be seen as penal measures in their own right, as intermediate sanctions, fitting into the tariff between prisons and probation. The Criminal Justice Act 1991 was preceded by considerable consultation, research and discussion and represented the culmination of a process of change in the approach to sentencing.

This chapter will first look at the rise of rehabilitative theories, starting with the ideas of early rehabilitationists and influential penal reformers. Having failed to live up to their early promise we will examine the practical and theoretical limitations of rehabilitative strategies. The next section of the chapter will explore the growth of the 'back-to-justice' movement, its main ideas and growing influence. The arguments of the prison reductionists will then be considered, followed by a discussion of whether penal policy should pursue an aim of seeking alternatives to prison or intermediate sanctions. Finally, the theoretical underpinnings of the CJA 1991 will be explored, representing, as it does, an articulation of the contemporary theoretical approach to sentencing and the current penal paradigm.

## THE ERA OF REHABILITATION

During the 20th century, penal policy throughout Europe and the USA has been strongly influenced by the theory of rehabilitation. This moved away from earlier emphases on retribution and deterrence which were less concerned with the causes of crime and its treatment than with the justification for and distribution of punishment. Crime was seen as an immoral act which was in need of punishment which was justified primarily on deterrent or retributive grounds. To rehabilitationists, however, crime, like any other social problem, could be studied scientifically to establish its causes. In what came to be described as a medical model, crime was likened to an illness which could be diagnosed and treated, and through work with individual criminals and social reform, eventually cured. Thus from the start of the 20th century experts from the world of medicine, the growing professions of psychiatry and social work, educational specialists and social reformers became increasingly involved in the courts and penal system. Rehabilitation offered the promise that crime could be almost eradicated by these scientific and professional approaches – an orthodoxy which dominated penal policy until the 1960s.

There were many different views on how rehabilitation could be achieved which led to a variety of different strategies. First, the medical model stressed the need to diagnose, treat and cure criminals. This led to a growing involvement of doctors and psychiatrists in the criminal justice process, providing medical and psychiatric reports to the courts and working in prisons and other institutions. Secondly, others believed in the value of discipline and work, and advocated methods such as industrial and vocational training to encourage offenders to develop self-discipline and good work habits. Unlike medical and psychiatric treatment these measures aimed not to

242

reform offenders from within but to equip them with better skills which would, it was hoped, keep them from committing crimes. Thirdly, the growing profession of social work advocated the use of case work and counselling for offenders both inside prisons and through the work of the Probation Service. This led to the widespread use of pre-sentence reports outlining the circumstances of offenders, and also influenced the growth of after care provision for ex-prisoners. Fourthly, many believed in the power of moral awakening, either through religion, or more recently by confronting the offender with the harm they had done. Early prison regimes encouraged offenders to contemplate on their wrongdoing and religion has always played a role in prisons. Fifthly, others welcomed rehabilitationist strategies as a more humane way to treat prisoners which ameliorated the degrading and brutalising aspects of prison life. Thus penal reformers, who had for long sought to improve the conditions of prisoners and who felt that prison could make people worse, supported rehabilitative measures enthusiastically. Lastly, rehabilitation was linked to the ideas of social engineers who identified social deprivation as the root of all social problems and put their faith in growing affluence and the welfare state.

In England and Wales, the rehabilitative paradigm was officially recognised in 1895 in the report of the Home Office Departmental Committee on Prisons chaired by Herbert Gladstone (Home Office 1895). The committee found that 'the moral condition in which a large number of prisoners leave the prison, and the serious number of re-committals have led us to think that there is ample cause for a searching inquiry into the main features of prison life'. It went on to state, 'we start from the principle that prison treatment should have as its primary and concurrent objects deterrence and reformation', and in what became one of the most influential statements about the aims of prison continued that:

> . . . prison discipline and treatment should be more effectually designed to maintain, stimulate or awaken the higher susceptibilities of prisoners, to develop their moral instincts, to train them in orderly and industrial habits, and whenever possible to turn them out of prison better men and women, both physically and morally, than when they came in.

> (Home Office 1895: 8)

The first decade of the 20th century saw the development of many rehabilitative policies such as the introduction of Borstal in 1908, of probation in 1907, special provision for child offenders in 1913 and new arrangements for the mentally deficient offender in 1914. Welfare officers, psychiatrists and psychologists were recruited into the prison service and in 1919 the prison warder was replaced by the prison officer, a title which marked a changing role. The annual reports of prison commissioners revealed a new mood in which prisons were increasingly seen not negatively, as institutions for incarcerating the bad, but positively, as institutions which could act as agencies of human change.

Although our focus here is on penal philosophy, the growth of rehabilitative policies, especially in prisons, was strongly influenced by individuals. One particularly influential individual was Alexander Paterson, who was involved in social work with the Oxford Medical Mission in Bermondsey where he also worked as an elementary school teacher. Although never chairman of the Prison Commission he was its most dominant figure and his liberal reform values were evident in penal documents from 1921 until his death in 1947. This was a period in which the approach embodied in the Gladstone Report began to crystallise into the dominant penological paradigm. Thus Lionel Fox commented that 'it was in 1921 that gusts of fresh air began to blow through the pages of the reports of the prison commissioners' (Fox 1952). The 1930s were characterised as an age of optimism in penal reform (Hood 1974).

This spirit of optimism is illustrated in extracts from Paterson's evidence to the 1931 Persistent Offenders Committee. This committee also provides a good example of how changing views about the role of prisons legitimated the participation of medical experts. Of the 68 people who gave evidence to the committee, 13 were drawn from the medical world, working within the system as medical superintendents in prisons or in psychiatric hospitals. The growing influence of the medical model and the treatment approach is confirmed in Paterson's evidence. Thus:

> The English Courts today, facing a young offender under 21 in the dock, are not concerned like their predecessors to weigh out a dose of punishment appropriate to the proved offence, but exercised rather to diagnose his condition and to prescribe the right form of training or treatment for the condition. This more thoughtful, sensible and expensive way of dealing with the young offender has inevitably resulted in a marked fall in the number of professional recidivists.
>
> (Evidence to Persistent Offenders Committee 1931: vol. 3: 669)

The significance to rehabilitation of other measures was also noted. Thus Paterson comments:

> There has ensued in the last 25 years a whole series of changes in law and practice. The Children's Courts have been established to discover and check the potential tendency of the child offender; the probation system has emerged as a common-sense alternative to the imprisonment of the first offender of any age; the reformatories and industrial schools are no longer convict prisons for turbulent children, but take their place among other educational agencies, as special schools for the backward and the forward; the adolescent offender is sent in increasing proportion for training in a Borstal Institution rather than confinement in a prison.
>
> (Evidence to Persistent Offenders Committee 1931: vol. 3: 669)

Paterson was well aware of some of the problems and what have come to be called the 'pains' of imprisonment and the full impact on the individual offender and their families of a period of imprisonment.

> Imprisonment is to be avoided whenever possible. It is often but a clumsy piece of social surgery, tearing a man away from the social fabric of home and work and

club and union that has woven round himself, causing distress to others and rendering his replacement in social and industrial life a matter of grave difficulty.

(Evidence to Persistent Offenders Committee 1931: vol. 3: 675)

He wished to abolish prisons, and replace them with other institutions which were primarily concerned with reform – thus he also wrote:

I propose to abolish all prisons.

I propose to replace the prison commission with a Board of Welfare, whose members shall under a director administer:

   a) Probation and Aftercare

   b) Reformatory and Industrial Schools

   c) Borstal Institutions

   d) Examination Clinics

   e) Training Centres

   f) Places of detention

There shall be no more places called prisons.

(Evidence to Persistent Offenders Committee 1931: vol. 3: 675)

Whilst Paterson's ambition of the abolition of prisons was not achieved, his thinking, and the goal of rehabilitation, was paramount in the penal approach. However, the result of rehabilitative policies may have had a surprising outcome: an increase in prison sentence lengths. As we saw in Chapter 8, one implication of rehabilitative theory is that sentence lengths should be flexible and responsive to the needs of the offender. From this came the argument that sentences should be indeterminate along with the idea that offenders needed to be sent to prison for a sufficient time for treatment and training to take effect. Thus Paterson said, 'if we are concerned to train him, a few weeks in prison will be an idle pretence...' (Prison Commission 1927) This was a view clearly held by those running the prison system in the inter-war years. Thus the Report of the Commissioners of Prisons for 1925/26 stated:

. . . the short sentence remains an outstanding defect in our penal system and difficulty in prison administration. Repetition on this point is not amiss.

The highest administrative and judicial authorities have taken the same view, and have drawn attention to the uselessness of the short sentence. The International Penitentiary Congress in August 1925 passed a resolution to the same effect. There is not doubt but that the prospect of prison has a strong deterrent effect on those who have never yet passed its gates; nor that, once the disgrace of imprisonment has been incurred, much of that effect has been lost. It can also be readily understood that an impediment to the development of a sound system of prison training is the presence of a number of men who only come in for a few days, and cannot therefore be taught any work other than the simplest. The difficulty, of course, is to find proper alternatives. The most hopeful prospect lies in the development of the probation system. A point may be reached where many offenders can be so well supervised in the open that, if they fail, a period of custodial training of substantial length will be justified.

(Prison Commission 1927: xiii)

245

This extract makes it clear that the prison commissioners did not seek longer sentences for all prisoners. Indeed they advocated non-custodial alternatives for less serious offenders. However, if offenders were to go to prison, the logic was clearly that short sentences would not allow sufficient time to treat and train them to lead a good and useful life. The Prison Rules, first introduced in 1949, took the view that the task of the Prison Service was to, 'encourage and assist the inmate to lead a good and useful life'. In their Annual Report for 1949, the commissioners also exhort the need for longer sentences in the context of discussing the new Criminal Justice Act 1948. Thus they argue, 'the purpose of the Act was not to provide some new form of training but to give the courts power to pass sentences long enough to enable the methods of training already developed in training prisons to be effectively applied'. This can be contrasted vividly, as we shall later see, with theories based on punishment and deterrence where the 'short sharp shock' or the 'clang of the prison gates' is urged as the most effective part of imprisonment. The effect of this policy is shown in Figures 9.1 and 9.2, which shows prison terms from 1913 to 1975 in absolute and percentage figures.

Figure 9.1 shows that average sentence lengths increased between 1913 and 1975. This is partly explained by the increasing use of non-custodial sentences from 1913 which meant that fewer petty criminals were sent to prison for short periods of time – thus increasing the average sentence length. The figures also include offenders of all ages, and are therefore affected by the growing use of Borstal and detention centres for those under 21, and by statutory restrictions on sending younger offenders to prison. A major factor in the increase however is the influence of the rehabilitative arguments outlined above. By 1975, over 28 per cent of inmates were serving lengths of imprisonment of over 12 months, compared with less than 1.5 per cent in 1913. Thus policies based on rehabilitation appear to have led to longer prison sentences.

The 1979 May Report on the Prison Service also noted these longer sentences and commented:

> However, confidence in the treatment model as it is usually called has now been waning throughout the Western world for some years. The drive behind the original borstal ideas has fallen away and there is now no belief that longer sentences may be justified because they make actual reformative treatment more possible.
>
> (Home Office 1979: 63)

This last quote indicates that certainly by 1979, the influence of rehabilitation had waned: the reasons for this will be discussed below.

### Rehabilitation reassessed

Rehabilitation fell out of favour largely because its promise was not achieved – it became a faith dashed on the rocks of the unprecedented rise in

246

**Fig 9.1** Length of prison sentence imposed (males and females)[1]   *

|  | 1913 | 1938 | 1948 | 1958 | 1968 | 1975 |
|---|---|---|---|---|---|---|
| Up to 2 weeks | 80,961 | 8,820 | 3,366 | 3,030 | 2,932 | 3,161 |
| Over 2 weeks up to 5 weeks | 30,359 | 7,475 | 5,595 | 4,922 | 3,765 | 5,069 |
| Over 5 weeks up to 3 months | 16,862 | 7,043 | 8,925 | 8,398 | 6,930 | 10,126 |
| Over 3 months up to 6 months | 5,070 | 3,947 | 6,447 | 6,710 | 7,801 | 7,483 |
| Over 6 months up to 12 months | 2,873 | 1,881 | 4,775 | 4,843 | 5,858 | 7,418 |
| Over 12 months up to 18 months | 1,033 | 694 | 2,361 | 2,085 | 3,179 | 4,546 |
| Over 18 months up to 3 years | 774 | 581 | 2,478 | 2,906 | 4,059 | 6,197 |
| Over 3 years up to 5 years | 231 | 158 | 617 | 733 | 1,086 | 1,749 |
| Over 5 years | 120 | 47 | 123 | 348 | 364 | 532 |
| Life | 13 | 14 | 30 | 40 | 95 | 153 |

* Including periods imposed in cases of fine default but excluding sentences of corrective training or preventive detention.

(Home Office (1977) *Prisons and the Prisoner*. London: HMSO: 157)

**Fig 9.2** Analysis of length of prison sentence expressed as percentages (males and females)*

|  | 1913 | 1938 | 1948 | 1958 | 1968 | 1975 |
|---|---|---|---|---|---|---|
| Up to 2 weeks | 58.6 | 28.7 | 10.0 | 8.9 | 8.1 | 6.0 |
| Over 2 weeks up to 5 weeks | 21.9 | 24.4 | 16.7 | 14.5 | 10.5 | 10.9 |
| Over 5 weeks up to 3 months | 12.2 | 23.0 | 24.7 | 24.7 | 19.2 | 21.8 |
| Over 3 months up to 6 months | 3.7 | 12.9 | 18.3 | 19.7 | 21.6 | 16.1 |
| Over 6 months up to 12 months | 2.1 | 6.1 | 14.3 | 14.2 | 16.2 | 16.0 |
| Over 12 months up to 18 months | 0.7 | 2.3 | 7.1 | 6.3 | 8.8 | 9.8 |
| Over 18 months up to 3 years | 0.5 | 1.9 | 7.4 | 8.5 | 11.3 | 13.3 |
| Over 3 years up to 5 years | 0.2 | 0.5 | 1.0 | 2.1 | 3.0 | 3.8 |
| Over 5 years | 0.1 | 0.2 | 0.4 | 1.0 | 1.0 | 1.2 |
| Life | – | – | 0.1 | 0.1 | 0.3 | 0.3 |

* Including periods imposed in cases of fine default. Excluding court martial prisoners.

(Home Office (1977) *Prisons and the Prisoner*. London: HMSO: 158)

recorded crime in the post war years. As this coincided with the growing post-war affluence of the 1950s, it also challenged reformers' claims that crime would be reduced with the growth of social welfare. Thus a 1959 White Paper, *Penal Practice in a Changing Society*, lamented, 'It is a disquieting feature of our society that in the years since the end of the war, rising standards in material prosperity, education and social welfare have brought no decrease in the high rate of crime reached during the war: on the contrary, crime has increased and is still increasing.'

There were several main sources of the declining influence of rehabilitation. The medical model, whose influence has been illustrated above, began to come under considerable criticism. By the 1960s it was apparent that it could justify a range of treatments which seemed far from humane. Many feared the development, for example, of the use of surgery and drug treatment which could readily be used to produce docile inmates. When medical intervention took these more dramatic forms many of the liberal reformers, who supported rehabilitation as a more humane approach, came to realise that punishment might be a better alternative. In addition, the increase in sentence lengths mentioned above, along with the use of indeterminate sentences, made rehabilitative treatments appear harsher than those which would be justified by retributive approaches. Hence, the support from liberal and civil rights groups in the 1970s for the back-to-justice movement, to be discussed below.

A further problem with rehabilitation was its link, seen most clearly in the medical model, with a view that criminality resulted from the pathologies of individual offenders. Yet despite a large volume of research attempting to discover how the characteristics of individual offenders could be related to their criminality, the pathological causes of crime proved hard to find. As seen in Chapter 2 there were also many other approaches to explaining crime, and many offenders possess no clearly identifiable pathology. In addition, from a labelling perspective, excessive intervention risked increasing crime, and adherents advocated the use of minimal intervention (Schur 1973). Thus the promise to diagnose and therefore to devise suitable treatments for offenders was never fulfilled.

One of the greatest problems with the rehabilitative strategies was that they failed to live up to the claim that they would reduce recidivism. The lesson that prisons were not likely to reform offenders was slow to be learned. The results of research seeking to establish the impact of rehabilitative measures led to the gloomy conclusion that 'nothing works' (Lipton et al 1975). During the 1960s the coalition of interests that made up the rehabilitative lobby in Europe and North America began to fall apart.

By the 1980s Prison Service policy documents had abandoned the ambitious mission statements of previous penal epochs, and referred to the much more basic functions of prison. Thus in 1988, a statement by the Prison Service contained the message that 'Her Majesty's Prison Service serves the public by keeping in custody those committed by the courts'. They had not abandoned, but diluted, the rehabilitative aspirations of the prison and strengthened the concern with humane conditions. 'Our duty is to look after them (inmates) with humanity and to help them lead law-abiding and useful lives in custody and after release.' (Prison Service Briefing, November 1988).

## THE JUSTICE APPROACH

The declining faith in rehabilitation along with the continuing rise in recorded crime led to a reappraisal of sentencing aims in the late 1960s and 1970s. Extremely influential in this process was what came to be known as a back-to-justice policy which affected legislation throughout the 1980s and most particularly the CJA 1991. There was no one single and comprehensive formulation of the justice model, but it developed out of a number of publications by American academics such as K C Davies, D Fogel, M Frankel and Andrew von Hirsch (Davies 1969; Fogel 1975; Frankel 1973; von Hirsch 1976). In the USA, where the justice model developed and influenced policy more directly, it was influential in shaping reforms of the juvenile courts and the introduction of determinate sentencing laws in California in 1976. These reforms were strongly influenced by the problems of rehabilitative sentencing policies. The long and seemingly harsh sentences associated with rehabilitation, the uncertainty produced by indeterminate sentences and the individualisation of sentences were seen to conflict with the rights of offenders to receive predictable and proportionate sentences. Thus the justice model argues that sentencing should be fair and not aim to achieve anything other than punishing offenders in proportion to the harm they have done. It developed directly out of a critique of rehabilitation and as Messinger and Johnson comment 'it represented . . . an outright rejection of previous sentencing policy and seems to be based on the opposite assumptions in every respect'. (Messinger and Johnson 1978).

The justice model is often linked to and is not logically incompatible with retributive theories; however it emphasises fairness while retribution is often popularly distorted to support demands for vengeance or harsher sentences. Thus while the justice model stresses punishment as an end in itself it was not called 'back-to-punishment', and von Hirsch described it as 'vengeance with fairness'(von Hirsch 1976). This approach is incompatible with rehabilitation as a primary goal of punishment. It can however be included as a secondary task for sentences, provided it does not distort the length or type of sentence in terms of the principles of just deserts. While no one set of clearly articulated theories set out a just deserts model, four main sets of arguments can be isolated. These include assumptions about human behaviour, the objective of punishment, the distribution of punishment, and the extension of due process into the prisons.

## Assumptions about human behaviour

To advocates of the justice model, individuals are responsible for their own behaviour. Criminal behaviour therefore, like any other, is thus a result of conscious decisions made by responsible, autonomous, self-determined individuals. Thus the rehabilitationist notion that criminality results from some individual pathology or is attributable to the offender's social, economic or personal circumstances was rejected. While it was accepted that these factors could affect behaviour they should not neglect what is seen as the moral imperative of regarding human action as primarily attributable to individual choice. Thus offenders have made a free choice to commit crime, and should therefore be punished. Where they have not been able because, for example, of age or mental disability, to make a free choice, they are not fully responsible for their actions and need not be punished.

## The objective of punishment

Punishment is therefore seen as an end in itself and a just and condign reward for morally wrong behaviour. It does not have to be justified by social protection or on the grounds that it is likely to reduce the future likelihood of crime. It should therefore be based simply on the notion of just deserts: culpable criminals should be punished in amounts proportional to or commensurate with the seriousness of the harm done.

This raises important questions. By whom, and how is culpability to be assessed? What constitutes the proportionate level of punishment for each offence and who should determine this? Thus there can be moral and political objections to this approach. In unequal or unjust societies, just deserts may be determined by those in power and may be far from just to those at the receiving end. In addition, in pluralist societies, cultural differentiation makes shared agreement as to what is right or wrong difficult to assess. Thus decisions as to how serious a crime is and what its 'just' punishment should be may open up a wider debate on moral, social and political issues. It might not be easy, for example, to distinguish between different offences in terms of seriousness. How can the respective seriousness of rape, burglary or tax fraud be assessed? As we have seen, the public may have very different views over what should be criminalised, let alone how serious some offences are. Is there likely to be any agreement over this, let alone over what might represent just punishment? However, even if agreement cannot be reached as to what is 'just', it does keep the debate about punishment associated with issues of morality and justice. This point is well made by C S Lewis:

> The humanitarian theory removes from punishment the concept of Desert. But the concept of Desert is the only connecting link between punishment and justice. It is only as deserved or undeserved that a sentence can be just or unjust ... we may very properly ask whether it is likely to deter others and to reform the criminal. But neither of these two last questions is a question of justice.
>
> (Lewis 1953)

Von Hirsch, discussing the twin objectives of deterrence and deserts makes it clear that the deserts principle is more important for decisions about the distribution of punishment. Thus he argues:

> . . . we think that the commensurate deserts principle should have priority over other objectives in decisions about how to punish. The disposition of convicted offenders should be commensurate with the seriousness of their offences, even if greater or less severity would promote other goals.
>
> (von Hirsch 1976)

## The distribution of punishment

Once culpability is established the main determinant of the type or amount of punishment will be the seriousness of the offence. A secondary consideration once this has been established is the degree of responsibility. Thus both mitigating and aggravating circumstances in relation to both the offence and the offender form part of the consideration of the sentence to be given.

Proponents of the justice model aimed to reduce individualised sentencing strategies, which as we have seen underlie sentencing disparities, and to eradicate indeterminacy. Thus they wished to see fixed and determinate sentencing with an established tariff for each offence, and uniformity of sentences for offenders committing the same offence under similar circumstances. Hence the move towards more constraints on judicial discretion at the sentencing stage throughout much of the USA and the UK.

## Legalism: the extension of due process

Indeterminate prison sentences created a situation whereby the length of a prison sentence depended on discretionary decisions made within the prison. This led to many problems, which, especially in the USA, were associated not only with increasing sentence lengths and thus an increase in the prison population, but also with unrest within prisons. Prisoners could not predict how long their sentences were to last nor could they always predict what they had to do to ensure an early release. This could also lead to a situation where release dates and parole decisions could be used as a means of control within the prison system. It also led to apparent injustices as offenders sent to prison for similar offences could in effect serve very different lengths of sentence. This not unsurprisingly led to much discontent and feelings of inequity. Thus a major argument of the justice model was to extend the principles of due process into the prison system. The clearest impact on prison regimes was achieved by David Fogel, who, as commissioner for prisons in Minnesota from 1971–73, attempted to apply the principles of the justice model to prisons. He advocated reforms which would involve more due process; greater openness in decision making and accountability according to the demands of natural justice. His reforms emphasised prisoners' rights and a belief that in the world of the prison community there should be an atmosphere of justice and fairness. This view was later echoed in the Woolf Report 1991 into prison disturbances in 1990, which will be discussed in Chapter 10.

In the UK the justice approach made its mark in a more diffuse way than in the USA. By the end of the 1970s aspects of prison policy were being scrutinised by the courts and greater attention was paid to prisoners' rights. The indeterminate sentence of Borstal training was replaced by the determinate sentence of youth custody in 1982. Also, as we have seen in Chapter 8, increasing guidance was given to courts to reduce sentence disparity. The 1990 White Paper and the subsequent legislative reforms in the CJA 1991 gave the clearest message that just deserts should be the primary principle for sentencing decisions in England and Wales.

## THE PRISON REDUCTIONISTS

The declining influence of rehabilitationist arguments and the growing attention to a justice model were accompanied by arguments that the use of prison should be drastically reduced. It was gradually accepted by most commentators, policy makers and administrators that despite the good intentions of penal reformers prisons had not achieved the goals claimed by their protagonists and were not likely to rehabilitate offenders. Today prisons are primarily justified by notions of retribution and denunciation, the uncertain impact of deterrence and a claim to incapacitate. The existence of violence, gangs and drug use within the prisons means that even the claim to incapacitate is optimistic.

In addition prisons are costly institutions and there have been recurrent concerns over the overcrowding of existing prisons and conditions within them. Many prisons in the UK were built in Victorian times and have few modern facilities. Concerns about overcrowding on the part of the Prison Officers' Association were evident in Britain as early as the 1940s and the Prison Commissioners' Annual Reports repeated the warning from 1955 until their demise in 1964. The degrading conditions within prisons also caused considerable concern and were described as an 'affront to civilised society' by the Director General of Prisons in the Annual Report of the Prison Department in 1980.

Out of these concerns grew what came to be known as the 'prison reductionist' movement. Some focused on degrading conditions and overcrowding, while others focused on the adverse effects of prisons and claimed that sentencers were sending too many people to prison. By the 1970s liberal and welfare oriented groups who had supported rehabilitation came to argue for a reduction in the use of prison. Their message was underlined by media stories of overcrowded cells, antiquated conditions and incidents of unrest in prisons. Thus there has been a theme in the British press over the last 20 years of prisons in crisis.

Of course, one solution to problems of overcrowding and degrading conditions would be to build more prisons. Moreover, the argument that sentencers send 'too many people' to prison is a difficult one to evaluate given the different aims underlying a prison sentence. Nonetheless, the argument of the reductionists, who shared a common view that the size of the prison population should be reduced, became an influential one. A key part of this argument was that as prison could no longer be seen to rehabilitate and indeed could have an adverse effect on prisoners their use should be curtailed.

This influence was evident in the parliamentary debate on the 1967 Criminal Justice Bill. Thus Roy Jenkins, then Home Secretary, echoed the reductionist position in his speech on the Bill in which he stated that 'the main range of the penal provision of the bill revolves round the single theme, that of keeping out of prison those who need not be there ... the overstrain upon prison resources, both of buildings and men, is at present appalling'.

From the 1960s official documents started to move away from the grander claims made during the heyday of rehabilitation, and towards an acceptance that prisons were not appropriate places to reform individual inmates. It began to be argued that prisons had an adverse effect on inmates, making them reliant on institutional life, and could further deepen their commitment to crime as they mixed freely with other criminals: the prison as the university of crime. In addition, ex-prisoners faced considerable stigma, making it more difficult for them to gain housing or employment. Thus a more limited rehabilitative rationale emerged in arguments that if rehabilitation was sought by sentencers it was not likely be achieved in prison. This was made most apparent in the arguments in the Green Paper, *Punishment, Custody and the Community* in 1988 and the subsequent White Paper of 1990.

During the late 1980s and early 1990s the reductionist message was paramount. The arguments of those who wished to see prisons reduced on the grounds that they were ineffective and inhumane were echoed by more pragmatic reductionists concerned with the costs, efficacy and the strains caused by the numbers in the system. Thus from the 1980s onwards, as we have seen successive legislation and policy initiatives began to encourage more consistency in sentencing and imposed limitations on the use of imprisonment such as the introduction of statutory criteria on the use of prison in the Criminal Justice Acts 1982, 1988 and 1991.

In 1990, explicit recognition was given in a White Paper to the idea that imprisonment has a limited role to play in penal policy. The report is discussed in Chapter 10. Changing prison regimes alone however could not alleviate the problems of the prison system and the White Paper argued that prison overcrowding could not be solved in isolation from sentencing policy. Hence the search for sanctions which could be used instead of prison, not necessarily to act as an alternative sentence, but to be placed on the tariff below prison. These sentences should it was argued be less severe than imprisonment, but be demanding enough to encourage sentencers to use them for the less serious offences that had previously attracted a prison term.

## Alternatives to custody or intermediate sanctions?

If prison is to be used less often, then alternative sentences need to be used more often. But what is an alternative to prison? Many of the new types of sentences introduced from the 1960s onwards, such as the community service order, were presented as alternatives to custody. That is they were to be regarded as equivalent to custody, and only imposed in circumstances where a prison sentence would have been considered. This implies that the sentences can be substituted for prison and are equivalent. And indeed the Court of Appeal established that 190 hours of community service were equivalent to 9–12 months of imprisonment (*R v Lawrence* 1982). When the community service order was originally introduced, courts were enjoined to indicate whether the order was a direct alternative to custody or not, and to record that fact in the court register (Home Office 1986: 43).

The problem with this kind of approach is that many sentencers and the public simply do not see community penalties as in any way equivalent to prison. Thus there was a tendency for the new, so called alternatives to prison to be used instead as alternatives to probation. In addition, the mixed rationales underlying the community service order made it difficult to approach in terms of the tariff – how, for example, did such sentences match the seriousness of the offence? If however the use of imprisonment was to be reduced while at the same time maintaining a notion of tough sentences, new approaches to community sentences were necessary.

Such new approaches were influenced by the justice model. The logic of just deserts and proportionality implied that penalties should be differentiated according to the severity of the crime and the culpability of the offender. In practice, prison terms are measured in terms of the degree of restriction on the offender's liberty. Community sentences could also, it was argued, be justified in this way. It was suggested that community penalties could be made tougher. This could be done by increasing sentencing options and introducing tougher penalties between probation and prison, thus producing a continuum or gradation of penalties which would reflect sentencers' needs for sanctions proportionate to the seriousness of the offence. Intermediate sanctions, that is sentences that in terms of punitiveness are regarded as between a probation order and custody, were seen as one answer to the problems of reconciling the prison reductionists' case and the public demand for tougher penalties in the context of increased incidence and fear of crime. This was one of the themes reflected in the CJA 1991, which we shall now consider as a whole, describing and analysing the ways in which changes in penal thinking influenced its formation and subsequent amendment.

## CRIMINAL JUSTICE ACT 1991

By the 1980s therefore many factors suggested that there was a need for a review of penal policy. It had been largely recognised that the individualised sentencing associated with rehabilitation had produced disparities and what were seen by proponents of a justice model as injustices. It had become associated with longer and indeterminate sentences, far out of proportion to the crime committed. At the same time, whether or not rehabilitation had produced a rise in the prison population, there were also strong arguments in favour of substantially reducing the use of imprisonment, both on the grounds of the relative ineffectiveness of prison in terms of rehabilitation or deterrence, and also on the grounds of its cost effectiveness. At the same time however, public concern over rising crime rates, particularly in offences of violence suggested that reducing the use of imprisonment could be seen as paying insufficient regard to the protection of the public. Community sentences lacked credibility. These issues were reflected in a series of discussion documents and government papers (notably the 1988 Green Paper, *Punishment, Custody and the Community*, and the 1990 White Paper, *Crime, Justice and Protecting the Public*) preceding the CJA 1991, which promised to be one of the most thorough overhauls of sentencing policy. We have already outlined many of the changes brought about by this legislation, some to be quickly overturned in the CJA 1993. This section will place these changes in the context of the shifting penal paradigms outlined above.

The difficulties of the deterrent approach to sentencing was developed in the White Paper:

> Deterrence is a principle with much immediate appeal. Most law abiding citizens understand the reasons why some behaviour is made a criminal offence, and would be deterred by the shame of a criminal conviction or the possibility of a severe penalty. There are doubtless some criminals who carefully calculate the possible gains and risks. But much crime is committed on impulse, given the opportunity presented by an open window or unlocked door, and it is committed by offenders who live from moment to moment; their crimes are as impulsive as the rest of their feckless, sad or pathetic lives. It is unrealistic to construct sentencing arrangements on the assumption that most offenders will weigh up the possibilities in advance and base their conduct on rational calculation. Often they do not.
>
> (Home Office 1990a: 6)

According to Ashworth, 'The origins of the new law were in the government's White Paper of 1990, which stated that desert should be the primary aim of sentencing, that rehabilitation should not be an aim of sentencing but should be striven for within proportionate sentences, and that deterrence is rarely a proper or profitable aim for a sentencer' (von Hirsch and Ashworth 1993: 285–286). The White Paper rejected deterrent sentencing and while it saw a role for rehabilitation, rejected any notion that rehabilitation should be a primary goal. Denunciation was also seen as significant: thus the 1990 White Paper stated that 'the first objective for all sentences is denunciation of and retribution for the crime'. (Home Office 1990a: 6). The emphasis on just deserts meant that the seriousness of the offence was to be the primary criteria for determining the sentence, and it was also envisaged that it should limit the severity of a sentence. This can be seen in the following extract:

> . . . the severity of the sentence in an individual case should reflect primarily the seriousness of the offence which has been committed. Whilst factors such as preventing crime or the rehabilitation of the offender remain important functions of the criminal justice process as a whole, they should not lead to a heavier penalty in an individual case than that which is justified by the seriousness of the offence or the need to protect the public from the offender.
>
> (Home Office 1991)

This extract also shows that while just deserts is a major principle, the protection of the public is also important, thus the Act contained an important incapacitative element. What is often known as bifurcation or a twin track approach was introduced on the principle that for most offenders the sentence was to be based on the seriousness of the offence, except in circumstances where, as, for example, with sexual and violent offenders, incapacitation was seen to be necessary. This was described largely in terms of distinguishing property offences from those involving violence. While the courts were to be encouraged to use non-custodial sentences for property offenders where possible, prison terms, and terms longer than the offence itself merited, could be used for violent offenders.

These key themes were evident throughout the Act. Thus what was to become one of the most controversial provisions of the Act provided that previous convictions should not be looked at when assessing seriousness, the only exception being where earlier offences were taken as aggravating features of the current offence. The offender was to be sentenced on the basis of the current offence and not previous convictions and with the multiple offender, each offence was to be considered individually so that in effect only one offence (the most serious) and only one other would determine the sentence in typical cases. This was, as had been intended, given a very narrow interpretation by the courts, but was heavily criticised as limiting the powers available to courts when sentencing the persistent offender whose offences taken individually were not counted as 'so serious'. As we have seen the CJA 1993 altered this position by removing the s 29 limitation on considering previous offences and the requirement to consider only two current offences when sentencing the multiple offender.

A second implication of the approach was that any restriction on liberty should be commensurate with the seriousness of the offence, which affected the use of both custodial and community sentences. As we have seen, the 1990 White Paper made it clear that imprisonment should not be used for rehabilitative or deterrent motives but might be justified in particular cases on retributive, denunciatory and incapacitative grounds. This is the significance of the statutory criteria to restrict the use of imprisonment, particularly aimed at property offenders. Just deserts was also used to determine lengths of custodial sentences.

In addition, the element of indeterminacy implied by parole was also changed with the introduction of provisions to clarify release dates from prisons with the reform of the system of parole and remission, discussed in Chapter 10.

The Act also changed the role, function and organisation of community sentences. Indeed the 1990 White Paper devoted four out of nine chapters to exploring the role of community penalties. As outlined above, these had primarily been seen as rehabilitative. Probation, for example, had not hitherto been a sentence, but had been seen as an alternative to a sentence. Encouraging the courts to use community sentences more and prison less, and to make these changes acceptable to the public meant that they had to be tied into the just deserts approach, and had to be credible punishments in

256

their own right. Under the CJA 1991 community sentences were placed on the tariff between a fine or discharge and imprisonment and the penalty chosen had to be proportionate to the seriousness of the offence. Thus the 1990 White Paper referred to a continuum of penalties involving an increasing degree of restriction on the offender's liberty with custody at one end and probation at the other with a range of intermediate punishments in the community. This new approach was based on the assumption that the punishment was to be the degree of restriction on the offender's liberty.

Thus it was argued that imprisonment should be retained as the means of punishment for the most serious offences, and fines and discharges for the least serious offences. The Green Paper clarified this point, 'Liberty under the law is highly valued by all of us. The deprivation of liberty is the most severe penalty available to the courts' (Home Office 1988: 8). Apart from financial penalties, most court disposals place restrictions on offenders' freedom of action. The degree of restriction on the offender's freedom of action thus provides the link between community based forms of punishments and imprisonment. Custody is at one end of the continuum of restrictions on offender's freedom of action:

> The effect of custodial sentences is to restrict offenders' freedom of action by removing them from their homes, by determining where they will live during the sentence, by limiting their social relationships and by deciding how and where they will spend the 24 hours in each day.
>
> (Home Office 1988: 3.3)

A new sentence was introduced, the combination order (discussed in Chapter 8). This allowed a term of probation to be combined with a community service order, but with a maximum of 100 hours. Statutory restrictions on mixing different types of community sentences were repealed to allow the sentencer greater flexibility. Restrictions on liberty could also be placed without resorting to custody, thus a new curfew order was introduced with the possibility of using electronic monitoring as a means of surveillance and other restrictions on liberty such as restrictions on associations and home curfews.

The White Paper also highlights the need to confront offenders with their behaviour, 'to enable offenders to see the damage and pain they have caused to their victims, their families and friends, and themselves; and to encourage offenders to develop more responsible attitudes'. (Home Office 1990a: 36). This represents a shift towards a more demanding and challenging approach to offenders, consistent with a deterrent or denunciatory model.

Given that the majority of offenders already stay in the community, who would the new, more demanding, community sanctions be for? It was made clear that they should be for offenders, who in terms of the tariff, would have previously been given a short prison term, which effectively means that the target population were those convicted of non-violent property offences. The White Paper claims, 'The aim is to ensure that the more restrictive, and usually more expensive, community sentences are used for more serious offenders, such as persistent thieves and non-domestic burglars, and not for those who have committed minor offences.'(Home Office 1990a: 19). The problem remains however of what to do with the persistent property offenders. There are, 'About 10,000 of those in custody sentenced for burglary, theft, handling, fraud and forgery, who have three or more previous convictions.' (Home Office 1990a: 21).

Thus the CJA 1991 was a logical development in the context of the shifting penal paradigms explored above. In addition, it stated, more clearly than before, the main principles to be used by sentencers, and thus hoped to encourage consistency. Consequently an editorial in the *Criminal Law Review* on the introduction of the Act commented that 'it can be claimed that the 1991 Act differs from its predecessors in one significant respect: its sentencing provisions have some fairly coherent themes' (Ashworth 1992: 229). Ashworth comments, 'it introduced a primary rationale for English sentencing (desert) and clarified the extent to which other "aims" such as public protection, rehabilitation and deterrence should play a part'. (Ashworth 1994b: 853).

The aims and principles of the Act were welcomed by many though the details of its implementation, for instance, the system of unit fines, led to opposition in some quarters. Of course, not everyone accepted a sentencing policy based primarily on a just deserts approach which fitted sentences to the seriousness of the offence. One of the problems was that the Act gave little guidance on how this seriousness is to be assessed. There is an assumption, for example, that violent and sexual offenders are more serious than property ones, but in practice the delineation of seriousness is far more complex, and perhaps leaves space for both individualisation in terms of judging offence seriousness and discretion. In addition, some argue that just deserts policies can lead to an increase in the tariff. This can come about by very different calculations about what kind of sentence is appropriate for different levels of offence. This is not inevitable however – just deserts models have led to more severe sentencing approaches in California (Davies 1989), but not in Scandinavian countries (Ashworth 1994b; Hudson 1993). Much depends on exactly how maximum sentences are conceived and how actual sentencing lengths are determined in practice.

## SENTENCING FOR WHOM?

We have seen above how penal policy has changed, and how new policies and the philosophies underpinning them are based on criticisms of the policies they replace. Shifts in the penal paradigm usually represent a change in the balance between the claims of many different theories and considerations. One of the questions that underlines the different theories of punishment is whether it is possible for sentencing decisions to reconcile the different needs of the offender, victim and community. We could also question who sentencing is for – the offender? the victim? or the wider community?

The dilemmas of sentencing policy are often popularly encapsulated as seeking a balance between the offender and the offence. Thus should the punishment fit the crime? or should punishment fit the offender? Many discussions of sentencing policy focus on the individual offender or on the individual offence as is evident in the just deserts approach. But denouncers and those who stress public protection would argue that this focus neglects the wider role of sentencing policy in expressing the public's disapproval of crime and recognising their need for protection. Others see the victim as a forgotten player in the drama of crime and punishment.

It is not surprising that a criminal justice system based on adversarial principles should produce a sentencing policy that is geared towards the individual offence, offender and the circumstances of the case. The criminal justice system is after all primarily concerned with implementing the rules which determine criminal liability and it deals with individual cases and individual offenders. Thus as Judge Rhys Davies comments, 'Judges . . . must look at the person before them, and all the circumstances, and do what they know to be right conscientiously. That's their duty.' (*The Times*, 28 June 1994: 11). To sentencers therefore what is fair in the individual case is likely to take priority over abstract principles of justice. This is compounded by the tendency to judge each case on its merits and the case law tradition of English law in which as we have seen there are no penal codes stating general principles.

The individualisation of sentencing has also of course been justified by the offender instrumental approach which argues that sentences should aim to prevent further criminality. Also in the adversarial system, defendants have the opportunity as required by due process to present factors in mitigation. All of this encourages a focus on the circumstances of the convicted criminal.

This individualisation however neglects a key person in many offences – the victim. While there is a focus on the harm done, the victim would appear to be little involved in sentencing other than as the potential recipient of a compensation order. As we have seen some argue that there should be a victim impact statement and others have gone so far as to argue that victims' opinions be sought. This might seem fair in some respects but is often rejected also on the grounds of fairness and justice. It is, for example, regarded as a key part of criminal law that punishment is undertaken by the state on behalf of the general public (see, for example, Ashworth 1994b). An offence, unlike a civil dispute, is not a private matter, it is a public one. Therefore, the victim should have no role in sentencing, other than when compensation or reparation is considered. In addition, such victim involvement might further compound disparities when different sentences are given to similar offenders on the basis of victim participation. This would add yet further individualised circumstances, this time based on the opinion of the victim, and could produce highly unpredictable sentencing decisions, further undermining any notion of fairness.

In terms of considering fairness therefore current discussions focus on fairness to individual offenders and fairness in terms of the sentence being proportionate to the crime. In recent years the balance has shifted with more weight being given to the seriousness of the offence and less to the needs and risks of individual offenders. However, the justice approach does restrict the severity of sentencing and encourage consistency, thus increasing justice to offenders. A major advantage of including in the aims of sentencing the retributivist concern with just desert is that it sets, in principle, limits on that system as to who, how and when it can act against an individual and thus provides the justification for civil rights within the criminal justice system.

But as we have seen fairness to individual offenders is not easy to achieve. How much for example should their individual circumstances be a factor in sentencing? And how might this lead to other kinds of inequities in sentencing? This can be seen when, as in Chapter 8, we look at the sentences given to those from different socio-economic backgrounds. Thus offenders' domestic, financial, and social circumstances may mean that they are judged favourably or adversely by the court. They may affect how they can present themselves, whether or not they can pay a fine, and the kind of mitigating factors they may present. In addition, sentences may have an unequal impact on these different groups.

Some of the above points indicate that sentencing policy cannot hope to include what some would see as the root causes of crime if these lie in social inequalities and the individual circumstances. This brings us back to the failure of offender instrumental approaches to make any inroads into the volume of crime. How far therefore can the public be protected or reassured through sentencing policy?

In answer to this it could be argued that tougher policing and tougher sentencing policies are only likely to have a marginal effect on crime prevention. This is because as we have seen only a minority of cases reach the courts in comparison with the totality of crime. Approximately 100,000 cases reached the Crown Court annually in recent years, and the number is falling, whereas the British Crime Survey suggests that 15 million crimes are committed each year. Even if the police force caught twice as many criminals, the courts could only be dealing with less than 1 per cent of those responsible for criminal acts. Currently, the Home Office figures on attrition suggest that only 2 per cent of known crimes result in a conviction (see Figure 3.3) and of these the overwhelming majority are offences that do not result in a prison sentence. Thus the offender instrumental approach can at best have only a marginal impact on the amount of crime that the community is subject to. Furthermore, as we have seen, the promise of rehabilitation that crime could be cured and the arguments of deterrent theorists that it could be prevented have not been fulfilled.

Thus the criminal justice process appears to have an intrinsically limited role to play in reducing or preventing crime. What implication does this have for sentencing policy particularly in respect of its credibility with the public? The furore caused by unpopular sentencing decisions and the unit fines introduced by the CJA 1991 illustrates however that the public do perceive sentencing policy as important. To the denunciation model, as we have seen, punishment is not only a matter for offenders and victims but also involves the community's expectations about standards of behaviour and appropriate punishment. The criminal endangers their civil liberties by threatening their property, physical well-being and shared values.

The CJA 1991 also recognised the denunciatory role of punishment. Thus the 1990 White Paper stated that, 'Punishment can effectively denounce criminal behaviour and exact retribution for it. The sentence of the court expresses public repugnance of criminal behaviour and determines the punishment for it.' (Home Office 1990a: 5). The CJA 1991 therefore could be seen as advocating what has been described as a denunciatory-retributivist perspective which by focusing on the morality of the act looks at the consequences of punishment for society as a whole rather than on the convicted criminal (Davies 1993).

Sentencing, after all, is a judgment about an appropriate sentence for a wrong done and is in effect morality in action. The judge condemns the offender in the name of the community and so re-enforces standards of morality. Thus a denunciatory-retributivist approach to sentencing recognises the moral censuring role of sentencing; and that in a democracy the tariff of sentencing should reflect and articulate the moral concerns of the community as well as ensuring fairness to the individual offender before the courts.

Denunciation could add a more positive dimension to a sentencing policy which in many ways has accepted the rather gloomy prognostication that 'nothing works'. One strength of rehabilitative and deterrent arguments was that they appeared to do something positive, they focused on the future rather than on the past. Just deserts focuses on the harm done in the past and therefore could be seen as negative – punishment, however fair, for its own sake. Denunciation on the other hand stresses the key role of punishment in focusing public attention onto issues of morality and right and wrong. This in turn draws attention to the social function of punishment. Thus David Garland comments:

> In designing penal policy we are not simply deciding how to deal with a group of people on the margins of society – whether to deter, reform, or incapacitate them and if so how. Nor are we simply deploying power or economic resources for penological ends. We are also and at the same time defining ourselves and our society in ways which may be quite central to our cultural and political identity. An important part of a society's penal rhetoric is taken up with the suggestion of a social vision.

> (Garland 1990)

Thus the importance of punishment for community and society should be recognised. The values embodied in the criminal law demonstrate a society's moral views of right and wrong and those who breach the laws are doing more than just the physical and financial damage they do to the individual victim, they are challenging the values of society, and threaten the individual's definition of normality. Therefore, the purpose of punishment for the denouncer is not directed at the criminal act or the criminal actor; but at the values which define the rules embodied in the criminal law. The audience is neither the criminal nor victim but the public at large.

Thus the link between punishment and the public involves more than protecting individual citizens from individual criminals, though it is one essential role of the criminal justice system. Thus crime does more than threaten the individual, it is a threat to the community itself. 'The real significance of crime', wrote Joseph Conrad, 'is in its being a breach of faith with the community of mankind.'

## CONCLUSION

This chapter has looked at how sentencing policy must be placed within the context of changing views about the causes of crime and the role of the penal system, especially prison. Thus the rehabilitative model was based on the idea that the problems which caused crime could be established and therefore alleviated. A sentence of imprisonment could be likened to a period of hospital treatment, an approach which had great appeal to reformers who also saw it as more humane. After decades of influence however the key ideas of rehabilitation were discredited. Rehabilitative policies were criticised as inhumane and inefficient. To some indeed they represented another way in which the powerful in society could enforce their values on others. Where for example did rehabilitation stop and enforced conformity or brainwashing begin? Did offenders who were effectively sentenced to be helped not have rights? Were these sentences fair?

The justice model aimed to provide an answer to the many problems of rehabilitation and other instrumental policies. Punishment should not aim to do good, but to do as little harm as possible. Harsher sentences on the grounds of rehabilitation or deterrence could be limited by an approach which stressed linking the sentence to the harm done by culpable offenders. Yet as we have seen, the application of the justice model raises questions about what is meant by justice and fairness in relation to sentencing.

A key feature of sentencing policy has also been an acceptance of the prison reductionist's aim, whether for idealistic or practical reasons, to reduce the use of imprisonment. This involved stressing the punitive nature of community sentences so as to make them credible to the police and sentencers. Whether or not this will be successful either in terms of reducing the use of imprisonment or making community penalties acceptable as a punishment, remains to be seen.

262

Changes in penal policy reflect the efforts of policy makers to find a balance between the various aims of sentencing as well as the aims of the criminal justice process as a whole. There is a constant tension between the need for due process, which extends beyond conviction to the sentencing process and the penal system, and the often conflicting claims of public protection. While the CJA 1991 defined the primary aim of sentencing as just deserts it also, with the twin track approach, allows for incapacitation through larger sentences for some violent and sexual offences. Incapacitation may conflict with the interests of due process, particularly where an assessment needs to be made of the circumstances in which a particular offender is assessed as dangerous enough that a sentence out of proportion to just deserts is justified.

The declining role of rehabilitation and offender instrumental strategies may require a re-evaluation of existing sentencing practices and penal sanctions. How for example might this affect prisons? How will the new emphasis on punishment in the community affect the operation of community sentences previously seen as rehabilitative? And how far is the community served by the criminal justice process and sentencing policy? Some of these issues will be taken up in the next two chapters. Chapter 10 will look at prisons and Chapter 11 will explore community sentences and other aspects of crime prevention in the community.

## Review questions

1. Explain why the principles of individualisation and indeterminacy followed from a rehabilitative approach to sentencing.
2. What is meant by the term 'disparity' and explain how it is affected by individualistic strategies?
3. What are the main elements of a justice approach to sentencing?
4. Explain the difference between a rationale for community penalties that aims to achieve an 'alternative to custody' and a rationale that seeks an intermediate sanction.

## Further reading

Cavadino P and Dignan J (1992) *The Penal System: An Introduction*. London: Sage

Davies M (1993) *Punishing Criminals: Developing Community-based Intermediate Sanctions*. Connecticut: Greenwood

Duff A and Garland (1994) *A Reader on Punishment*. Oxford: Oxford University Press

von Hirsch A and Ashworth A (eds) (1993) *Principled Sentencing*. Edinburgh: Edinburgh University Press

# CHAPTER 10

# PRISONS

Origins of the Penitentiary
Prisons in England and Wales in the 1990s
Prison Population
Impact of Imprisonment on Inmates
Aims of the Prison Service: Do Prisons Work?
Woolf Report into the 1990 Prison Disturbances

## INTRODUCTION

In October 1993 in a speech to the Conservative Party Conference, the Home Secretary, Michael Howard, stated that:

> Let us be clear. Prison works. It ensures that we are protected from murderers, muggers and rapists – and it makes many who are tempted to commit crime think twice.

He went on to announce the building of six new prisons, and continued:

> A rumour got out over the summer that I don't think prison should be a picnic. Well I'll let you into a secret. I don't. That is why I am determined to ensure that conditions are decent, but austere.

The considerable public debate which followed demonstrated conflicting views about the role, aims and functions of prison along with continuing concerns about aspects of prison regimes, conditions and security. In general terms prisons have credibility with the public as an institution for punishment – the punishment being loss of liberty. This serves a retributive and denunciatory purpose. Prisons are also seen as a potential deterrent for the general public and they incapacitate dangerous and persistent offenders for the period of time they are incarcerated. Whether prisons can rehabilitate inmates or deter them from committing further offences is far less obvious in the light of statistics on recidivism. Indeed some argue that it may increase the likelihood that offenders will continue their life of crime – not only have prisons been characterised as schools of crime but they remove offenders from the stabilising effect of their families and the likelihood of obtaining gainful employment. Yet others feel that the prison experience is insufficiently punitive – sentiments echoed in the Home Secretary's reference to prison being a 'picnic'.

On the other hand, it has often been argued that prison *is* the punishment, and is not *for* punishment. Poor conditions within prisons have been blamed for riots, violence within prisons and for inhibiting prospects for rehabilitation. To those who run prisons, the day-to-day problems of security – ensuring that prisoners do not abscond, and control – attempting to prevent riots and violence, may well take precedence over more abstract goals of rehabilitation or deterrence.

This chapter will explore many of these issues. It starts by examining the origin of the penitentiary, and how the use and aims of prison have developed over the last century. We will outline the current organisation of the prison system in England and Wales, and we will look at the numbers and characteristics of the prison population. We will examine the experience of imprisonment, the aims of prisons, and explore the issues involved in assessing whether or not prison can be said to work as the Home Secretary implies. Finally, we will look at a review of the prison system in the 1991 Woolf Report.

## ORIGINS OF THE PENITENTIARY

The prison as we know it today is a relatively recent social experiment which began 200 years ago. Before that time people were not usually given a sentence of imprisonment. The prisons, dungeons and gaols were owned by a variety of municipal and private bodies, and were used to hold debtors or people who had been arrested and were awaiting trial at the quarter sessions (quarterly sittings of the court). They also held those awaiting the implementation of a sentence. For serious offenders, transportation or execution was the main punishment. For lesser offenders, prison was used to encourage a person to pay a fine and short periods of confinement were prescribed for offenders too poor to pay a fine.

John Howard in his survey of prisons in the 1770s estimated a prison population of 4,084. His census of 1776 calculated that the prison population was made up of debtors (59.7 per cent), felons awaiting trial, execution and transportation, along with a few serving a prison sentence (24.3 per cent), and petty offenders (15.9 per cent). Howard was appointed to the post of High Sheriff for Bedfordshire in 1773. One of his duties, usually neglected by other sheriffs, was to report on the prisons in his county. The conditions he encountered so shocked him that he undertook a more widespread review of prison conditions that was printed in 1777, entitled *The State of the Prisons*.

Punishment in the 18th century for those convicted of misdemeanours consisted of the stocks, corporal punishment or fines. For serious offenders the sanction was the death penalty, or a substitute. During the 18th century, the number of capital offences rose from 50 to 225, and the death penalty became the prescribed punishment for most offences classified as felonies. Juries, however, were often reluctant to convict a person knowing that they would be executed. 'Pious perjury' according to William Blackstone became more popular after 1750. By re-evaluating the value of goods stolen to less than a shilling, juries convicted offenders for petty larceny rather than the capital offence of grand larceny. Despite the growth in the number of capital offences, the number of executions declined over the century and transportation became the typical sentence by the end of the 18th century. As Figure 10.1 shows, in the five years from 1765-69, 70 per cent of criminals sentenced at the Old Bailey were transported.

The Transportation Act 1717, providing for transportation to the American colonies as a punishment, was introduced with the purpose of deterring criminals and supplying the colonies with much needed labour. It became increasingly popular to commute a death penalty to transportation. Although transportation did not stop immediately with the American Revolution of 1776, prisoners began to be housed in hulks which were permanently moored old ships. A House of Commons Committee review of transportation in 1779 recommended the continued use of hulks and that two new penitentiaries be built. The idea of the penitentiary was therefore seen at this time as a way forward, even though alternative locations were also being examined to permit the continuation of transportation.

Transportation came under scrutiny because some felt it was not a sufficient deterrent. Indeed it was said that some committed crime in order to be transported, despite the health hazards of the journey. A Transportation Act was passed in 1784 at a time when there was nowhere to send convicts although the Beauchamp Committee of 1785 reported favourably on the practice and cited its potential for reform, its cheapness and the advantages to the colonies of a convict workforce. Alternatives considered included Algiers, Tristan de Cunha and sending convicts down the coal mines but Australia was preferred.

Transportation to Australia reached its peak in the 1830s and 1840s with between 4,000 and 5,000 convicts being sent each year. There were also periods in the early 19th century when 70 per cent of convicted felons were imprisoned in hulks. The use of hulks and transportation declined after the prison building programme of the 1840s. By 1853 the idea of penal servitude as a substitute for transportation was introduced for those sentenced to under 14 years. In 1857 the last prison hulk went out of service and transportation ended formally in 1867.

Ideological and practical considerations changed the conditions within, and the function of, prison. In the new penal ideas emerging at the end of the 18th century the penitentiary style of prison was seen as a place to change criminals' behaviour by making them penitent. Places of detention were to be transformed from gaols for holding criminals into penitentiaries for

266

**Fig 10.1** Distribution of punishments, Old Bailey 1760–94

| Year | Per cent death sentence | Per cent transported/ hulks | Per cent whip/brand/ fine | Per cent imprisoned |
|---|---|---|---|---|
| 1760–64 | 12.7 | 74.1 | 12.3 | 1.2 |
| 1765–69 | 15.8 | 70.2 | 13.4 | 0.8 |
| 1770–74 | 17.0 | 66.5 | 14.2 | 2.3 |
| 1775–79 | 20.7 | 33.4 | 17.6 | 28.6 |
| 1780–84 | 25.8 | 24.1 | 15.5 | 34.6 |
| 1785–89 | 18.5 | 50.1 | 13.2 | 13.3 |
| 1790–94 | 15.9 | 43.9 | 11.7 | 28.3 |

(Ignatieff M (1975) *A Just Measure of Pain.* New York: Columbia University Press: 81)

transforming them into law-abiding citizens. This new ideology was influenced by a combination of ideas about religious salvation, humanitarian concern with the conditions of prisons and control concerns about the growing urban population. The penal ideology of the era was also shaped by the theories of rehabilitation which we discussed in Chapter 9. These involved isolating the offender from the bad influences of the community in 'total institutions' (Goffman 1961) which cut off the inmate from the environmental sources that were considered by some to be the cause of crime (Rothman 1980). This penal ideology also focused on the importance of surveillance and styles of discipline which could transform prisoners into self-disciplined workers (Bentham 1791; Foucault 1977).

These new ideas were prevalent across the emerging industrial societies of Europe and the USA. They were embodied in reforms influenced by Quaker thinkers in Pennsylvania and prison reformers such as John Howard and Elizabeth Fry in England (Rothman 1980). They also represented a shift in views about how to control problem groups in the community (Scull 1977). By the end of the 18th century not only prisoners, but orphans, mentally ill, sick and unemployed were being assigned to new style institutions such as prisons, orphanages, asylums, hospitals and workhouses. The grand Georgian and late Victorian style of institutions were invented at this time as the solution to deal with 'problem' categories of the population.

The Penitentiary Act 1779 provided the first indication of the new role for prisons as institutions to reform and deter criminals. The influence of John Howard, Sir William Blackstone and William Eden was apparent in the new direction to penal policy. This positive role for prisons was re-echoed in the report of the May Committee on prisons as late as 1979, and in the statements of the Chief Inspector of Prisons in the 1990s, Judge Stephen Tumin. Many ideas on prisons and their roles were utopian – such as Jeremy Bentham's panopticon, a model discussed below. However, these ideas offered a way forward for a penal system which faced three main practical problems.

First, the concern about growing numbers of migrants coming to the cities in search of work. The old style welfare system, based on parish relief, was no longer viable as the new factory system needed a more mobile labour force. It was no use having large pools of unemployed workers in isolated rural areas away from the new sources of work. Hence, the problem of how to care and control those who were moving to rapidly expanding urban areas. This encouraged the search for innovative solutions and the invention of new institutions to cope with those deemed to be either a threat or inadequate – thus the workhouse, asylum and orphanage as well as the penitentiary.

Secondly, there was the practical problem after 1776 that transportation to the colony of Virginia was no longer available as a result of the American Revolution. Thirdly, there was growing disquiet amongst reformers and thinkers such as Blackstone, Romilly and Beccaria about the large numbers of capital offences. The ideas of Cesare Beccaria about the use of the death penalty influenced debates in the House of Commons. He attacked the widespread use of capital punishment arguing that the death penalty brutalised rather than deterred the population. His views were espoused by William Eden in the reform debates in Britain. Eden's book, *Principles of Penal Law*, was published in 1771. Sir Samuel Romilly took the lead in the parliamentary campaign to reduce the number of capital offences. He realised that to relinquish one mode of punishment the public and Parliament would need to be reassured that a satisfactory alternative was available. Thus some promoters of the penitentiary argued that it was a more humane alternative to the death penalty, not that it was more efficient, as Bentham and Howard were to argue.

It took 50 years for prisons to become the main mode of punishment used by the criminal courts in Britain. The views of Howard and Bentham influenced prison policy for the next two centuries. Prison became not merely a substitute for the death penalty and transportation but a positive institution in which regimes, if sufficiently constructive, could rehabilitate those sent to them. Regimes were also to be sufficiently austere to deter future lawbreakers. The principle of 'less eligibility' implied that prison conditions were not to be more favourable than those found in the homes of the honest poor lest it encouraged crime.

The most celebrated of the novel ideas for bringing about constructive rehabilitation of convicts was the panopticon design proposed by Jeremy Bentham. The panopticon style prison involved a central viewing tower with rings of cells on each floor facing inwards to be visible to the observation tower. Observation and inspection were the keys to Bentham's approach to a more humane and effective mode of punishment. The panopticon would permit surveillance to allow prison officials to make assessments of prisoner's rehabilitation by constantly monitoring their behaviour.

The coliseum style and circular design of the panopticon was to prove difficult to build and was also inefficient. Pentonville was opened in 1842, and became the model for most Victorian prisons. It had stacked galleries on landings along a central straight corridor. Each corridor met at a central location in a fan shaped floor plan with a central control and observation point permitting uninterrupted observation of each wing.

This systematic approach to prison design and administration reflected a growing interest in penal reform, which was wider than that of mere philanthropy. As the 19th century progressed a growing number of professional experts such as architects and doctors began to take an interest in penal affairs. The intervention of central government into penal policy meant that resources were made available to those who appeared to offer a solution to the problems of crime. Government involvement had been spurred by the problems of where to ship those sentenced to transportation. Having resorted to housing increasing numbers of prisoners in the hulks, it was then necessary for the government to find them work such as river dredging.

**Fig 10.2** The Panopticon

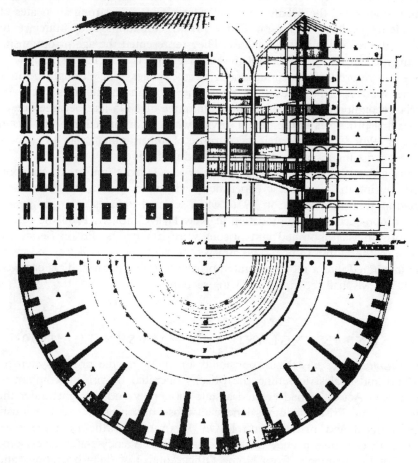

(Bowering (1843) The Works of Jeremy Bentham, Volume IV, 172–3 cf p.201)

For the next 200 years, the government became increasingly concerned in the administration of prisons. The second half of the 19th century saw the gradual transfer of responsibility for monitoring conditions and the administration of prisons to central government. This process began with the Gaol Act 1823, in which Peel's administration set out the first comprehensive statement of principles about the running of local prisons. The Act imposed health requirements; required inspection by visiting justices; banned the consumption of alcohol and demanded the classification of inmates and the segregation of different categories. There were to be five classes of inmates with male separated from female prisoners and an annual report on the prison had to be submitted to the Home Secretary.

In 1877 all prisons were nationalised in a Prison Act which brought all prisons under central government control. The government established the Prison Commission to run prisons and the first of a number of influential chairmen of the commissioners was appointed, Sir Edmund Du Cane. Some commissioners led the debate on penal reform and were strong advocates of a modern penology based on better prison conditions and strategies to achieve the rehabilitation of inmates. They represented the age of optimism, documented in Chapter 9, about the positive aspects of penal institutions as places of reform. This commitment to the belief that through positive regimes inmates could be encouraged to lead good and useful lives was given official recognition in the Gladstone Committee of 1895 and became one of the leading principles of the prison service when incorporated into the Prison Rules in 1949. This states that the purpose of imprisonment was 'to encourage and assist the inmate to lead a good and useful life'.

During the 1930s the treadmill and arrows on convict uniforms were abolished. During this period also experiments with open prisons for adults were started at Wakefield Prison in 1936, when selected inmates from the prison slept in non-secure accommodation at New Hall Camp. In 1963 the Prison Commission was abolished and prisons were run by the Prison Service, a branch of the Home Office. The aim was to allow penal policy to be more fully integrated into a more general approach to crime control. This changed in 1993 as we shall see in the following section.

## PRISONS IN ENGLAND AND WALES IN THE 1990s

The *Prison Service* has the responsibility of operating the prison system in England and Wales, including the prisons operated by private companies. The Prison Act 1877 had created a state monopoly and brought under the control of the Prison Commissioners all those prisons that had previously been in local and private control. On 1 April 1993 the Prison Service became an executive agency of the Home Office. Agency status gives some degree of independence from Home Office control of daily operations and responsibility for budget and expenditure. The first director of the Prison

Service under these new arrangements was Derek Lewis, previously an executive in the private sector.

In January 1994 there were 132 prison establishments in England and Wales. The range of prisons reflects the variety of tasks they are used for. Some need to be near criminal courts in urban areas to house those remanded in custody while awaiting trial or sentence. Others deal with specialist populations such as young offenders or females. Others hold inmates for relatively short periods while others need to offer a regime for those prisoners who might spend the rest of their life inside a prison. Some can pay less attention to security because they house prisoners who have shown they can be trusted, while others must contain inmates convicted of serious violent offences who would be a danger to the public if they were to escape, and remain a danger to those inside prison while they are there. The Prison Service classifies prisons as local, training and dispersal prisons, young offender institutions, remand centres and women's prisons. Closed prisons have most security and surveillance to prevent escapes, whereas open prisons have more relaxed security.

*Local prisons* are used to hold those remanded in custody awaiting trial or sentence. After conviction and sentence to a period of incarceration the observation, classification and allocation unit in the local prison carries out an initial assessment and classification. This determines which prison the prisoner will be sent to, depending on security categorisation, the length of sentence and the training, medical and other needs of the inmate.

Those sentenced to a short period in prison will probably stay in the local prison. This is usually near to where they live and so helps facilitate family visits. The local prisons tend to be the older prisons built in the Victorian era and found in urban built-up areas. A new local prison, Belmarsh in East London, was opened in 1991, but this is unusual as most expenditure on prison building went on new training prisons. These are convenient for proximity to the courts and to the prisoners' families but are often the most overcrowded with the oldest facilities. All 37 local prisons are closed establishments.

*Remand wings and centres* are used in addition to local prisons for holding remand prisoners. In 1992 there were 31 remand centres or local prisons with adult remand wings for males. Remand centres were created specifically for young offenders in response to growing concerns about mixing young remand prisoners with adults and, in particular, about the level of suicides and self-inflicted harm amongst remand prisoners under 21.

*Dispersal prisons* have regimes designed to ensure no escapes as they hold prisoners with the maximum security classification. All sentenced prisoners on arrival in a prison are given a security rating. This ranges from category A for those whose escape would constitute a serious risk to the public, to category D for those who can be sent to open prisons.

The escape of the Soviet spy, George Blake, from Wormwood Scrubs prison in 1965 led to an inquiry by the Mountbatten Committee. Their report in 1966 recommended that all high risk inmates be held in one maximum security prison. This recommendation was not approved and, after a further proposal from a committee chaired by Leon Radzinowicz which reported in 1968 it was decided that high security prisoners should be dispersed amongst a number of prisons with maximum security facilities; hence the term 'dispersal prisons' of which there were six in 1994. Three of these have special security units for those category A inmates most likely to try to escape, such as IRA prisoners.

The need for security classifications was another of the recommendations of the Mountbatten Report. Initial classification is based on the crime committed and the reports made by the assessment unit in the local prison. These categories are reassessed at regular intervals and most inmates are reclassified downwards during their prison term. Category A is for prisoners whose escape from custody would be highly dangerous to the public or to the security of the state. In March 1992 there were 395 category A prisoners. Category B is used to classify inmates who do not constitute such a serious risk. Category C is applied to prisoners who cannot be trusted in open prisons but are deemed unlikely to make an effort to escape, and category D is for prisoners who can be trusted to serve their time in open prisons where the security aspect of the regime is minimal.

*Training prisons* hold long-term inmates. There are 71 training prisons and they can be open or closed. They provide training facilities, vocational courses and the opportunity to work in the prison industries. At Coldingley Prison, a closed prison, inmates can work making motorway signs or in the large industrial laundry that has a contract with hospitals in the region. Grendon Underwood offers a specialist regime based on the therapeutic community concept pioneered by Maxwell Henderson in psychiatric hospitals.

*Young offender institutions* – On 30 June 1992 there were 8,296 inmates aged 14–16 and young adults (aged 17–21) in young offender institutions run by the Prison Service. The breakdown of this population can be seen in Figure 10.3.

Young offender institutions hold offenders aged between 15 and 21 years of age. There are 29 young offender institutions. Places for incarcerating younger offenders have changed over the years since the Victorian era when the first efforts to separate younger inmates from adults were made with the introduction of reformatories and industrial schools. Borstals were introduced in 1901 and made fully available after the Prevention of Crime Act 1908. Detention centres were introduced in the Criminal Justice Act 1948. In Chapter 5 we described the changes since 1982 to the name of institutions holding younger offenders. The names may have changed more rapidly than the nature of the regimes that the changes were supposed to signify.

*Women's prisons* hold less than 4 per cent of the total prison population (average daily population of 1,577 in 1992) and the majority are serving sentences of less than 18 months. Female prisoners are held in one of 13

**Fig 10.3** Population of young offenders in prison service establishments in England and Wales (30 June 1992)

Number of persons

| Sex and age | All custody types | Type of custody | | | | |
|---|---|---|---|---|---|---|
| | | Detention in a young offender institution | Section 53 C & YP Act 1933 and custody for life | In default of payment of a fine | Untried | Convicted un-sentenced |
| All males and females | 8,296 | 5,273 | 217 | 82 | 1,958 | 766 |
| All males | 8,094 | 5,146 | 208 | 79 | 1,923 | 738 |
| All juveniles* | 336 | 237 | 26 | – | 54 | 19 |
| Aged 14 | 16 | 14 | 1 | – | – | 1 |
| Aged 15 | 95 | 69 | 7 | – | 14 | 5 |
| Aged 16 | 225 | 154 | 18 | – | 40 | 13 |
| All young adults | 7,758 | 4,909 | 182 | 79 | 1,869 | 719 |
| Aged 17 | 965 | 426 | 36 | 1 | 386 | 116 |
| Aged 18 | 1,610 | 922 | 33 | 8 | 451 | 196 |
| Aged 19 | 2,078 | 1,300 | 30 | 20 | 494 | 234 |
| Aged 20 | 2,291 | 1,499 | 48 | 33 | 538 | 173 |
| Aged 21 | 814 | 762 | 35 | 17 | – | – |
| All females | 202 | 127 | 9 | 3 | 35 | 28 |
| All juveniles | 8 | 5 | 3 | – | – | – |
| Aged 14 | – | – | – | – | – | – |
| Aged 15 | 1 | 1 | – | – | – | – |
| Aged 16 | 7 | 4 | 3 | – | – | – |
| All young adults | 194 | 122 | 6 | 3 | 35 | 28 |
| Aged 17 | 19 | 10 | - | – | 5 | 4 |
| Aged 18 | 46 | 31 | 2 | – | 6 | 7 |
| Aged 19 | 57 | 37 | - | 1 | 11 | 8 |
| Aged 20 | 52 | 26 | 3 | 1 | 13 | 9 |
| Aged 21 | 20 | 18 | 1 | 1 | – | – |

* Juveniles are inmates aged 14, 15 or 16

(*Prison Statistics England and Wales 1992*: 58)

penal establishments. Most are in all female prisons, the biggest being Holloway. It holds almost a third of all female prisoners with an average population of 483 inmates in 1991/92. Four prisons hold both men and women. Three are local prisons: Exeter which is used for emergencies only, Risley which held on average 74 female inmates in 1991/92, and Low Newton with 33 female inmates on average in 1991/92. Durham is a closed prison which has a high security female wing and held on average 23 female prisoners in 1991/92.

*Special hospitals* are used for offenders who need treatment for mental disorders under conditions of special security because of their violent or criminal behaviour. These offenders can be sent to one of three special hospitals, Broadmoor, Rampton or Ashworth. These have maximum security facilities similar to a dispersal prison. Special hospitals are run by the Department of Health. All the other types of prisons mentioned above are the responsibility of the Prison Service.

The Prison Service is not now the only agency allowed to run prisons. The Criminal Justice Act 1988 allowed for private companies to take over the operation of remand prisons, a sector of the prison establishment where the worst conditions were usually found. Since then companies such as Group 4 have been involved in operating prisons. The Prison Service has overall responsibility for the 'contracted out' prisons run by the private sector. All contracted out prisons have a Prison Service controller of governor grade to monitor the delivery of the contract with the Prison Service, and to undertake adjudications for prisoners charged with offences against disciplinary rules.

First to open was The Wolds private remand centre near Hull. Others include Blakenhurst near Redditch, Hereford and Worcester and Doncaster which opened in June 1994. The government's aim to break down the Prison Service monopoly in this area was not only influenced by their ideological belief in the virtues of competition. Two other factors played their part. First, a desire to inject new ideas into the running of remand prison regimes, and secondly, after a series of industrial disputes, a determination to undermine the powerful trade union, the Prison Officers' Association, that represents prison officers.

The influence of the Prison Officers' Association has been apparent in a number of industrial disputes over the years. The Labour government of James Callaghan established an inquiry to look into questions associated with the administration of prisons and in particular resources and staff relations with management. The resulting Home Office report published in 1979 (*Committee of Inquiry into the UK Prison Service*, Cmnd 7673). It was chaired by Mr Justice May and its report was known as the May Report. More than one Home Secretary would have agreed with Merlyn Rees, Home Secretary between 1976 and 1979, when he said, 'As Home Secretary I did not control the Prison Service.' (University of London Conference, 26 April 1980).

The May Committee was set up after a long period of deteriorating industrial relations in prisons in England and Wales. It examined the prison population, objectives and regimes, the organisation of the system, resources, the roles of prison officers and governors, pay and allowances, industrial relations and working conditions. It concluded that, 'Central administration ought to have shown itself more responsive to growing feelings of dissatisfaction with the organization and management and service as a whole, especially in the field of personnel management.' With reference to the importance of having clear and agreed aims for prisons – discussed later in this chapter – it commented:

> A great deal of the evidence we received maintained that at the present time these objectives (of imprisonment) were unclear or confused or both, and that this had brought about or contributed not only to a lack of incisive and purposeful leadership but also to indecision, frustration and the consequent lowering of morale throughout the prison service . . .

(Home Office 1979: 1961)

The May Report found that over a quarter of junior prison officers were working more than 60 hours overtime a week, boosting a modest basic salary into reasonably high average earnings. In response to these staffing costs, a new higher basic wage for a 39-hour working week was introduced for prison officers in exchange for abandoning some of the expensive shift work practices.

Fresh Start, as the initiative was called, was introduced in 1987 in an attempt to overcome these staffing costs. The Prison Officers' Association agreed to the scheme because of the rise in basic pay, pension benefits, and officers were allowed to, and given financial inducements to, buy their own living quarters. This created a longer-term problem for the Prison Service as it reduced geographical mobility due to the lack of affordable accommodation in some regions.

Industrial disputes were not overcome by the Fresh Start programme and the government sought other ways of curtailing the influence of the Prison Officers' Association. The introduction of 'contracting out' of Prison Service work to private companies should be seen in this context. The CJPOA 1994 curtailed the right of prison officers and governor grade staff to go on strike.

In 1993/94 the average cost of imprisonment was calculated at £22,006 per inmate per year. However, this does not mean that sending one less person to prison would save this amount as most of these costs are relatively fixed. Three-quarters of prison service expenditure is attributable to staffing costs. In 1992/93 the Prison Service employed 39,314 people, of which 23,050 were uniformed officers. This represents a ratio of just over two inmates per officer and compares with a ratio of three to one in 1980. This is a very generous ratio of officers to prisoners compared with prison services around the world. In 1994, there were 1,020 governors.

The Prison Service is open to inspection by the *Inspectorate of Prisons*, established by statute in 1982 after a recommendation in the 1979 May Report. The Chief Inspector is currently Judge Stephen Tumim, co-author of the second part of the Woolf Report 1991 which made numerous recommendations for improving the prison system. Members of the inspectorate can make unannounced visits as well as having a number of scheduled visits to certain prisons each year. After a visit a report is made highlighting the strengths and weaknesses of the establishments visited. Some reports have been very damning about conditions in prison establishments and the treatment of prisoners.

Each prison has a *Board of Visitors*, who oversee the administration of the prison, made up of lay members of the local community, usually JPs, doctors and other local people. Until 1992 the Board of Visitors adjudicated on matters of discipline where an inmate might be liable to lose remission for disciplinary offences. As a result of the CJA 1991 prison governors have the right to order up to 14 'added days' for disciplinary offences. The Board of Visitors at Wandsworth prison in the 1980s were one of the first to publish a public report, describing the insanitary conditions associated with slopping out and the health hazards of a cockroach infestation near the kitchen area.

In April 1994, the Board of Visitors at Whitemoor prison in March, Cambridgeshire published a report about the conditions and regime in the prison, which holds 514 inmates, 20 per cent of whom were classified as category A. These included Dennis Nilsen and IRA terrorists. Another 20 per cent were life sentence prisoners. It was in this prison that Leslie Bailey, a paedophile convicted of serious sexual offences against children, was found strangled in his cell in October 1993. The report describes the prison as dirty and the Board of Visitors condemned the illegal brewing of 'hooch' by inmates. The main concern expressed by the Board in their report was that management had lost control of the situation and they quote a governor who was of the opinion that the prisoners and not the staff were virtually in control of the prison. An allegation that was to be prescient in the light of the subsequent escape attempt in September 1994 by five convicted IRA prisoners who were able to obtain guns in which one prison officer was shot and wounded. All the prisoners were recaptured within hours of the escape. In the same month, quantities of the explosive Semtex were found at Whitemoor. These incidents raised many questions about why no action had been taken and led to demands for the resignation of the Home Secretary, as did the escape in January 1995 of three category A offenders from another dispersal prison, Parkhurst, on the Isle of Wight.

## PRISON POPULATION

We saw in Chapter 9 that concerns over prison overcrowding, conditions and the size of the prison population led to policies to reduce the numbers sent to prison. At the same time a prison building programme started in 1982 designed to improve facilities and reduce cell sharing. The routine of 'slopping out' caused by the lack of toilet facilities in the cells of the Victorian prisons led to the daily morning practice in the cell blocks of prisoners forming a queue to the washrooms to dispose of the contents of their chamber pots. The Prison Service accepted the February 1996 deadline set by Lord Woolf for an end to slopping out. In fact most prisons completed their programme of modernisation to end this practice by 1994.

The daily population in prison varies depending on the time of year. It usually drops in December and rises to a high point in March. The average daily prison population in England and Wales in 1993 was 44,600. This was over 1,000 lower than the year before and the lowest population since 1984. The prison population peaked in 1988 at 49,900 and then fell to the 1993 level (see Figure 10.4). Since 1993, the prison population has steadily risen, reaching the 50,000 figure in October 1994. The prison population on 31 January 1995 was 49,408 (Home Office 1995). The average prison population for 1994 was 48,621. The Home Office long-term population projection for the year 2001 is 56,600.

276

## Categories of prisoners

Not all inmates held in Her Majesty's Prisons are of the same status. As we have seen in Chapter 5 some defendants are remanded in custody and held in prison. These unconvicted prisoners have rights distinguishing them from other inmates such as daily access to visitors. There are also those who have been convicted but have not yet been sentenced. In Figure 10.4 these two groups are identified as unsentenced prisoners and constitute approximately one-fifth of the average prison population. Figure 10.4 also distinguishes between young offenders below the age of 21 sentenced to detention in young offender institutions and short and long-term inmates defined by sentence lengths of over four years for men and three for women.

## Fine defaulters in prison

In the average daily population of the Prison Service, fine defaulters form a small proportion of the inmates, but if looked at in terms of receptions into prison each year they form a considerable proportion of new arrivals and departures. The reason for this is the short period of time they remain in prison, typically one week.

On 30 June 1991 there were 409 fine defaulters in prison, forming 1.2 per cent of the total sentenced population. Nearly 19,000 fine defaulters were received into Prison Service establishments during 1991. Receptions of female fine defaulters totalled 976 in 1991. Receptions of fine defaulters as a proportion of all receptions under sentence increased from 20.5 per cent in 1988 to 26.2 per cent in 1991, higher than for any of the previous 10 years. Most fine defaulters serve only very short periods of detention or imprisonment. In 1991, the average time served in Prison Service establishments was 7.5 days for males and 6.8 days for females. As a result, even though the number of receptions is large (26 per cent in 1991), because of the comparatively short periods served, fine defaulters form a very small proportion of the average daily prison population.

What were the original offences of those sent to prison because of an unpaid fine? Prison Department Statistics show that for males in 1991 the biggest categories were motoring offences (29 per cent), theft and handling (17 per cent) and drunkenness (4 per cent of receptions in 1991 compared to 11 per cent in 1981). (*Prison Statistics, England and Wales 1991*. Cmd 2157: 111)

The number of offenders sentenced to a fine (excluding motoring offences) has been between 500,000 and 600,000 a year in the last decade whilst the numbers received in default has tended to fall so that receptions per 1,000 fined has fallen from over 30 in the early part of the period to 23 to 24 in the three years from 1988 to 1990. However, in 1991 there was a reversal of these trends and the ratio rose to 28 per 1,000 fined.

Fine defaulters are not automatically sent to prison as Mark Romer, a

**Fig 10.4** Population in custody* 1988–93 in England and Wales (annual averages)

Number of persons[2]

| Type of prisoner | Males | | | | | | Females | | | | | |
|---|---|---|---|---|---|---|---|---|---|---|---|---|
| | 1988 | 1989 | 1990 | 1991 | 1992 | 1993 | 1988 | 1989 | 1990 | 1991 | 1992 | 1993 |
| **Prisoners on remand** | | | | | | | | | | | | |
| Untried | 9,346 | 8,304 | 7,771 | 7,922 | 7,805 | 7687 | 430 | 375 | 300 | 292 | 271 | 285 |
| Convicted unsentenced | 1,587 | 1,727 | 1,749 | 1,845 | 1,902 | 2592 | 77 | 93 | 84 | 97 | 112 | 110 |
| **All remand prisoners** | **10,933** | **10,031** | **9,521** | **9,768** | **9,707** | **1,0279** | **507** | **468** | **384** | **389** | **383** | **395** |
| **Prisoners under sentence** | | | | | | | | | | | | |
| Adults | | | | | | | | | | | | |
| Up to 18 months | 8,279 | 7,648 | 7,111 | 7,501 | 7,417 | 7,073 | 427 | 391 | 358 | 364 | 380 | 396 |
| Over 18 months up to 4 years (males) and 3 years (females) | 10,613 | 10,818 | 9,443 | 9,075 | 9,153 | 8,194 | 273 | 257 | 206 | 169 | 188 | 187 |
| Over 4 years (males) and 3 years (females) (inc life) | 9,958 | 11,076 | 11,647 | 11,975 | 12,325 | 11,922 | 387 | 40 | 502 | 497 | 489 | 414 |
| **All adults** | **28,850** | **29,543** | **28,201** | **28,551** | **28,894** | **27,189** | **1,086** | **1,117** | **1,066** | **1,030** | **1,057** | **998** |
| Young offenders | | | | | | | | | | | | |
| Up to 18 months | 4,495 | 3,605 | 3,147 | 3,129 | 2,829 | 2,670 | 112 | 104 | 88 | 72 | 64 | 79 |
| Over 18 months | 3,660 | 3,451 | 2,974 | 2,594 | 2,507 | 2,324 | 79 | 72 | 55 | 64 | 67 | 58 |
| **All young offenders** | **8,156** | **7,056** | **6,121** | **5,723** | **5,336** | **4,994** | **190** | **176** | **143** | **136** | **133** | **137** |
| All sentenced prisoners | 37,006 | 36,599 | 34,321 | 34,274 | 34,230 | 32,183 | 1,276 | 1,293 | 1,209 | 1,166 | 1,189 | 1,135 |
| Non-criminal prisoners | 221 | 214 | 197 | 294 | 303 | 543 | 6 | 6 | 4 | 6 | 5 | 31 |
| **Total population in custody** | **48,160** | **46,843** | **44,039** | **44,336** | **44,240** | **43,005** | **1,789** | **1,767** | **1,597** | **1,561** | **1,577** | **1,560** |

[1] Including prisoners held in police cells. The following breakdown has been estimated and numbers included with those held in prison service establishments under the relevant type of prisoner.

[2] Components may not tally with totals because they have been rounded up independently

(Home Office (1994) *Home Office Statistical Bulletin* 16/94: Table 1)

Metropolitan Stipendiary Magistrate explained in a letter to the *Independent*:

> Fine defaulters are not imprisoned because they cannot pay their fines but because, often after many attempts to get them to pay, they will not. Magistrates are forbidden by law to imprison fine defaulters unless either they refuse to pay or, having had the means to pay and other methods of enforcing payment (eg by a bailiff's warrant) having failed, they do not pay.

*(Independent, 5 March 1995: 24)*

## Life sentence inmates

In contrast to those who enter prison for a week or two the offender given a life sentence has a very different situation to face. In 1990, 246 offenders were given a *life sentence*. This figure includes younger offenders given a sentence of detention during Her Majesty's Pleasure and custody for life. On 30 June 1991, 2,900 persons were serving a life sentence of which 93 per cent were males and 80 per cent were sentenced for murder. The population of lifers inside prisons has risen steadily in recent years as more lifers are sentenced than released. In 1991, for example, 72 were released whereas 246 were received.

Life sentence prisoners spend some time after sentence at a life sentence unit to undergo counselling and preparation for their future life in prison or on licence. They have no entitlement to automatic release but are eligible to apply for *release on licence*. This is discretionary and if released the person is on licence for the rest of their life and may be recalled to prison at any time. The time spent inside a prison on a life sentence is set by the Home Secretary. The actual time served will be based primarily on the type and nature of offence and the views of the Lord Chief Justice. The trial judge may also make a recommendation as to the minimum time to be served in prison. After the tariff date for the individual life sentence has been served release will depend on the assessment of risk and rehabilitative factors. On release into the community the life offender becomes known as a life licensee.

Home Office data shows that between 1972 and 1991 1,329 inmates were released on life licence for the first time (*Home Office Statistical Bulletin*, issue 18/94, 31 July 1994). Subsequently, 225 were recalled and 21 given another life sentence. Using the Home Office Offenders Index database about 10 per cent were reconvicted for a standard list offence and 2 per cent were reconvicted of a grave offence. Fourteen of the life licensees were reconvicted for homicide.

The time served before release on licence varies depending on the nature of the crime and the perceived risk to the community of releasing a life sentence inmate. Some inmates may never be released. Such is likely the situation of Ian Brady, the Moors murderer, convicted with Myra Hindley in 1966 at Chester Assizes for the murder of Lesley Anne Downey, aged 10, and Edward Evans, aged 17. Hindley later confessed to her role in the murder of three other children. Both have now been in prison for nearly 30 years. The majority of lifers serve a time in prison of between 7 and 13 years before release, the average time being between 11 and 12 years.

The actual time served by inmates is rarely the same as the sentence given by the court. In the case of life sentence prisoners this is because most will be released on licence at some time. All other inmates with a determinate or fixed sentence length will be eligible for release before the end of their sentence length. The details of the rules governing early release are explained in the next section of this chapter.

## Time served

The time served in prison is not usually the amount of time imposed by the judge or magistrate for three reasons. First, time is deducted for pre-sentence periods in custody awaiting trial or sentence while on remand. Secondly, because prisoners (except for those serving four years and over) are entitled to remission or what is now called automatic release, and thirdly, because of parole.

The Prison Act 1898 allowed the use of remission of part of the sentence for the good conduct of inmates. The maximum remission, for those given penal sentences, was a quarter for men and a third for women. In the 1940s, this was changed to a third for all inmates. Parole was introduced in 1967 and allowed inmates to apply for early release in addition to remission. This was a discretionary element and unlike remission was not automatic. Prior to the changes brought about by the CJA 1991, parole release time was in addition to the one-third deduction from sentence length for remission. Thus with remission (one-third) and parole eligibility starting at the one-third stage of the sentence, before the changes brought about by the CJA 1991, an inmate might be released soon after the one-third stage of their sentence.

## Time actually served prior to the Criminal Justice Act 1991

Let us take an example of a prisoner who had been given a custodial sentence of six years. The deductions from that six-year period would be a one-third deduction for remission as the earliest date of release: four years is the most the prisoner would have served unless days of remission were lost for breaches of the prison rules. With a deduction for time on remand in custody prior to sentence, of four months, for example, the actual maximum time served would have been three years and eight months. However, the prisoner would have been eligible to apply for parole at the one-third stage of sentence, ie after two years. In this example the prisoner was held on remand in custody for four months and therefore would be eligible to apply for parole in 20 months time.

Thus although the court had sentenced the offender to six years in prison, the longest time in prison from time of sentence would be three years eight months, and if immediately successful with an application for parole, the prisoner could have been released in 20 months. The situation for prisoners serving under 12 months was different and they were released at the 50 per cent stage of sentence time.

## Sentence calculations after the Criminal Justice Act 1991

Sentence calculations changed with the abolition of the terms remission and parole by the CJA 1991. Every inmate was now to serve half of their sentence with full allowance for time held on remand in custody. For breaches of prison rules the inmate may serve up to 14 'added days'. Three sets of rules govern release as a consequence of the CJA 1991.

- *Those serving a sentence of under 12 months*: would be automatically released at the 50 per cent stage as before. This is referred to as automatic unconditional release (AUR).
- *Those sentenced from one to four years*: will serve 50 per cent of the time but on release will be supervised in the community until the three-quarter period of time. So a person sentenced to two years will be released after one year, allowing for time spent on remand in custody, and supervised for a further six months. This is known as automatic conditional release (ACR).
- *Those sentenced to four years and over*: must serve half their sentence, with an allowance for time spent in custody while on remand. But they must still apply after the 50 per cent stage of sentence for release. This is a discretionary decision. They might not be successful in which case they will serve up to the two-thirds stage of sentence time. Whether they are released at the earliest opportunity (50 per cent stage) or serve all their time to the two-thirds stage, the released prisoner will be supervised in the community after release until the three-quarters stage.

Thus a prisoner sentenced to 10 years who had spent six months awaiting trial and sentence would, from the time of sentence, be able to apply for release after a further four years six months. If successful the prisoner would be supervised on release in the community for a further two years and six months, ie to the three-quarter stage. If unsuccessful in a bid for early release the prisoner would be released finally at the two-thirds stage. That is at six years eight months minus the six months served on remand. The prisoner would then be supervised in the community for a further one year and four months, ie a total period either in prison or under supervision in the community of seven and a half years for a sentence of ten years.

The length of time served is one calculation that the sentenced inmate will be keen to work out soon after reception. However, other considerations will affect the nature of the prison experience that the inmate will face during their prison term. Having explained the quantity of time that an inmate will have to serve, what factors influence the quality of time served?

# IMPACT OF IMPRISONMENT ON INMATES

For 200 years since the introduction of the penitentiary the impact of prison life on the inmate has been debated. As we saw in Chapter 9, some believed that prison life could provide a positive and constructive experience that would rehabilitate, while others argued that the consequence of imprisonment is to lock an offender further into a life of crime. Recent opinion, as expressed in the 1990 White Paper, *Crime, Justice and Protecting the Public*, makes it clear that the effect of imprisonment is unlikely to be beneficial in rehabilitative terms. It is important to bear in mind, however, that individual inmates vary in character and that generalisations about the impact of prison regimes will not hold for every inmate. Empirical studies of how inmates experience and adapt to prison help to shed light on the consequences of being incarcerated, and explain why they have not matched the good intentions of those who saw prison as a means of re-socialising inmates.

Toleration of life in prison varies from inmate to inmate. Some will feel their conviction or sentence was unjust, others will accept it, and others will be grateful that the sentence length was no longer. Each prisoner will bring a range of pre-existing impressions and knowledge of prisons. The National Prison Survey 1991 showed most (57 per cent) sentenced inmates had been in prison before (Walmsley et al 1993). The survey of 4,000 inmates was conducted in January and February 1991 and covered the background characteristics of inmates and asked questions about the regimes and the conditions of imprisonment from the inmates' perspective.

Cell sharing was most evident amongst the remand population where only 18 per cent had a cell to themselves, compared with 52 per cent of the total sample. Overcrowding was most apparent in local prisons, with 13 per cent of prisoners in cells accommodating three people. The average time locked up in a cell was 14 hours. Most, 66 per cent, said they had unlimited access to baths and showers and a further 12 per cent reported that they had three or more baths or showers in the preceding week. Questions about the quality of food revealed that 51 per cent thought the quality was bad and 13 per cent thought it was good.

Asked about how they got on with staff, 9 per cent said they had been treated badly but most (41 per cent) said the prison staff treated them well. Personal safety questions showed that while most (71 per cent) agreed with the statement that 'most prison officers treat prisoners fairly here' a quarter also expressed agreement with the statement that 'some prison officers assault prisoners here'. They expressed concern about their personal safety – 18 per cent replied that they did not feel safe from being injured or bullied by other prisoners and 9 per cent reported that they had been assaulted by another inmate in the last six months.

These physical aspects of the regime such as food, overcrowding, the time locked up in a cell, access to bath and toilet facilities and staff attitudes are vital to the trouble-free running of a prison as will be shown in the final section of this chapter which looks at the findings of the Woolf Report on the riots in 1990 (see also Figure 10.6 below).

## Inmate adaptation to prison life

How do people cope with being deprived of their liberty? Prisoners do not have the same degree of freedom to decide their daily routines, eating habits, social contacts and sleeping arrangements. Studies of how inmates adapt to prison life illustrate its impact on the inmate and how this is likely to affect their potential for successful rehabilitation. These sociological and psychological studies of prison life give clues about the causes of prison disturbances and riots that we will look at in the final section of this chapter (Cohen and Taylor 1972; Fitzgerald 1977; King and Elliott 1977).

How people cope with prison depends on a number of factors. First, if they have had prior experience of prison, they will have some understanding of the routines of prison life. For the novice initial acquaintance with prison life might be overwhelming and intimidating. Erving Goffman uses the term 'mortification', to describe the induction process in which supports for the person's individuality such as personal name, clothing and hair style are replaced by a prison number, uniform and hygiene requirements (Goffman 1968). This can be lessened and some prison administrators have introduced regimes to normalise some aspects of prison life by, for example, less insistence on uniforms and less restrictions on what might be allowed in a cell, although this might conflict with the needs of containment and security as was suggested in the case of the IRA prisoner escape from Whitemoor Prison.

Prisoner adaptation, whether the inmate is an old hand or a novice, will depend on their individual circumstances. Most important is the length of sentence. The nature of the crime committed also influences the prison experience. Thieves, fraudsters and robbers are often regarded with relative degrees of respect and contempt by other inmates, but they will not suffer the fear felt by those convicted of sexual crimes, especially those where the victim was a child. To avoid attacks from other inmates, the 'nonces', as they are called in prison argot, often request to be housed in vulnerable prisoner units and segregated for their own protection under Prison Rule 43, which states:

> Where it appears desirable for the maintenance of good order or discipline or in his own interest, that a prisoner should not associate with other prisoners, either generally, or for particular purposes, the governor may arrange for the prisoner's removal from association.

At the end of March 1992 there were 1,877 adult male and 13 adult female prisoners segregated for their own protection plus 149 male and one female prisoner aged under 21.

Another factor influencing prisoners' adaptation is relationships in the outside world. One of the realities of prison life is that inmates are cut off from ordinary routine interactions with the outside world. Goffman calls prisons, along with other institutions such as monasteries, mental hospitals and boarding schools, total institutions. They are 'total' in that all aspects of life such as sleeping, eating, working and leisure are conducted within the one organisation (Goffman 1968). This means that the array of contacts and opportunities are severely confined and the impact of the outside world is limited. However, this does not mean that there is no outside contact and weekly visits, access to telephones for prisoners and outside visits in pre-release schemes have all been extended in recent years. Of course, the main leisure activities such as watching television, listening to the radio and reading newspapers and magazines mean that inmates in prison can keep up with events that interest them. Regimes will vary between prisons and some, such as open prisons, allow inmates two days a month out of the prison for 'town visits'.

The loss of daily contact with the home or workplace is no hardship for some inmates. Others suffer mental anguish when they think about their outside lives, homes and families. The shame of imprisonment on the family and themselves will have an impact on some of those sentenced to imprisonment. Some argue that these factors are of particular significance to women prisoners, especially where they have children (Eaton 1993).

A further factor shaping the way in which an inmate adapts to prison life is their attitude towards their offence and sentence. While some accept their guilt and feel ashamed, others feel no remorse. This might be because they are professional thieves who have made a career out of criminal activity and regard imprisonment as an occupational hazard. Individual inmates will vary in their response to conviction. Those incorrectly convicted are entitled to feel outrage and anger. Others are outraged because of the type of person they are. Some are resigned to their fate and 'do their time'. Others will be influenced by the type of company they come into contact with in the prison. Although there is no one factor that determines how a prisoner responds, a number of research studies have indicated patterns of adaptation (Cohen and Taylor 1972).

Some theories accounting for offender adaptation have stressed the importance of institutional traditions and opportunities, particularly focusing on the impact of inmate subcultures and the deprivations associated with a 'closed' institution. Theorists in this tradition include Donald Clemmer, Gresham Sykes and Erving Goffman. Other theorists have focused on the 'importation' model, where the prisoner's adaptation will depend on their pre-institutional careers and lifestyles (Shrag 1944). Schrag's work showed how the social role adopted in prison depended on the inmate's previous lifestyle before imprisonment.

John Irwin's study, *The Felon* (1970), found three types of responses amongst inmates in California prisons 'jailing', 'doing time' and 'gleaning'. These responses tended to reflect the prisoner's personal history, although

Irwin makes the caveat that inmates did not always fit into only one response model and that the three main response patterns did not cover every inmate. Thus 'jailing' was characteristic of 'state raised youth' who had prior institutional contacts from an early age and knew how to exploit the opportunities in a total institution to achieve maximum benefits and status through the rackets and gangs. Prison was not too burdensome for them as they usually had little status outside the institution other than in gang life, which continued in prison. The professional and more mature thieves who were career criminals adopted a different response. Their predominant aim was to get through their sentence as quietly and quickly as possible. Therefore they were not interested in the rehabilitative programmes of the institution except where it meant an easier life inside or the chance to get out of prison more quickly. Nor were these inmates interested in campaigning or confrontation with the authorities as were the 'jailing' inmates. The third pattern of adaptation described by Irwin was 'gleaning'. These inmates engaged in the opportunities offered by education, counselling, therapy and work programmes to increase their opportunities of being granted parole and of changing their lifestyles.

In a later study, *Prisons in Turmoil* (1980) Irwin points out that the models of inmate subcultures were easier to identify in the traditional style of penitentiary with more rigid and authoritarian regimes. Clemmer's study in 1940 found a very distinctive and conformist prisoner culture, with an inmate code, defined and enforced primarily through the inmates (Clemmer 1958). Since that time the nature of the prison experience has become more diversified, as new types of inmate and values have been brought into prison. The commitment to rehabilitative strategies in the 1950s brought about more liberal regimes with less emphasis on the convict culture found in many prisons before 1950. The new mix of inmates also undermined the single inmate culture. In the USA in the 1960s, as with the British prisons during the period of World War I, political prisoners objecting to the war generated a more articulate and politically sophisticated inmate. In the USA the black power movement created another form of politically orientated inmate. Younger inmates convicted of drug and gang related crimes were not so easily impressed by either the formal or informal cultures of prison life and had their own support and reference groups as gang and drug activities meant that prison contacts became an extension of street life.

More recent theorists and studies have stressed the greater diversity of inmate culture as less strict regimes and more diverse pre-institutional lifestyles become more apparent in prison in the 1990s.

If prisons were no longer to be regarded as institutions seeking to rehabilitate offenders, then what was their purpose? The next section will set out the aims of the Prison Service in 1990 and asks do prisons work?

# AIMS OF THE PRISON SERVICE: DO PRISONS WORK?

Does prison work as Michael Howard asserted in the quote at the beginning of this chapter? To answer this it is necessary to ask what the goals of imprisonment are. In clarifying these goals we must distinguish between the function of imprisonment within the criminal justice system, that is to carry out the sentence of the court and the specific goals of prisons as institutions.

Thus prisons work in one sense if they deprive offenders of their liberty for the period of time specified by the court. Hence the main purpose of imprisonment is in terms of sentencing goals. When assessed in terms of whether prisons fulfil this function they are successful if general deterrence, denunciation and just deserts goals are achieved; and at the minimum they fulfil an incapacitative function of keeping away from the community offenders who would, and will, when released, continue criminal activities.

However, the Prison Service has its own institutionally specific goals reflecting the penal paradigms explored in Chapter 9. In 1979 the report of the May Committee referred to the loss of faith in the treatment objective in prison and recommended the rewriting of Prison Rule 1 and adopting the idea of custody which is both 'secure and yet positive'. 'Positive custody' was defined in four ways. It should:

- create an environment which can assist them (the inmates) to respond and contribute to society as positively as possible;
- preserve and promote their self-respect;
- minimise, to the degree of security necessary in each particular case, the harmful effects of their removal from normal life;
- prepare them for and assist them on discharge.

(Home Office 1979: 67)

In the 1990s the Prison Service set out the following goals of imprisonment in its mission statement:

> Her Majesty's Prison Service serves the public by keeping in custody those committed by the courts. Our duty is to look after them with humanity and help them lead law-abiding and useful lives in custody and after release.

Therefore, in terms of the institutional goals the Prison Service has set itself, prisons can claim to work, first, in the sense that those sent by the courts are retained until the proper release date. The escape and absconder rates from prison establishments in England and Wales could be looked at to test whether they are serving the courts effectively by holding those sent there by the courts.

Between 1 April 1991 and 31 March 1992, 310 inmates escaped from closed establishments. A further 155 escaped from their escort outside of the prison, often on their way to court. Most escapes are from open prisons but are referred to by the Prison Service as absconders. In addition to the 473 who were officially classified as escapers in 1991/92 there were an additional 1,743 absconders from open prisons or from outside working parties or while on an outside visit. Most escapees and absconders are caught within the year.

Secondly, the prison service aims to look after inmates with humanity. This requires providing decent conditions for inmates and meeting their physical needs. The aspiration to look after inmates with humanity also implies a style of regime that allows inmates the opportunity to lead a full and responsible life within the constraints imposed by costs and security. Apart from basic material and medical needs a measure of the success of prisons, in terms of their declared aims, could include the number of inmates and the average time devoted to educational, work and leisure activities.

The goal of humanity can be audited in general terms by such contra-indicators as overcrowded cells, poor food, insulting behaviour by staff, time allowed out of the cells and slopping out. Slopping out is condemned as unacceptable by the criteria set in the European Prison Standards. (Casale 1984; Stern 1987; Morgan 1994).

Thirdly, do inmates lead law-abiding lives while in prison? One measure would be to look at inmate-on-inmate assault rates. In October 1993, Leslie Bailey, an inmate at Whitemoor Prison in March, Cambridgeshire was strangled in his cell. He was a convicted paedophile, a category of offender frequently the target of attacks in prison by other inmates. A murder in prison is unlikely to support a view that inmates are secure from physical assault; surely a first condition for humane containment is the personal safety of those sent to prison. Therefore the number of assaults on inmates and staff is one aspect of any measure of the success of the goal of helping inmates to lead law abiding lives while in custody. The *Prison Service Annual Report and Accounts* 1995 recorded 3,204 assaults on staff and 2,440 attacks were by prisoners on other prisoners.

Fourthly, do prisons work to achieve the aim of helping inmates to lead law abiding and useful lives after release? The Prison Service seeks to offer a positive environment so that offenders have an opportunity to address their offending behaviour. The 1990 White Paper made it clear that judges should no longer use imprisonment as a sentence if they seek to bring about the rehabilitation of the offender. Prisons, the report concludes, are counter-productive in this regard. The report states:

> It was once believed that prison, properly used, could encourage a high proportion of offenders to start an honest life on their release. Nobody now regards imprisonment, in itself, as an effective means of reform for most prisoners ... however much prison staff try to inject a positive purpose into the regime, as they do, prison is a society which requires virtually no sense of personal responsibility from prisoners. Normal social or working habits do not fit. The opportunity to learn from other prisoners is pervasive. For most offenders, imprisonment has to be justified in terms of public protection, denunciation and retribution. Otherwise it can be an expensive way of making bad people worse.

> (Home Office 1990a: 6)

The Green Paper *Punishment, Custody and the Community* can be seen as a formal recognition of the limitations of prisons as places for rehabilitating offenders (Home Office 1988a). They have not achieved the ambitious goals claimed by the protagonists for the penitentiary 200 years ago. If custody is to be used it should be for purposes other than a belief that it will help the offender to lead a 'good and useful life' or even a 'law-abiding and useful life'. The Green Paper cites the many unintended consequences of imprisonment which made them counter-productive in rehabilitative terms.

Paragraph 1.1:

. . . they are not required to face up to what they have done and to the effects on their victim.

Paragraph 1.1:

. . . if they are removed in prison from the responsibilities, problems and temptations of everyday life, they are less likely to acquire the self-discipline and self-reliance which will prevent re-offending in the future.

Paragraph 1.6:

Imprisonment is likely to add to the difficulties which offenders find in living a normal and law-abiding life. Overcrowded local prisons are emphatically not schools of citizenship.

Paragraph 2.15:

[With regard to young offenders] Even a short period of custody is quite likely to confirm them as criminals, particularly if they acquire new criminal skills from more sophisticated offenders. They see themselves labelled as criminals and behave accordingly.

(Home Office 1988a)

However, it might be correct to recognise that whilst prisons do not work to re-socialise offenders, it is important to prevent further de-socialisation whilst in prison. Therefore projects within prison that encourage self-responsibility and help inmates to maintain their links with the family and the outside world might help to achieve this. Treating inmates with respect can also be an aspect of a positive regime. With this in mind it might be worth fostering constructive and positive goals in rehabilitative terms because it might encourage staff to treat inmates with some degree of decency.

The test of the proposition that prisons reduce the future criminality of those released from prison – whether through rehabilitative strategies or via the impact of individual deterrence – can be tested by an examination of recidivism rates. They measure what proportion of offenders have been reconvicted for a further offence in a two-year period from release. These figures are not entirely accurate as measures of re-offending as, first, they include some 'pseudo-reconvictions' being convictions recorded after the original sentence, for offences committed before (Lloyd et al 1995).

**Fig 10.5** Reconviction rates

| *England and Wales 1987* | | | | | | *Percentage* |
|---|---|---|---|---|---|---|
| *% reconvicted after 2 years* | *Number of previous convictions* | | | | | |
| *All ages* | *None* | *1 or 2* | *3 to 6* | *7 to 10* | *11 or more* | *All* |
| Probation plus other requirements | 41 | 58 | 69 | 74 | 74 | 67 |
| Other probation | 31 | 48 | 58 | 66 | 67 | 52 |
| All probation | 32 | 49 | 60 | 62 | 69 | 53 |
| Community service | 36 | 48 | 62 | 67 | 69 | 55 |
| Immediate custody | 22 | 44 | 61 | 65 | 74 | 57 |

(Adapted from, Home Office (1994c) *Probation Statistics, England and Wales* 1993: 110)

Secondly, they will not include offences committed by those in the sample which remain unknown, unsolved, or unsuccessfully prosecuted. Figure 10.5 shows the reconviction rate for those discharged from custody or commencing probation and community service orders.

These figures show that, going to prison is likely to be related to future re-offending. However, they also show that non-custodial sanctions are not much better at reducing the likelihood of re-offending. Perhaps sentencing an offender, whether to prison or in the community, has little to do with the influences on offending behaviour. Certainly it is difficult to accept the proposition that prisons work to reduce criminality in the sense of their impact on individual offenders. The usefulness of imprisonment should be assessed in terms of its functions other than those to do with its effect on individual offenders.

So the answer to the question of, whether prisons work is that it depends on what we expect of them. The failure to meet the original high expectations of those who pioneered the idea that the penitentiary would be an institution to change offenders into law-abiding citizens is apparent. But prisons meet other demands, particularly as the most credible way to achieve retribution, denunciation, general deterrence and incapacitation.

Finally, no doubt the 'success rate' of imprisonment, in terms of any of its aims could be improved if more money is spent on the prison system. What would be the cost of ensuring no escapes? Would the taxpayer wish to pay this cost? For those who think prisons have failed in all or most respects, the onus is on them to say what they would put in its place as the major institution symbolising punishment.

# WOOLF REPORT INTO THE 1990 PRISON DISTURBANCES

On April Fool's Day 1990, prisoners rioted at Strangeways, a local prison in Manchester. Strangeways was built in 1868 and at the time of the riot had 1,647 inmates. The riot started during the Sunday morning chapel service and resulted in violent attacks on prison officers and Rule 43 prisoners. It took 25 days for the prison authorities to gain control of the prison. The damage to the prison was valued at £30 million. Rioting was not to be confined to Strangeways as prisoners at other institutions followed their example. The worst were at two other local prisons at Bristol and Cardiff; at the category B training prison, Dartmoor; and at the young offender remand centres at Glen Parva and Pucklechurch.

An independent public inquiry was established under the chairmanship of Lord Justice Woolf to look at the causes of these riots and to make recommendations. The report *Prison Disturbances, April 1990* was published in 1991. The first half of the report written by Lord Justice Woolf examined the causes of the riots. The second half of this extensive 600 page report was written by Lord Justice Woolf and Judge Stephen Tumim, Her Majesty's Inspector of Prisons, and provided an overview of prison conditions and made 12 key recommendations and 204 specific proposals.

The inquiry gathered data from a number of sources including inmates' perceptions as to the causes of the riots. A content analysis of the letters submitted by prisoners indicated six possible causes of the riots: physical conditions, particularly poor sanitation and overcrowding; prisoners being locked in their cells for long periods of time and limited association, referred to as being 'banged up'; complaints about food; the attitude of staff towards inmates and, finally, the letters indicated the 'copycat' influences on the riots as bored or hostile inmates emulated actions in other prisons. Figure 10.6 shows the perceptions of inmates in the six different prisons at the time of the riots and their views about the causes of the disturbances.

Woolf's conclusions about the causes of the riots pointed to individual reasons at each prison. For example, at Bristol the combination of prisoners being locked in their cells for long periods and limited facilities had fuelled inmate grievances, added to which was the influx of prisoners from Dartmoor prison to a wing which already housed many disruptive prisoners.

**Fig 10.6** Prisoners' letters on the causes of the1990 riots

| Complaints | Strangeways % | Glen Parva % | Dartmoor % | Bristol % | Cardiff % |
|---|---|---|---|---|---|
| Sanitation | 55 | 7 | 22 | 24 | 20 |
| Overcrowding | 50 | – | – | 16 | 18 |
| 'Bang up' | 43 | 4 | 15 | 26 | 24 |
| Poor food | 40 | 20 | 37 | 16 | 10 |
| Poor staff attitudes | 27 | 13 | 39 | 22 | 22 |
| Copycat | N/A | 32 | 21 | 26 | 16 |

Results from letters submitted to the public inquiry from prisoners involved in the disturbances. The results indicate the main sources of complaints within prisons.

Note: Results from Pucklechurch have not been included because the total set of responses from this establishment was too small.

(Woolf, Lord Justice (1991) *Report of the Inquiry into Prison Disturbances 1990.* Cmd 1456 London Home Office)

The riot spread quickly because keys were taken from two officers attacked at the beginning of the riot. Their keys opened all the doors on the wing. In addition to the individual factors that played their part in each of the disturbances, the report made a general comment on the way to achieve a more stable prison system:

> The achievement of this role, however, depends on there being a proper balance within prisons between security and control on the one hand and humanity and justice on the other

(Home Office 1991a: 245)

The Woolf Report made 12 major recommendations aimed to reduce future conflicts between inmates and the prison authorities. These recommendations not only apply to the internal running of prisons but make the point that prisons should work more closely with other agencies in the criminal justice system. They recognised that prisons are at the back-end of the system and that prison managers have very little control over the numbers who are received into prisons, making it difficult to plan ahead to provide adequate and appropriate facilities. The 12 major recommendations are:

- Closer co-operation between the different parts of the criminal justice system. For this purpose a national forum and local committees should be established.
- More visible leadership of the Prison Service by a Director General who is and is seen to be the operational head and in day-to-day charge of the Service. To achieve this, there should be a published 'compact' or 'contract' given by ministers to the Director General of the Prison Service, who should be responsible for the performance of that 'contract' and publicly answerable for the day-to-day operations of the Prison Service.
- Increased delegation of responsibility to governors of establishments.
- An enhanced role for prison officers.
- A 'compact' or 'contract' for each prisoner setting out the prisoner's expectations and responsibilities in the prison in which he or she is held.
- A national system of accredited standards, with which, in time, each prison establishment would be required to comply.
- A new prison rule that no establishment should hold more prisoners than is provided for in its certified normal level of accommodation, with provisions for Parliament to be informed if exceptionally there is to be a material departure from that rule.
- A public commitment from ministers setting a timetable to provide access to sanitation for all inmates at the earliest practical date, not later than February 1996.
- Better prospects for prisoners to maintain their links with families and the community through more visits and home leaves and through being located in community prisons as near to their homes as possible.
- A division of prison establishments into small and more manageable and secure units.

- A separate statement of purpose, separate conditions and generally a lower security categorisation for remand prisoners.
- Improved standards of justice within prisons involving the giving of reasons to a prisoner for any decision which materially and adversely affects him; a grievance procedure and disciplinary proceedings which ensure that the governor deals with most matters under his present powers; relieving Boards of Visitors of their adjudicatory role; and providing for final access to an independent Complaints Adjudicator.

(Home Office 1991a: para 15.5)

In response, Kenneth Baker, the Home Secretary at the time of the publication of the Woolf Report, had already begun to introduce some of the proposals recommended by Woolf to improve conditions within prisons. An increase in visits, letters and access to telephones was implemented together with the start of a programme of works to meet the Woolf deadline of February 1996 for ending the practice of slopping out. The planning and building of new prisons also continued in order to reduce the overcrowding described in the Woolf Report. By early 1994 the prison service could claim that there were no cases of three inmates having to share a prison cell designed for one. Sentencing planning for inmates was introduced on 1 October 1992 for inmates serving four years and over and for category A inmates. For inmates serving between 12 months and less than four years the scheme started on 1 November 1993. The CJA 1993 removed the disciplinary powers of the Board of Visitors in line with the recommendations of the Woolf Report; and National and Area Criminal Justice Consultative Councils were established. However, there has been less development with regard to community prisons and a national system of accredited standards.

## CONCLUSION

We can see from this chapter that prisons have been expected to perform many functions. The rehabilitative paradigm discussed in Chapter 9 influenced the design, organisation and regimes of prisons from their inception to around the 1960s. Thus prisons were seen not as degrading and punitive institutions but as institutions where inmates should be encouraged and assisted to lead a good and useful life through a regime of treatment and training. These ideals however were not achieved, and some of the reasons why prisons may not be able to achieve rehabilitation have been noted. They are after all institutions in which inmates are deprived of their liberty, which may have an adverse effect on their sense of individuality and purpose. Some prisoners are wedded to a life of crime, others, particularly those on long sentences, may simply wish to forget the outside world and see no hope for the future. Prisons indeed may have a damaging rather than a positive effect.

292

The demise of rehabilitative goals however had a profound effect on the institutions making up the prison system. At the same time conditions within prisons worsened due to the increasing numbers which the system had to deal with. One attraction of rehabilitative goals to penal reformers was that it held out the promise of treating prisoners with humanity. With its demise, these conditions also declined, many training programmes ceased and prisoners were locked up for longer periods in their cells. These conditions arguably contributed to the disturbances in the early 1990s.

As we have seen it is important to distinguish between the aims of sentencers in sending offenders to prison and the aims of the prison system itself. Thus while sentencers and policy makers talk of incapacitation and the deprivation of liberty, these do not provide constructive goals for the institutions who must carry out these aims. Reducing the goal of prison to that of simply keeping offenders from escaping until they are due to be released ('warehousing') might further distance staff from inmates and undermine programmes aimed at reforming them. Rehabilitation, while ultimately unsuccessful, did give prisons a goal other than containment, and its demise leaves institutions without any incentive to consider the impact of regimes on offenders.

Prisons are likely to face many problems in the future. They must deal with those whom the courts send to them and attempt to prevent them escaping and creating disturbances. Yet the interests of security and control may run counter to humane conditions, especially in a cost conscious climate with strong public reaction likely to be provoked if, as the Home Secretary's comments above indicate, they are likely to be seen as 'holiday camps'. These issues also affect other parts of the penal system and will be looked at in relation to community sentences in Chapter 11.

## Review questions

1. What are the different categories of prisons run by the Prison Service in England and Wales?
2. Calculate the actual amount of time served by an inmate if he or she is sentenced for (a) eight months, (b) two years, and what rules apply to the prisoner sentenced to over four years.
3. What are the different aims of imprisonment? What kind of evidence should be examined to explore whether or not these aims are being achieved?
4. What arguments are involved in considering whether more prisons should be built or greater efforts should be made to reduce the prison population?

**Further reading**

Cavadino M and Dignan J (1992) *The Penal System: An Introduction.* London: Sage

Harding C, Hines C B, Ireland R and Rawlings P (1985) *Imprisonment in England and Wales.* London: Croom Helm

Morgan R (1994) 'Imprisonment' in Maguire M, Morgan R and Reiner R (eds) *The Oxford Handbook of Criminology.* Oxford: Clarendon Press: 889–948

Player E and Jenkins M (1994) *Prisons After Woolf: Reform Through Riot.* London: Routledge

# CHAPTER 11

# COMMUNITY AND CRIME

Probation Service and Community Sanctions
Community Policing
Crime Prevention and Safer Cities
Victims
Vigilantes

## INTRODUCTION

Crime has an enormous impact on the community in general, on individual victims, local neighbourhoods and on business and commercial life. As we have seen however, the agencies and formal processes of the criminal justice system have a limited effect on the volume of crime. They deal with only a small minority of offences and offenders and have little impact on their criminality. Previous chapters have illustrated conflicts over the role and function of criminal justice agencies, many hinging around the extent to which the system should aim to prevent, reduce or punish crime and whether its main focus should be on the offender irrespective of the impact of crime on victims or the community.

In recent years a number of policy initiatives have invoked the notion of the community. As we have seen, sentencing policy has recently emphasised the significance of community sentences. Problems involving relationships between the police and communities influenced the development of community policing. Pessimism about the ability of the police and courts to have a real impact on crime reduction has led to the growth of community crime prevention. Government publicity has indicated that preventing crime is a joint responsibility between the public and the police with talk of 'partnerships' and that 'together we can crack crime'. Effective policing of course, relies on the public and victims of crime providing information about and reporting offences, but in recent years victims have voiced dissatisfaction with many aspects of their experiences – thus victims are a major group within the community whose needs should be considered. Finally, those most frustrated by the limited impact of the criminal justice system on crime may be tempted to engage in crime prevention and even retribution – to become vigilantes.

These seemingly diverse developments have a number of common elements. The growing pessimism surrounding the impact of rehabilitation prompted a desire to find new approaches which might have a positive impact on crime. The growing concern with the victims of crime and the fear of crime, found in the British Crime Survey, led to policies to tackle these issues. The rising cost of the criminal justice process and its agencies led to a search for more cost effective ways of reducing crime. Community sentences are cheaper than imprisonment and crime prevention measures can be simple and economical. If community policing can secure the co-operation of the public, it may enhance the effectiveness of the police. In addition, many policies are consistent with the view that individual citizens and communities must share not only the cost of but the responsibility for protecting themselves from crime – they involve the notion of the 'active citizen'. Other policies encourage members of the community to assist the police, and to help both victims and offenders by being involved as volunteers in community projects, victim support schemes and as lay visitors to police stations.

This chapter will start by looking at the operation of community sanctions and the probation and after care service. It will then go on to examine community policing and community crime prevention. Victims' experiences in the criminal justice process will then be explored along with policies providing victims with support and compensation. Finally, a brief section will outline the issues surrounding the willingness of citizens to take the law into their own hands by engaging in actions to apprehend and punish criminals in their community.

## PROBATION SERVICE AND COMMUNITY SANCTIONS

Chapters 8 and 9 outlined the growing emphasis on and the main provisions for community sentences, and this section will focus on probation, community service and combination orders. The Probation Service is responsible for implementing community sentences.

The idea that offenders can be dealt with in the community has a long history. In the late 19th century many juvenile offenders were saved from prison by police court missionaries who agreed to be responsible for them – the forerunners of the probation service. The Probation of Offenders Act 1907 provided that the courts could appoint probation officers who were to advise, assist and befriend offenders where either the character of the offender or the nature of the offence rendered punishment inexpedient. The Criminal Justice Act 1925 formalised the role of probation officers.

Since then the work of the probation service has expanded. Probation officers became responsible not only for work in the criminal courts but also for civil work involving divorce. They provided social inquiry reports to the court giving information about offenders' circumstances and attitude to offences and gave the court advice about what sentence would be appropriate. They also began to work with ex-prisoners, reflected in the name Probation and After-Care service. Their role was linked to the rise of rehabilitation and the service became professionalised and was linked to the development of social case work in the penal system. Most probation officers are trained as social workers.

At the end of 1991, there were 55 probation areas in England and Wales employing 7,153 probation officers. This represents an increase of 28 per cent since 1981 (Home Office 1993: 71). The scope of work carried out by the Probation Service is illustrated in a recent National Probation Survey (May 1992). This found that a typical probation officer spent 23 per cent of his or her time on probation and other criminal supervision, 8 per cent on community service orders and 14 per cent on after care which includes work with offenders before and after release. Court duties took up 15 per cent of their time and the preparation of social inquiry reports (now called pre-sentence reports) a further 11 per cent. Office duties occupied 3 per cent of time and civil and other work 26 per cent. The precise activities of the individual probation officer will depend however on whether they are part of a team attached to a court, a prison, a bail project or are one of several area teams working with offenders in the community.

Once on probation, community service or combination orders, offenders face a variety of experiences. These may include a programme of meetings with their supervising officer or attendance at counselling or therapy sessions for alcohol and drug abuse or anger management. Some will require help finding accommodation and work, others with welfare and social security applications. Others may participate in a variety of projects such as motor projects which provide offenders who have been involved in car crime with an opportunity to drive and work with cars legitimately. Other offenders are sent on programmes involving physical exercise to improve their ability to use leisure time constructively and co-operate within teams and groups.

An example of the latter kind of project is Essex Challenge run by the probation service (*Daily Telegraph*, 23 October 1994). In this scheme persistent criminals are introduced to windsurfing, potholing and sailing. Offenders spend one week at a 'spartan' hostel and the next four weeks on outdoor sports. Intended as a last chance for offenders aged between 17 and 21, it is not, argued a council spokesperson, a soft option and aims to break the cycle of offending behaviour.

In a community service scheme in Manchester, offenders undertake a variety of decorating jobs which involve learning a trade. One such was in a nursery school. According to a senior probation officer this scheme puts offenders in contact with disadvantaged groups in the community such as the elderly or the disabled. This, he argues, means that offenders are put in contact with people coping with worse conditions than their own. Indeed, he adds, some carry on working as volunteers and others have obtained permanent jobs. At the same time however it is a punishment – if their work is unsatisfactory or they fail to comply they can lose hours and be sent back to court (*Guardian*, 23 October 1994).

These kind of schemes have attracted criticism on the grounds that they are insufficiently punitive, comments which reflect an underlying tension in the role of community sentences. This role has always been problematic. When, for example, community service was introduced during the 1960s discussions referred to 'treatment in the community'. In the discussion papers preceding the CJA 1991 however, the predominant phraseology was 'punishment in the community'. This changing emphasis indicates some potential conflicts.

What is the role of the probation officer? Is it primarily to help offenders, who in the past were described as clients, or to serve the court and the public by ensuring that offenders do not re-offend? This care or control dilemma refers to the tension between the rehabilitative, and the control and penal aspects of probation. Similar tensions can be identified in the aims of community service orders. As seen in Chapter 8, these can involve restitution, deterrence, rehabilitation and retribution. While the tradition of the probation service has been mainly rehabilitative, seeing what they offer as 'treatment' and offenders as 'clients', we saw in Chapter 9 how the CJA 1991 stressed the deprivation of liberty and an element of punishment. Nonetheless community services continue to be seen as soft. This was particularly evident during 1994, when much publicity was given to a small number of offenders who were sent abroad or to holiday camps as part of their community sentences. The strong reaction this provoked led to further measures to toughen up community service further, illustrating the shift towards a more punitive role.

As noted in Chapter 9, many have seen the role of community sentences as being to reduce the prison population. These arguments influenced the introduction of new measures during the 1960s and 1970s. Parole and the suspended sentence were introduced in 1967 and the Criminal Justice Act 1972 introduced community service orders (CSOs), made available nationally in 1975. CSOs proved popular because they combined so many sentencing aims, and by 1988 they accounted for 8 per cent of all sentences for indictable offenders. While the legislation itself made no specific reference to their use for those who would otherwise have been sent to prison, they were expected to be used primarily as an alternative to prison (Cavadino and Dignan 1992). Later policies were also influenced by the disillusionment with rehabilitation which in some ways left the probation service without a clear function.

Throughout the 1970s and 1980s the trend towards a more punitive role for community sentences continued. In 1973 provisions were made that offenders on probation could be required to attend day training centres. The Criminal Justice Act 1982 provided that courts could require full-time attendance at day centres for a maximum of 60 days. Day centres were viewed with concern by many probation officers who saw their use as increasing their control function (May 1994). Other policies during the 1970s involved targeting selected offenders for intensive probation supervision and during the 1980s some schemes involved tracking offenders. In these schemes offenders are required to keep regular contact with a voluntary tracker, supervised by the Probation Service.

During the 1980s the Home Office policy sought to reduce local variations in community sentences and to increase their punitive elements. They thus attempted to exert greater control over community sentences seeing the strong welfare orientation within the Probation Service as an impediment (May 1994). In 1984 a Statement of National Objectives for Probation (SNOP) was issued which stated that the priorities of the probation service were to provide alternatives to custody and prepare social inquiry reports for the court. A major theme was that offenders with a high risk of imprisonment were to be targeted, signalling yet a further shift away from the traditional role of the service as dealing with offenders who would benefit from treatment, help or support (May 1994). In 1988 an Action Plan called on every local probation area to develop its own strategy for targeting more intensive supervision on young adult offenders.

Changes were also made to community service orders. In 1989 a set of national standards for community service was introduced which encouraged the adoption of more exacting procedures for dealing with lateness, non-compliance and unsatisfactory behaviour. A strong preference for manual labour was indicated, laying emphasis on tasks such as cleaning up graffiti.

The CJA 1991 was a further illustration of this changing emphasis which can also be seen in recent changes since that Act. In addition to the concerns about holiday camps, controversy was also aroused by the sentencing of a wife batterer to an 'anger management' course run by the Probation Service. The Home Secretary expressed these concerns in an address to the annual conference of the Central Probation Council in May 1994, where he commented that 'probation services are working with offenders but for the community and not the other way round'. The courts and the public he went on to say, must have confidence in community sentences as punishment, and, while he was in favour of programmes making demands on offenders they should not be given 'privileged access to opportunities which law-abiding members of the community cannot afford'.

A number of proposals made in 1994 also illustrate this focus. There have been for example suggestions that probation officers' training should be changed from a primarily social work training to a more practical course to attract ex-police and army officers. In August 1994 the government announced new national standards including a ban on safari and domestic holidays and requirements that work on community sentences should be demanding and physical. Other proposals aimed to introduce stricter supervision and provisions that offenders will be sent to prison if the terms of a sentence are not met. Offenders will receive two formal warnings if they fail to comply with the terms of an order which will be followed by a penalty. Offenders are to be made more aware of the effect of their crimes and it is proposed that all pre-sentence reports are to include an assessment of the risk of re-offending.

The many criticisms of community sentences imply that they may not be very effective. Given the different aims of community sentences however it is not entirely clear how they should be evaluated. Is their effectiveness to be judged in terms of how well they provide an alternative to prison? Or in terms of how many offenders are diverted from further crime? Alternatively, given the high costs of imprisonment and pressures for cost effectiveness should we subject community sentences to a cost benefit analysis? Finally, irrespective of any of these measures, should we look at the extent to which offenders are helped by these schemes, whether or not they re-offend?

In relation to the first question – their effectiveness as alternatives to prison, evidence is mixed. As we saw in Chapter 8, the prison population continued to rise despite the introduction of measures which aimed to reduce it, and it appeared that the so-called alternatives to prison acted instead as alternatives to existing non-custodial sentences. This may even have resulted in more people being sent to prison – if, for example, they failed to comply with an order or committed further offences, they could be sent to prison – thus moving more rapidly up the tariff than they might otherwise have done. What appeared to be happening was that the courts, viewing community sentences as too soft, were not prepared use them for offenders that they would otherwise have sent to prison. Cavadino and Dignan, reviewing the available research, conclude that only 45-50 per cent of those who received community service orders would otherwise have been imprisoned (Cavadino and Dignan 1992). As we also saw in Chapter 8, the use of community sentences rose immediately after the implementation of the CJA 1991, but has more recently fallen. Their use as alternatives to prison may therefore be somewhat limited.

One of the major arguments in favour of community sentences is that they are cheaper. In terms of cost this cannot be disputed. The National Probation Survey for example found that probation orders cost £1,060 per annum in 1990/91, and community service orders £1,020 (May 1992). Compare this with the high costs of imprisonment seen in previous chapters, and it is evident that community sentences offer a cheaper alternative – but how effective are they in reducing recidivism?

Statistics on community sentences are difficult to compare with those on prison as the measure of success is often the number of offenders who successfully complete orders, or who are taken to court for breaching orders. In 1991, 29 per cent of offenders on community service orders and 20 per cent on probation orders were the subject of breach proceedings, indicating that the majority of offenders on community sentences comply with their orders (Home Office 1993: 56). While these might be regarded as a success by those familiar with the problems of dealing with offenders, from another per-spective they represent a failure of offenders to complete the sentence given by the court; a sentence usually proposed in the pre-sentence report by the probation service.

Statistics on re-conviction indicate that 53 per cent of offenders given pro-bation orders in 1987 were reconvicted within two years. The equivalent figure for community service orders was 55 per cent. Reconviction rates were highest for those who had previous custodial sentences or a large num-ber of previous convictions (see Figure 10.5). In general these figures indicate that community sentences may be no more successful than prison in terms of rehabilitation, but at the same time they are no less successful and involve less cost. These figures however are very limited. They only relate to a follow-up period of two years since discharge from prison or commence-ment of a community sentence. In addition, as only two in every 100 crimes result in a conviction, their use as a measure of re-offending must be seri-ously questioned. These figures tell us little about any positive help the offender may have received.

It is also important to consider the conflicting pressures on community sentences. The increasing emphasis on cost effectiveness and the deprivation of liberty may have an impact on how offenders respond to some schemes. For example, pressures of cost effectiveness may lead to more offenders being placed on any one scheme reducing opportunities for individual work. The recent stress on tough and demanding work may also have an effect. A report on community service schemes in Scotland found that offenders responded better to schemes which provided contact with those who bene-fited from their work, where provision was made for the acquisition of new skills and where the work was seen to be useful (McIvor 1991). The author questions the stress in the National Standards on hard manual labour which is less likely to be seen by offenders as useful and which provides few oppor-tunities for direct contact with the community and learning new skills. It has also been argued that if community service becomes more punitive offenders will become more hostile and resistant–making them less likely to comply (May 1994; Vass 1990).

While some in the Probation Service remain committed to the ideal of rehabilitation through community penalties, their lack of success in rehabili-tative terms undermines these claims. The rationale of community penalties has moved on from an alternative to custody approach towards an interme-diate sanction rationale in which success will be measured in terms of just deserts and denunciatory goals. In this respect the shift reflects a greater sen-sitivity to the concerns of the community rather than the needs of the offenders. Whether judges, magistrates and the public have accepted com-munity penalties as anything other than a soft option to imprisonment is however doubtful. The concepts of community used in these discussions is synonymous with the phrase 'not in prison'. Whether a more profound link between the notions of community and punishment is likely to develop along the lines discussed in Chapter 9 with regard to the denunciatory approach to sentencing has yet to be seen.

## COMMUNITY POLICING

Effective policing requires the co-operation and support of the community, and in Chapter 4 it was seen how changes in policing and in the nature of communities led to what was seen as a decline in police community relations in some areas. This led to the growth of a number of initiatives described, somewhat loosely, as community policing, which includes both the more familiar policing tasks of patrolling and investigating crime and strategies aimed at crime prevention and reducing the fear of crime. Schemes often involve the police working with local authorities, businesses and voluntary organisations.

It is difficult to define what, exactly, is meant by the phrase community policing, which emerged in the late 1970s. A pioneer of the concept was Chief Constable John Alderson of the Devon and Cornwall force, who argued:

> community policing would exist in its purest form where all elements in the community, official and unofficial, would conceive of the common good and combine to produce a social climate and an environment conducive to good order and the happiness of all those living within it.
>
> (Alderson 1978)

In Alderson's version the community constable is seen as a 'social leader' working with the community and the emphasis is firmly placed on preventive rather than reactive policing. In theory, community policing is based on ideas that the police should consult and seek co-operation with the public and in 'general notions of creating a tranquil and safe environment' (Bennett 1994b: 6). On the basis of informal conversations with police officers Bennett found that these broadly conceived aims included stressing the benefits of public contact and reassurance along with deterrence, prevention, intelligence gathering and reducing the fear of crime (Bennett 1994a).

Many advantages are claimed for community policing. In addition to the obvious benefit of improving police relations with the community, it can also add to the effectiveness of the police in relation to law enforcement. Thus it is argued that if the community have more confidence in the police, they may be more likely to come forward with information and co-operation.

In practice, community policing encompasses a wide variety of different schemes and Bennett identifies five models or styles (Bennett 1994a). First, many schemes involve area based policing, known variously as neighbourhood, zonal, team or sector policing. This involves a small team of managers, supervisors and officers being allocated to a local area. Sector policing has recently been introduced in the Metropolitan Police area and has been adopted by many other forces – Bennett cites a 1990 survey which found that over one-quarter of all forces operated some form of sector policing. These generally involve allocating community constables to small areas on a semi-permanent basis. In the Metropolitan Police Area, teams of officers, under an inspector are responsible for a small community area, or sector. This inspector, according to the Commissioner's Annual Report for 1991/92 will be responsible for:

> ensuring that the policing arrangements are adequate and effective. The Senior Inspector, in consultation with the local community, will determine the style of policing for the sector, and set its priorities . . . Over a period of time the officers will come to identify more closely with that community and as a result will be more responsive to its needs. They will feel greater ownership of the community's problems, and will help to address underlying causes, rather than merely responding to the symptoms.

(Metropolitan Police Commissioner 1992)

Bennett's second model of community policing refers to the multi-agency approach, in which the police work in partnership with local authorities and voluntary agencies. These initiatives may be centred around law enforcement by, for example, targeting particular crimes, or may be more concerned with crime prevention or victim support. In an example of partnership policing in the King's Cross area of London the police and local authorities developed a co-ordinated range of environmental and policing initiatives to reduce prostitution and drug dealing. Local authority departments cleaned the streets, improved lighting and closed off places where drug dealers and prostitutes operated. High profile policing, including videos of drug dealers carrying out their trade, led to an increase in convictions. It was claimed that drug dealing was reduced by two-thirds (*Guardian*, 16 February 1994).

Another project in South London targeted a high rate of street robbery. In an area where there had been poor relationships between the police and the community a range of strategies were developed involving the police, the local authority, schools and community consultative groups. Safe routes were created and video cameras installed on selected streets; school campaigns against bullying and carrying knives were launched and the Department of the Environment funded a crime shop which offered help and advice on a local estate. Summer projects aimed to keep young people involved in sport. As a result it was claimed that robbery fell by 38 per cent (*Guardian*, 4 April 1994).

A major focus of these schemes is crime prevention, the focus of Bennett's third theme. Community crime prevention partnerships include neighbourhood watch schemes, which will be discussed in the following section on crime prevention. Bennett's fourth model identifies schemes which involve police contact with the public. This may be through foot patrols or setting up shops on estates and high streets away from the police station. It may also involve the police knocking on doors to contact the public directly.

Fifthly, community policing refers to the consultation mechanisms outlined in Chapter 4 and the introduction of lay visitors to police stations.

Despite the many potential benefits of community policing it has not proved easy to implement. Full implementation would, argue many, involve a total reorganisation of police forces in which prevention and service roles take precedence over law enforcement and public order roles. As was seen in Chapter 4, however, the law enforcement role of the police is often priorit-ised and seen within the police culture as real police work. Some have discerned a tendency for community police functions to be 'bolted on' to existing organisations and seen as an addition to, rather than the main pur-pose of, organisations (Bennett 1994a). Attempts to change styles of policing may encounter resistance from officers on the ground and it has been argued that they cannot be effective if they do not carry the support of these officers (Fielding 1988).

In addition, given the vast number of tasks which the police are expected to perform, there may simply not be enough officers to allocate to beats on a semi-permanent basis. In times of emergency they may be called off the beat to deal with football disturbances, public order incidents or other duties. This means that the community cannot rely on consistency of cover. In addition community constables spend much time on administrative duties and in the police station, and relatively small amounts of time on 'commun-ity contacts' (Bennett and Lupton 1992). Moreover, in organisations where community policing has a low status officers may be keen to move on from such roles meaning that few gather sufficient experience. Community polic-ing has also been found to be more successful in smaller, suburban middle class communities than in inner city areas where the greatest problems have occurred (Fielding et al 1989).

A study attempting to measure the impact of community policing found no change in public attitudes or rates of victimisation (Irving et al 1989 cited in Bennett 1984a). The reasons for this limited success of schemes may be that they did not fit well with other organisational priorities and faced resist-ance from officers. Some positive results have been associated with foot patrols – Bennett, for example, found that a scheme involving the police seeking direct contact with the public had little effect on crime or reporting rates but did lead to substantial improvement in public satisfaction with the police (Bennett 1991).

These results should not however be taken to indicate that all schemes are ineffective and there are examples of highly committed community officers. Much more thorough research and evaluation is clearly needed to unravel what makes a scheme successful and how it can be fairly evaluated. It may be, for example, that some schemes have little impact on crime or victimisa-tion rates but reduce people's fear of crime. Some on the other hand may have an immediate success which is difficult to sustain over time as enthu-siasm wanes. The limited evidence of success to date however raises important questions about the role of the police – to what extent should they be fostering community relations or focusing on law enforcement and public order?

Public order concerns and the frustrations with the criminal law led Coventry City Council to seek a civil law solution via a High Court injunction against two convicted burglars, John and David Finnie. They were ordered to keep out of the Stoke Heath Estate, Coventry, described as 'crime-ridden' (*Daily Telegraph*, 25 February 1995: 6) where their mother lived and where they had grown up. The search for a safer environment has stimulated a variety of initiations in crime preventions.


## CRIME PREVENTION AND SAFER CITIES

It is a well-known adage that prevention is better than cure and much attention has recently turned to the development of schemes designed to prevent crime. There is now a vast industry surrounding crime prevention which started in the late 1970s and expanded during the 1980s. Many organisations have responsibility for crime prevention, including multi-agency partnerships involving central government, local authorities, the police, voluntary organisations, business and commerce. A wide variety of measures are involved from simple strategies such as improving locks or installing gates in alleyways to high tech computer and close circuit television (CCTV) screening and changing aspects of environmental design.

There are generally assumed to be three main models of crime prevention, primary, secondary and tertiary. Primary crime prevention refers to strategies aiming to prevent crime not involving offenders – for example, by encouraging better security. Secondary crime prevention involves policies which target people considered to be at risk of becoming offenders. Thus a variety of educational and sports schemes aim to divert youth in high crime areas from criminal activity. Tertiary crime prevention aims to prevent those already convicted of crime from continuing with their criminal careers mainly through the sentences of the court.

The 1990 Blue Ribbon Report in California identified different crime prevention strategies and stressed the importance of social and economic factors and the general welfare of the population in preventing crime:

> . . . good education, health care, shelter, nutrition, recreation, and employment opportunities represent forms of primary prevention. Unemployment and the lack of formal education are significant contributing factors to the level of criminal conduct in contemporary society. A well-educated and working population are much less likely to be involved in crimes such as robbery, the trafficking of narcotics and other illegal drugs, and certain property crimes such as burglary.
>
> (California State Government (1990): 12)

The report goes on to point out that secondary prevention targets individuals who are at risk and have been identified by criminal, welfare or educational agencies as likely to require intervention to prevent a drift towards crime.

Tertiary prevention deals with those who have been found guilty of committing an offence, and involves efforts to rehabilitate them.

Recently attention has shifted from tertiary crime prevention through sentencing policy to primary and secondary measures (Pease 1994). What is often known as community crime prevention mainly deals with the primary and secondary aspects.

Greater interest in primary crime prevention developed during the 1970s as a result of the declining faith in attempts to both explain crime and reduce offending as detailed in Chapter 9. New approaches argued that crime could be prevented by focusing not on individual offenders but on the situations in which crime is committed. Offenders choose to commit a crime and will be more likely to so choose when faced with an opportunity in which there is a small likelihood of being caught (see also Chapter 2). Reducing these opportunities can therefore reduce crime.

In an influential publication the Home Office Research and Planning Unit detailed the potential of a variety of measures for crime prevention (Mayhew et al 1976). Some of these involve target hardening which means making the target of a crime, for example a car, bank or telephone kiosk, harder to steal, break into or vandalise. Many of these ideas are relatively simple and inexpensive to implement. Other schemes involve altering aspects of the environment – better street lighting for example may deter muggers as it increases the likelihood of their being observed and identified. It also reduces the fear of crime among residents. At a more fundamental level re-designing housing schemes may produce more public space – space which people occupy and feel responsibility for. This prevents crime as it means that strangers can be more readily observed and therefore deterred. In any situation in which a crime may occur, levels of surveillance are crucial. Surveillance can be increased informally, by altering the design of buildings to ensure greater surveillance by employees or residents, or formally by employing security guards or installing video cameras. Vandalism in schools, for example, could be reduced by using schools in the evening for other activities. An example of this kind of approach is outlined in Figure 11.1 below, which is an extract from an architect's plan for the renovation of King's Square in Hammersmith.

The potential of these kind of schemes was quickly recognised and they had a wide appeal. They inspired a more positive approach to crime prevention indicating that something as opposed to nothing worked (Pease 1994). The slogan 'together we can crack crime' captured this mood. They were consistent with prevailing government policy in that they encouraged the community, industry and commerce to play a part as 'active citizens' in crime prevention, bearing some of the cost and responsibility themselves. The Home Office Crime Prevention Unit, set up in 1983, played a major role in developing many policy initiatives. Other departments such as Transport, Health and Social Security also became involved with crime prevention initiatives and the Department of the Environment plays a crucial

**Fig 11.1** Community and crime prevention strategies

---

### STREETS, SPACES, AND NATURAL SURVEILLANCE

A pavement or a street is much more than just a thoroughfare, a way of carrying pedestrians, it is one of the city's vital organs: the most common place of social contact and the key to sustaining a robust and healthy public realm.

By using pavements people become active participants in the dynamics of a city. Successful urban areas are those where people – residents, shop keepers, shoppers, visitors – feel comfortable and able to interact freely with those around them. This sense of safety and comfort is never produced by some external policing agent, it is a function of the multiple interactions which take place in that particular public space throughout the day. Safe streets and pavements are self-policing, through the intricate, almost unconscious network of voluntary controls, checks and balances, sanctions and licences, enforced by the people them-selves: the passers by, the people watchers and those whose daily business involves contact with the street, even if this is only through visual contact.

There are a number of important pre-conditions if streets and pavements are to be allowed to police themselves:

(i)   There should be a clear demarcation between public and private space. This means that everyone has an equal and unambiguous relationship with the public space they are using and an equal responsibility towards it.

(ii)  There must be eyes on the street, a kind of unconscious surveillance. This means, for example, providing places and opportunities for people watching and encouraging visual contact between the indoors and the outdoors. Shops, bars, restaurants, markets play an important role in this respect.

(iii) The pavements must have people on them continuously, across different times of the day. This often means giving people reasons to visit or pass through in those important bridging hours, for example, between leaving work and coming back into town for a recreational purpose.

One of the natural laws of street life – so frequently misunderstood by planners and urban designers – is that the sight of people attracts still other people. They are more likely to be drawn to the buzz of unordered activity than neat, ordered half-empty precincts. Underneath the apparent messiness and disorder of a mar-ket or busy pavement there is a subtle order, a set of checks and balances, a mixture of watchers and users, a myriad of social interactions: in short the most effective antidote to crime and fear of crime.

Activity is the key objective: volume of activity, variety of activity and activity across different times of the day.

---

(Urban Cultures Ltd and John Lydall Architects (1993) 'Kings Square: Hammersmith and the Safer Cities Project' December 1993) role, as much crime prevention involves environmental change in public areas and housing estates (Heal and Laycock 1986).

By the late 1980s many schemes appeared successful and new initiatives were launched. In 1988 Crime Concern was launched; a charity funded partly by the Home Office and partly by private enterprise. This organisation has been responsible for a large number of crime prevention projects in conjunction with both commercial and public organisations. 1988 also saw the launch of the Crack Crime campaign and the Safer Cities Programme, outlined below. In 1993 a National Board for Crime Prevention was established to bring together representatives of central and local government, business, voluntary agencies, the media, the police and the probation service. The Morgan Report 1991 recommended that local authorities be required by statute to set up community safety departments. While never fully implemented this report was influential and many local authorities have set up community safety units.

Other schemes aim to prevent crime by targeting particular crimes or groups of victims. Thus the Home Secretary, Michael Howard, told the 1994 Annual Conference of the Association of Chief Police Officers, 'Hard facts suggest that targeting crimes, targeting offenders and targeting victims could contribute substantially to the fight against crime' (*The Times*, 7 July 1994: 5). This is based on a number of studies which showed the importance of concentrating on repeat victimisation (see, for example, Pease 1994). It has been found that victims have a statistically higher chance of becoming a victim in the future than those who have not been a victim. One

**Fig 11.2** Campaign against driving and drinking

**SCREENING BREATH TESTS AND NUMBER POSITIVE OR REFUSED BY MONTH (ENGLAND AND WALES 1993)**

*Numbers and percentages*

| Month | Total tests | Positive/ refused | % Positive/ refused |
|---|---|---|---|
| January | 45,600 | 6,100 | 13 |
| February | 37,800 | 6,400 | 17 |
| March | 39,400 | 6,500 | 16 |
| April | 40,300 | 7,300 | 18 |
| May | 38,400 | 7,300 | 19 |
| June | 41,400 | 7,000 | 17 |
| July | 58,900 | 8,500 | 15 |
| August | 47,000 | 8,100 | 17 |
| September | 44,800 | 7,200 | 16 |
| October | 47,300 | 8,300 | 18 |
| November | 52,900 | 7,900 | 15 |
| December | 105,800 | 8,600 | 8 |
| TOTAL | 599,600 | 89,200 | 15 |

(Home Office (1994) *Home Office Statistical Bulletin 14/94*: Table 3)

study found that once a house had been burgled it was four times more likely to be burgled again than a house that had not been burgled (Pease 1991). The 1992 British Crime Survey estimated that 43 per cent of all crime was committed against 4.3 per cent of people who had been the victim of a crime on five or more occasions in a 12-month period.

Another example of successful crime prevention is the Drink-Driving Campaign, as shown in Figure 11.2. In 1993, 599,600 motorists in England and Wales were given, or asked to take a breathalyser test. The percentage of motorists who gave a positive test, that is one which indicates that they have consumed an excess amount of alcohol, or who refused the test was 15 per cent (89,400 motorists). During the Christmas period there is considerable publicity about the dangers of driving and drinking. In December the police carry out more than twice as many tests than in a typical month (105,800). However the number of those who tested positive or refused to take the test was 8,600 – a rate of 8 per cent, not much greater than in those months in which fewer motorists are tested. So that in July 1994 with 58,900 motorists tested, 8,500 tested positive or refused the test producing a rate of 15 per cent.

## Safer cities

A major crime prevention initiative followed a series of programmes in the five towns of Bolton, North Tyneside, Croydon, Swansea and Wellingborough, known as the Five Towns Initiative. This was followed by a Safer Cities, a larger programme which was linked with the Action for Cities initiative set up to facilitate the regeneration of inner cities. It incorporates a total of 20 projects funded by the Home Office. Each programme, set up in one local area, consists of a co-ordinator, an assistant co-ordinator and a personal assistant. They work under the guidance of a local steering group made up of representatives of local authorities, the police and probation services, voluntary organisations, ethnic minority business and community interests (Tilley 1993).

The Safer Cities initiative has three stated goals:

- to reduce crime
- to lessen the fear of crime
- to create safer cities where economic enterprise and community life can flourish.

Safer Cities therefore incorporates not only crime prevention but a concern with other related aspects of community safety. It includes the growing concern for victims of crime and the recognition that many live in fear of crime. These issues are interlinked in that a focus on crime prevention inevitably affects the public's estimation of the risks of victimisation. Indeed, some crime prevention schemes can increase the fear of crime by drawing attention to these risks (Tilley 1993). Economic enterprise and community life are also related. If crime rates are high in a particular area and the population have a high fear of crime, they will avoid public places, local shops and community activities. Therefore crime is related to wider socio-economic activity – as indicated in the extract reproduced as Figure 11.1.

The structure of Safer Cities, with its local steering committees and organisers, has meant that it has been involved in a very wide range of programmes. The Annual Safer Cities Progress Report of 1992/93 reported that up to 1993, more than 3,300 crime prevention and community safety measures had been initiated involving £20.4 million Home Office funding. This report also indicated the variety of activities undertaken under the Safer Cities umbrella which included:

- projects to improve security in homes, businesses and public facilities;
- helping young people as potential offenders, offenders and victims of crime;
- schemes to tackle domestic violence and other women's safety issues;
- action on car crime and racial harassment.

(Home Office 1993b: 7)

Considerable success has been claimed for these projects. The progress report revealed, for example, that one scheme succeeded in reducing victimisation rates from 19 per cent to 1 per cent. Another scheme was claimed to have accounted for a 62 per cent reduction in burglaries and yet another for a 75 per cent reduction. One alarm system installed in empty properties had reputedly saved £14,000 in reduced vandalism and lost rent.

The use of CCTV has also been a popular method both for preventing and investigating crime. The example in Figure 11.3 gives details of a scheme used on London Underground, as set out in a report on the scheme to the Safer Town Centre Committee, Hammersmith.

## Neighbourhood Watch

Neighbourhood Watch emerged in the early 1980s, based on the principle that the police and the community can work together to prevent crime. Based in local areas, these schemes involve the public looking out for and reporting anything suspicious – being the 'eyes and ears' of the police. By 1987 there were 35,000 neighbourhood watch schemes, and the British Crime Survey estimated that in 1988 as many as 14 per cent of households were members (Mayhew et al 1989). By 1994 there were 130,000 Neighbourhood Watch schemes with five million members.

The organisation of individual schemes varies enormously, however they normally involve groups of residents with a local co-ordinator. Members produce and distribute newsletters and leaflets giving general crime prevention advice, often supported by local businesses. Some schemes encourage property marking and security surveys and members are asked to display their membership by the now familiar stickers on doors.

**Fig 11.3** Closed circuit television and crime prevention

---

### THE OPERATION OF CCTV ON LONDON UNDERGROUND BETWEEN GOSPEL OAK AND HAMMERSMITH STATIONS.

In October 1991, a CCTV system began operating in eight stations on the western end of the District Line, with a monitoring and control room at Ladbroke Grove Station. Before its installation, seven stations on the District line – Gospel Oak, Westbourne Park, Latimer Road, Ladbroke Grove, Shepherds Bush, Goldhawk Road and Hammersmith – had the highest rates of crime.

Each station has between ten to eighteen fixed wide-angle lens cameras, covering the platforms and stairways from the booking halls. An operator at the Ladbroke Grove control room has a bank of eight screens showing one picture from each station. The operator can move from camera to camera at each station to show activity at different parts of the stations. Four screens monitor events if a passenger Help/Emergency Line button is pressed at any of the stations. In what is known as a time lapse recording, recordings are made onto a video tape every four stations. A further monitor, with four-way split screen capability, allows playback from the tapes covering the 150 cameras that are in place. Eight time lapse video recorders, one for each station, cover the pictures sent out every four seconds from each camera. Two time lapse video recorders record pictures sent when the help line button is pressed. The tapes are kept for two weeks. Identical time lapse recordings are made at the British Transport Police office at the Broadway, St James's Park station. As well as recording incidents the operator can alert the British Transport Police or the Metropolitan Police if an incident is seen taking place.

The equipment includes:
- 8 Visual Display Units
- 4 Emergency real time VDU monitors
- 1 Playback, split screen monitor
- 10 time lapse recording VCR machines
- 1 Multiplexer, playback machine
- Radio link with every station

The system cost three and a half million pounds to install. Each time lapse playback video recorder cost £3,500 in 1994, and 24 hour monitoring requires three employees, which is the main operating cost. Other operating costs include top quality video recording tapes and a service contract with Siemens Plessey.

The system provides for a police response to emergency situations and criminal incidents, provided by the British Transport Police. A squad of 20 officers, three sergeants and one inspector covering the seven stations are based at Hammersmith station. At any one time there are typically five officers on duty in mobile police vehicles ready to respond to an emergency. The police have promised a 3–4 minute arrival time for response to the most serious category of incident. Following advice and consultation with the Crown Prosecution Service and the Metropolitan Police as to how tapes could be used in support of criminal investigation and prosecution, a form was designed to permit the tapes to be used in evidence in a court. In a contested case this might involve the control room operator being called to give evidence in court.

**Fig 11.3** Continued

---

Overall, the scheme has proved successful with the manager of the stations involved commenting that 'It has surpassed expectations.' Inspection visits have been made to the CCTV control centre at Ladbroke Grove by representatives of transport systems from Bilbao, Hong Kong, Liverpool, and a Dutch travel authority. What are its main achievements?

**Crime Investigation:**
Following a murder on the Sunday of the 1993 Notting Hill carnival, the suspect escaped on the underground. His picture, taken from the time lapse recordings, was printed in the *Evening Standard* the following day leading to his arrest.

**Crime Prevention:**
On Christmas Day 1993, the operator in the control room at Ladbroke Grove noticed unauthorised personnel at Royal Oak station with spray cans. By using the public address system he was able to announce that the police had been called and were on the way. The potential graffiti was avoided. Now the seven stations have no graffiti on them. The trains are still subject to graffiti but the stations have remained clear since the introduction of the scheme.

**Deterrence:**
Police data on recorded crime shows that in the first full year of its operation, recorded crime was reduced by 83%. From 1991 to 1993 the seven stations have changed from having the highest, to the least, number of recorded crimes for all the London Transport station areas.

**Public/Employer Safety:**
All staff are issued with a radio and this is thought to have led to an enhanced feeling of safety amongst employees.

Travellers have access to help points on the station that allow for immediate contact with the control room. Visual and radio contact is made with the operator who can call for police backup if necessary.

**Public Information:**
The public can use the helpline for passenger information about waiting times for trains. This provides them with useful information and reassures them that someone is available if they need assistance for whatever purposes.

**Prosecution:**
Evidence from the time lapse recordings was used in the successful prosecution of two offenders for serious crimes.

In support of the claims made for this CCTV project it was pointed out by Alan Green, the station manager of the seven stations, that ticket revenue has increased on this section of London Transport's operation and that police recorded crime statistics are down for this sector.

---

(Report presented by the Criminal Justice Centre, TVU, to the Safer Town Centre Committee, Hammersmith, 5 April 1994)

Despite its popularity the success of Neighbourhood Watch has been limited. One of its major limitations is that schemes are easier to set up and operate more effectively in the areas in which they are least needed. Thus the British Crime Survey found that schemes were most common in affluent suburban areas, with members being drawn from high status and higher income groups (Mayhew et al 1989). The population in multi-racial areas and poorest council estates on the other hand were least likely to join. This survey also found that areas where membership was lower also tended to be those where burglary risks were higher. This may have the effect that schemes divert police resources from high crime to low crime areas (Heal and Laycock 1986).

In addition, the British Crime Survey also found that while members of schemes were more likely than non-members to take crime prevention measures, many had done so before they joined. Membership of a Neighbourhood Watch scheme may in reality mean very little and involvement often falls off after initial launch meetings (Bennett 1990). Three-quarters of members interviewed by the British Crime Survey had put stickers or posters in their windows but 21 per cent had neither attended progress meetings nor knew the name of their co-ordinator. Members reported matters to the police more often than non-members, and felt a greater sense of security. Many however found it difficult to pinpoint any specific benefits of schemes although there are some indications that burglary risks were lower after joining Neighbourhood Watch.

Despite the claims made for specific projects and the enthusiasm for crime prevention in general, its effectiveness is difficult to assess. This is partly because we may never know how much crime would have occurred had any initiative not been introduced, and whether any apparent improvement is temporary or long term. Another major problem besetting evaluation is the extent to which crime may have been displaced to other areas. Evaluation methods can rarely measure this effect (Pease 1994; Bennett 1994a). For example, a successful Neighbourhood Watch scheme might prevent crime in one group of streets, but crime may rise in an adjoining area without such a scheme. One kind of crime may also be replaced by another. Thus would-be burglars deterred by security alarms may turn to vandalism. It might well be that the benefit of schemes such as Neighbourhood Watch is to reassure the community that someone is trying to do something about crime.

These problems are related to the assumption underlying much crime prevention that crime is essentially opportunist. If, on the other hand, a sizeable proportion of offenders are motivated in some way to commit crime, they will find a way around prevention measures. Thus a major limitation of all crime prevention schemes is that they may neglect the underlying roots of crime. If crime is related to diet, family breakdown or unemployment and inner city degeneration, crime prevention measures may offer a slight improvement but can do little to solve these underlying causes.

On a more practical level, the multi-agency partnerships which have been so popular also have problems. In essence these require very different agencies with different patterns of organisation, ways of working and cultural backgrounds to work together. Communications, deciding who is responsible for implementing initiatives and full co-operation have all produced difficulties. There have also been reports that the agencies involved may mistrust each other. Community groups may mistrust the police who in turn may mistrust the social services (Bennett 1994a). In addition, crime prevention may not be a priority for participating agencies. Heal and Laycock for example found that prevention remained a poor relation within police organisation, and like community policing it may not be seen as 'real police work' (Heal and Laycock 1986).

Others point out that crime prevention measures are only targeted at some kinds of crime. Stanko, for example, comments that they play on women's fears of 'stranger danger' by focusing on safer streets and public areas, whereas most rapes and domestic violence take place in the home or workplace (Stanko 1990). And while there have been some initiatives in the prevention of commercial fraud, crime prevention measures and safer cities programmes have not so far targeted environmental or corporate crimes which also endanger the safety of the community. This can be seen in concerns about transport safety and pollution.

Finally, others have criticised the focus of many crime prevention measures on the 'technological fix' of locks bolts and video cameras. These may well reduce the fear of crime but can in themselves have an adverse effect on the environment. Estate residents for example may find themselves living in mini fortresses and gates, locks, bolts and bars can themselves inhibit the development of neighbourliness or community spirit (Young 1994). CCTV means that we are all under far more surveillance than hitherto leading to some fears of unduly pervasive policing and a threat to civil liberties.


## VICTIMS

It is often said that victims are the forgotten element in the criminal justice process and recent decades have seen a greater emphasis on them. A major focus of crime prevention initiatives is on reducing the risk of victimisation, and a variety of measures have been introduced to support individual victims. Some of these involve the formal agencies of the system, others involve volunteers drawn from the community. In addition as we saw in Chapter 8, some policies aim to involve victims more directly in sentencing through reparation, or by including an assessment of the harm done in the information available to courts.

What came to be called the victim movement drew attention to the problems faced by victims at all stages of the criminal justice process. A number of studies during the 1970s and 1980s, including the British Crime Surveys, revealed that victims were often dissatisfied with many aspects of their treatment by criminal justice agencies (see, for example, Maguire and Pointing 1988). Once they had reported their case to the police, little else seemed to happen. Yet victims require both practical help such as reinstating locks and repairing damage and emotional support to get over the trauma involved in the offence. In addition victims complained that they were often unaware of the progress of their case, were not informed when cases were to be tried unless they were called as witnesses, and if called as witnesses were often given little information about what was expected of them.

In court, they could find themselves confronted by offenders' friends and relatives in the waiting room. Giving evidence might involve re-living the offence, and cross-examination could be particularly traumatic as one feature of the adversarial system is that the defence may attempt to discredit the victim's story. This can be particularly acute for female victims of rape or sexual assault, whose own history and character can be called into question (see, for example, Walklate 1989). Victims may also feel aggrieved if they feel that sentences do not reflect the harm they had suffered.

At the same time as sentencing policy was being reviewed the government signalled a greater attention to the needs of victims by the publication, in 1990, of the Victim's Charter which stated that victims had a right to expect among other things information about the progress of a case, trial dates and bail and sentencing decisions (Home Office 1990). In addition it gave a commitment to improve facilities for victim witnesses called to court, to reduce waiting times and to take the special needs of victims into account in new court buildings, by providing for example separate waiting rooms. A number of disparate movements led to this recognition of the needs of victims and measures to improve their situation.

Women's groups who drew attention to the plight of women victimised by rape, sexual assault and domestic violence formed part of this movement. They not only campaigned for better treatment but set up a number of initiatives themselves. In 1972 Erin Pizzey established the first refuge for victims of domestic violence in Chiswick. Rape crisis centres were also developed during the 1970s, and by 1988 there were 40 such centres (Zedner 1994). These, staffed mainly by volunteers, offer a helpline and a 24-hour counselling service. Many police forces also developed specialist units to provide a better service for women and child victims, and some set up special interview suites in police stations staffed by trained teams of female officers. A Home Office Circular (69/1986) to chief police officers offered advice on better treatment for victims of rape and domestic violence. This included the provision of suitable private facilities for the examination of victims, reference to advice and counselling services, and police training. It also expressed an overriding concern for the safety of victims of domestic violence and the need to reduce any risk of further violence. In addition the CJA 1988 contains tougher provisions to ensure the anonymity of rape victims. The woman's identity is safeguarded, subject to the oversight of the courts, from the moment of allegation, whether or not any proceedings follow, and for the rest of her life.

Victims' needs were supported by other developments, particularly by the growth of victim support schemes, first set up in Bristol in 1974. Nationally, these are regulated by the National Association of Victim Support Schemes (NAVSS) which receives financial support from the government. Funding has risen from £1.5 million in 1987/88 to over £2.5 million in 1988/89 and approaching £4 million in 1989/90 (NAVSS). By 1991, 370 schemes were affiliated, and in 1990, a total of 7,000 volunteers contacted almost 600,000 victims (Zedner 1994). Victim Support is a charity which in addition to providing individual support for victims aims to influence the provision of services for victims and campaigns on matters relating to compensation and provision for the victim in court. It has also launched a special initiative on children affected by crime.

The major role of victim support is to provide services, on a voluntary basis, to individual victims at the local level. Each victim support scheme is run by a management committee and a co-ordinator collects details of victims from the police. Under local agreements the police give the local victim support scheme information about victims, including their name and address unless the victim asks them not to. These details are then distributed to a pool of volunteers who contact victims either by letter, telephone or doorstep visits.

Schemes provide help over practical matters or the provision of information. The emphasis of victim support has mainly been on short-term help and support on a 'good neighbour' principle by providing a shoulder to cry on (see, for example, Gill and Mawby 1990). Until recently, the emphasis was mainly on victims of burglary, robbery or theft although victim support has now expanded its work to include more long-term work with the victims of sexual and violent crime, the families of murder victims and some schemes include a service for those involved in serious motor accidents.

Victim support has also been involved with the provision of schemes to help victims in court, arising out of victims' complaints about their experiences. Initially a number of pilot schemes were set up. One such scheme is described by Rock, who found that the main role of volunteers was to offer 'companionship and solace' during the long periods of waiting and confusion (Rock 1991). These have been followed by a growing number of court schemes and the appointment of court staff with specific responsibility for liaising with victims.

Despite the recognition of the needs of victims in the Victim's Charter, progress towards better provision has been slow. In October 1993, the Home Secretary announced that the government had accepted recommendations made by the Royal Commission on Criminal Justice including the provision of better information on the progress of cases, better consultation with victims and better court facilities. In addition he announced extra funding for victim support to enable witness support schemes to be set up in all 78 Crown Court Centres by the end of 1995.

When considering the role of victims in court a major issue is whether they should have any role in sentencing. The Right Honourable Lord McCluskey, a former Solicitor General for Scotland, argued for a sentencing reform which would hand over the sentencing decision to the jury who tried the case (*Guardian*, 13 December 1994: 26). At present in England and Wales there are, as we saw in Chapter 8, provisions for compensation orders which involve the victim being directly compensated by the offender. Other proposals for bringing the victim into the sentencing stage have been made. In the USA, for example, there are provisions in some states for victim impact statements to precede the courts' consideration of compensation and sentencing. In some cases victims may state an opinion about the sentence.

These ideas have some strengths. Lucia Zedner, for example, argues that they recognise the victim's role in the dispute and could psychologically benefit the victim. In addition victims might be encouraged to co-operate with the police and the court would have better information about the harm suffered by the victim, thus assisting their assessment of how the sentence can be made proportionate to the harm done. On the other hand, continues Zedner, further victim involvement may limit the prosecutor's discretion and there is a danger that the victim's subjectivity would undermine the objectivity of the court. Disparities in sentencing could result whereby those guilty of similar offences received very different sentences. Finally, she argues, victims may not wish to be involved as it might prove yet a further burden (Zedner 1994). Others such as Ashworth have pointed out that a victim's participation in sentencing undermines one of the most fundamental principles of criminal law – that of culpability and intent (Ashworth 1993). It is what the offender intends, not what the victim suffers, that should be the basis of the sentence.

Principles of restitution and reparation have become more popular in recent years. There has also been a growth in mediation schemes, which involve meetings between offenders and victims which often agree some form of compensation. This may be an alternative to the formal trial process, it may be part of a community sentence, or it may be carried out while the offender is in custody. In one example, a victim whose car had been stolen and damaged, and who had himself been run down when he tried to intervene, met twice with the offender. These meetings were arranged at the local social services department, after the offender had given himself up to the police and had agreed to attempt mediation. In the first meeting, offender and victim confronted each other, with the victim expressing strong feelings about his experience. In the second meeting the offender agreed to compensate the victim for the damage to his car (*Guardian*, 24 August 1994).

While these schemes clearly help some individual offenders and victims, their potential may be somewhat limited. They may be more appropriate for less serious offences than for those involving serious loss and especially physical injury. Not all victims might wish to confront offenders. It can also be asked who benefits most from such schemes. Walklate comments that they

317

may benefit offenders who receive a reduced sentence or have their case diverted. They may benefit the state by being cheap. But while they may benefit some individual victims, they are of dubious benefit to others (Walklate 1989). Where the loss has been great either in monetary or in physical terms, such schemes are unlikely to provide anything like adequate compensation, which may either be impossible or well beyond the offender's means.

The use of compensation orders has increased rapidly in recent years. Provisions for compensation orders were made in the CJA 1972, which provided that courts could make an ancillary order for compensation in addition to the main penalty in cases where injury, loss or damage had resulted. The CJA of 1982 provided that a compensation order could be the sole penalty, and, where it was used with a fine, would take priority over the fine. The CJA 1988 required the courts to consider a compensation order in every case of death, injury, loss or damage. To increase the use of compensation it also requires courts to give reasons why they have not made orders when they could have done. The police have been asked to ensure that the information on the victim's injury or loss is obtained and the Crown Prosecution Service will present it to the court. The CJA 1991 increased the maximum sum which can be awarded by magistrates' courts from £2,000 to £5,000. In 1991, 26 per cent of offenders convicted of indictable offences in magistrates' courts were ordered to pay compensation, and 12 per cent in the Crown Court. The figure for the Crown Court is lower as compensation is not normally combined with a custodial sentence. The average amount of compensation in magistrates' courts was £161 for indictable offences and in the Crown Court, £882 (Home Office 1993: 20).

While compensation orders are clearly seen as important elements in sentencing, their effect can be somewhat limited. Like fines, they may not be paid. A *Mail on Sunday* investigation claimed that as many as two in three orders result in no payment, following which the Home Office undertook to investigate this problem (*Mail on Sunday*, 26 June 1994). Compensation orders may also be limited by the offenders' means and the nature of the offence. Where, for example, non-monetary harm is involved, they may be inappropriate or inadequate. Both mediation schemes and compensation orders may therefore be more applicable to minor property crimes and are difficult to apply to more serious crimes where the trauma suffered by the victim cannot readily be translated into a monetary value. (See also Moxon et al 1992).

Victims of violent crimes may receive compensation from the Criminal Injuries Compensation Board (CICB). This was set up in 1964, and gives awards to victims of unlawful violence. Claims are evaluated on the basis of criteria which include an assessment of the victim's co-operation with the police, whether or not the victim precipitated an incident and a consideration of the character and conduct of the applicant. Victims with previous convictions may well not receive an award. The system therefore embodies the notion of a 'deserving victim' (Walklate 1989).

From its inception the scheme received an increasing number of applications – during 1989/90 applications reached 22,000. Not all applicants receive awards and indeed the proportion of successful applications fell from 80 per cent in 1980 to 52 per cent in 1990. Applications take a long time to be processed with only a fifth of claims being settled within one year. The costs of the scheme however rose steadily, with £109 million pounds being paid in 1990/91 – an increase of 50 per cent over the previous year (Zedner 1994).

The CJA 1988 provided for a statutory scheme to replace this 'voluntary' system. This was to provide for compensation for victims of violent crime on an individual basis as if the victim had privately sued the offender. This was never in fact brought into force and in 1993 the Secretary of State proposed a new non-statutory scheme whereby payments would be made according to a set tariff. This would move away from considering applications on a case-by-case basis to a system under which awards would be based solely on the type and severity of injury. Twenty-five tariff bands were to be introduced – from £1,000 to a maximum of £25,000. These proposals attracted vehement criticism and opposition. Particularly controversial was the proposal to exclude any consideration of either medical expenses or loss of earnings in the calculation of compensation. This would reduce the compensation received by many victims and reduce the cost of the scheme – following persistent questioning the government estimated that around 6,600 victims would receive less compensation. It would also have a severe effect on victims whose injuries have led to loss of employment. One example cited by Victim Support, one of the opponents of the proposed changes, was that of a nurse who had given up work as result of her injuries. She received £125,000 under the old scheme which would have been reduced to a mere £5,000 under the new scheme (*Daily Telegraph*, 26 February 1994). Those whose jobs make them vulnerable to attack, such as the police, prison officers and health workers were those who would be most severely affected by the change. Accordingly, the proposals were challenged in court by trade unions and attracted opposition in the House of Lords which, in an amendment to the Criminal Justice and Public Order Bill, required the government to incorporate the existing scheme in legislation (*Guardian*, 17 June 1994). In *R v Home Secretary, ex parte Fire Brigades Union and others* (1995) the Court of Appeal held that the Home Secretary had no power to replace the scheme agreed by Parliament by an extra-statutory measure, and had acted unlawfully: a decision upheld by the House of Lords.

# VIGILANTES

Many of the issues and policies reviewed above have developed out of the recognition that the formal agencies of the criminal justice system have in reality a limited effect on the incidence of crime. One result of this perceived inadequacy may be that the public may quite literally decide to take the law into their own hands – by patrolling streets, apprehending offenders and punishing them. Extreme versions of such vigilantism can involve groups conducting their own trials and sentencing processes. In Northern Ireland, for example, there have been cases where informal justice has been carried out by paramilitaries of both sides against burglars, thieves and robbers. While their punishments – which have included injuring and 'knee capping' alleged offenders – have been severe they have enjoyed a degree of popular support (Johnston 1992). Other individuals who have sought to take the law into their own hands have received some sympathy as seen in Figure 11.4.

Whereas Neighbourhood Watch and other schemes involve members of the public working with, and under the supervision of, the police, vigilantism may not involve the police and raises the possibility that small groups of untrained citizens could be involved in patrolling and preventive duties. The

**Fig 11.4** Vigilantes

## Man who electrified car to deter thieves wins jury's sympathy

An engineer who electrified his high-performance car to protect it against persistent thieves was cleared of assault and weapon offences by an Old Bailey jury yesterday.

As Roderick Minshull, 48, left court he said he would swap the Ford Sierra Cosworth for a diesel van. A lawyer described the case as another example of the public showing sympathy for people who risked the law to fight crime or defend themselves.

He said his only intention was to protect his property and, as a qualified electrical engineer, he made sure the car was safe and would not cause serious injury.

Mr Minshull took action after thieves tried at least ten times to steal the car.

Mr Minshull used a £200 device known as an ESB200. The equipment, which could deliver a peak power of 10,000 volts, was placed in the boot and linked to the car battery.

Guy Holloway, a guard at the Hilton, saw a wire and heard ticking. . . .When he investigated further he touched the wire and received a shock through his hand into his chest.

After the case Steven Kay, secretary of the Criminal Bar Association, said: 'I don't know whether it will encourage others but the interesting thing is the public and juries are probably under-

standing more why people take steps to protect their property. They are becoming more sympathetic. I think this is disturbing as a trend, particularly as innocent people could get themselves injured.'

Kevin Delaney, the RAC's traffic policy manager, said: 'In this case the victim was someone who was quite robust. What if a small child had touched the car or an old person fallen against it? What we are seeing in this case is the frustration of the ordinary man in the street with car crime.'

The frustration felt by Mr Minshull to protect his car was obviously the same frustration felt by the jury that acquitted him at the inability of society to deal with car crimes.

(*The Times*, 30 June 1994 © Times Supplements Limited, 1994) concern is that such groups can take the law into their own hands. The *Sunday Times* reported that vigilantes have attacked and threatened 'known trouble makers' on the Bellamy Road Estate in Mansfield. The secretary of the Tenants' Association is quoted as saying 'It's very frustrating. When you report an incident, nothing is done. Most of the known criminals are under age, so they escape with a caution. I can understand those who deal with the criminals themselves. It is the only thing they can do.' (*Sunday Times*, 26 February 1995: 5).

Johnston identifies a number of different circumstances which may give rise to vigilantism. It may be a response to harassment and racially motivated crime by ethnic minority groups who feel a threat to their cultural identity. Thus Johnston gives the example of Jewish youth who formed groups to defend themselves against attack. In other situations, residents, often middle class, have joined together to protect their streets from invasion by prostitutes and pimps as happened in Birmingham. Vigilante groups may also emerge where the police response to crime is seen as inadequate (Johnston 1992).

The borderline between vigilantism and community involvement in policing can be seen in the response to proposals to involve citizens not only in Neighbourhood Watch but in patrolling duties. In 1994 the Home Secretary, Michael Howard, introduced an initiative to extend citizen involvement with police work. He announced firstly, that members of Neighbourhood Watch schemes would be allowed to patrol areas acting as the 'eyes and ears' of the police. They would have no powers of arrest, would not wear a uniform or carry equipment and would not receive any self-protection training. Experiments in Washington DC and Sandwich in Kent were cited as a prototype for this development.

The Home Secretary also indicated an intention to use volunteers to supplement regular police manpower. He planned to increase the number of special constables from 19,000 in 1994 to 30,000 by 1996. Special constables receive expenses but are not paid. They have uniforms and are trained and sworn in as police constables with a warrant for the area covered by the police force to which they are attached and to adjoining police forces.

A third means of using volunteer citizens to help with police work is through the extension of the parish constable or parish warden schemes, by resurrecting the parish constable to patrol villages without a police presence. This would involve training unpaid volunteers who would conduct their police work in uniform and would have the power of arrest. The parish warden scheme would require parish councils to establish a list of volunteers who would have no powers of arrest and would merely patrol and record any incident and report it to the police. In 1994, 20 experiments were established to monitor the effectiveness of parish constable and parish wardens.

The police have objected strongly to proposals that citizens should play a major part in patrolling. A Police Federation statement commented that:

voluntary work can never replace police officers and we are totally opposed to patrolling, uniformed or otherwise by members of volunteer groups. The dangers of vigilantism are obvious.

(*Guardian*, 19 April 1994)

Another problem is how effective such groups are likely to be. Johnston summarising research on the effectiveness of such groups, including the well-known Guardian Angels in the USA, comments that it is doubtful whether they have any long-term effect in reducing crime, although they may have some effect on reducing the fear of crime (Johnston 1992). Like many community crime prevention measures, they are locally based, and may work for a short time, but not in the long term.

In addition vigilantism arouses many, often conflicting issues. On the one hand, it could lead to the genuine involvement of the community in the tasks of criminal justice, leading to a more genuine community justice. On the other hand, however, it is often seen as a threat to communities as it can all too easily get out of hand. Major fears of vigilantes involve the key issue of who such groups are accountable to and the dangers of untrained and unaccountable citizens attempting to intervene in dangerous situations.

## CONCLUSION

Many of the strategies outlined above emerged as a response to pessimism about the ability of the criminal justice process to affect the spread of crime or to rehabilitate individual offenders. At the same time, the costs of the criminal justice system rose along with crime rates. Many of the measures described above therefore represent attempts to find cheaper and effective ways of doing something positive about crime. Thus community sentences, while they may not have fulfilled the rehabilitative aims often associated with them, do provide a cheaper alternative to prison. Community policing aims not only to improve community relations but to improve the effectiveness of the police by improving the quality of information they receive from a more supportive public. Crime prevention also arose out of a desire to prevent and cut the amount of crime. Other schemes aim at the victim of crime which also gives the appearance of positive action.

The effectiveness of these measures is far less easy to assess, especially given their diffuse aims. Cynics might argue that they ultimately represent little more than public relations exercises – giving the appearance of doing something positive but at little cost and with little effect. Community sentences have little proven rehabilitative potential and community policing would appear to have a limited impact on crime. The effectiveness of crime prevention is similarly difficult to assess and it may merely displace crime. Victims may be better supported and involved in the system, but as we have seen progress is slow and they may often be inadequately compensated. One response to this further pessimism may be the growth of vigilante groups although it is more likely that citizens will be encouraged to assist the police in some of their functions.

On the other hand, many measures do appear to have success in achieving some of their aims. Community sentences, while producing no fewer recidivists, may be a far more humane and possibly more productive way of dealing with offenders without the disruption that prison involves. Community policing may in certain circumstances make the public less worried about crime and more confident in the police. Crime prevention may well reduce crime in some areas and divert potential offenders, albeit for short periods of time. And to the extent that many individual victims have been helped by the many support schemes they may have fewer sources of dissatisfaction.

How far these schemes address the relationship between the criminal justice process and the community in the wider sense discussed in Chapter 9 is far less certain. Many schemes do contain the potential for a much wider community participation in the criminal justice process, and a much closer co-operation between the agencies of the system and the wider community. Community sentences hold out the prospect that offenders could become more integrated into the community by working within it. Yet the emphasis in recent years on the deprivation of liberty and on toughening up community sentences to make them more credible may mean that the community has become simply a place for punishment (May 1994). Some of the ideas behind community policing see the police and the community working together to secure some form of social harmony. Yet community policing is also justified as a better way of gathering intelligence and exercising surveillance over the community – ideas which reflect the police priority of law enforcement.

Community crime prevention has enormous potential to involve the whole community in reducing crime at the same time as improving their wider environment and community life. Yet at the same time many of its strategies involve yet more surveillance and in themselves adversely affect the environment. To the extent however that it may reduce victimisation in some areas it goes some way to reassuring victims and potential victims as do the improvements in support and compensation for victims. Vigilantism, often seen as the ultimate threat to justice in the community because of its lack of due process, could also be seen as leading to a genuine involvement of the community in all aspects of criminal justice. But great dangers also accompany its growth which may involve untrained and inexperienced members of the community taking the law into their own hands.

Many of these measures are of relatively recent origin and it may be too early to assess them adequately or predict their future course. They represent a continuation of the shifting perceptions about crime and its control seen in Chapter 9, and a recognition of the limitations of the formal agencies of criminal justice looked at in earlier chapters. These trends, and some of the remaining issues facing criminal justice as it approaches the 21st century will be outlined in Chapter 12.

## Review questions

1.  What are the main tasks carried out by the Probation Service?
2.  Outline the different forms of community policing and discuss how their success can be assessed.
3.  Outline the main forms of community crime prevention. What are their major strengths and limitations?
4.  Describe the main ways in which victims of crime are helped in England and Wales.

## Further reading

May T (1991) *Probation: Politics, Policy and Practice.* Milton Keynes: Open University Press

Bennett T H (1994a) 'Recent Developments in Community Policing' in Stephens M and Becker S (eds) *Police Force, Police Service: Care and Control in Britain.* London: Macmillan

Zedner L (1994) 'Victims' in Maguire M, Morgan R and Reiner R (eds) *The Oxford Handbook of Criminology.* Oxford: Clarendon Press: 1207–1246

Clarke R V (1993) (ed) *Crime Prevention Studies.* Vol 1. Monsey, New York: Criminal Justice Press

# CHAPTER 12

# CONCLUSION

Scarcely a week goes by without a crime story or issue hitting the headlines and occasioning considerable public debate about such topics as violent crime, persistent young offenders, football hooligans, soft sentences or lapses in prison security which enable drugs and explosives to be smuggled in, and inmates to get out. The suicide of Frederick West on New Year's Day 1995 in Winson Green Prison brought together concerns over suicides in prisons and concerns that West's death denied the opportunity for justice to be done as it prevented a trial and a chance for the community to express its collective horror at West's alleged activities. West of Cromwell Street, Gloucester had been accused of 12 murders. But it is not just the crime stories of murder and mayhem that capture the headlines. Vying for space on the front page is news of reviews, commissions and inquiries into the activities of criminal justice agencies and new legislation giving additional tasks to them.

The effects of the CJPOA 1994 remain to be fully assessed. Many of the more far-reaching suggestions of the Woolf Report and the Royal Commission on Criminal Justice 1993 are still under review. Further changes to the organisation and functions of the police, the courts, the Crown Prosecution Service and community sentences are envisaged. Thus virtually every agency in the criminal justice system is under continual review. It is hoped that the analysis of previous chapters may help the reader to place these current events in the context of past and continuing developments in criminal justice policy.

In this chapter we will explore the themes and trends which continue to influence criminal justice policies in the 1990s and look at how these affect the key parts of the system – policing, prosecution, the criminal courts and trial process, sentencing, penal policy, prisons and community sentences. We started by asking if British criminal justice was the best in the world – finally this chapter will return to the issue of public confidence in the system.

# THE CRIMINAL JUSTICE SYSTEM UNDER SCRUTINY

In Chapter 1 we looked at the essential elements of criminal justice and at the goals of the system and its agencies. Successive chapters have shown how the multiple and sometimes conflicting goals affect the criminal justice process from the moment offenders are suspected to the end of their sentence. We have also seen the importance of exploring how each stage of the process relates to others and the relationships between agencies, not only those within the system but including the growing private and voluntary sectors. Similarly we have seen the necessity of looking not only at the formal rules and procedures but at the informal considerations which affect their implementation. This includes the working cultures of those who work in the system and the attitudes and backgrounds of defendants. In addition we outlined how different models could be used to explore and analyse criminal justice.

In Chapter 2 we set out a definition of crime and criminal culpability and looked at ways of explaining criminal behaviour. In Chapter 3 we examined the impact and volume of crime. It is evident that only a small proportion of offences and offenders come to the attention of the criminal justice system and that an even smaller proportion are eventually convicted and sentenced, a proportion affected by efforts to divert offenders. These considerations alone mean that the direct impact of the criminal justice system on offenders is inevitably limited. This recognition has led to a re-evaluation of the role of agencies and the formulation of policies aimed at crime prevention strategies which focus on the situations in which crime occurs rather than on the motivation of offenders.

This raises the issue of how effectively the system can achieve the aims identified in Chapter 1. The explanations of crime in Chapter 2 also underlines the limited potential of the system to directly affect the overall level of crime. Even where the causes of crime are thought to have been identified the solution will often be beyond the scope of the criminal justice system. The offender-instrumental theories such as rehabilitation and deterrence, that sought to reduce if not eradicate crime, which were popular with policy makers in the early part of the century seem less plausible by the end of the 20th century.

Chapter 3 indicated the problems of measuring the extent of crime. Nevertheless, the rise in reported crime and the fear of crime keeps crime control high on the political agenda. The spiralling costs of law enforcement means that 'law and order' policies must also be assessed in terms of value for money. This, coupled with the perceived weaknesses of welfare and interventionist policies, which for a period after World War II promised to cure crime through social engineering, has led to a reappraisal in recent years with policy makers seeking to play down the role of the state. Thus we have seen a devolution of responsibilities towards private and voluntary agencies and the mobilisation of the local community, the Special

Constables or part-time police officers and the awakening of the 'active citizen' in the 'war on crime'.

Throughout the system we see the competing pressures of due process, crime control, bureaucratic efficiency, and the need to take into account the requirements of denunciation, rehabilitation and concerns about inequality and discrimination. Thus police, prosecutors, courts and sentencers have to balance compliance with rules derived from due process with crime control pressures which seek to ensure that the guilty are convicted and that the public are protected from further victimisation. Due process can in some ways be seen as a constraint on crime control with its emphasis on the presumption of innocence at the trial stage and the many rules and procedures necessitated by the adversarial system. This may produce pressures at all stages to short circuit the rules to enable the conviction of offenders who the police 'know' are guilty, and can persuade others in the system that this is so. Crime control pressures may also lead to restraints on individuals suspected of criminal activities before they have been convicted by detaining them in police custody, prisons or mental hospitals, and may lead to the incapacititative policies which run counter to the principles of just deserts.

Implementing crime control or due process is not cheap and financial pressures may conflict with both. Many apparent departures from both crime control and due process, such as the encouragement of diversionary policies and guilty pleas, can be justified on the grounds that they speed up the process and are more cost effective. Many of the reviews of the performance of criminal justice agencies have arisen because of the need to limit public expenditure.

This re-examination has also been strongly affected by the demise of the rehabilitative model discussed in Chapters 8 and 9. We have seen how its influence conflicted with other models, particularly its emphasis on considering the individual offender, irrespective of the justice or fairness which this might involve. Sentences were often criticised as being too soft but could also conflict with the limiting principle of just deserts. In the penal system it gave rise to the as yet unresolved conflicts between care and control which affect both prison and community sentences. It also led to disparities in sentencing, which in turn gave rise to criticisms on the grounds of inequity.

Whatever solutions are sought, policy makers must also recognise the crucial role of the criminal justice process in expressing the public's concern about crime and morality and a desire to censure criminal behaviour. Principles of denunciation may therefore conflict with other considerations. The public and victims, for example, may be considerably aggrieved if offenders are not seen to be publicly held accountable for their offences when they are not tried and punished. Thus diversionary policies which appear to be sympathetic to the offender may also appear to neglect the public's concerns about crime and thus are likely to face resistance.

While due process and just deserts approaches stress the equal application of rules to all offenders, critics whose arguments derive from the power or the class domination model stress the unequal impact of the system on different groups of offences and offenders. As we have seen, allegations of overt discrimination on the grounds of race, gender or class are difficult to substantiate, although these factors may affect, albeit indirectly, the treatment of different groups of offenders in the system. Hence, the proposal that anti-discrimination legislation, similar to that applying to areas such as housing or employment, be applied to criminal justice (see, for example, Ashworth 1994b).

Policy makers also need to recognise the interdependency between parts of the system; thus prison policy, at the back-end of the system, cannot ignore what happens at the front-end. Here we have the police, the gatekeepers of the system whose decisions about where to police, how to police, who to stop, search, arrest and charge affect the intake of the system. They also determine what a suspect should be charged with, a decision which may have considerable implications for the eventual outcome – whether they will be convicted and how they will be sentenced. The information they provide affects the decisions of the CPS and crucial decisions about remand, bail, custody, mode of trial and plea, which as we have seen are strongly interrelated. Defendants' decisions are also crucial here, either taken alone or with the advice of lawyers or the police. Defendants' decisions on plea may be affected by negotiations with the police and their estimation of the effect of how long the process will take, their calculations as to where they are most likely to be held awaiting trial, whether or not they will be given bail, whether or not they will be convicted and the type of sentence they might receive.

Policies directed at one part of the system also affect other parts. Thus if more offenders are diverted by means of no further action or cautions, fewer offenders will be tried and sentenced and passed on to prisons or community sentences. Those remaining, to proceed on to the next stage of the system, will represent the more serious offenders. This will affect the proportions receiving different kinds of sentences and the way in which these sentences are implemented. Prisons and those managing community sentences can therefore expect to receive higher proportions of more serious offenders.

In evidence to the Woolf Inquiry, Brian Cubbon, a former Permanent Secretary at the Home Office, described the 'geological fault' that existed in terms of the unpredictability and volatility of the prison population. The Woolf Report agreed with him and made their first major recommendation: the establishment of a criminal justice consultative council to promote greater co-operation, communications and co-ordination across the criminal justice system (Home Office 1991a: para 10.169).

Interdependency is also evident in terms of the information flows from one agency to another. Thus the CPS rely on information provided by the police and defence lawyers also start with this information. Probation officers provide yet more. Sentencers receive this information and their interpretation of it may be affected by their attitude towards the agencies providing it.

Implementation of policy also depends to a large extent on inter-agency co-operation and in recent years we have seen the development of more partnerships both between agencies in the system and with private or voluntary agencies. Thus crime prevention and safer community schemes may involve the police, businesses, volunteers, private agencies and the probation and social services.

The way in which agencies perceive their role may influence key decisions and the implementation of formal rules. Thus the police are affected by their views of what does or does not constitute real police work and which offenders deserve to be taken forward to the court. The CPS while technically reviewing the decisions of the police may come to share some of the police working rules and be affected by their information. In individual decisions, the police and prosecutors may be affected by the circumstances of the individual offence and offender, allowing their subjective perceptions of just deserts to come into play. The police may also be affected by a host of circumstances such as their immediate judgment of the suspect's demeanour and attitude. The choice of the charge itself may be coloured by the defendant's first response to an approach from the police. Breach of the peace, drunk and disorderly, threatening behaviour, resisting arrest and assaulting a police officer represents a spiral of seriousness that can be quickly climbed depending on the defendant's and police officer's response to a street encounter. Judges, magistrates and court personnel can also be influenced by the attitude and demeanour of the person in front of them.

Inter-agency co-operation may be enhanced or hindered by the attitudes of and relations between the different agencies and participants in the system. The intentions of policy makers may be undermined by the informal priorities derived from the working cultures of those who operate the system. Thus police officers committed to a view of 'real police work' as involving law enforcement may resist initiatives emphasising the crime prevention or community policing role. Sentencers, feeling that sentencing is ultimately a matter of human judgment may resist attempts to limit their discretion. Probation officers, still emphasising their rehabilitative role, may resist the shifting emphasis of their work towards punishment and control.

Any considerations of policy reform must therefore take into account all of these different factors which may affect the implementation and therefore the effectiveness of policies. It must not be forgotten however that the adversarial system requires that an aspect of conflict is built into the trial stage and it would not do for there to be too much collusion between the prosecuting and defence counsels. We will now look at recent policy developments and consider how they affect the major parts of criminal justice system.

# POLICY DIRECTIONS

As we have seen, there has been an explosion of policy initiatives in recent years and an almost unprecedented number of reviews, many still in progress, covering virtually every aspect of criminal justice. This has in some cases been a response to perceived crises, in law and order, policing, in the courts challenged by miscarriages of justice, and in the prison system. The extent to which the system can be said to be in crisis is open to debate but dramatic language informs policy discussions on criminal justice, in part because they are crucial issues in a democratic society about how much authority to give agencies that have the power to arrest, judge and imprison citizens.

Apart from this underlying theme other historically specific factors have shaped policy developments in recent years. Among these is the recognition of the limited impact of rehabilitation on individual offenders and of the criminal justice system as a whole in stemming the rising rates of recorded crime. Thus doubts have been cast about the ideas that dominated the penal paradigm during the first half of the 20th century. Doubts about the rehabilitative effects of imprisonment; an awareness that rehabilitation is more difficult to achieve than was previously assumed; a concern about the unfairness of sentencing disparities; a shift in penal rationales from deterrence and rehabilitation to just deserts; and an awareness that prisoners have civil rights. These have led to reforms seeking to achieve greater uniformity in sentencing decisions; providing for community crime prevention initiatives; and taking more account of the victims' needs.

These influences are not restricted to England and Wales and there have been remarkable similarities in criminal justice policy in different countries. Criticism of the so-called treatment ideology of the 1960s has led to the development of the back-to-justice approach, resulting in a greater emphasis on punishment and incapacitation than on rehabilitation as a sentencing rationale. These similarities can also be found in respect of the greater concern with the impact of crime on communities and the growing emphasis on crime prevention strategies to combat crime; the politicisation of criminal justice issues; and a cost-benefit management driven reorganisation of agencies in the 1980s.

This convergence was commented on in *Crime, Justice and Protecting the Public* which noted the universal trend of common law countries to move towards sentencing policies based on just deserts. It commented that 'Other common law jurisdictions, for example, in the United States, Canada and Australia are moving in this direction or are thinking of doing so.' (Home Office 1990a: 5).

This new thinking about crime control involved a new realism in which economic costs, community fears and political realities shaped developments in a way not apparent before. A good example was the government's commitment in the 1990 White Paper to get tough on crime, while wanting to make less use of imprisonment because of the costs involved. Hence, the search for community based intermediate sanctions.

As we have seen throughout, cost considerations have become a major factor overtly influencing policy. For example, the first paragraph in the introductory section of the White Paper 1990 which preceded the CJA 1991 makes it clear that the criminal justice system has grown over the decade and is very expensive to run. 'A price cannot be put on justice, but it is not without its costs' states the report and emphasises that the criminal justice system in England and Wales which costs £7 billion annually 'has increased by 77% in real terms in the last ten years'. (Home Office 1990a: para 47.1).

Cost effectiveness is also one of the rationales underlying the current emphasis on privatisation although this has an ideological as well as an economic basis. The effects of privatisation can be seen across the system, from recent suggestions to remove many of the functions of the police to private agencies, to the privatisation of remand centres and prisons and aspects of community sentences. It is argued that privatisation is cost effective as it allows competition and thus a reduction in costs, cuts down bureaucratic procedures, cuts staffing costs and allows far greater flexibility. On the other hand many argue that claims about cost effectiveness are exaggerated, that private organisations, often lacking skilled, experienced and trained staff, are less effective; that the exigencies of cost effectiveness mean that there will be less rather than more flexibility; and that private institutions will attempt to avoid dealing with more dangerous, hard core or high tariff offenders. Public organisations will be left therefore with responsibility for the most serious crimes and the most hard core and dangerous offenders. Ultimately it could be argued, the drive to privatisation has been fuelled by political and ideological considerations such as a belief in free enterprise and the wish to reduce the power of criminal justice professions such as the police and most particularly the prison service.

The prediction that the private sector may be used for less serious offenders, and the public sector for the most serious would be a further example of a trend noted across the system – a trend towards bifurcation. This involves a division between more and less serious offenders, with less serious offenders being diverted at different stages. As we have seen diversionary policies may apply before prosecution and before punishment. With privatisation we may see more of the less serious offenders being diverted to the private sector.

This can of course conflict with notions of just deserts and denunciation and with the interests of victims who see offenders being apparently unpunished. It also creates yet another dilemma for governments wishing to be seen to be tough, while at the same time cutting costs by reducing the system's workload. This can be managed by yet more bifurcation – increasing the punishments for the serious offenders while increasing diversion for the lesser ones. Thus the introduction in the CJPOA 1994 of secure units for young offenders and greater controls on bail, while appearing tough on crime, will only affect a small minority of serious offenders.

We will now examine the influence of these policies on key agencies in the system, looking at their influence on current policy and attempting, without engaging in too much crystal gazing, to identify the major trends that will shape those agencies as we move towards the next century.

## POLICE

Chapter 4 explored the many different roles of the public police and it could be asked whether they should continue to be responsible for such a wide range of functions. Can they continue to attempt to prevent, detect and investigate crime along with acting as social workers, traffic controllers, peace keepers, crowd controllers and protectors of the safety of citizens, royalty, governments, businesses, and local neighbourhoods? Should others participate in the policing function and what should their role be?

In discussing the role of the police, we should first distinguish between policing by the private and the public police. Private security agencies have been increasingly employed to police particular areas. Particularly significant is the growth of what Shearing and Stenning call 'mass private property' such as large shopping centres, leisure parks, industrial estates, private housing estates and apartment blocks all of which have a variety of security arrangements and in which the role of the public police may be minimal. Thus Robert Reiner comments:

> A police officer is seldom if ever seen in Disneyland or indeed Brent Cross (except as a customer) ... instead control is maintained by architecture, the technology of surveillance and informal social mechanisms with even the specialist input of private security personnel being vestigial, and primarily concerned with maintaining perimeter security.
>
> (Reiner 1992b: 80)

According to Johnston 'everyday policing' is undergoing a complex process of restructuring involving the growth of many different kinds of policing agencies (Johnston 1994). These include private security organisations contracted to protect residential property who are hired to patrol particular streets. Local authorities are increasingly employing security companies and some have their own municipal security – this is common, for example, in parks and some have extended this to council property, housing estates and public places. Some have proposed that police forces themselves set up private security companies. Other arrangements involve the extension of Neighbourhood Watch and citizen patrols (Johnston 1994).

Any discussion of the future role of policing must therefore take this proliferation of private policing into account, and it is likely that its growth will continue, as it is consistent with the current emphasis on cost effectiveness and privatisation. As Johnston comments this could lead to a situation in which policing could be bought and sold in the market. As we saw in Chapter 11, a major problem with private policing is how it can be rendered accountable and regulated. A major issue for policy makers is therefore how the boundaries between public and private policing are to be defined.

As seen in Chapter 4, the role of the public police is under review. It has often been popularly assumed, for example, that the police can affect crime rates – thus the assumption that with more police the crime rate would decline. There is an increasing recognition however that their role in curbing crime is limited. As Reiner comments:

> . . . the police should be seen primarily as managers of crime and keepers of the peace; they are not realistically a vehicle for reducing crime substantially. Crime is the product of deeper social forces largely beyond the ambit of any policing tactics and the clear up rate is a function of crime levels and other aspects of workload rather than of police efficiency.

> (Reiner 1994: 755)

In managing crime, what should their function be? We have already seen how their organisation has been changed in an attempt to make them more efficient and cost effective. A good illustration of this is the growth of civilian employees to do clerical and administrative tasks previously carried out by police officers.

In 1994 the Posen Inquiry began a review of police functions. The task of this inquiry was to identify the core and ancillary tasks of the police, with a view to removing ancillary tasks to civilians and private agencies. As part of this chief officers were asked to categorise 95 police tasks, ranging from hunting terrorists to visiting schools as core or ancillary. Some 36 tasks have already been identified as ancillary, including executing warrants, transcribing interviews and coroner's duties. Other duties might also be included as non-core such as crime prevention advice, liquor licensing, missing persons and community safety education. One proposal is to transfer the Police National Computer, with confidential data on over three million people, into the private commercial sector.

Were these suggestions to be adopted it would leave the police responsible for what can be seen as the inner core tasks of foot and vehicle patrol, riot control and operations targeting crime (Loveday 1994). These early indications provoked strong reactions from the Association of Chief Police Officers (ACPO) who see any such dispersal of tasks as a threat to many service functions which they see as providing regular and positive police contacts. They also fear that it will lead to a reduction in establishments (Loveday 1994). In support of this they cite the precedent of the privatisation of prisoner escort, which is claimed to have cost the Metropolitan Police 272 constables (*Observer*, 10 July 1994:1). Johnston also comments that implementing the proposed aims of the Posen Inquiry could result in reforms with a potential for saving up to £200 million (Johnston 1994).

Underlying the ACPO objections is also a fear of further privatisation and many see the review as overwhelmingly driven by a concern with costs rather than efficiency. In addition, many fear the removal of the service function which is seen as an important element in overall policing. Thus as a comment in the *Observer* points out in respect of the inquiry:

> Restating the founding principles of Sir Robert Peel, Scarman said that the first job of the police was not catching criminals but preserving tranquillity: and they should do this by digging deep roots in communities, to achieve policing by consent. Hard-boiled detectives, no less than liberal police graduates, have come to appreciate the benefits: the old lady whose cat is rescued by her sector bobby finds time to mention the strange late-night visits to a house up the road, leading to the arrest of a drug dealer – there is a wealth of research to show that crimes are most frequently solved not by police but by the public.
>
> (*Observer*, 10 July 1994: 24)

A comment by Tony Butler, Chief Constable of Gloucestershire, interviewed by David Rose of the *Observer* also illustrates this theme:

> We are being pushed into becoming a purely law-enforcement body. That would lose sight of the fact that we can use our authority in law-enforcement because citizens respect it – because last week we helped an old lady get into her flat when she'd locked herself out, or brought home a little girl.
>
> That is what policing a democratic society is about. Then you turn to the Home Office and you say, 'Well, how are you going to reflect that in your review?' And they say. 'Oh, it's easy, we identified 95 tasks the police do: 19 of them are mixed and 36 of them are supposedly ancillary'.
>
> What do they mean by ancillary? There's a notion you can measure the time police spend on things which are not law enforcement, and give that to someone else (to do). If you do that, you reduce the time available to spend on what public surveys tell us the public want, and the reason they respect police officers – their humanity.
>
> (*Observer*, 10 July 1994: 2)

Whatever the results of the inquiry it is clear that the role of the police continues to excite controversy and also that increasing attention must be paid to the relationship between the police and the private and voluntary sectors. This issue is taken up by Rod Morgan and Tim Newburn in an article reporting on the deliberations of an Independent Committee on the Role and Responsibilities of the Police, who point to the danger of ending up with an increasingly centralised police service armed with growing legal powers working alongside an increasingly anarchic unregulated array of private agencies (Morgan and Newburn 1994). A major question is therefore what powers should be restricted to the police. They suggest a limiting principle whereby only constables or other Crown servants should have powers to arrest, detain and search, search and seize property, bear arms and use force and have rights of full access to criminal records and intelligence.

Some ways of introducing more citizen involvement are suggested within a framework of accountability. These include the appointment of designated patrol officers within constabularies who could be authorised to execute limited street powers. They would wear a uniform, thus encouraging public confidence and would have limited powers of arrest for minor public order offences and carefully defined property offences.

Another possibility is that there may be a centralised force dealing with more serious offences, with others being left to local forces. Reiner points out, for example, that the British police are unique in having responsibility for crime prevention, detection, peace keeping, order maintenance and the preservation of state security, functions which in other countries are divided between different bodies. He predicts that there may be greater fragmentation in the future, with a move more towards a more international pattern of specialist national units for serious crime, terrorism, public order, large scale fraud and other national or international problems. Local police will be responsible for local communities where there may be a service style in stable suburban areas and a more watchman style for others (Reiner 1992; 1994). Fragmentation will also occur in that those who can afford it will increasingly employ private security in residential areas and where middle class leisure and work takes place. This human policing he argues will form a smaller part of an array of impersonal control processes built into environmental, technological control and surveillance devices and the guarding and self-policing activities of ordinary citizens. Thus, 'The police will be replaced by a more varied assortment of bodies with policing functions' (Reiner 1994: 757). This parallels a wider process of social fragmentation. Thus to Reiner the role of the public police will be a rump – of maintaining public order amongst the lower classes or the underclass.

## PROSECUTION AND DIVERSION

Policy reviews and reforms have affected the prosecution agencies and the courts. As seen in Chapter 5, for example, there has been an increasing emphasis on diversionary policies, under which less serious offenders are diverted from the system, and the role of the Crown Prosecution Service is seen as to being weed out cases which it is not in the public interest to prosecute. This raises the fundamental question of how many offenders should be prosecuted and on what grounds. If not all offenders who admit their guilt are to be prosecuted, how should they be dealt with? This in turn raises the question of what the prosecutor's role should be.

The recent emphasis on diversion is partly cost driven. There is also a recognition that prosecuting many offenders serves little purpose especially if their crimes have been trivial and only a small sentence would result. In addition, the claims of labelling theorists that early intervention may in fact escalate offending may also have had some impact.

It is likely that diversionary policies will increase. What should then happen to diverted offenders? As we have seen there has been an increase in cautions and encouragement to use these for adult as well as young offend-ers. There are schemes known as caution plus – in which cautioned offenders participate in activities run by the probation service or voluntary agencies. Reparation may also be a form of diversion. There have been other suggestions to increase the use of diversion. These include ideas that prose-cutors should have powers, like regulatory bodies, to impose different kinds of regulatory sanctions, as in the Scottish prosecutor fine system. We have also seen that regulatory bodies may choose not to prosecute in situations where offenders have made some efforts to recompense victims or have per-suaded them that re-offending is unlikely. Other proposals include dealing with more trivial offences by forms of mediation which are more like civil proceedings. Thus minor disputes between those who know each other could be dealt with in a neighbourhood mediation centre. In more serious cases, where this was unacceptable to either side or where the offender denied guilt, the case could go to court.

The net effect of diversionary policies can lead to some public disquiet on the grounds that offenders may be being let off too lightly and denunciation-ists might argue that offenders should be publicly tried. In addition diversionary policies raise issues of justice and due process. Would wealthier offenders be more likely to escape prosecution by paying off their victims? Prosecution decisions affected by victim and offender mediation would be made in private and would thus be less accountable. Offenders may be encouraged to accept a caution and thus clear up the books on the promise of not being prosecuted. This bifurcation may also disadvantage those who choose to contest their guilt and who may receive a harsher disposition as a result. It also raises questions of the degree to which some minor offences are in effect being decriminalised.

## THE COURTS AND THE ORGANISATION OF THE TRIAL

Crucial questions can also be asked about the organisation and role of the courts, and the conflict between crime control and due process is seen parti-cularly in respect of court proceedings. On the one hand, from the perspectives of crime control and cost effectiveness, court procedures are lengthy and costly. Too much emphasis is placed on the defendant, the right to silence and their right to mitigation. On the other hand, from the perspec-tive of the power model and due process, what are seen as incursions into the rights of defendants to elect for jury trial, the right to silence and the provision of legal representation are fiercely resisted.

Plea negotiations may particularly undermine due process, leading to a sit-uation where defendants may 'play the game' and plead guilty, in order to obtain a sentencing discount. Thus they are sentenced not on the basis of what they have done, and therefore the seriousness of the offence but on the basis of what they have decided to admit to, so as to secure a lighter sentence. This infringes the principle of just deserts.

As we have seen a major thrust in policy has been a focus on the role of the victim, who has often been seen as being neglected in court procedures, other than as a witness whose evidence is subjected to cross-examination. While there have been many initiatives to improve the victim's court experience and an extension of reparation and compensation, victims may still feel excluded in that the impact of the offence on them is not a factor in sentencing.

Despite the 1990 Victim's Charter, Helen Reeves, Director of Victim Support believes that victims have legal rights. She told a Victim Support conference in February 1995, 'Offenders have clear rights in our system of justice but victims have no enforceable rights under the law. Victims should have the right to be protected and respected and know what is happening in their case and why.' (*The Times*, 22 February 1995: 7).

More legal rights, whether for victims or defendants, adds to the complexity of procedures in the system and usually results in additional delays and costs. This runs counter to the efforts to streamline the administration of justice so as to achieve speedier and cheaper proceedings. To avoid injustices these countervailing tendencies need to be carefully balanced. It was the issue of injustices which led to the establishment of a Royal Commission to examine ways of avoiding miscarriages of justice.

The term miscarriages of justice has come to be associated with a number of high profile cases: those of the Birmingham Six, the Guildford Four and Judith Ward. These have been concerned largely with those convicted of IRA terrorist offences. Subsequent court rulings have overturned the original convictions. The question might be asked therefore why they were termed miscarriages. In any system there will be mistakes and the appeal procedure is designed to cope with and remedy such errors. The reason the above cases attracted criticism was the failure of the normal appeal procedure to isolate the defects involved. Lengthy prison sentences were served before the accused were released. Different problems arose in these cases. There was over-reliance on expert evidence that was flawed. There was the tampering of evidence by the police or a failure to abide by PACE and other procedural rules including the use of oppressive interview techniques. Above all there was the failure of the police to consider that they may have got the wrong suspect.

A central recommendation of the Royal Commission was that a review body be established to investigate alleged miscarriages of justice. The Criminal Appeal Act 1968 gave the Home Secretary the right to refer cases to the Court of Appeal where there were grounds for believing that a conviction was unsafe. The problem with this arrangement was that it gave judicial power to a member of the executive who was inevitably also a high profile politician. The Royal Commission of 1993 recommended the establishment of an independent commission to fulfil this task. In February 1995, with the support of Lord Chief Justice Taylor, the Home Secretary announced the establishment of a Criminal Cases Review Commission to start in 1996. It would have a staff of 60 and will comprise at least 11 commissioners, each of whom will be appointed for a five-year term. The new commission will still rely on the police to conduct any inquiries into alleged miscarriages of justice. (*The Times*, 24 February 1995: 8).

To some commentators the miscarriage of justice errors suggested that the criminal justice system in England and Wales was fundamentally flawed; to others it was the result of pressure on the police in notorious cases to find the perpetrators and to make an accusation stick; to others the problem high-lighted yet again the general conflicts within the system. All these criticisms relate to features of the adversarial system. This led some commentators to hope that the review of criminal justice undertaken by the Royal Commission 1993 would carefully examine the case for a fundamental change of the system of criminal justice in this country. The Royal Commission set out what it saw as the difference between the adversarial and the inquisitorial system found in European countries.

> The criminal justice system of England and Wales, in common with other jurisdictions which have evolved within the 'Anglo-Saxon' or 'common law' tradition, is often categorised as 'adversarial'. This is in contrast to the so-called 'inquisitorial' system based on the 'Continental' or 'civil law' tradition. In this context, the term 'adversarial' is usually taken to mean the system which has the judge as an umpire who leaves the presentation of the case to the parties (prosecution and defence) on each side. These separately prepare their case and call, examine and cross-examine their witnesses. The term 'inquisitorial' describes the systems where judges may supervise the pre-trial preparation of the evidence by the police and, more important, play a major part in the presentation of the evidence at trial. The judge in 'inquisitorial' systems typically calls and examines the defendant and the witnesses while the lawyers for the prosecution and the defence ask supplementary questions.
>
> It is important not to overstate the differences between the two systems: all adversarial systems contain inquisitorial elements, and vice versa. But it is implicit in our terms of reference that we should consider whether a change in the direction of more inquisitorial procedures might not reduce the risks of mistaken verdicts and the need for subsequent re-examination of convictions which may be unsafe. For the reasons set out below we do not recommend the adoption of a thoroughgoing inquisitorial system. But we do recognise the force of the criticisms which can be directed at a thoroughgoing adversarial system which seems to turn a search for the truth into a contest played between opposing lawyers according to a set of rules which the jury does not necessarily accept or even understand. In some instances, such as our approach to forensic science evidence, our recommendations can fairly be interpreted as seeking to move the system in an inquisitorial direction, or at least as seeking to minimise the danger of adversarial practices being taken too far. But we have not arrived at our proposals through a theoretical assessment of the relative merits of the two legal traditions. On the contrary, we have been guided throughout by practical considerations in proposing changes which will, in our view, make our existing system more capable of serving the interests of both justice and efficiency.
>
> (Royal Commission on Criminal Justice 1993: 3)

338

The Royal Commission therefore did not recommend a move to an inquisitorial system. However, the debate will continue as the tensions, conflicts and criticisms remain, as does the difficulty of evaluating and reconciling the issues and principles involved. For instance, are too many cases discontinued or acquitted? It is after all the role of the courts to establish guilt beyond reasonable doubt and prosecutorial reviews may not be able to weed out appropriate cases. Therefore a high acquittal rate may show the courts are doing their job. A trial remains the ultimate safeguard against unfair prosecution, although as the current spate of miscarriage of justice cases reveals, there are considerable concerns that due process may be undermined in practice by over zealous law enforcers and prosecutors whose actions are not detectable by the court.

The Court of Appeal has ruled, in line with the principles of due process, that the convictions of those prosecuted for the bombings and murders in Birmingham and Guildford were unsafe. But these miscarriages of justice cases raise other questions of profound importance for public confidence in the effectiveness of criminal justice system. These are, 'Who was responsible?' and 'Who should be punished?' for the callous killings of innocent civilians in Guildford and Birmingham.

## SENTENCING AND PENAL POLICY

We saw in Chapters 8 and 9 how sentencing policy has been affected by all the processes discussed above. We have also seen that despite the aim of the CJA 1991 to state clear principles many of its provisions were vehemently opposed and that what have been described as panic measures followed to overturn some of its key provisions. The CJPOA 1994 also reflects an increasing tendency to be tougher on crime. It remains to be seen whether the desired consistency of approach, the primacy of just deserts and a reduction in the use of imprisonment will be achieved. Questions have also been raised about the extent to which it did encourage consistency and the more far-reaching implications of a move away from rehabilitation. Thus while stressing the primacy of just deserts it allowed for the twin track or bifurcatory approach to sentencing. This raises questions about which offences are to be seen as most serious and who is to make these assessments. The just deserts approach raises similar questions, particularly in relation to its implementation. How, for example, are sentences to be approximated to the seriousness of the offence?

As we saw in Chapter 2 there are no absolute standards of what represents a serious offence and public attitudes and tolerance may change. A survey of public attitudes published in *British Social Attitudes*, found that in 1983, 72 per cent agreed with the statement, 'People who break the law should be given stiffer sentences.' The latest report (1994) found 85 per cent agreed with this statement (Jowell 1994: 78). How are these shifts to be reflected in judgments of seriousness? This raises questions of equity. We have seen that some offences, such as white collar offences, may be viewed less seriously because of a lack of intent directly to harm a victim. Other apparently victimless crimes raise similar problems. All such judgments have an element of subjectivity and are thus affected by the problem of establishing clearly agreed criteria that can be applied fairly and equally.

In addition, a clear emphasis in sentencing policy has been to downplay the role of rehabilitation. But what are the implications of this for those who implement sentencing policies? What are to be the aims of prison and probation officers dealing with what are likely to be the most hard core offenders? It may well be that rehabilitation while much discredited should continue to be sought within the framework set by just deserts (see, for example, the May Report 1979 and Hudson 1993). This can be seen when we examine the effect of recent policies on prisons and community sentences.

## PRISONS

The effect of prison reductionist arguments along with the recognition that prisons have only a limited rehabilitative potential raises important questions for prison regimes. If they are increasingly to be used for more serious, hard core offenders, for largely incapacitative purposes, how should regimes be organised and what should they aim for? Clearly security and control are crucial, popularly expressed as 'keeping them in and keeping them quiet'. Focusing on these aims alone however leaves inmates and officers without constructive goals, a situation regarded as undesirable by the May Report 1979. Stan Cohen warned of the dangers of prisons becoming in effect 'human warehouses' for those effectively expelled from society for a period of time (Cohen 1985).

In addition, while the prison reductionist argument may have had some effect, there are other pressures at work which create demands for more imprisonment such as the Court of Appeal guideline cases which indicated that rapists should receive custodial sentences. The prison population is projected to rise and overcrowding may slow down the improvements suggested by Lord Justice Woolf. Thus Morgan, citing government projections that numbers will rise to 57,500 by the year 2000 comments that 'If that were to happen it seems improbable that the structural reforms recommended by Lord Justice Woolf would be implemented' (Morgan 1994: 936).

Some of Woolf's recommendations in any event have so far not been implemented. While some actions have been taken to alleviate the worst conditions, his proposals in relation to community prisons have received little attention. He proposed that there should be community prisons which would enable prisoners to maintain their links with their family and other community ties and be able to easily contact local services. This might also mean that local prisons, which typically enjoy the poorest conditions would house

340

remand and sentenced prisoners, men and women (Morgan 1994). This however would involve considerable difficulties in relation to having some prisons overused and others underused.

In prisons as elsewhere in the system, we have also seen the effect of privatisation, and it is proposed that new secure units for young offenders should be run by private companies. There are many arguments in favour of privatising prisons, in addition to the general arguments outlined above. It could be seen as a quick and cost effective solution to the problems of conditions and overcrowding. Thus more prison accommodation can be provided quickly and cheaply and with appropriate regulation it could strengthen the accountability of those responsible for running prisons. It was also argued that it could achieve more flexible working practices (Cavadino and Dignan 1992). Indeed, some early advocates of privatisation argued that it could provide more humane conditions and more innovative regimes. Privatising prisons was also popular in the USA where prisons were, according to Logan, not meant to be used instead of existing facilities but to enhance or support the system (Logan 1990). In addition it was envisaged that they could involve more flexibility and innovation with the introduction of entrepreneurial skills commonly found in running a small business.

Despite the claims made for the benefits of private prisons, they also raise many problems. Many object on moral grounds, for example, to the implication that profit can be made from human misery or from taking away people's liberty (Borna 1986). In addition, US experience suggests that cost savings are not always achieved and that conditions may not be improved (Cavadino and Dignan 1992). Privatisation may also be counter-productive in respect of achieving any reduction in prison numbers. Indeed the provision of private facilities may encourage an expansion in numbers. Thus what has been described as the commercial corrections complex, consisting of corporations supplying correctional equipment and services along with government agencies and professionals working in the criminal justice sphere may have a vested interest in maintaining a high – even expanding – prison population. There are also dangers in a cost based approach to prisons. In order to maximise cost effectiveness, private prisons often rely on electronic surveillance to cut down staffing costs. This may lead to a reduction in the quality of the regime.

Thus, despite the influence of the prison reductionists' arguments, it is likely that the prison population will rise. Some have criticised the CJA 1991 for not introducing further measures to limit its use and argue for more measures including placing ceilings on the population of individual prisons. Indeed some, echoing the sentiments of Alexander Paterson expressed in Chapter 9, argue that prisons should be virtually abolished, and that a reliance on prisons as the ultimate back-up punishment should cease (see, for example, Mathiesen 1991; Carlen 1990).

Others have suggested drastically limiting the use of prison for restricted categories of offenders, as has been done, for example, with children and young persons. Thus Carlen (1990) argues that the abolition of prison as a 'normal sentence' for women may be more acceptable on the grounds that women are imprisoned, she claims, for less serious crimes than men, receive lower sentences and have lower recidivism rates. She has therefore proposed that only 100 places be reserved for female prisoners. There seems little likelihood however that such proposals will be acceptable and it is much more probable that the prison population will continue to rise until such a time as a credible non-prison form of punishment becomes available that is acceptable to judges, magistratres and the public.

## PUNISHMENT IN THE COMMUNITY

We have seen how the search for cost effective alternatives to prison has led to a changing emphasis on the role and function of community sentences. It was pointed out in Chapter 11 that this had important implications for the probation service whose role has hitherto been seen primarily rehabilitative. A major question regarding community sentences is therefore how far these changes will signal a move towards a 'punishment administrative' rather than a 'professional therapeutic' rationale and how this will be viewed by probation officers (May 1994: 881). Will they become in effect, a new breed of surveillance officers, in what Vass sees as a move towards greater control and the deprivation of liberty within the community? (Vass 1990). Some change is inevitable in view of the clear emphasis on the deprivation of liberty and provisions for curfew orders and electronic surveillance in the CJA 1991 and CJPOA 1994.

This change was also illustrated by the Home Office proposal in 1995 that the probation service should seek more recruits from those leaving the armed services and that there should be a reduction in emphasis given to the social work component of probation officer training. That this shift is likely to be unpopular with existing probation officers is indicated in a survey carried out by May (May 1991). He asked probation officers about two scenarios for the future of the service, one envisaging a more coercive and authoritarian style, the other placing a value on the rights of the offender in a more libertarian and participatory society. Only two of the probation officers surveyed felt that the authoritarian path should be followed and some feared that they would become more like probation and parole officers in the USA, who carry guns and act more like law enforcement officers. A greater emphasis on surveillance was particularly unpopular, and officers also feared that privatisation might lead to an increase in non-professional officers taking on surveillance tasks. This would result in declining job satisfaction and many felt that they would leave the service.

It is also likely that privatisation will affect the operation of community sentences. The CJA 1991 for example contains a provision for contracting out electronic tagging and May argues that punishment in the community will be increasingly privately rather than publicly administered (May 1994). It may also lead to a change in the kind of offenders that the probation service deals with. Vass for example argues that the logic of privatisation will mean that private agencies dealing with the implementation of curfew orders will wish to restrict themselves to less serious offenders who present less of a risk. This would leave the probation service dealing with more high tariff offenders (Vass 1990). In addition Vass queries whether privatisation will lead to any real savings as these new schemes will require regulation and organisation thus creating new costs. The emphasis on surveillance and costs also he argues will lead to a reduction in the standards of service.

It is likely therefore that the future of community sentences will see probation officers working alongside private sector security agencies and that many tasks of a more caring nature, formerly carried out by probation officers, may be carried out by volunteers. May points to the irony in this:

> It would be ironic that in the era of punishment in the community, voluntary groups may expand to fill a gap in provision as the probation service transforms to control, rather than care for, offenders and their families. The voluntary police-court missionaries, who were the first probation officers, could then return for the same reasons they first appeared. This time, however, it will be in a different guise.
>
> (May 1994: 882)

While probation officers might have one set of concerns about their future role so do the public, particularly with the credibility of community sentences. The Chief Inspector of Probation in his annual report for 1992/93 wrote:

> The service will have to work hard to demonstrate its effectiveness in the face of such factors as the James Bulger case, juveniles in balaclavas taunting and abusing the community, an apparent 'out of control' crime wave and media hysteria. . .
>
> . . . A second issue relates to the credibility of the probation order. Although the inspection found that this problem related most to the traditional 'straight' order with no additional requirements, there was some evidence as well that courts were not able to perceive attendance at a probation centre or an offending behaviour programme as sufficiently demanding and restrictive to constitute a punishment. Nevertheless it is worth acknowledging that there are large numbers of relatively serious offenders being given probation orders.
>
> (HMI of Probation 1993, *Annual Report 1992–93*: 42–43)

In response to these concerns the Home Office in March 1995 published a Green Paper *Strengthening Punishment in the Community*. Its aim was to overcome the problems associated with the piecemeal development of community sentences, the perception that these were soft options and the problem of how different community sentences fitted in the framework of proportionality required by the CJA 1991. The report sought consultation so as to develop a 'comprehensive new framework for community sentences, which have been added to the statute book in a piecemeal way over many years.' (Home Office, 1995: 1). The report states, 'Probation supervision is still widely regarded as a soft option. Although in many cases this perception may be misconceived, it must be addressed. Both courts and the public have found some difficulty in squaring their concept of the probation order (with its additionally high social work content) with the notion of a punishment involving a significant restriction of liberty.' (Home Office, 1995: 11–12).

The Green Paper sets out a number of proposals for consultation which include a single integrated community sentence to replace existing sentences and to allow magistrates more discretion in determining the content of community sentences and providing for more feedback on the outcome of these sentences to magistrates. Another proposal is to remove the requirement that offenders have to give their consent if a community sentence is to be imposed. This would bring community penalties into line with custody and fines where the convicted person's consent is not required. These proposals aim to allow for more flexible 'sentences with elements of both punishment and rehabilitation.' (Home Office, 1995: 1–7). The magistrates decide how to balance the requirements for restriction on liberty, reparation and preventing re-offending. The Green Paper expressed 'the view of the Government that the role of community sentences is poorly understood and – perhaps as a result they have failed to command the confidence of the public. . .' (Home Office 1995: 11).

## PUBLIC CONCERN

We started this book by asking whether British justice was the best in the world. After looking at many aspects of criminal justice, we should consider how the criminal justice system is viewed by the public. The public is, after all, one audience for the decisions made throughout the criminal justice process, and increasingly may take a more overt role in many of the functions currently undertaken by professionals. To some extent this is seen as desirable in that the community and citizens play their part in collective efforts to control crime. However, where this takes the form of vigilante groups punishing those they see as criminals, there is concern that this will escalate with more groups taking the law into their own hands. Mike Bennett, chairman of the Metropolitan Police Federation, commented, 'There is growing evidence of disenchantment with the criminal justice system, which is making people take the law into their own hands. We cannot condone it, but it is something the authorities have to get to grips with.' (*Sunday Times*, 26 February 1995: 5).

Crime is an issue that is of great moment to the British. A survey of 6,500 people published in 1994 showed that Britons were far more worried about crime than people in other European countries. Over half the British respondents said it is the issue that worried them most. In Britain the fear of crime has doubled over the past three years. The survey found that 56 per cent of British people were most concerned about crime, compared with 13 per cent

344

in Spain, 14 per cent in France, 37 per cent in Italy and 43 per cent in Germany. James Murphy, the editor of the journal that published the survey, said, 'This is a phenomenon which, perversely, unites and defines British society.' (*Frontiers*, 9 June 1994).

If concern about crime is indeed a phenomenon which 'unites and defines' British society, it is clear that the issues we have discussed in this book will remain matters of social concern and high on the political agenda for the foreseeable future.

# APPENDIX

## EXERCISE NO 1   CRIME DATA EXERCISE

You should consider how crime is defined. Look at various sources of information about crime, particularly at the media and official sources. Why are some kinds of crime seen as more serious than others? To understand the creation and interpretation of official data about crime, you will need to examine the processes underlying the reporting of crime – by the public, victims and the police. The reliability of official criminal statistics will depend upon these factors.

Students may wish to consult the following general reading:

Bottomley K and Pease K (1986) *Crime and Punishment - Interpreting the Data.* Chs 1, 2 and 6. Milton Keynes: Open University Press

Heidenson F (1989) *Crime and Society.* Ch 1. London: Macmillan

Home Office (1993) Digest 2: *Information on the Criminal Justice System in England and Wales.* (G Barclay ed.) London: HMSO

Home Office (annually) *Criminal Statistics in England & Wales.* An annual report. London: HMSO

Hough M and Mayhew P (1983) *The British Crime Survey: First Report Taking Account of Crime.* London: Home Office Research Study

Maguire M, Morgan R and Reiner R (eds) (1994) *The Oxford Handbook of Criminology.* Oxford: Clarendon Press

Mayhew P, Elliot D and Dowds L (1988) *The 1988 British Crime Survey.* London: HMSO

Mayhew P, Maung N and Mirrlees-Black C (1995) *The 1994 British Crime Survey.* London: HMSO

# INTERPRETING CRIME STATISTICS

Consult extracts from the criminal statistics and answer the following questions, illustrating your answers with figures taken from statistics. Specify your source of information. Give the title of the publication you consulted and indicate which year the data covers:

Title:....................................................
Year:.............

(a) By how much has the total volume of crime known to the police increased in recent years?

(b) What percentage of all crimes reported to the police do the following constitute?

murder
rape
robbery
theft
fraud
car theft

Consider which crimes are likely to be proportionately over represented and why?

Which crimes are likely to be under-represented and why?

(c) Give examples of the variations in the rate at which different kinds of crimes are 'cleared up' by the police.

What does it mean to say that a crime is 'cleared up'?

Why are some offences more likely to be 'cleared up' than others?

(d) Which groups in the population are most 'at risk' from 'personal crime'?

Should we be more afraid of strangers, acquaintances or family? Why?

(e) What percentage of known offenders are male?

Taking into account the process of 'creating' statistics – how accurate do you think the ratio of male to female known offenders is?

# EXERCISE NO 2  VICTIM SURVEY

You should use the following 'Crime Victim Questionnaire' and interview eight people (four male, four female). Note their age. Try to include a range of people.

Consider the following:

1. Which offences are respondents most/least likely to be the victims of? Are there any significant age/gender differences?

2. Which offences are more likely to be reported?

3. What reasons do victims give for not reporting crimes?

# CRIME VICTIM QUESTIONNAIRE

| In the last two years, how many times have you been the victim of the following crimes? | If so, was this reported to the police? | If not reported, why not? |
|---|---|---|
| Theft | ............ | .......................... |
| of a motor car | ............ | .......................... |
| from a motor car | ............ | .......................... |
| of a bicycle | ............ | .......................... |
| at work | ............ | .......................... |
| from your person | ............ | .......................... |
| Burglary | ............ | .......................... |
| Assault | | |
| with injury | ............ | .......................... |
| no injury | ............ | .......................... |
| Robbery | | |
| in street | ............ | .......................... |
| in bank/post office | ............ | .......................... |
| Insulted/bothered by strangers | ............ | .......................... |
| Any other? | | |
| describe briefly | ............ | .......................... |

# EXERCISE NO 3 MAGISTRATES' COURT OBSERVATION REPORT

We recommend you observe a morning session of a magistrates' court, which will normally start at 10 am and go on until lunchtime. If you are unable to attend during the week it may be possible to find inner urban courts that sit on Saturday and there is at least one evening court in the London area.

1. Name:

   Location of magistrates' court:

   Date of visit:

   Time of arrival:

   Time of departure:

2. Before you go give some impression of what you expect to see in a magistrates' court.

3. How many courtrooms were there?

   How many cases were scheduled to be heard in each?

4. After 10 minutes, from your time of arrival at the magistrates' court, describe your initial impressions.

5. Can you identify the following:

   Please tick

   - Bench          ( )
   - Clerk's desk    ( )
   - Advocates' seats ( )
   - Dock            ( )

- Witness box        ( )
- Press box        ( )
- Usher's seat        ( )
- Public seating        ( )
- Seating for defendants on bail or summons ( )

6. **Personnel in the courtroom**

   How many magistrates were there?

   Name the other functionaries.

   Who else was in the court?

7. **Defendants**

   How many defendants appeared while you were in the court?

8. What sort of cases did you observe?

                                               Please tick
   - a remand        ( )
   - a decision as to mode of trial        ( )
   - an adjournment        ( )
   - a decision to grant bail        ( )
   - a remand in custody        ( )
   - a probation order being made        ( )
   - a disqualification from driving being ordered ( )
   - a guilty plea being entered        ( )
   - a trial        ( )
   - a fine being imposed        ( )

9. How would you describe the types of defendants you saw?

10. Were there some defendants who seemed unable to understand the proceedings?

11. Outcomes

How many cases were disposed of, from plea to sentence?

How many defendants were remanded in custody?

How many defendants were given bail with conditions?

How many defendants were given bail without conditions?

How many defendants were committed for trial to the Crown Court?

How many cases were adjourned to a future date?

If they were adjourned, give the reasons why.

12. What were your impressions of the performance of the Crown Prosecutor?

13. What was your impression of the magistrates?

14. What was your impression of the defence lawyer?

15. Using keywords, describe your general impression of the magistrates' court.

16. What time did the court commence business?

17. Was the conduct of the court efficient in your view? If not explain why not.

18. Are there any other comments you wish to make about your observations?

# EXERCISE NO 4   SENTENCING AIMS IN COURT OF APPEAL DECISIONS

In the following three extracts from Court of Appeal decisions on sentencing cases, see if you can identify the aims of sentencing that are referred to by the court. Identify the statement and indicate which theory it represents.

1.  R v Decino

2.  R v Meggs

3.  R v Knight (Colin)

Extract 1

# Kiosk theft justifies jail
## Regina v Decino

The offence of theft of money from a telephone kiosk was capable of being so serious that only a custodial sentence could be justified, within the terms of section 1(2)(a) of the Criminal Justice Act 1991.

The Court of Appeal (Lord Justice Beldam, Mr Justice Connell and Mrs Justice Ebsworth) so held on April 21 when allowing an appeal by Nicholas Decino against a sentence of 12 months imprisonment imposed on January 8, 1993 by Mr Recorder Williams at Cardiff Crown Court, following his conviction on December 8, 1992 at West Berkshire Magistrates Court of theft of £40.20 from a telephone kiosk.

For that offence he was sentenced to two months, and suspended sentences totalling ten months for burglary and possession of a controlled drug were activated consecutively. The sentences were made concurrent, reducing the total to ten months.

LORD JUSTICE BELDAM says that this was the kind of offence which was capable of depriving members of the public of the use of the public telephone which, to many people, was a lifeline. Of necessity telephone boxes were left unprotected. It was a matter of public policy to deter thefts from such boxes.

There was evidence that the appellant and two other young men provided themselves with the necessary tools and went on a deliberate expedition to rob telephone boxes of their contents.

In their Lordships' view it was, as the recorder has said, an offence capable of being so serious that only a sentence of custody could be justified for it.

(*The Times* 10 May 1993 © Times Supplements Limited, 1993)

Extract 2

# Sentencing in cases of incest
## Regina v Meggs

Before Lord Lane, Lord Chief Justice, Mr Justice Kennedy and Mr Justice Hutchinson.
[Judgment February 21]
Cases of incest varied so enormously the one from the other that it was very difficult to derive any assistance from the previous instances which had appeared before the Court of Appeal.

The Lord Chief Justice so stated when giving the judgment of the court on an appeal by Eric William Meggs, aged 50, against prison sentences totalling 10 years passed at the Central Criminal Court by Sir James Miskin, QC, the Recorder of London, on pleas of guilty to specimen counts of incest with two of his daughters, extending in the case of the elder, for more than 22 years.
Sentence of three years on one count, which had been made consecutive, was ordered to run concurrent with the other sentences, totalling $7\frac{1}{2}$ years.

Mr William Clegg, assigned by the Registrar of Criminal Appeals for the appellant.

THE LORD CHIEF JUSTICE said that, having made the elder girl pregnant twice the appellant caused her to have abortions. For a time they had lived as a married couple which according to Mr Clegg, was what the neighbours thought they were.

The elder daughter became pregnant by her boy friend but the appellant did not desist from having sexual intercourse with her throughout.

The appellant, throughout interviews with the police, denied that anything improper had occurred.

Such cases varied so enormously from one to the other that it was very difficult to derive any assistance from the previous instances which had appeared before the court.

The court had to mark its disapproval and the disapproval of the community of such behaviour. It had to endeavour to deter other men from behaving in such a way.

It had to punish the appellant for using his two daughters, in particular his elder daughter, simply as a chattel to satisfy his own sexual appetite, regardless of the damage he might do to her welfare and happiness and, perhaps most important of all, her ability to enjoy a happy married life herself.

Mr Clegg submitted that insufficient regard was given to the plea of guilty and that overall the totality was too great despite the horrifying features of the case.

He pointed out that the appellant was disowned by his family, which was not surprising, but the effect was that he received no visits and was serving his sentence isolated to a great extent from his fellow prisoners.

They were all matters to be taken into account and their Lordships had concluded that Mr Clegg was correct in stating that the totality was too high.

There was nothing wrong with the individual sentences but their Lordships were concerned with the overall total and the proper course was to order that the sentence on a count ordered to run consecutively should, instead, run concurrent, so that the sentence was reduced by three years.

(*The Times* 22 February 1989 © Times Supplements Limited, 1989)

Extract 3

# Punishment for perjury

**Regina v Knight (Colin)**

Before Mr Justice McCowan and Mr Justice Leggatt.

(Judgment delivered 26 January).

Punishment for perjury had to be condign and commensurate with the gravity of the offence to prevent conviction of another for which the perjury was committed. The Court of Appeal so stated in dismissing an appeal by Colin Charles Knight, aged 32, against a three-year prison sentence passed at the Central Criminal Court by Sir James Miskin, QC, Recorder of London on a plea of guilty to perjury in that, being lawfully sworn as a witness on the trial of a man called Tobin at the Central Criminal Court, the appellant knowingly falsely described a man who jumped down from a crane.

Mr C Y Nutt, assigned by the Registrar of Criminal Appeals, for the appellant.

MR JUSTICE LEG-GATT said that the crane was driven by Tobin into the back of a security van to gain access to it by a group of professional armed robbers. The jury disagreed at his first trial.

At the second trial the appellant not called at the first trial, gave perjured evidence in saying that he had been in the area at the time of the robbery and described a man different from Tobin getting down from the crane. In the event Tobin was convicted.

In mitigation of the appellant's offence it was suggested that there had been some inducement and threat by an intermediary.

In passing sentence on the appellant, Sir James Miskin had said that armed robbery, planned with exquisite skill by intelligent, determined men forhigh profit was one of the most serious crimes known to the courts and there was a great deal too much of it. Those who intentionally gave false testimony on behalf of such men did so intending to mislead the jury into returning a verdict contrary to true justice and the evidence.

Not having seen one whiff of what had happened and for reward the appellant had entered the witness box and told a whole string of purposive lies. Account was taken of the plea of guilty and good character and implicit show of steel on the part of the intermediary. However, perjury was difficult enough to detect and much more difficult to prove. When it occurred it demanded instant prison.

Three years was imposed so that the appellant might be seen to be punished and, even more importantly, so that every single person in this age who contemplated events like giving false evidence in any case, let alone a serious one, or was minded to tamper with a jury, might know it would always be met by immediate, condign punishment.

Their Lordships agreed with every word of the judge in sentencing and, in particular that punishment had to be condign. The purpose of the appellant's perjury was to avoid conviction for a grave offence. The punishment had to be commensurate with the gravity of that offence. The maximum penalty was seven years' imprisonment. The judge having made such allowance as could have been made for the appellant's antecedents and plea of guilty, the sentence was unimpeachable. The appeal was dismissed.

(*The Times* 4 February 1984 © Times Supplements Limited, 1984)

# EXERCISE NO 5  SENTENCING

In respect of the following triable-either-way case consider the sentence you think a court would impose.

Look at the charge(s) in the light of the Magistrates' Guidelines for Mode of Trial. Where should the case be tried? Depending on that decision, what are the court's powers? How would you assess the seriousness of the offence? Consult Figure 8.2 for relevant sentencing guidelines. Is there any mitigation on the part of the offender? Impose your sentence.

## AFFRAY

| | |
|---|---|
| <u>Accused:</u> | DARREN SMITH (22)<br>KEVIN JONES (19) |
| <u>Charge:</u> | On 31 January, 1994, used unlawful violence towards others and their conduct was such as would cause a person of reasonable firmness to fear for his personal safety; Section 3 Public Order Act, 1986 |
| <u>Maximum Penalty:</u> | On indictment: 3 years, imprisonment and/or fine<br>Summarily: 6 months, imprisonment and/or £5,000 fine |
| <u>Pleas:</u> | Both accused consent to summary trial<br>Smith pleaded NOT GUILTY but was convicted after a trial in the magistrates' court<br>Jones pleaded GUILTY |
| <u>Facts:</u> | The accused with a group of others who have not been traced, were passing a hamburger restaurant when they saw a group of Asian men eating there. The group entered the restaurant and began using terms of racial abuse towards the Asians. The restaurant manager (R Mcdonald) asked the accused to leave. They refused. An altercation ensued in which Mr Mcdonald was pushed over, injuring his back. Although the two accused used their fists and a chair as a weapon, no injuries were occasioned to the Asians because of the intervention of other customers. The police were called and arrested the two accused whilst the rest of the group ran off. |

Previous Convictions:

**SMITH:**

| | | |
|---|---|---|
| 3 years ago | Magistrates' Court: Criminal damage, possession cannabis | Conditional discharge 12 months, £80 compensation |
| 2 years ago | Magistrates' Court: Threatening behaviour (fight in pub) | Fined £75 and £35 costs |
| 3 months ago | Magistrates' Court: Assault actual bodily harm | Probation order 1 year, condition to attend Probation Centre, compensation £250 |

**JONES:**  No previous convictions

Pre-Sentence Reports:

**SMITH:**

Left home when he was 16 because of violence from his step-father. Became involved in alcohol and drug abuse. Drink was involved in last two convictions. He had been drinking before current incident.

Attends Probation Centre under probation order imposed 3 months ago. Also does voluntary work in local psychiatric hospital. Owes compensation from last conviction. Unemployed, on benefit. Lives with girlfriend in rented accommodation. Proposes another probation order.

**JONES:**

No previous convictions, does not need supervision. Community service available, but suggests financial penalty. Earns £150 per week and has expenses (board, travel to work etc) of £70 per week. Lives with parents.

Mitigation: Both regret stupid behaviour, recognise alcohol partly to blame. Deny they have racist views.

# BIBLIOGRAPHY

Advisory Council on the Penal System (1968) *The Regime for Long Term Prisoners in Maximum Security (Chaired by Sir Leon Radzinowicz).* London: HMSO

Advisory Council on the Penal System (1978) *Sentences of Imprisonment: A Review of Maximum Penalties.* London: HMSO

Alderson J (1978) *Communal Policing.* Exeter: Devon and Cornwall Constabulary

Allen R (1991) 'Out of Jail: The Reduction in the Use of Penal Custody for Male Juveniles', *Howard Journal,* Vol 30/1: 30–53

Alschuler A (1992) *New Law Journal.* 3 July: 937

Ashworth A (1989) 'Criminal Justice and Deserved Sentences', *Criminal Law Review*: 340–355

Ashworth A (1992) *The Youth Court.* Winchester: Waterside Press

Ashworth A (1992) *Sentencing and Penal Policy.* 2nd edn. London: Weidenfeld and Nicholson

Ashworth A (1993) 'Victim Impact Statements and Sentencing', *Criminal Law Review*: 498–509

Ashworth A (1994a) *The Criminal Process.* Oxford: Clarendon Press

Ashworth A (1994b) 'Sentencing' in Maguire M, Morgan R and Reiner R (eds) *The Oxford Handbook of Criminology.* Oxford: Clarendon Press

Baldwin J and Bottomley A (eds) (1978) *Criminal Justice: Selected Readings.* London: Martin Robertson

Baldwin J and McConville M (1979) *Jury Trials.* Oxford: Clarendon Press

Barclay G (ed) (1993) *Digest 2: A Digest of Information on the Criminal Justice System.* London: HMSO

Becker H S (1963) *Outsiders: Studies in the Sociology of Deviance.* New York: Free Press

Bennett T (1984) *Burglars on Burglary: Prevention and the Offender.* Farnborough: Gower

Bennett T (1990) *Evaluating Neighbourhood Watch.* Aldershot: Gower

Bennett T (1991) 'The Effectiveness of a Police-Initiated Fear Reducing Strategy', *British Journal of Criminology*, Vol 31: 11–14

Bennett T (1994a) 'Recent Developments in Community Policing' in Stephens M and Becker S (eds) *Police Force, Police Service: Care and Control in Britain*. London: MacMillan

Bennett T (1994b) 'Community Policing', *Criminal Justice Matters*, No 17. Autumn 1994: 6–7

Bennett T and Lupton R (1992) 'A National Activity Survey of Police Work', *Howard Journal*, Vol 31/3: 200–223

Bentham J (1791) *Panopticon: or the Inspection House*. London: Payer

Bentham J (1830) *The Rationale of Punishment*. London: Hewood

Block B, Corbett C and Peay J (1993) 'Ordered and Directed Acquittals in the Crown Court. A Time of Change?', *Criminal Law Review 95*

Blom Cooper L (1988) *The Penalty of Imprisonment*. London: Prison Reform Trust

Blumberg (1967) *Criminal Justice*. Chicago: Quadrangle Books

Borna S (1986) 'Free Enterprise goes to Prison', *British Journal of Criminology*, Vol 26/4

Bottomley K and Pease K (1986) *Crime and Punishment – Interpreting the Data*. Milton Keynes: Open University Press

Bottoms A and McClean (1978) in Baldwin and Bottomley (eds) (1978) *Criminal Justice: Selected Readings*. London: Martin Robertson

Box S (1987) *Recession, Crime and Punishment*. London: MacMillan

Braithwaite J (1989) *Crime, Shame and Re-integration*. Cambridge: Cambridge University Press

Braithwaite J and Pettit P (1990) *Not Just Deserts: A Republican Theory of Justice*. Oxford: Clarendon Press

Brogden M, Jefferson T and Walklate S (1988) *Introducing Police Work*. London: Unwin Hyman

Burton A (1994) 'The Demise of Criminal Legal Aid', *New Law Journal*, Vol 28 October 1994: 1491


Cain M (1973) *Society and the Policeman's Role*. London: Routledge and Kegan Paul

Campbell B (1993) *Goliath: Britain's Dangerous Places*. London: Methuen

Carlen P (1976) *Magistrates' Justice*. London: Martin Robertson

Carlen P and Worrall A (eds) (1987) *Gender, Crime and Justice*. Milton Keynes: Open University Press

Carlen P (1990) *Alternatives to Women's Imprisonment*. Milton Keynes: Open University Press

Carson W G (1974) 'Symbolic and Instrumental Dimensions of Early Factory Legislation: A Case Study on the Social Origins of Criminal Law', in Hood R (ed) *Crime Criminology and Public Policy*. London: Heinemann

Casales (1984) *Minimum Standards for Prison Establishments.* London: National Association for the Care and Resettlement of Offenders

Cavadino M and Dignan J (1992) *The Penal System: An Introduction.* London: Sage

Cavadino P (1994) 'Recent Developments in England and Wales: A Background Paper.' Presented to the Goethe Institute Conference 9/10 June 1994, London

Chibnall S (1977) *Law and Order News.* London: Tavistock

Clarke R and Mayhew P (1980) *Designing Out Crime.* London: HMSO

Clarke R V (ed) *Crime Prevention Studies. Vol 1.* Monsey, New York: Criminal Justice Press (1993)

Clemmer D (1958) *The Prison Community.* New York: Holt, Rinehart and Winston

Cloward R and Ohlin L (1960) *Delinquency and Opportunity: A Theory of Delinquent Gangs.* New York: Free Press

Cohen A K (1955) *Delinquent Boys: The Culture of the Gang.* New York: Free Press

Cohen N (1991) *Independent.* 4 September 1991 and 17 September 1991

Cohen P (1979) Policing the Working Class City in Fine B (ed) *Capitalism and the Rule of Law.* London: Hutchinson

Cohen S (1980) *Folk Devils and Moral Panics.* Oxford: Martin Robertson

Cohen S (1985) *Visions of Social Control.* Cambridge: Polity Press

Cohen S and Taylor L (1972) *Psychological Survival.* Harmondsworth: Penguin

Condon P (1994) Metropolitan Police Commissioner. Address to meeting of British Society of Criminology. London, January 1994

Cressey D (1986) 'Why Managers Commit Fraud', *Australian and New Zealand Journal of Criminology,* Vol 19: 195–209

Crime Concern (1994) *Counting the Cost.* A briefing paper on financial losses arising from crime. Swindon: Crime Concern

Croall H (1988) 'Mistakes, Accidents and Someone Else's Fault: the Trading Offender in Court', *Journal of Law and Society,* Vol 15(3): 293–325

Croall H (1989) 'Who is the White Collar Criminal?', *British Journal of Criminology,* Vol 29 No 2: 157–174

Croall H (1991) 'Sentencing the Business Offender' in *The Howard Journal,* Vol 30/4: 280–294

Croall H (1992) *White Collar Crime.* Milton Keynes: Open University Press

Crown Prosecution Service (annually) *Annual Report.* London: HMSO


Davies K (1969) *Discretionary Justice: A Preliminary Inquiry.* Baton Rouge: Louisiana State University Press

Davies M (1989) 'An Alternative View: Square Deal Punishment in the Community: It Is Cheaper But Who Will Buy It?' in *Punishment, Custody and the Community: Reflections and Comments on the Green*

*Paper.* Rees H and Hall Williams E (eds). Suntory Toyota International Centre for Economics and Related Disciplines.

Davies M (1993) *Punishing Criminals: Developing Community-based Intermediate Sanctions.* Connecticut: Greenwood

Dicey A (1959) *Introduction to the Study of the Law of the Constitution.* London: Macmillan

Ditton J and Duffy J (1983) 'Bias in the Newspaper Reporting of Crime News', *British Journal of Criminology,* Vol 23: 129

Dixon D, Bottomley A, Coleman C, Gill M and Wall D (1989) 'Reality and Rules in the Construction and Regulation of Police Suspicion', *International Journal of the Sociology of Law,* Vol 17:

Downes D (1966) *The Delinquent Solution.* London: Routledge and Kegan Paul

Duff A and Garland D (1994) *A Reader on Punishment.* Oxford: Oxford University Press


Eaton M (1986) *Justice for Women?* Milton Keynes: Open University Press

Eaton M (1987) 'The Question of Bail: Magistrates' Responses to Applications for Bail on Behalf of Men and Women Defendants' in Carlen P and Worrall A (eds) *Gender, Crime and Justice.* Milton Keynes: Open University Press

Eaton M (1993) *Women after Prison.* Milton Keynes: Open University Press

Eden W (1777) *Principles of Penal Law.* London: B White and T Cadell

Evans R and Wilkinson C (1990) 'Variations in Police Cautioning Policy and Practice in England and Wales', *Howard Journal,* Vol 29/3: 155–176

Eysenck H J (1977) *Crime and Personality.* London: Routledge and Kegan Paul


Farrington D (1992) 'Juvenile Delinquency' in Coleman J (ed) *The School Years.* London: Routledge

Farrington D (1994) 'Human Development and Criminal Careers' in Maguire M, Morgan R and Reiner R (eds) *The Oxford Handbook of Criminology.* Oxford: Clarendon Press

Farrington D and Dowds E (1985) 'Disentangling Criminal Behaviour and Police Reaction' in Farrington D and Gunn J (eds) *Reactions to Crime: the Public, the Police, Courts and Prisons.* Chichester: Wiley

Farrington D and Gunn J (eds)(1985) *Reactions to Crime: the Public, the Police, Courts and Prisons.* Chichester: Wiley

Farrington D and Morris A (1983) 'Sex, Sentencing and Re-conviction', *British Journal of Criminology* 23: 229–248

Fennell P (1991) 'Diversion of Mentally Disordered Offenders From Custody', *Criminal Law Review:* 333–348

Fielding N (1988) *Joining Forces: Police Training, Socialisation and Occupational Competence.* London: Routledge

Fielding N, Kemp C and Norris C (1989) 'Constraints on the Practice of Community Policing' in Morgan R and Smith D (eds) *Coming to Terms with Policing*. London: Routledge

Fitzgerald M (1977) *Prisoners in Revolt*. Harmondsworth: Penguin

Fogel D (1975) *We Are the Living Proof: the Justice Model for Corrections*. Cincinatti: W H Anderson Co

Foster J (1989) 'Two Stations: An Ethnographic Study of Policing in the Inner City' in Downes D (ed) *Crime and the City*. London: Macmillan

Foucault M (1977) *Discipline and Punish*. Harmondsworth: Penguin

Fox L (1952) *The English Prison and Borstal System*. London: Routledge and Kegan Paul

Frankel M (1973) *Criminal Sentences: Law without Order*. New York: Hill and Wang


Garfinkel H (1956) 'Conditions of Successful Degradation Ceremonies', *American Journal of Sociology* 61(2): 420-424

Garland D (1990) *Punishment and Modern Society*. Oxford: Oxford University Press

Gelsthorpe L and Morris A (1994) 'Juvenile Justice 1945-1992' in Maguire M, Morgan R and Reiner R (eds) *The Oxford Handbook of Criminology*. Oxford: Clarendon Press

Gill M and Mawby R (1990) *Volunteers in the Criminal Justice System. A comparative study of probation, police and victim support*. Milton Keynes: Open University Press

Goffman E (1961) *Asylums: Essays on the Social Situation of Mental Patients and Other Inmates*. Golden City, New York: Doubleday

Goffman E (1968) *Stigma: Notes on the Management of Spoiled Identities*. Harmondsworth: Penguin

Graef R (1989) *Talking Blues: The Police in their Own Words*. London: Collins-Harvill

Graef R (1990) *Talking Blues: The Police in their Own Words*. London: Fontana/Collins-Harvill

Graef R (1992) *Living Dangerously: Young Offenders in their Own Words*. London: Harper-Collins

Graef R (1993) 'Cutting Down On Crime Doesn't Always Work', *Daily Telegraph*, 20 July 1993

Gross H (1979) *A Theory of Criminal Justice*. New York: Oxford University Press

Grubin D (1991) 'Unfit to Plead in England and Wales 1976-1988: A Survey', *British Journal of Psychiatry*: 540-548


Hall S, Critcher C, Jefferson T, Clarke J and Roberts B (1978) *Policing the Crisis: Mugging, the State and Law and Order*. London: Macmillan

Hall S and Jefferson T (1976) (eds) *Resistance Through Ritual*. London: Hutchinson

Harding C, Hines B, Ireland R and Rawlings P (1985) *Imprisonment in England and Wales*. Beckenham: Croom Helm

Harman H and Griffith J (1979) *Justice Deserted: The Subversion of the Jury*. London: NCCL

Hart H L A (1968) 'Prolegomenon to the Principles of Punishment' in *Punishment and Responsibility*. Oxford: Clarendon Press

Hawkins K (1984) *Environment and Enforcement: Regulation and the Social Definition of Pollution*. Oxford Socio-Legal Studies: Clarendon Press

Heal K and Laycock G (1986) *Situational Crime Prevention: From Theory to Practice*. Home Office Research and Publication Unit: HMSO

Hedderman C and Moxon D (1992) *Magistrates' Court or Crown Court? Mode of Trial and Sentencing Decisions*. London: HMSO

Hedderman C and Hough M (1994) *Does the Criminal Justice System Treat Men and Women Differently?* Home Office Research and Statistics Department No 10. London: HMSO

Heidensohn F (1985) *Women and Crime*. London: Macmillan

Heidensohn F (1989) *Crime and Society*. London: Macmillan

Heidensohn F (1992) *Women in Control? The Role of Women in Law Enforcement*. Oxford: Oxford University Press

Heidensohn F (1994) Gender and Crime in Maguire M, Morgan R, and Reiner R *The Oxford Handbook of Criminology*. Oxford: Clarendon Press

Hirschi T (1969) *Causes of Delinquency*. Los Angeles: University of California Press

HM Inspector of Constabulary (1992) *Annual Report for the Year 1991*. London: HMSO

HM Inspectorate of Probation (1993) *Annual Report 1992–93*. London: HMSO

HM Prison Service (1995) *Annual Report and Accounts 1993–94*. London: HMSO

Hobbs D (1991) 'A Piece of Business: The Moral Economy of Detective Work in the East of London', *British Journal of Sociology* 42: 4

Holdaway S (1983) *Inside the British Police*. Oxford: Basil Blackwell

Hollin C (1989) *Psychology and Crime: An Introduction to Criminological Psychology*. London: Routledge

Home Office (1895) *Report from the Departmental Committee on Prisons*. Chaired by Herbert Gladstone. London: HMSO

Home Office (1959) *Penal Practice in a Changing Society*. London: HMSO

Home Office (1966) *Report of the Inquiry into Prison Escapes and Security* by Admiral of the Fleet, Earl Mountbatten of Burma. London: HMSO

Home Office (1968) *Report on the Regime for Long-term Prisoners in Maximum Security*. Chaired by Sir Leon Radzinowicz. London: HMSO

Home Office (1979) *Report of the Committee of Inquiry into the Prison Service*. Cmnd 7673. London: HMSO

Home Office (1984) *Criminal Justice: A Working Paper*. London: Home Office

Home Office (1986) *The Sentence of the Court*. London: HMSO

Home Office (1988a) *Punishment, Custody and the Community*. Cmnd 424. London: HMSO

Home Office (1988b) *The Parole System in England and Wales: Report of the Review Committee* (Carlisle Committee). Cmnd 532. London: HMSO

Home Office (1990a) *Crime, Justice and Protecting the Public*. London: HMSO

Home Office (1990b) *Victim's Charter: A Statement of the Rights of the Victims of Crime*. London: HMSO

Home Office (1991a) *Prison Disturbances, April 1990*. Report of an inquiry presented to the Home Office by Lord Justice H Woolf and Judge Stephen Tumin. Cmnd 1456. London: HMSO

Home Office (1991b) *A General Guide to the Criminal Justice Act 1991*. London: HMSO

Home Office (1992) *Survey of Prisons in England and Wales*. London: HMSO

Home Office (1993a) *Digest 2: Information on the Criminal Justice System in England and Wales*. Barclay G (ed). London: HMSO

Home Office (1993b) *Safer Cities Progress Report 1992–93*. Home Office Crime Prevention Unit London: HMSO

Home Office (1994a) *Home Office Research Findings*. 14. London: HMSO

Home Office (1994b) *Home Office Statistical Bulletin*. Issue 15/94. London: HMSO

Home Office (1994c) *Probation Statistics, England and Wales 1993*. London: Government Statistical Service

Home Office (annually) *Criminal Statistics, England & Wales*. An annual report. London: HMSO

Hood R (1965) *Borstal Re-assessed*. London: Heinemann

Hood R (1972) *Sentencing the Motoring Offender*. London: Heinemann

Hood R (1974)(ed) *Crime, Criminology and Public Policy*. London: Heinemann

Hood R (1992) *Race and Sentencing*. Clarendon: Oxford University Press

Hough M and Mayhew P (1983) *The British Crime Survey: First Report Taking Account of Crime*. Home Office Research Study. London: HMSO

Hudson B (1989) 'Discrimination and Disparity: The Influence of Race on Sentencing', *New Community*, Vol 16: 23–34

Hudson B (1993) *Penal Policy and Social Justice*. London: Macmillan

Ignatieff M (1975) *A Just Measure of Pain: The Penitentiary in the Industrial Revolution 1750-1850*. London: Macmillan

Irving B, Bird C, Hibberd M and Wilmore J (1989) *Neighbourhood Policing: The Natural History of a Policing Experiment*. London: The Police Foundation

Irwin J (1970) *The Felon*. Englewood Cliffs: Prentice-Hall

Irwin J (1980) *Prisons in Turmoil.* Toronto: Little, Brown and Co

Jefferson T (1990) *The Case Against Paramilitary Policing.* Milton Keynes: Open University Press

Jefferson T and Walker M (1992) 'Ethnic Minorities in the Criminal Justice System', *Criminal Law Review* 83: 88

Jefferson T, Walker M and Seneviratne M (1992) 'Ethnic Minorities, Crime and Criminal Justice: A Study in a Provincial City' in Downes D (ed) *Unravelling Criminal Justice* London: Macmillan

Johnston L (1992) *The Rebirth of Private Policing.* London: Routledge

Johnston L (1994) 'Current Developments in Private Policing'in *Criminal Justice Matters* No 17. Autumn 1994:

Jones T, McClean B and Young J (1986) *The Islington Crime Survey.* Aldershot: Gower

Jones T and Newburn T (1994a) *How Big is the Private Security Industry?* Policy Studies Institute

Jones T and Newburn T (1994b) 'Policing and Democracy', *Criminal Justice Matters* No 17. Autumn 1994:

Joutsen M (1990) *The Criminal Justice System of Finland: A General Introduction.* Helsinki: Ministry of Justice

Jowell R, Curtice J, Lindsay B, Ahrendt D with Pork A (eds) (1994) *British Social Attitudes. 11th Report.* Aldershot: Dartmouth Publishing Co

King M (1981) *The Framework of Criminal Justice.* London: Croom Helm

King R and Elliott K (1978) *Albany: The Birth of a Prison, the End of an Era.* London: Routledge and Kegan Paul

King R and Morgan R (1980) *The Future of the Prison System.* Farnborough: Gower

Landau S F and Nathan G (1983) 'Selecting Juveniles for Cautioning in the London Metropolitan Area', *British Journal of Criminology,* Vol 23 No 2: 128–149

Lea J and Young J (1984) *What Is to Be Done about Law and Order?* Harmondsworth: Penguin

Lea J and Young J (1992) *What Is to Be Done about Law and Order?* 2nd edn London: Pluto Press

Lemert E (1967) *Human Deviance, Social Problems and Social Control.* Englewood Cliffs: Prentice Hall

Leng R, McConville M and Sanders A (1992) 'Researching the Discretions to Charge and to Prosecute', in Downes D (ed) *Unravelling Criminal Justice.* London: Macmillan

Levi M (1987) *Regulating Fraud: White Collar Crime and the Criminal Process* London: Tavistock

Levi M (1989) 'Suite Justice: Sentencing for Fraud', *Criminal Law Review:* 420–434

Levi and Pithouse (1992) 'The Victims of Fraud', in Downes D (ed) *Unravelling Criminal Justice*. London: Macmillan

Lewis C S (1953) 'On Punishment', *Res Judicatae*, Vol 6 1952–54

Light R (1993) *Car Theft: The Offender's Perspective*. Home Office Research and Planning Unit Report No 130. London: HMSO

Lipton D, Martinson R and Wilks J (1975) *Effectiveness of Correctional Treatment*. Springfield, Mass: Praeger

Lloyd C, Mair G and Hough M (1995) *Explaining Reconviction Rates: A Critical Analysis*. London: HMSO

Logan C (1990) *Private Prisons: the Cons and Pros*. Oxford: Oxford University Press

Loveday B (1992) 'Right Agendas: Law and Order in England and Wales', *International Journal of the Sociology of Law*, Vol 20: 297–319

Loveday B (1994) 'Policing the Future', *Criminal Justice Matters*, No 17. Autumn 1994: 4


Maguire M (1994) 'Crime Statistics, Patterns and Trends: Changing Perceptions and their Implications', in Maguire M, Morgan R and Reiner R (eds) *The Oxford Handbook of Criminology*. Oxford: Clarendon Press

Maguire M, Morgan R and Reiner R (eds) (1994) *The Oxford Handbook of Criminology*. Oxford: Clarendon Press

Maguire M and Pointing J (eds) (1988) *Victims of Crime: A New Deal?* Milton Keynes: Open University Press

Mann K (1985) *Defending White Collar Crime*. New Haven and London Yale University Press

Mars G (1982) *Cheats at Work, an Anthropology of Workplace Crime*. London: George Allen and Unwin

Mathiesen T (1990) *Prison on Trial*. London: Sage

Mathiesen T (1991) 'The Argument Against Building More Prisons' in Muncie J and Sparks R (eds) *Imprisonment: European Perspectives*. Hemel Hempstead: Harvester Wheatsheaf.

Matza D (1964) *Delinquency and Drift*. New York: Wiley

May C (1992) *The National Probation Survey 1990*. Home Office Research and Planning Unit Paper 72. London: HMSO

May T (1991) *Probation: Politics, Policy and Practice*. Buckingham: Open University Press

May T (1994) 'Probation and Community Sanctions' in Maguire M, Morgan R and Reiner R (eds) *The Oxford Handbook of Criminology*. Oxford: Clarendon Press: 861-888

May Sir John (1979) *Report of the Committee of Inquiry into the UK Prison Service*. Cmnd 7673. London: Home Office

Mayhew P, Clarke R, Sturman A and Hough J (eds) (1976) *Crime as Opportunity*. Home Office Research Study No 34. London: HMSO

Mayhew P, Elliot D and Dowds L (1989) *The 1988 British Crime Survey*. London: HMSO

Mayhew P, Maung N and Mirrlees-Black C (1993) *The 1992 British Crime Survey*. London: HMSO

Mayhew P, Maung N and Mirrlees-Black C (1995) *The 1994 British Crime Survey*. London: HMSO

McBarnet D (1981) *Conviction: Law, the State and the Construction of Justice*. London: Macmillan

McCabe S (1988) in Findlay M and Duff P (eds) (1988) *The Jury Under Attack*. London: Butterworths

McIvor G (1991) 'Community Service and Custody in Scotland', *Howard Journal* 29/2: 101–113

Merton R K (1938) 'Social Structure and Anomie', *American Sociological Review* 3: 672–682

Messinger S and Johnson P (1978) 'California's Determinate Sentencing Statute: History and Issues' in *Determinate Sentencing: Reform or Regression*. National Institute of Law Enforcement and Criminal Justice. Washington DC: Government Printing Office

Metropolitan Police Commissioner (1991) *Annual Report*. London: HMSO

Morgan P (1992) *Offending While on Bail – A Survey of Recent Studies*. London: HMSO

Morgan R (1989) 'Policing by Consent: Legitimating the Doctrine' in Morgan and Smith (eds) (1989) *Coming to Terms with Policing: Perspectives on Policy*. London: Routledge

Morgan R (1994) 'Imprisonment' in Maguire M, Morgan R and Reiner R (eds) *The Oxford Handbook of Criminology*. Oxford: Clarendon Press: 889–948

Morgan R and Newburn T (1994) 'Backing up the Police', *Criminal Justice Matters* No 17, Autumn 1994: 3

Morgan R and Jones (1992) '*Bail or Jail?*' in Stockdale E and Casales S (eds) (1992) *Criminal Justice under Stress*. London: Blackstone

Morris A and Giller H (1987) *Understanding Juvenile Justice*. London: Croom Helm

Moxon D (1993) 'Use of Compensation Orders in Magistrates' Courts'. Home Office Research Bulletin 33/1993. London: HMSO

Murphy P (1992) *A Practical Approach to Evidence*. London: Blackstone Press

National Audit Office (1992) *The Administration of Legal Aid in England and Wales*. HC 90 (1991–92). London: HMSO

Packer H (1968) *The Limits of the Criminal Sanction*. Stanford: Stanford University Press

Parker H, Sumner M and Jarvis, G (1989) *Unmasking the Magistrates*. Milton Keynes: Open University Press

Paterson (1927) Report of the Prison Commission. London: HMSO

Pearson G (1983) *Hooligan: A History of Respectable Fears*. London: Macmillan

Pearson G (1987) *The New Heroin Users*. London: Blackwell

Pearson G (1994) 'Youth, Crime and Society' in Maguire M, Morgan R and Reiner R (eds) *The Oxford Handbook of Criminology*. Oxford: Clarendon Press

Pease K (1991) 'Preventing Burglary on a British Public Housing Estate' in Clarke R (ed) *Situational Crime Prevention: Successful Case Studies*. New York: Harrow and Heston

Pease K (1994) 'Crime Prevention' in Maguire M, Morgan R and Reiner R (eds) *The Oxford Handbook of Criminology*. Oxford: Clarendon Press: 659–704

Peay J (1994) 'Mentally Disordered Offenders' in Maguire M, Morgan R and Reiner R (eds) *The Oxford Handbook of Criminology*. Oxford: Clarendon Press: 1119–1160

Phillips C (1981) *Report of the Royal Commission on Criminal Procedure*. The Phillips Commission. Cmnd 8092. London: HMSO

Pullinger H (1985) *Home Office Research and Planning Unit, Paper 36*. London: HMSO

Pollack O (1950) *The Criminality of Women*. New York: A S Barnes/ Perpetua

Prison Commissioners (1925) *Annual Report*. London: HMSO

Prison Service (1988) *Briefing*. November 1988. London: HMSO

Prison Service (1993) *Report on the Work of the Prison Service 1991-92*. London: HMSO


Reiner R (1992a) *The Politics of the Police*. London: Harvester Wheatsheaf

Reiner R (1992b) 'Policing a Postmodern Society', *Modern Law Review* 55/6: 761–781

Reiner R (1994) 'Policing and the Police' in Maguire M, Morgan R and Reiner R (eds) *The Oxford Handbook of Criminology*. Oxford: Clarendon Press: 705–772

Rock P (1991) 'The Victim in Court Project at the Crown Court at Wood Green', *Howard Journal*, Vol 30/4: 301–10

Runciman Lord (1993) *The Report of the Royal Commission on Criminal Justice 1993*. The Runciman Report. London: HMSO


Sanders A (1985) 'Class Bias in Prosecutions', *Howard Journal* 24: 176–99

Sanders A (1994) 'From Suspect to Trial' in Maguire M, Morgan R and Reiner R (eds) *The Oxford Handbook of Criminology*. Oxford: Clarendon Press

Sanders A and Young J (1994) *Criminal Justice*. London: Butterworths

Sanderson J (1992) *Criminology Textbook*. London: HLT

Schlesinger P and Tumber H (1994) *Reporting Crime: The Media Politics of Criminal Justice*. Oxford: Clarendon Press

Schrag (1944) Social Types of a Prison Community. Quoted in Ditchfield J (1990) *Control in Prisons: A Review of the Literature*. London: HMSO

Schur E (1969) *Our Criminal Society*. Englewood Cliffs: Prentice-Hall

Schur E (1973) *Radical Non-Intervention. Rethinking the Delinquency problem*. Englewood Cliffs: Prentice-Hall

Scull A (1977) *Decarceration: Community Treatment and the Deviant – A Radical View*. Englewood Cliff: Prentice-Hall

Skolnick J (1966) *Justice without Trial*. New York: John Wiley

Smith D J and Gray J (1985) *Police and People in London: the PSI Report*. Aldershot: Gower

Smith D J (1994) 'Race, Crime and Criminal Justice' in Maguire M, Morgan R, and Reiner R *The Oxford Handbook of Criminology*. Oxford: Clarendon Press:

Solicitors Journal (1993)*Solicitor's Journal Justice Survey*. 9 July 1993: 650

Soothill K (1993) 'Sex Crime in the News Revisited.' Unpublished paper presented to the British Criminology Conference, Cardiff. July 1993

Soothill K and Walby S (1991) *Sex Crime in the News*. London: Routledge

Sprack (1992) *Emmins on Criminal Procedure*. 5th edn. London: Blackstone Press

Stanko E (1990) 'When Precaution is Normal: A Feminist Critique of Crime Prevention' in Gelsthorpe L and Morris A (eds) *Feminist Perspectives in Criminology*. Milton Keynes: Open University Press

Stephens M and Becker S (eds) (1994) *Police Force Police Service: Care and Control in Britain*. London: Macmillan

Stern V (1987) *Bricks of Shame*. Harmondsworth: Penguin

Sutherland E (1949) *White Collar Crime*. New York: Holt, Rinehart and Winston

Sveri K (1990) 'Criminal Law and Penal Sanctions' in Snare A (ed) *Criminal Violence in Scandinavia: Selected Topics*. Oslo: Norwegian University Press

Tarling R and Weatheritt M (1979) *Sentencing Practice in Magistrates' Courts*. Home Office Research Study No 56. London: HMSO

Taylor Lord Chief Justice (1993) *17th Leggatt Lecture – What Do We Want from Our Judges?* University of Surrey, Guildford

Thomas D A (1979) *Principles of Sentencing*. London: Heinemann

Tilley N (1993) 'Crime Prevention and the Safer Cities Story', *Howard Journal* 32/1: 40–57

Tonry M (1987) *Sentencing Reform Impacts*. Washington DC: US Department of Justice

Uglow S (1988) *Policing Liberal Society*. Oxford: Oxford University Press

Utting D, Bright J and Henricson C (1993) *Crime and the Family: Improving Child Rearing and Preventing Delinquency*. Occasional Paper 16. Family Policy Studies Centre

Vass A (1990) *Alternatives to Prison: Punishment, Custody and the Community*. London: Sage

Vennard J (1985) 'The Outcome of Contested Trials' in Moxon D (ed) *Managing Criminal Justice*. London: HMSO:

Von Hirsch A and Ashworth A (eds) (1993) *Principled Sentencing*. Edinburgh: Edinburgh University Press

Von Hirsch A (1976) *Doing Justice – the Choice of Punishment.* York: Hill and Wang

von Hirsch A (1986) Past or Future Crimes: Deservedness and Dangerousness in the Sentencing of Criminals. Manchester: University Press

Walker M (1987) 'Interpreting Race and Crime Statistics', *Journal of the Royal Statistical Society*, Part 1: 39-56

Walker N (1985) *Sentencing: Theory, Law and Practice.* London: Butterworths

Walklate S (1989) *Victimology: The Victim and the Criminal Justice Process.* Unwin Hyman

Walmsley R  Howard L and White S (1993) *The National Prison Survey 1991: Main Findings.* Home Office Research Study No 128. London: HMSO

Warburton F (1992) 'Bail Bandits – A Persistent Minority or the Usual Suspects?', *Criminal Justice Matters* No 10. Winter 1992/93: 7

Wasik M (1993) *The Magistrate.* October 1993

Wasik M and Taylor R (1994) *Criminal Justice Act, 1991.* London: Blackstone Press

Weigend T (1980) 'Continental Cures for American Ailments: European Criminal Procedure as a Model for Law Reform', *Crime and Justice.* Vol 2: 1980

Wells C (1988) 'The Decline and Rise of English Murder; Corporate Crime and Individual Responsibility', *Criminal Law Review*: 789–801

Wessley S (1995) *The Times.* 7 February: 17

West D (1965) *Murder Followed by Suicide.* London: Heinemann

West D (1969) *Present Conduct and Future Delinquency.* London: Heinemann

West D J and Farrington D (1973) *Who Becomes Delinquent?* London: Heinemann

West D J and Farrington D (1977) *The Delinquent Way of Life.* London: Heinemann

Williams K (1991) *Textbook on Criminology.* London: Blackstone Press

Wilson H (1980) 'Parental Supervision: A Neglected Aspect of Delinquency', *British Journal of Criminology*, Vol 20: 20

Woolf Lord Justice and Tumin S (1991) *Report of the Inquiry into Prison Disturbances, April 1990.* Cmnd 1456. London: HMSO

Young J (1994) 'Incessant Chatter: Recent Paradigms in Criminology' in Maguire M, Morgan R and Reiner R (eds) *The Oxford Handbook of Criminology.* Oxford: Clarendon Press: 69-124

Zander M (1992) *The Police and Criminal Evidence Act 1984.* 3rd edn. London: Sweet & Maxwell

Zedner L (1994) 'Victims' in Maguire M, Morgan R and Reiner R (eds) *The Oxford Handbook of Criminology.* Oxford: Clarendon Press

# INDEX